THE HARD WORK OF HOPE

THE HARD WORK OF HOPE

A Memoir

Michael Ansara

ILR PRESS

AN IMPRINT OF CORNELL UNIVERSITY PRESS

ITHACA AND LONDON

First published 2025 by Cornell University Press

Library of Congress Cataloging-in-Publication Data
Names: Ansara, Michael, 1947– author.
Title: The hard work of hope : a memoir / Michael Ansara.
Description: Ithaca : ILR Press, an imprint of Cornell University Press, 2025. | Includes bibliographical references and index.
Identifiers: LCCN 2024049169 (print) | LCCN 2024049170 (ebook) | ISBN 9781501782145 (paperback) | ISBN 9781501782152 (ebook) | ISBN 9781501782169 (pdf)
Subjects: LCSH: Ansara, Michael, 1947– | Political activists—United States— History—20th century. | Protest movements—United States—History— 20th century. | Community organization—United States—History— 20th century. | Activism—United States—History—20th century.
Classification: LCC HN65 .A6947 2025 (print) | LCC HN65 (ebook) | DDC 303.48/40973—dc23/eng/20250117
LC record available at https://lccn.loc.gov/2024049169
LC ebook record available at https://lccn.loc.gov/2024049170

Contents

List of Illustrations   vi

"Hard Work" from *After That*, poems by Kathleen Aguero   ix

Author's Note   x

Preface   xi

1. Getting on the Bus   1

2. A New Left and the Start of the Student Movement   23

3. Creating Room for Dissent   39

4. The Not-So-Radical Personal Life of a Sixties Radical   58

5. Taking it to a New Level: 1966–67   63

6. Sitting In and Armies of the Night   85

7. 1968   95

8. Shutting Down Harvard   115

9. Strange Days: 1969–70   130

10. Days of Rage   150

11. A March in Lowell   167

12. Dorchester and The People First   177

13. How Does a War End?   191

14. To Be an Organizer   201

15. Massachusetts Fair Share   217

16. The End of My Long Sixties   243

Epilogue: From the Vantage of Fifty Years   250

Acknowledgments   261

Notes   263

Selected Bibliography   275

Index   277

Illustrations

1. In the 1950s all public schools routinely had civil
defense drills   2

2. Planning Stay Out for Freedom, June 1963   13

3. The 1963 March on Washington for Jobs and Freedom   15

4. I had desperately wanted to be one of these Freedom
Summer Volunteers, here completing their training   18

5. The SDS Vietnam protest in Washington, April 15, 1965   35

6. Our first local march against the war, October 1965   42

7. Search and destroy mission, Battle of Ia Drang   47

8. McNamara and I on the hood of a car   64

9. In 1966 images like this brought home the reality
of the war   68

10. Detroit, July 25, 1967   76

11. Troops moving into Detroit, July 1967   77

12. Draft card being burned inside the Arlington
Street Church, October 16, 1967   86

13. Outside the Pentagon, October 21, 1967   88

14. Napalm became a searing image of the war   89

15. Rudi Dutschke, 1968   98

16. April 4, 1968—after Rudi Dutschke was shot,
"More than 20.000 policemen had trouble with
student-demonstrators."   100

17. Students marching in Paris, May 1968   102

18. My Harvard commencement. Protesting, Amy is
in the center   103

19. In 1968 we organized thousands to protest on
Election Day   111

20. Our signs said "Don't Vote"   111

21. Inside occupied University Hall   120

22. Police beating a student in Harvard Yard, early morning,
April 10, 1969   123

23. Thousands of members of the Harvard community
rally in the stadium   125

24. I (second from right) was among those ratifying strike
demands in Harvard Stadium   126

25. Harvard strike poster   128

26. Image that haunted us. The South Vietnamese National
Police chief executes a suspected Vietcong officer,
February 1, 1968   131

27. The iconic picture of a young girl and others fleeing a
napalm attack, 1972   132

28. Hard Hats rally in New York to support the war, just before
attacking antiwar high school and college students   134

29. Injured paratroopers of the 101st Airborne make their way
down "Hamburger Hill"   141

30. Marching on MIT's iLab   151

31. By 1970 we usually marched with National Liberation
Front flags   151

32. *New York Daily News* front page, August 26, 1969. Headline:
"SIR, MY MEN REFUSE TO GO!"   153

33. October 15, 1969, the moratorium on the Common   155

34. Ten thousand marched the day after the Chicago verdict was
announced   158

35. Photographer's caption was "Police attack demonstrators,"
Northeastern, 1970   159

36. Injured police at Northeastern, 1970   160

37. Harvard Square as night fell   160

38. Caption by photographer: "Massachusetts State Troopers
in riot gear assault a protester at an anti–Vietnam War
demonstration in Harvard Square"   161

39. Full-blown riot in Cambridge   162

40. Younger kids hanging at Ronan Park   179

41. Gathering signatures to demand the judge Jerome
Troy be removed   189

42. The People First (TPF) protesting Judge Troy   190

43. Pushing a US helicopter into the sea after the fall of Saigon   192

44. Vietnam Veterans Against the War marching in
East Boston, 1971   193

45. VVAW. From left to right: Al Hubbard, John Kerry,
Bestor Cram, Art Johnson   194

46. Police dragging protester at federal building sit-in,
May 11, 1972   196

47. Frustrated police pulling those sitting in by their hair,
May 11, 1972   196

48. Me in 1972   202

49. CAP-Energy protest   206

50. Fair Share leaders at the State House filing petitions
for the referendum   212

51. As executive director of Mass Fair Share   220

52. Mass Fair Share picketing the phone company   223

53. Typical Fair Share member   232

Hard Work

Kathleen Aguero

Hope springs eternal, but
I couldn't imagine how
hope, before it gets to that bubbling place,
forces itself through miles of dirt packed hard,
then around, over, under rocks,
willing itself not to dry up in the desert
or to merge with the sewer of a city street,
waiting for frozen prairie to thaw,
resisting the warm and mindless absorption
of mud, moss, sand, swamp
until it finds the small trembling
where, welcome or not, it gathers the last of its strength
and breaks through to the surface
the way a laboring woman, stinking,
exhausted, summons one last grunt and push
to force the baby into the world
where it takes its first, sharp breath.

I bow my head to the hard work of hope.
I let it place its dull and heavy hand upon my neck.
I submit to its dour blessing.
I give up. I begin
its thankless, necessary pilgrimage.

Author's Note

This book was completed months before the catastrophic election of November 5, 2024, which has the potential to profoundly erode American democracy, possibly even end it. Tragically, billionaires financed an effort that convinced millions of hard-pressed working Americans to vote for Trump as the "change" candidate. Millions more stayed home and did not vote at all.

The results were driven in part by the specific dynamics of the post-Covid period. Across the globe, every governing party that presided over the inflation-wracked recovery has lost large vote shares. As well, the results sadly reflect the fact that there are millions of Americans who simply will not vote for a woman for president, especially one who is Black and South Asian, no matter how skilled, smart, or qualified.

Longer term trends were also at work: the failure of Democrats to speak to the challenges and anguish of so many working Americans and their families, the rise of a media ecosystem that propagates rightwing misinformation and lies, the degeneration of our politics into billion dollar marketing campaigns, the vast increase in economic inequality, the increased power of the insanely rich, white backlash, and finally the fear that has always followed waves of immigration.

Immediately after the election, gripped by waves of sadness, I wondered if this book had any relevance for the new period we have entered. Upon reflection, I think it is even more relevant. Organizers and organizing built the civil rights movement. Organizers and organizing built the student and antiwar movements. This moment calls out for a new generation of thousands of young organizers willing to reach out, not just to those who voted Democratic, but to those who did not vote and even those who voted for Trump; to listen to them, connect with them and organize them to fight for democracy and for an economic populism similar to that of Mass Fair Share (described in this book.) The Trump regime will inflict enormous damage. If organizers are there, connecting with people, year-round, not just in the weeks before an election, there can be a powerful response to that damage.

We have entered a desperate and dark period. The hard work of hope is rarely easy. It has never been more imperative.

—Michael Ansara, November 11, 2024

Preface

> **I think that the past is all that makes the present coherent, and
> further, that the past will remain horrible for exactly as long as we
> refuse to assess it honestly.**
>
> —James Baldwin

America seems to be on the verge of flying apart. Increasingly the conflicts over race, gender, culture, and politics are so profound that it seems hard to see how the country can survive. Decades ago, in a similar moment, the country riven and roiling, I was young, and I marched. Marched first in support of civil rights, marched then against the war in Vietnam. Marched and then organized marches of tens of thousands. Sat in and then organized sit-ins of thousands.

For over two decades I devoted myself to changing America. I felt part of a movement much larger than myself, a movement of the young attempting to shape a better future, our future, a future furiously resisted by the old men at the commanding heights of power. I moved from protest to resistance to seeking systemic change. I marched and marched but perhaps more importantly, fitfully, immersed in baptisms of fire, I learned the craft, the art of organizing.

Now, in another time of extreme polarization and backlash, the young have been marching again. African Americans are marching for the right to live, to not be killed by the police. A new generation of students, shaped by school shootings and "active shooter drills" are marching and organizing against gun violence. Young "Dreamers" are fighting for the right to stay in their own country, America. Thousands of young people are demanding that old people take responsibility and act now to save the planet from the catastrophes of climate change. Young people are again protesting wars in far-off lands. Young women and men are marching to protect reproductive freedom. Tens of thousands are working to preserve American democracy.

Once again, the young are fighting for the future, fighting to have a future. Once again, they are furiously opposed by old men desperately clinging to old ways, protecting the wealth and power of the few. Increasingly, in our America, those old white men, resisting change knowing that they are not in the majority, are doing what they can to create the conditions for minority rule.

More than the young have been marching and organizing. Vast marches of women. Thousands of suburban women creating Indivisible groups. Black women spearheading voter registration and mobilization. The amazing outpouring after the murder of George Floyd when twenty million Americans took to the streets.[1] Tens of thousands of women organizing to resist the rollback of their rights enacted by a Supreme Court packed with conservative judges. A new wave of union organizing.

I wrote this book for the activists of today and of tomorrow. I have little doubt that they will learn to organize and to struggle for power in new ways that I cannot even imagine. Still, my hope is that they can learn from my experiences.

This memoir is not a history of the sixties. Nor is it an activist guide. It is an intensely personal remembering of two decades of organizing and activism. I was privileged to be part of powerful movements: the Civil Rights Movement, the student New Left, the antiwar movement. I was able to learn the skills and craft of organizing and apply it to leading a community-based economic justice organization. I made many mistakes, learned painful lessons, and was part of memorable moments.

I did not take notes. I kept no papers. I have consulted contemporaneous newspapers, especially the *New York Times*, the *Boston Globe*, the *Washington Post*, and the *Harvard Crimson*. I have read histories and memoirs of the period. At times I have searched the internet. But this is primarily a work of remembering.

Much of the dialogue is a creative effort at reconstruction. A couple of scenes are amalgams; a very few are creative attempts at representation. I have done my best to remember as accurately as possible. Of necessity, I have had to be highly selective, leaving out many important events and people.

While this memoir is primarily a personal story, it is also grounded in the shared experiences of many of my generation. I was born in 1947, part of the foaming front edge of the demographic wave that would come to be known as the Baby Boom. Growing up in the immediate aftermath of the Holocaust and the Second World War, we knew from an early age that evil walked our world. We were also the first generation to experience thirty years of exceptional, sustained economic growth. We were the first generation who grew up with the atomic bomb and with television.

As a boy, lying on the floor of my room at night, peering surreptitiously through the crack in the door as my parents watched *Gunsmoke, Have Gun—Will*

Travel, or going to the movies to see *Shane* and *High Noon,* I absorbed the lesson that "being a man" meant standing up for others, taking that walk in the dust at high noon, overseeing the long winding wagon train. In 1956, watching young "freedom fighters" take on Soviet tanks in Hungarian streets, absorbing the deeply etched image of young people hurling Coke bottle Molotov cocktails at massive tanks, I absorbed the lesson that to rebel was good.

I also grew up earnestly believing in America, believing that we were the most democratic, most generous, the tallest, and most athletic people in the world. As did so many of my generation, I believed in the unique promise of American democracy. I took our history seriously and thrilled to the words of the Declaration of Independence, believing indeed that "all men are created equal . . . endowed with certain unalienable Rights . . . life, liberty, and the pursuit of happiness." It was the remarkable inclusion of "the pursuit of happiness" that made me confident America was unique.

I realized everything was not perfect. Even at a young age I was aware of how Black people were treated—in Virginia, where I lived as a boy, there were still segregated schools despite the Supreme Court's *Brown* decision. The shadow of nuclear weapons cast a pall over us. Living in a world of mutually assured destruction seemed the height of irrationality and madness.

Our generation was constantly made aware of our numbers and our power. We were a demographic bulge and as we progressed through time, we altered everything. Our sheer size drove markets, and hence the media, to focus on us. As we entered our teenage years many of us felt distant from the dominant culture. Our music was subversive, our attitude rebellious. Many of us were rebels without a clear cause but rebels none the less. We felt the strength of our numbers. We knew the future belonged to us.

Yet the future that we have now is radically different from any that we imagined. We succeeded in some ways, abolishing Jim Crow and opening doors for a new Black middle class, preparing the ground for profound change in the possibilities for women, laying the foundation for increasing freedom and equality for the LGBTQ+ community, seeding a long-lasting environmental movement. We have failed in larger ways, failing to stop ever greater economic inequality, never succeeding to drive a stake into the beating heart of American white supremacy, rarely creating a political force that could effectively fight for the more democratic future we once believed in.

Now it is up to those younger than me to fight for a better future, to save America and the world from catastrophe, to preserve American democracy and reinvent it in new ways. I want to provide them with a glimpse at the amazing experience that was the Civil Rights Movement. I want them to know how we built a large student movement, how we organized against a war that was originally supported by over 90 percent of the American public. How events and our efforts built a massive, sprawling, disruptive movement against that war. I want them to understand that it was *organizing*, engaging with people, countless discussions, connecting with people on a personal level, building relationships, constant outreach, and education, that made possible the demonstrations that most people associate with the 1960s.

I hope that the activists of today and of tomorrow can learn from our mistakes, particularly those made in 1968 and 1969 when we chose militancy over strategy, experienced a profound failure of political imagination. I hope they can also benefit from the story of how I learned the craft of organizing so that they may find their own way to reinvent organizing and change America.

This book, the story of one organizer and activist, is dedicated to all those who will march and organize, who dream of decency and a democratic future, who resist barbarism, racism, and hatred, who will create new movements that will, to adapt Theodore Parker's phrase often used by Martin Luther King, Jr., bend the moral arc of the universe toward justice.

THE HARD WORK OF HOPE

GETTING ON THE BUS

In the fall of 1960, a loaf of bread cost twenty cents. "Only the Lonely" by Roy Orbison was on all the AM radio stations. In twenty-six states it was illegal for men and women of different races to marry. Jim Crow segregation was the law in all Southern states. John F. Kennedy and Richard Nixon were competing for the presidency. And, at age thirteen, I started high school in Brookline, Massachusetts.

Civil defense drills were common to every school across America. Periodically, we were told there would be a drill to practice what to do in the event of nuclear attack. The fire alarms would ring. Dutifully, we would troop down to the basement with its yellow and black "fallout shelter" signs, one of one million metal signs, visible from 200 feet, carefully designed by psychologists to direct us to safety.[1] Once in the basement, we would be ordered to "drop" and then assume the proper position, head down, "duck and cover." The one thing we are not to do, we were repeatedly told, is to look up at the time of the blast, as it would blind us. Drop. Head down. Duck and cover.

We are huddled down in the basement, some boys trying to tease the girls. Some of us are just bored. Some are frightened. We have seen the newsreels of Hiroshima and Nagasaki, the cindered bodies, the devastation. I veer from thinking it is all a joke to being terrified. But of course, I and all the other boys do not want to show how we feel. We want to be James Dean or Marlon Brando. We practice curling our lip. We need to be cool, and we are so not cool.

One chart on the wall catches my attention. It depicts concentric circles centered on a blast site. Each expanding circle demarks a zone of destruction. Within

FIGURE 1. In the 1950s all public schools routinely held civil defense drills. Keystone-France via Getty Images.

the inner zone everything is turned to ash; further out there is a vast firestorm and all the oxygen is consumed instantaneously; in the next zone most buildings are flattened, and in the next there is massive radiation contamination. I am supposed to have my head down between my knees, but I cannot keep my eyes off those circles, the mile radius markings clear.

I raise my hand and ask the obvious question: since Brookline High is located less than ten miles from the South Boston army base and since the active army base will be the logical target in any nuclear attack, isn't it completely clear that we would all be dead? I point to the chart. Why should we worry about not looking up? Why duck and cover when we will be either ash, or dead, because the firestorm has sucked all the oxygen out of the very air?

Questioning the teachers assigned to run civil defense drills is not well received. One teacher chirps, "Keep quiet, look down, do as your told."

I have no sense of optimism. I believe there is some sort of equation for sanity in a crazed world. If everyone around you, especially those in authority, is irrational, then the only reasonable response is to behave in a manner that may seem crazy. I think the world could actually end. I think I am a stranger in a strange land. (I have read Robert A. Heinlein of course.)

Out of despair, I refuse to duck and cover. I simply will not cooperate with lunacy. I will not sit down. I will look up. I will stand up.

Detention after school.

The next civil defense drill I pass out a leaflet explaining how wacky this is.

Double detention.

I join with two young women, Rika Alper and Harriet Hornstein, to form a small team protesting nuclear weapons. We enlist a few other kids and pass out leaflets on Saturday mornings to pedestrians along the busiest shopping streets in Brookline calling on both the Soviets and the United States to take "unilateral steps toward nuclear disarmament." I have no expectation that our gestures will have a real impact.

That first year of high school I was often on crutches, frequently in pain, frequently morose and resentful. I had spent much of the previous summer in Children's Hospital in Boston, immobilized in casts that had done nothing to ease the searing pain of an undiagnosed joint disease. Upon being sent home, I had fled into books, found escape into an alternative reality allowing me to shuck off, at least for a night, my failing body and my drab existence. I would find an author who excited me and then read every one of their books. Increasingly I was drawn to American history. I devoured all the novels of Kenneth Roberts. I spent hours browsing in the *American Heritage Book of the American Revolution* or lost in a book of photographs from the Civil War. Our history came alive for me. Curled amid the disheveled blankets and sheets at two in the morning, I did not so much read books, I lived books. My reading confirmed that I was born in the wrong century. Everything had already been explored. All the important battles had already been fought. Born into the wrong body, the wrong time.

The first day of school, I had hobbled along on crutches awkwardly navigating unfamiliar halls, acutely aware of my pimples and flab, found my cubby, greeted some of the kids I knew, and generally wished I were anywhere else. The one thing I was looking forward to was the American history class. The teacher, a short, balding man with a round, bespectacled, froglike countenance, passed out the syllabuses and explained that our grades would be determined solely by how well we did on weekly tests. There would be no essays, only multiple-choice tests.

I was outraged.

After class, with the insolence of the eager young, I explained that multiple-choice history tests were the stupidest idea I had ever encountered. What— George Washington was A) our first president, B) our first general, or C) a liar?

He was not pleased. The tests were what the school used, he said, and I would have a hard time getting the answers right. Arrogant and morosely cocky, I replied that I would not open a textbook all fall and would still get an A. He became furious, sputtered that I was wrong, that I was outrageous, and that I would most certainly fail the class if I did not do the assigned reading. His frog face turned red.

I swung away on my crutches, disdainful, convinced that teachers were clueless. I did not open the textbook. My score ended up being a hundred for the semester. I stopped doing any homework. I detested my classes, refused to take them seriously.

With adolescent certainty, I was determined to not conform to a system that was intellectually bankrupt. I was driven by despair. Wrong century. Wrong school. Wrong life. Wrong body.

I had grown up in a strange family. As a child, of course, I did not think it strange. I was determinedly oblivious. I remembered my early years as idyllic, spent in the new Virginia suburbs of Washington surrounded with woods, creeks, and even a few remaining farms. But after we relocated to Massachusetts and I became a precocious adolescent, I noticed that my parents, unlike the parents of my friends, rarely went out, never had guests over for dinner. Our house was crammed with books. But we were always scrabbling for money. Each home of ours had my mother's paintings on the walls but she had stopped painting before I was born. I was raised to think of myself as a Syrian Lebanese American. My father's family had immigrated from what is now Lebanon. My mother's brother and sisters were Jewish, but she maintained that her family was not Jewish, that they had converted because of their marriages. In fact, despite my mother's vehement assertions to the contrary, her family had been part of the great wave of Russian Jewish immigration to the United States in the first years of the twentieth century.

I do not remember political discussions growing up. In my teenage years I would learn that both my parents had been active in left politics in the 1930s and that in 1947 my father had been fired from his job at the State Department as a security risk.

My father had trouble staying in a job for long. He went through a string of them, rarely lasting more than three years. In the end, despite a Harvard degree, he became a cab driver, hated it, and did poorly at it. Desperate for money, my mother started tutoring children in our kitchen. At twelve, I went to work at the Brookline Public Library shelving books.

While others thrilled to the generational summons of a young JFK, I thought we lived in an irrational world with crazy leaders, including the new president, who was testing nuclear weapons that put radioactivity in the milk I and millions drank every day. The whole world was crazy, bleak, and hopeless. I was in the iron grip of adolescent despair.

I walk, slightly limping, down Harvard Avenue into Coolidge Corner with its stores and restaurants. Walking past Woolworth's, I see a small group of picketers circling, back and forth, carrying signs. After watching for a few minutes, I ask a tall young man what they are doing. He says they are supporting "Negro" students in North Carolina who were refused a cup of coffee at a Woolworth's and so are sitting at the lunch counter until they get served. Segregation has to go, he says. America is the land of the free, he says. Everyone has a right to life, liberty, and the pursuit of happiness, he says. "Negroes" are Americans too.

Sunlight filters on the sidewalk. I step into the slow-moving line, step into "the movement," step out of adolescent despair and bleakness and into a new life.

I do not think about what I am doing. With impetuous certainty I know my place is in that line. Only much later will I consider why I took that first step into a life of activism. I will recall attending the only integrated school in the Commonwealth of Virginia. I will remember a sweat-stained, tear-stained walk home from a lost fight in the Virginia twilight after a Little League practice when the other kids taunted me for "going to that n----- school on the hill." I will remember the burnished mahogany cheek of the gentle nurse who took care of me through polio, when at eight years old, I was confined to bed for months. I will feel ashamed that I do not remember her name.

Quickly I fall in love with "the movement." I am in awe of those who sit in at the lunch counters, ride on the freedom buses, and register people to vote. Their quiet courage in the face of hatred and violence is stunning. They possess a ferocious dignity. The Freedom Riders, those sitting in at lunch counters, those lining up to register to vote, those young Black bodies willing to be beaten, those new heroes of mine, are standing up to decades of terror and legalized discrimination.

Southern white people had woven a tight net of laws segregating and subjugating Black people. In 1960, it was illegal for Black people to drink from white-only water fountains or to swim in white-only pools, to attend white-only schools, to eat or even sit at white-only lunch counters. Black voters were disenfranchised. Over roughly eighty years, the Jim Crow system was enforced by unyielding terror. Routinely Black Americans were beaten, shot, even murdered, lynched. Killed for trying to sell their crops at market rates. Killed for not stepping off the sidewalk fast enough to let white people pass easily. Killed for trying to vote. Killed for being "uppity." Killed for looking the wrong way at a white woman.[2]

Then young Black students and slightly older African American ministers challenged that terror and the legal system of segregation. Sat in. Became Freedom Riders integrating buses. Marched. Registered people to vote. Challenged the decades old laws and violence. They were beaten. They were shot. They were jailed. Water hoses turned on them. Dogs unleashed on them. Bombs exploded on front porches and in Black churches. Some were murdered. And still, they would not stop. Despite the beatings, despite the arrests, despite the shootings, despite the deaths, they brought legal segregation to an end. They integrated the South. They won voting rights. They changed America.

How could I not fall in love with those young men and women only six, seven, and eight years older than I? How could I not dream of following in their footsteps? How could I resist the magnetic pull of such gigantic hope?

I could not. I dove into the movement. I plunged in, without any hesitation, and with fierce joy.

There was a constant buzz of civil rights activities in Boston. The Northern Student Movement organized high school and college students to tutor younger Black students, and I helped out. Activists from the South frequently came to Boston to raise awareness and support. I felt a particular connection with the young organizers of the Student Nonviolent Coordinating Committee (SNCC), the organization that emerged from and carried forward the sit-ins at the lunch counters. Soon courageous young African American students left their colleges to become full-time activists. They possessed a passionate intensity. They talked about organizing as well as sit-ins, wade-ins, and marches. And I listened, eagerly. Their moral gravity drew me the way a magnet attracts filings. At my home, I had a sense of things broken, space filled with unspoken despair. My moments with the SNCC organizers as they came to Boston bathed me in courage and optimism. For the first time I began to believe that there were causes worth fighting for. Perhaps I was not born into the wrong century after all.

Late in the spring of 1961, I let my parents know that the next year I would not be attending Brookline High. I was done with multiple-choice education. I had heard about a new, small, private school called the Commonwealth School that had started up three years earlier in Boston's Back Bay.

Walking into the two old townhouses that had been joined to create the school, I immediately felt at home. The entrance exam asked the applicant to choose three questions from a list and write a short essay about each one. I wrote one essay on why their questions were the wrong questions. Commonwealth loved it.

I was accepted with a huge scholarship and the newly created job of "assistant janitor" to pay the remainder of my tuition.

I loved Commonwealth and thrived there. The teachers wanted to teach. The classes were tiny—there were twenty-two students in my entire grade. The school was for my intellect as a rain forest is for orchids. I soaked in everything, blossoming in my own angsty adolescent way.

I made two close friends, Tim Dickinson and Ron Carver. Ronnie, in particular, was deeply antiauthoritarian—as budding activist teenagers should be.

I was as well—ideologically. But I felt I needed to be responsible and care for my family. At school, I wanted to excel, to please teachers who I respected, even loved. I wanted to change the world but did not want to change a thing about Commonwealth.

My education extended beyond school. St. Mark's Church and the affiliated Social Center in Grove Hall were the center of organizing for civil rights in Boston. Its youth marching band, instead of playing the music of John Phillip Souza, worked up freedom songs. Two dozen young Black kids high stepping to drums and singing "keep on walking, keep on talking, marching down to freedom land," sent my adolescent soul soaring.

I was mentored by a remarkably generous array of Black activists. Sarah-Ann Shaw, a slight young woman with the beginning of an afro, a social worker for St. Mark's, became one of the organizers in Boston for the Congress of Racial Equality (CORE). Byron Rushing, slender and soft spoken, was the organizer for the Northern Student Movement in Boston. Mel King was the large, overalls-wearing social worker at the South End Settlement House. The reverend Jim Breeden was the poised and handsome Episcopal priest at St. James Episcopal Church. Julian Houston was a tall and precociously dignified undergraduate at Boston University. They all became my mentors. The two most important and most generous were Noel Day, the lead social worker at St. Mark's who would spearhead the Boston Action Group and the Massachusetts Freedom Movement, and A. Robert Phillips, the organizer for both.

I do not know why they bothered, given how young, raw, and inexperienced I was, but they treated me with a respect that nourished. I was fourteen and fifteen and have no idea if they realized exactly how young I really was. I volunteered for any task: knocking on doors, producing flyers on mimeo machines, setting out chairs, whatever was needed. Miraculously they treated me as one of their own, invited me into their inner circle.

After a meeting, I could often be found sitting on the stoop of an old townhouse in the South End, a constant stream of activity on the street, mothers returning from shopping, drunks attempting to cadge enough money for yet another drink, kids biking. Everyone except me was Black.

Bob Phillips tilts back his head, his goatee militantly fashionable, looks me in the eye and takes me through what has happened and what is being planned.

"So how many doors have we knocked on so far?"

I have the list. "Seventy-three this weekend."

"And where does that put us toward our goal?"

"We've knocked a total of one hundred fifty-five out of our goal of seven hundred fifty."

"Well, I think we need to recruit more people to knock on doors this week and next weekend. Here is the list of people I will visit. If I get twelve new people for next weekend, I want you to be ready with the streets to assign, and make sure we have enough packets for them."

"Okay. I am on it."

"By the way, what did you think of Jean? I think she has a lot of potential. I think we can get her to play a bigger role. Perhaps we ask her to coordinate a team of the other women in her area. What do you think?"

He talks with me as if I am a fellow organizer—younger, in need of education and guidance but still in some way an equal. He stresses that the movement is the sea we swim in, but that organization is what matters; organizing will build power, sustain people.

Other times, I am sitting on a hard metal folding chair at St. Mark's after a public meeting, included in the evaluation and planning with Bob, Sarah-Ann, Noel, and Reverend Breeden. Noel, his round, golden-brown face glistening with sweat, dissects the meeting and takes us through the plan for what comes next. Interlaced with all the detail and logistics is a constant questioning: are we effectively changing people, changing their understandings, their relationships? Are we getting people to see that problems they think of as individual, as their own, are shared problems rooted in systems of power? Noel leads us into taking leaps, launching a boycott of Wonder Bread, planning a walkout of students, planning a march without a permit. I am thrilled that young as I am, white, pimply, and wide-eyed, I am allowed to be a small part of that "we."

From them, I gain optimism. I discard my despair. I shed my cynicism. I still hurt in most of my joints, but my body and its failures seem far less important.

I idolize Fannie Lou Hamer, a Mississippi sharecropper who has emerged as a civil rights leader. She radiates courage. I am awed as she describes being a sharecropper who never finished high school. She is "sick and tired of being sick and tired." She possesses moral weight and a deep well of determination. She is not fearless—she fears for herself, for her kids, for her people. She had no illusions about what awaited her when she stood up for the right to vote. She knew she would be reviled, beaten, and jailed. And still she not only stood up, but she is also organizing; she is a leader. She is the richest example to me of what happens when "ordinary people" step out of their day-to-day lives and join a movement for change: they can do extraordinary things. Out of darkness they kindle hope. It is happening even in the darkest regions of the Mississippi Delta.

Hamer and the organizers of SNCC impart to me a profound belief that history can be shaped, that history is in the hands of the children of Birmingham, in the hands of the organizers in small hamlets of the Mississippi Delta, in the hands of the swaying crowds in the churches. I know it is in our hands, and with love, passion, sacrifice, organizing, and courage it could, it would, be shaped toward justice. I do not just know it intellectually. I feel it.

As I sit in packed churches, African Americans of all ages around me, as I hear the stories of the South, as we sway, arm in arm singing, I fall in love with *organizing*, the idea that you could create social change by changing people, convincing them to come together to build organization. To change people, you first must talk with them, earn their trust, listen to them, get them to see that their individual problems were shared problems, social problems, and then get them to see the potential power that comes when people act together, have the courage to engage in direct action. Organizing is not as dramatic as the sit-ins, the bus rides, or the marches, but it is what makes direct action possible. Intrinsic to the concept of organizing is the belief that ordinary people matter, and that through working together in new democratic forms we can change society.

I know what I want to be in life: an organizer. I will toy with other paths from time to time—perhaps I will be an artist, perhaps I will be a journalist, for a few months, I even think I might be a college professor—but always, I will return to what I first saw in the young organizers of SNCC and the young African American organizers in Roxbury. I will be an organizer.

In 1962, when I am fifteen, Noel and Breeden test out the power of economic boycotts in Boston. Discrimination is not restricted to the South. All around us are companies that never hire Black workers or only hire them for the most menial of positions. Noel challenges us to mobilize the economic power of Boston's Black community to force changes in corporate behavior. At that time, Black people were averaging 53 percent of white wages and one out of three Black people in Boston made under $2,000 a year.[3]

We start months of canvassing, research, listening, recruiting block captains. We are building a new organization, the Boston Action Group (BAG). Volunteers meet at St. Mark's and go door to door talking about economic discrimination and asking families to fill out forms about what they buy. Particularly responsive people are asked to become block captains.

Normally we went door knocking in pairs. As time went on, I occasionally knocked on doors by myself, white and eager, and usually received a warm welcome.

Occasionally I met indifference. Certainly, I met people tired from their work and lives of worry and scarcity. But that did not stop them from inviting me in, taking time to talk with me.

A typical visit would start with my ringing doorbells of the brick townhouses on Mass Ave that once were elegant single-family homes for Boston's richest and most fashionable families. Now converted into apartments, they house multiple families amid flaking paint and failing plumbing.

I had to find one doorbell that worked so I could get into the building. I knock on the first door and as it opens a crack, I say: "Hi, I am Michael from the Boston Action Group, working with Noel Day and Reverend Breeden. Can I come in and talk with you about how we are planning to get better jobs for our community?"

The door swings open. Beneath a high ceiling with chipped decorative moldings, a large woman in a tan house coat and slippers, answers. "Hi, I'm Mrs. Johnson, come on in." She leads me to the kitchen table.

I explain, "We as a community can have power if we act together. One power we have is to decide together what we will buy and what we won't buy. It's not right that companies will take our money but not give us jobs. (I feel no incongruity in the use of that "we." She knows I am speaking of the Black community.)

"And that is not right. We gotta use our economic power. If they won't give us the jobs, they won't get our dollars. We need those good jobs just like everyone else."

"Yes indeed," she murmurs. "For sure."

I continue, "So BAG is going door to door. We want to find out what people are buying and ask if you will be willing to be part of a boycott. Just imagine what we can do if we all pool our buying power. May I go over this list of products to see what you buy?"

I show her a list of household products and food items organized by brand. We go over it and check off everything she buys. I ask her lots of questions not just about what she buys but how she feels about all that is happening. She is enthusiastic about a possible boycott. I explain how the boycott will work, that we will need every family to participate once we announce the target company at a large community meeting. I say that I am listing her as committed.

Mrs. Johnson is nodding her head. "You sure can."

I explain that we are setting up a system of block captains and once one is selected for her block, I will connect them. I remind her that when we all work together, we can make change happen.

"Great," says Mrs. Johnson, "time for some changes around here. Past time. You can count on me."

Frequently, I would be offered a piece of pie or cake, and we would sit talking about the community, family, their church.

Often, I find myself late on a Saturday evening alone in Roxbury or the South End. Usually, I am the only white person. I never once feel the slightest fear—and with good reason. Despite all that they have suffered at the hands of white people—the slights, the insults, the jobs denied, the restrictions as to where they can live, even relatives lynched—family after family not only listens to what this young white boy has to say, but because I am part of the movement, because Noel and the others vouch for me, I am embraced. I not only don't feel fear, I feel loved.

I know it is the message more than the messenger, but still, I feel a very personal, warm generosity.

The first company targeted is Continental Baking Company, makers of Wonder Bread, the ubiquitous whitest of white breads. Twelve percent of Wonder Bread's Boston sales are in the Black community.[4] But of 250 workers in their plant located in the heart of that community, only eight are Black and all restricted to the lowest paid, most menial positions. BAG meets with Wonder Bread executives and demands that the company hire Black people for five driver salesmen jobs, one long-distance driver, four clerks, and two bakery production positions. The executives refuse, saying that they have no open jobs.

We initiate the boycott. Black ministers are all in. Throughout the South End, Roxbury, and Dorchester, churches preach boycott. The block captains reach out to the families on their blocks. We have a distribution system that can get a mimeographed leaflet into the hands of virtually every Black family within forty-eight hours. With each day Wonder Bread sales fall. In less than a month, the company decides it is better to give in than continue to lose revenue.

The strategy outlined by Noel and Reverend Breeden works. Wonder Bread hires African Americans into positions previously reserved for white people. Other groups, especially the Congress of Racial Equality, pick up the strategy and soon a growing list of Boston companies, including the major banks, pressured with the threat of sit-ins and boycotts, are negotiating hiring practices with community leaders.[5] I see firsthand the power of collective action. I see firsthand the iron grasp of unreasoning racism being loosened and released.

In the summer of 1962, I volunteered for the campaign of Harvard professor H. Stuart Hughes, running as an independent candidate for the Senate seat vacated by President Kennedy. The Kennedys decided the seat should go to the younger brother, the totally inexperienced Ted Kennedy. Hughes ran on a remarkable platform of nuclear disarmament, civil rights, and economic justice.

The campaign needed to collect 72,000 signatures to get on the ballot. Those signatures had to come from every county across the state. Led by a graduate student, Chester Hartman, the campaign collected over 140,000 signatures in ten weeks. Along with dozens of others, I teamed up with Ron and we walked the streets, knocked on doors in Fitchburg, Leominster, Lowell, and Holyoke. Through the campaign, I met a group of older undergraduates and graduate students who became role models for me. They debated politics in a way I had never heard before. Lee Webb, a Boston University student, also from Brookline, impressed me immediately. He would go on to become national secretary of SDS. Another, a tall and soft-spoken Texan, John Maher, drove a sleek green Porsche and even let me drive it once. I was so much younger in so many ways than all of them but felt an immediate connection. Many were members of a small organization called Students for a Democratic Society (SDS). Because of them, I began to pay close attention to SDS, got on the mailing list, joined, and began to think of myself as part of a New Left. Through the Hughes campaign, I also met Jerry Grossman and Flora Donham, who would create an enduring political reform effort in Massachusetts and end up playing a significant role in both politics and the peace movement.

Just before the election, the Cuban Missile crisis brought the world close to the unthinkable. Hughes dared to call for a peaceful resolution, criticized President Kennedy, and suggested that the UN should play a role. Popular perception was that Kennedy "won" and that Nikita Khrushchev "blinked." Massachusetts voters overwhelmingly elected Ted Kennedy. Hughes received fewer actual votes than he had names on his nominating petitions.[6]

In April of 1963, Birmingham was rocked by the nonviolent civil disobedience campaign led by Dr. Martin Luther King, Jr., and Reverend Fred Shuttlesworth. Along with millions, I watched on television as water hoses were turned on the protestors, dogs unleashed on the marching Black children. King was arrested and wrote his "Letter from a Birmingham Jail."

In Boston that spring, Noel and Reverend Breeden, joined by SNCC's Peggy Trotter Dammond (Noel's wife) formed Citizens for Human Rights to organize a rapid response demonstration of 10,000 people on the Boston Common to support the Civil Rights Movement in Birmingham.[7] That day we raised enough money for King's Southern Christian Leadership Conference (SCLC) to pay for a voter registration bus.

Then they turned their organizing to the Boston public schools. The Boston NAACP tried to negotiate with the Boston School Committee to end de facto segregation. Those negotiations led nowhere.

June 11, 1963, George Wallace barred Black students from entering the University of Alabama.[8] President Kennedy, reading the new political climate created by the wave of direct actions and the brutal response across the South, delivered a speech declaring civil rights a moral issue.[9] In Mississippi, on June 12, Medgar Evers, the NAACP field secretary, was killed, gunned down in his driveway.[10] And in Boston, the NAACP staged a sit-in at the Boston School Committee demanding action on fourteen demands to end de facto segregation in the Boston public schools. The next day Noel and Jim called for a Stay Out for Freedom Day in which high school students would not go to school. Instead, they would attend alternative "Freedom Schools," where they would study African American history for the day.[11]

FIGURE 2. Planning Stay Out for Freedom. Right to left: Peggy Trotter Dammond, Noel Day, Reverend James Breeden, Reverend Vernon Carter, Reverend John Harmon. Photo by Leroy Ryan/*Boston Globe* via Getty Images.

On June 18, 1963, 100 percent of Boston's Black high school students stayed out of school. One thousand of them jammed into Freedom Schools where they sang "We Shall Overcome" and "Eyes on the Prize," studied the history of Black people in America (there was no African American History Month back then), and listened to the Celtics great Bill Russell. Russell also spoke at a rally for parents picketing the School Committee downtown.

When the call came for a long-expected march on Washington, I was tasked to be the assistant bus coordinator, working under a courtly, slightly portly, Harvard Divinity School graduate, Archie Epps, who was then teaching at Harvard. (Archie would become the first African American dean of students at Harvard and would be carried out of his office by protesting students occupying University Hall.)

We arranged to rent a few buses, then more and then still more. In the last two weeks we were frantically searching for additional buses, mapping routes and pickup spots. As the number of people determined to go to Washington kept increasing, we desperately worked to locate enough buses, and then rented whole trains to accommodate the growing river of those heeding the call.

Finally, Ron and I got on one of the very last buses out of Boston headed for Washington.

I remember approaching Washington, the front of the bus packed with Black hope, Black faces, and in the back among a handful of white students, there I was, exhausted, tearful in the dark, crying with a pilgrim's devotion, returning to the shrine of the back yards of my childhood, back when lightning bugs blinked small beacons in the Virginia sunsets, a time before schools allowed Black and white people together, back when Black and white people could not marry, back before a couple unbelievably named Loving did marry and were arrested in their bedroom; back when my sisters vied to be Scarlett, the three of us playing runaway slave, and I was the slave, hurtling over barbed wire on the last farm left, racing through rows of new ranch houses, urged on to run long and hard, in the shadows sneaking home to hide, tears watering my imagination. . . . But that was before and now I am coming back in a bus pulling into the Ellipse lined with more buses than I ever dreamed could pour into one city, a mighty, righteous river of buses.

On that day in DC, I marched out into unexpected brilliance: black, brown, copper, conked, and curled, marching, walking, clapping, keeping on keeping on, a frenzy of hope shooting us into the stream of history. Mississippi sharecroppers in overalls, Detroit church ladies in their Sunday dresses, collared and uncollared preachers of the miracle of redemption, and everywhere that day strode the young, possessed with our numbers, our freshness and vitality, and the words! Words that made words suddenly not mere words: I have a dream, life, liberty, and the pursuit of happiness, solid, felt, carried in our hands, in our stride, giving us confidence in the future, our future—a future that lay, unknown and unknowable, slumbering like a snake under a supple sun.

There among the singing, swaying, clapping throngs, at the age of sixteen, I felt fully grown, a new person, a righteous warrior for justice.

Given my connections to SNCC, I was riveted by the behind-the-scenes drama of John Lewis's speech. Lewis was then the head of SNCC and as such was to be a major speaker. His original draft was harshly critical of the Kennedy administration. Several SNCC friends relayed to me that he had been pressured by the march organizer, A. Phillip Randolph, and Dr. King, both of whom insisted that he tone down his remarks. Hearing this, I was, of course, totally on the side of SNCC. Still nothing could dampen the spirit of that day, the tangible reality of being part of something so large, that great throng of hopeful people demanding America should be America for all its citizens. I worked my way up toward the Lincoln Memorial, the sun warming me, and then thrilled to the music and

FIGURE 3.   The 1963 March on Washington for Jobs and Freedom. Everett Collection Inc / Alamy Stock Photo.

speeches. Even toned down, Lewis's speech called to me.[12] Like everyone else there, Dr. King's words lifted my hopes to new heights.

As thrilling as Dr. King's speech was, I firmly cast my lot with SNCC. I already believed that as important as the marches were, grassroots organizing would be the real engine driving social change. It would be organizing that built power, organizing that would change a world in desperate need of radical solutions.

Today I am amazed at how history has treated the March on Washington. Gone is any controversy. Dr. King's speech is now iconic. It feels as if the march must have been accepted, embraced by the whole country. King's words must have unified the nation. Nothing could be further from the truth.

In the weeks before the march, Gallup polled a national sample asking how many people had heard of the march.[13] Seventy-one percent said that they had heard of the impending march. Of those, only 23 percent had a favorable view of it, and most thought the march was dangerous, unwarranted, and should not happen. Politicians denounced it. No one was confident that such a large number of Black protestors would remain peaceful.

In May 1964, Gallup asked, "Do you think mass demonstrations by Negroes are more likely to help or more likely to hurt the Negro's cause for racial equality?" In response, only 16 percent of Americans—including just 10 percent of white people but 55 percent of nonwhite people—said such mass demonstrations would help the cause.[14]

Segregation was still rampant throughout the land, racist violence a common occurrence. That march and the organizing behind it was a courageous act of defiance.

Eighteen days later, the white supremacists of the South gave their answer to the march. Four members of the Klan blew up the 16th Street Baptist Church in Birmingham, intentionally injuring more than a dozen people and killing four young Black girls. More martyrs added to an already too long list. It was hard to believe that nonviolence could be sustained. However, the movement pressed on, and my hopes remained ebullient. I believed that it would be a long, hard slog, but the movement would transform the nation, no matter how much violence was thrown at it.

That November when President Kennedy was assassinated, everyone around me was shocked, grieving, bereft. I was not. I did not love the Kennedys. They had failed to protect the civil rights workers. Any progress that had been made had been forced by the movement, by those who risked death and beatings—not by the liberals in the Kennedy administration. Those same liberals had taken us to the brink of nuclear catastrophe over Cuba. I did not cry for the fallen president as I cried for the four Black children killed in their Birmingham Church by a racist bomb. I thought Malcolm X perhaps had it right when he talked of chickens coming home to roost.

I did not stop to reflect on the assassination, what it might mean for the nation. I was too busy learning at Commonwealth and on the streets of Roxbury. And soon, too busy falling in love.

In the fall of my junior year, Tim, Ronnie, and I frequently added a fourth companion to our excursions: Amy Merrill. She was the daughter of the headmaster. I had, of course, noticed Amy before, but she seemed to me aloof, apart, snobbish. For her part, she had found me to be insufferably earnest, cocky, and arrogant. Now suddenly she seemed alluring, mysterious, beautiful. She had long brown hair that tinted red when she sat in the light of a tall window. She wore sandals that laced up her shapely legs. She spoke French and Russian without effort.

Soon I was a regular visitor to the old brownstone building in the first block of Commonwealth Avenue where the Merrills lived. Increasingly I found myself there for dinners, walking Amy home after school, playing with her three younger brothers.

In addition to the house on Commonwealth, the Merrills owned a "farm" in Hancock, New Hampshire. That winter I was invited to Hancock with the family. Snow was on the ground. The sun went down early. Amy and I tobogganed down a steep snow-covered dirt road, somehow managing to overturn the toboggan on every run, flinging us together, flopping onto each other's well-padded but still exciting bodies. After dinner, we took a walk. Snow crunched underfoot. The air was crisp. The stars rotated about us. Being shy and responsible, I did nothing despite feeling the growing tension of desire. I was saved when Amy kissed me, and I discovered to my delight the mystery of tongues. We became a couple, inseparable, so very young and so very much in love.

The Merrills seemed to think that I was the perfect high school boyfriend for their second daughter. They welcomed me and had no qualms about what I was doing with her late at night in the library at the back of the house once everyone else had gone to bed. In that large library lined with volumes of books, we made the couch a place for languid and then not so languid exploration. Despite the long time we spent late and later in that library, there were never any interruptions, never any questions. I was determined to be a responsible boyfriend. Exploration was one thing; sexual intercourse would have to wait until we got married.

My senior year at Commonwealth, I had a clear plan: get into a college, then head to Mississippi in June to answer the call for a Freedom Summer. SNCC and the larger Council of Federated Organizations (COFO) had issued a call for one thousand white college students to come to Mississippi, that bastion of segregation, hate and endless violence against Black people. My friend Ron and I planned to go together.

I was more excited about Mississippi than I was about which college I would attend. I was confident that I would get into a good college—largely because I had the Commonwealth School teachers and headmaster working on my behalf. I needed a large scholarship, as my parents could contribute nothing. Both Amherst and Harvard accepted me and offered great packages of work, loans, and huge scholarships.

I pretended not to care whether I went to Harvard or Amherst, in the end opting for Harvard. There was no way that I could admit even to myself that I wanted to go to Harvard because it was the more prestigious, because it was the pinnacle of the elite. That conflicted with everything I claimed to believe in—but that is exactly why I chose it.

Ron and I made our plans to go south, looking forward to the training sessions that would start the Freedom Summer. I was excited but anxious. We both knew that Mississippi would be dangerous that summer. Anyone going, even Northern white students, would face arrests, beating and possibly worse. Still,

FIGURE 4. I had desperately wanted to be one of these Freedom Summer volunteers, here completing their training. Photo by Ted Polumbaum/Freedom Forum's Newseum Collection.

I urgently wanted to be part of the thousand young students descending on that retrograde state to force the eyes of the nation to focus on the violence that was an everyday occurrence for Black residents.

Before the final plans were set, my mother took me aside. She confessed that she was at her wit's end. My father was driving a cab but was terrible at it, not even taking home $100 for seven days of twelve-hour work. She was doing her best to make money by tutoring, but they were desperately short of what was required to pay the bills. The family needed me; she needed me. Could I once again crank up the student painting crew that had been so successful in past summers? While she was sorry, there was no way I could go South.

And that was that. The end of my Freedom Summer. Ron headed south without me. I was heartbroken. However, I knew my duty. I re-formed the student painting crew, once again hiring young women, as well as men, telling the women that it was fine to wear short shorts, the shorter the better—inevitably we received bigger tips at the end of the job when they did.

That spring, Noel became the first ever Black candidate for Congress in Massachusetts. Running as an independent, Noel challenged the powerful speaker of the House, John McCormack. I was totally surprised when I was offered the one paid staff position on the campaign. I talked with my painting crew who agreed that if I continued securing the jobs, I could draw a salary even as they did all the painting. That meant I could take the lower paying organizer job and with the money from the painting crew, still have enough to give my mother.

Noel was exceptional. He grew up in Harlem. His maternal grandfather, Frederick R. Moore, was an escaped slave who became a newspaper publisher, alderman, philanthropist, and unofficial "mayor" of Harlem. Noel entered Dartmouth in 1949, three months before his sixteenth birthday. There he became close friends with future fellow leader James Breeden. After graduate work at CCNY and teaching, Noel became the executive director of St. Mark's Social Center and was at the center of civil rights organizing in Boston.[15]

While I knew little of this background, Noel seemed larger than life to me. He was overweight but moved with the fluid grace of an athlete. Intensity marked everything he did.

I met with him on a hot, early June day in 1964.

"Michael," Noel began, "here's our strategy. As you know, the movement in Boston has proven that we can mount nonviolent direct action. We did that with the Stay Out for Freedom campaigns that had school kids walk out of school. We did it with the boycott of Wonder Bread. You were there. You know what we were able to pull off."

I smiled in agreement.

"But there are real challenges. Can we sustain the movement? The community is ready to act—but can that be on more than one issue? Can we create a community that is committed to real social change and not just amelioration? Can we surface multiple issues so that we can sustain action on a number of fronts instead of one issue at time?"

"So here is what we are doing. We are going to use a campaign for Congress not to win . . ."

Here Noel positively beamed at me.

"We know we cannot beat the speaker of the House. But we will use this campaign to create two Action Centers. The campaign is going to raise critical issues, issues of housing, of welfare, of lead paint, of education, of jobs, of community development. And the campaign is going to spell out a vision of social change. We are going to use running for office to build the foundation that can sustain a community committed to social change. So, everything you are going to do this summer is about organizing."

I was excited. "So, what is success?" I asked.

Noel leaned back. "If we create a new organization of welfare mothers, if we create at least ten new block organizations of tenants, if we start a campaign about lead paint poisoning our kids, and if we can create two ongoing Action Centers, one in Dudley Square and one in Washington Park, that will add up to success. Getting that done through this campaign will be your job. Are you up for it?"

Of course I was. I was thrilled.

Being the field organizer for the Noel Day Campaign in the summer of 1964 was my first paid organizing job. It was not Mississippi, but it meant that in my own way I was part of Freedom Summer.

Immediately I set to work on the campaign, kickstarting it with the formation of the two "Action Centers" that would be the focus for neighborhood-based work. Using many of the contacts made through BAG and the Massachusetts Freedom Movement, we were able to form groups working on lead paint poisoning, other tenant issues and going after slum landlords. We pulled together a feisty group of women on welfare to launch Mothers for Adequate Welfare. And we got Noel the signatures needed to be on the ballot.

I organized the door-to-door canvassing and signature gathering. In the white neighborhoods, we occasionally were heard to slip and refer to our candidate as "Noel O'Day." In the Black neighborhoods, there was rarely a need to explain who he was.

In the end, we received only 5 percent of the vote, but the Dudley Street Action Center was launched and continued after the campaign ended. Mothers for Adequate Welfare took off. Campaigns around slumlords and lead paint poisoning continued. That summer I felt I had finally become an organizer. That fall, while I was still committed to the campaign, I was heading to Harvard. I was also ready to try organizing something else: a new student movement.

I had the sense that with so many students, my generation, the baby boom, pouring onto campuses, with the heroic example of young Black students so vividly fresh in our minds, and the experienced organizers returning from Freedom Summer, the time was ripe to harness that power, to create a new student movement. There had been significant stirrings already in Berkeley and Ann Arbor.

That August of 1964 there were two events that would reverberate for years, significantly shaping my future. While at the time I paid them close attention, I had no idea how profound their impact would prove to be on the country and on my life.

In the Gulf of Tonkin off the coast of Vietnam, the United States claimed that its ships had been attacked by the North Vietnamese. The administration of Lyndon B. Johnson used the incident to have Congress pass a resolution giving the president authority to escalate the American intervention in Vietnam without a declaration of war and without additional congressional oversight. The resolution was opposed by only two senators, Senators Wayne Morse (D-OR) and Ernest Gruening (D-AK). The United States claimed that North Vietnam had launched two unprovoked attacks against our ships in the gulf. Even then it was unclear what the truth was. Years later documents would reveal that much of what Johnson used to justify the escalation was embellishment and fabrication.[16] I quickly added a section to our basic Day for Congress brochure opposing the air strikes in North Vietnam and the escalation that would lead to wider war.

That same month, I was transfixed by the Mississippi Freedom Democratic Party's (MFDP) challenge at the National Democratic Convention in Atlantic City. The convention was supposed to be a coronation of Johnson. The Freedom Summer organizers and the civil rights organizations in Mississippi pulled off a democratic election of an integrated delegation to the convention. They challenged the all-white "regular" delegation, which not only was segregated in violation of the rules of the national party but had already openly announced its support for Barry Goldwater, the nominee of the Republican Party! Those Mississippi Democratic Party "regulars" were intertwined with the White Citizen's Councils, the local sheriffs, and the forces of segregation. The same people who early that summer had brutally killed the three Freedom Summer volunteers, James Chaney, Michael Schwerner, and Andrew Goodman.

I was convinced that the MFDP would be seated, especially after the convention heard the moving testimony of its leaders, including Hamer. President Johnson, however, decided that he could not risk further alienating the already angry conservative Southern wing of the Democratic Party. Johnson forced the longtime civil rights supporters Senator Hubert Humphrey and Walter Reuther of the United Auto Workers to oppose seating the MFDP. They in turn convinced many liberals and even civil rights leaders, including Dr. King, to agree to a "compromise," seating only two leaders of the MFDP as token "at large delegates." The compromise was announced as a done deal without any consultation with the MFDP. This was a part of the price for Humphrey getting the vice presidency.

The MFDP refused. The parade of liberal leaders telling the MFDP to accept it was played out on national television. The political pressure was unrelenting. Yet the delegation from Mississippi led by Mrs. Hamer did not bend, did not break, did not yield.

I watched, riveted by the drama, as did tens of thousands of young people also getting ready to go to college. We saw the moral corruption of liberal leadership and its "pragmatism." In contrast, we saw the courage and moral fortitude of sharecroppers, of ordinary people who had had enough. No better example of the failure of liberal leadership could be presented to five million young people before we were to head off to our colleges and our new lives.

I knew in the core of my being which side I was on. It was not the side of President Johnson and the soon-to-be Vice President Humphrey and the national Democratic Party who had failed the moral test presented by the MFDP.

I was heading off to college. Our liberal leaders had made their choices, made them in Atlantic City, made them in Washington, made them in the skies over Indochina. The wrong choices. Looking back from today's vantage point, it is hard to remember how solidly America in 1964 was led by liberals, corporate liberals as we called them. There was a broad and "liberal" consensus that dominated American political thought. It was liberals who continued to test nuclear weapons. Liberals who told the Civil Rights Movement to slow down. Liberals who were sending bombers to Vietnam. I and my friends felt a profound alienation from liberal leaders. Despite the white supremacists of the South, we did not perceive a serious threat from the right. The kooks of the John Birch Society seemed only a joke. Our fight was with the liberals who dominated politics, the media, and the culture. We were rebels and we were rebelling against a liberalism whose moral bankruptcy was on vivid display in Atlantic City.

Now I would be part of a great river of young people sweeping onto the campuses of America. We felt our numbers. We saw the choices those in power in Mississippi, in the White House and in Congress had made. Now we would make ours.

A NEW LEFT AND THE START OF THE STUDENT MOVEMENT

When you have chosen your part, abide by it, and do not try to weakly reconcile yourself with the world. . . . Adhere to your own act and congratulate yourself if you have done something strange and extravagant, and broken the monotony of a decorous age.

—Ralph Waldo Emerson

In the late summer of 1964, I entered Harvard as an advanced placement sopho-more. I felt liberated, excited, and fully grown up. I moved into a tiny single in Greenough Hall, one street over from Harvard Yard. It had just enough room for a small bed, a desk, and a chair—yet I felt a new space around me, possibilities everywhere. My parents were living only three miles away in a small duplex on Aberdeen Avenue with the landlord on the first floor and his plaster statue of the Madonna in the tiny, low fenced front yard. Despite the geographical proximity, I was in another universe.

Suddenly I was surrounded by thousands of people my own age. Out of open dorm windows, the Beatles' "I Want to Hold Your Hand," the Supremes' "Come See about Me," and the Kinks' "You Really Got Me" floated out into the Septem-ber evening, thrummed through the air, provided a backbeat to 1,200 young men prowling the early fall evenings in the hope of something unsaid but desperately wanted. Everywhere you looked, there were masses of fresh-faced young men and women, excited, eager, curious. The energy of so many of us was palpable on the streets, in the dorms, in the dining rooms, in the classes. The music throbbed. The talk never stopped. We were so eager, so hopeful, so sure that the future was soon to be ours.

Along with a scholarship that paid 90 percent of the cost of my tuition, I was given two jobs, working in the freshman dining hall and selling peanuts and popcorn at football games. Between work, studying for my major in history and literature, visits to Amy who was down in Providence studying at Pembroke (the women's college at Brown), and my organizing work, I was living packed, eighteen-hour days.

I still had work to do on Noel Day's campaign, primarily recruiting college students to make the bus trip down Mass Ave into Roxbury to volunteer. Increasingly, though, I was focused on building a student movement, creating a New Left in America.

There are things one knows analytically. And there are things one knows instinctively. I knew in my bones in that fall of 1964 that we could build a new student movement. This belief was not based on data or reason—I felt it. I felt my generation. If young African Americans could overcome almost a century of terror and change the Jim Crow system, certainly my generation could and would remake America. It would take years, but we would start by building a student-based New Left. With the arrogance of the young, I was certain.

I did not want to work on one issue here and another there. I saw racism, inequality, poverty, nuclear weapons, a stifling materialistic culture as interconnected evils of a system that put more and more power in fewer and fewer hands. I wanted to be part of something brand new, something vibrant and only imagined—a New Left that was organized around extending democracy. I wanted a New Left that would tackle the unique problems of our age: bureaucracy, rapid technological change, materialism, the need to balance community and individual freedom, as well as the enduring challenge of economic inequality. All people should be able to make the decisions that affect their lives. It meant students should have a say in the decisions of their universities. Welfare mothers in the policies of the welfare state. Workers in some of the decisions at their factories. Residents in the decisions that would shape their neighborhoods.

I was sure that the old left, the withered Communist and Socialist Parties, the intellectuals who had come of age in the 1930s, even the organizers who had built the unions, all had nothing to teach us. I scorned old leftists with their embrace of foreign models, their excuses for authoritarian states—we wanted more democracy not less. Their ideology was too determinist, too focused on state control. I associated the old left with people like my parents, tired, beaten. They lacked humor, they lacked music, they lacked youth—they were old.

Liberal ideology dominated the country. I thought mainstream liberals excused too much, were too incremental, always urging any insurgency to go slower, rarely questioning the power of the corporate elites. They were locked into a Cold War framework that stifled new thinking and justified the American imperial role in the world. Although I had no sympathy for communist systems, I rejected the rigid anticommunism that Cold War liberals sought to impose as the test for all politics. Cold War liberals, too, seemed old.

Two years before, I had chosen Students for a Democratic Society (SDS) as my future political home. There was a lot of overlap between the small SDS group in Cambridge and the Friends of SNCC. I had spent a lot of time with the Friends of SNCC and gotten to know two white Southern couples. Bob Zellner had been the Student Nonviolent Coordinating Committee's (SNCC) first white field secretary. I met Bob and his wife Dottie during their many trips to Boston. Another couple were Robb and Dorothy Burlage. Robb was a graduate student at Harvard and Dorothy at the Divinity School. I had met Robb through my civil rights work and through him made my way to a regular gathering of SDS members. Episodically, when organizing and schoolwork allowed, on Thursday evenings, I headed over to Cronin's Bar on Mt. Auburn Street in Harvard Square to join a regular gathering there. A small group of young men debated the issues of the day and discussed what would constitute the vision of a New Left. I was particularly mesmerized by two Harvard students, Richie Rothstein[1] and Todd Gitlin,[2] who had far-ranging intellects and could bring a new perspective to almost any topic. They were frequently joined by Lee Webb from Boston University with whom I had canvassed for the Hughes campaign and Mike Appleby, the young staff person for the American Friends Service Committee.[3] Sometimes they were joined by others I had met during the Hughes campaign. I was the only high school kid there. I rarely said much. Too young to drink beer, I nursed a soft drink. My brain felt like a massive sponge.

These early SDS leaders were smart and moral and practical and inspirational—exactly the combination I was seeking. They kept returning over and over to issues of strategy. Because of them, I had started to read small magazines, *Root & Branch* and the British *New Left Review*. Because of them, I read the Port Huron Statement, and once I had read it, I knew I had found my political home.

The Port Huron Statement took its name from a meeting at the United Auto Workers camp in Port Huron, Michigan, where, in June of 1962, the leadership of SDS, then a tiny organization, met, rewrote, edited, and approved a draft largely written by Tom Hayden. It began with a generational appeal that immediately spoke to me:

> We are people of this generation, bred in at least modest comfort, housed now in universities, looking uncomfortably to the world we inherit.
>
> When we were kids, the United States was the wealthiest and strongest country in the world: the only one with the atom bomb, the least scarred by modern war, an initiator of the United Nations that we thought would distribute Western influence throughout the world. Freedom and equality for each individual, government of, by, and for

the people—these American values we found good, principles by which we could live as men. Many of us began maturing in complacency.

As we grew, however, our comfort was penetrated by events too troubling to dismiss. First, the permeating and victimizing fact of human degradation, symbolized by the Southern struggle against racial bigotry, compelled most of us from silence to activism. Second, the enclosing fact of the Cold War, symbolized by the presence of the Bomb, brought awareness that we ourselves, and our friends, and millions of abstract "others" we knew more directly because of our common peril, might die at any time. We might deliberately ignore, or avoid, or fail to feel all other human problems, but not these two, for these were too immediate and crushing in their impact, too challenging in the demand that we as individuals take the responsibility for encounter and resolution.[4]

The statement proceeded to discuss values, politics, technology, and the challenges of individualism and community, and to call for "participatory democracy." The statement tackled the economy, the military-industrial complex, the impact of rapid technological change, the individual in the welfare state, foreign policy and the Cold War, the rise of independence movements in the former colonial countries, and the rigidity and stultifying ideology of anticommunism.

Today, much of it is dated: the male only language, the dominance of liberal ideology, the problem of Southern Democrats' hold on power, the Cold War, and, of course, the absence of any analysis of the treatment of women and gays.

In other ways, it still seems relevant: the impacts of rapid technological change, the need for more democracy and more community. Its statement, "We can no longer rely on competition of the many to ensure that business enterprise is responsive to social needs. The many have become the few. Nor can we trust the corporate bureaucracy to be socially responsible or to develop a 'corporate conscience' that is democratic" is, if anything, even more apt today. As is "America should concentrate on its genuine social priorities: abolish squalor, terminate neglect, and establish an environment for people to live in with dignity and creativeness."[5] SDS leaders' willingness to be precise about the politics of the moment as well as visionary in their calls for the future, added up for me to a breathtaking call to action. I wanted to be part of this bold project.

By then, I considered myself a democratic socialist. Yet I agreed with the prevalent thinking in SDS not to use the term socialism. I believed that an economy run purely for private profit made no sense. Instead, we needed a new model where workers had a say in their work, where economic activity benefited society as a whole.

However, for most Americans still caught in Cold War thinking, socialism was associated with the authoritarian communist states, regarded as un-American. Better to not use the term and focus on the content of democratic participation.

As soon as I arrived at Harvard, I was part of a group reorganizing the SDS chapter, which, until then, had been tiny. I was confident that I could be an organizer that transformed the brilliant ideas that I had absorbed at Cronin's into concrete action.

We started by convincing those participating in single-issue efforts to come into SDS. I found that many students were already there. The antinuclear group Tocsin, the students returning from Mississippi, many of whom had been active in the Civil Rights Coordinating Committee, a few members of the Student Peace Union, and the students who had volunteered on the Day campaign all agreed to merge into a revitalized SDS. Conscious of my youth (having just turned seventeen), I worked hard to promote other, older students into formal positions of leadership.

In October, I attended a small meeting of SDS members from around the region to figure out how to organize across New England. A dozen of us sat in a typical, shabby student apartment with too few chairs, grappling with how to get more SDS chapters organized. Representing Harvard-Radcliffe, Tufts, Boston University, and MIT, we started listing all the other schools where we wanted SDS chapters. I mentioned that Amy would try to pull together students at Brown. Soon we had a list of twenty-five colleges. Someone said, "We obviously need a regional organizer in charge of starting new chapters." Everyone agreed. There followed an awkward silence. Someone finally asked, "Well, who wants to do it?" David Smith from Tufts spoke up, "I am willing to take it on."[6] He was two years older, clean cut, wearing khakis and a collared shirt. For reasons now that I cannot recall or fathom, I thought, *I can do this*, and said I wanted the job as well. There was another awkward silence until someone said, "Great—let's have two of you." And so, the group selected two regional organizers.

I look back and am amazed: I had just arrived at college, entering as a sophomore with a full academic load; I had to work at two student jobs to help pay for school and have some spending money; I was committed to organizing the SDS chapter at Harvard while pursuing "the love of my life" who was in Providence, while also helping the Day campaign and the Dudley Street Action Center—*and* I wanted to be one of the first unpaid regional organizers for SDS! But I was seventeen, arrogant, and sure there was nothing I could not master if I put my mind to it.

In the following months, I visited Boston College, Holy Cross, Simmons, Emmanuel, Northeastern, and BU, organizing SDS chapters. When visiting Amy,

I would work with her to get SDS groups going at Brown and the Rhode Island School of Design. At new colleges, I would often start by dropping by the campus newspaper to ask if anyone was already active. Sometimes, in the smaller schools, I could go to the library and look at the due date cards to see the names of students who had checked out the books by C. Wright Mills and Herbert Marcuse. I would check in with the campus ministry whose members almost always knew the names of activists or potential activists.

Once I had connected with them, it was often easy to convince these students to consider working with SDS. I would introduce myself as the organization's regional organizer and ask if they had heard of us. Usually, they had. Then I would ask about them—where were they from, what were they studying, how were they finding school. Often, I would be talking with first year students. They were politically conscious, and usually they had done something to support civil rights before coming to college. They would tell me about tutoring for the Northern Student Movement, raising money for SNCC, or marching in support of a local African American organization. Often, they had protested nuclear testing.

Many of the young people I connected with to form SDS chapters came from families that approved of their activism. Some were "Red Diaper Babies" having grown up in socialist, communist, and former communist families. Others had parents who had been politically active New Deal Democrats. In those families dissenting from the prevailing political orthodoxies was not seen as unpatriotic. It was easier for young people from these families to become activists. This first generation of SDS members would soon be swamped by a much larger wave of students who came from conservative and apolitical family backgrounds.

I had learned from my organizing with Boston Action Group (BAG) and Noel's campaign that I was not a "salesman." I was not "selling" SDS. I was connecting. We found points of common experience to talk about. How horrified we had been at the murder of James Chaney, Michael Schwerner, and Andrew Goodman. How shocking the betrayal of Fannie Lou Hamer and the Mississippi Freedom Democratic Party (MFDP) had been in Atlantic City. What "duck and cover" meant to us in high school. How appalled we were by the sterility of mass culture and crass consumerism. How inspired we were by Berkeley's Free Speech Movement. Then I would work the conversation around to what they were hoping to do at college. I would listen and see what openings they provided me for making the point that there was only one multi-issue, national student organization that was working on foreign policy, civil rights and for greater student power—SDS. I would ask if they had read the Port Huron Statement and if not, I would leave them several copies, along with other literature.

Many of the young men and women I met with quickly wanted to explore putting together an SDS chapter. Often, they were already meeting with a group of like-minded students, talking about what they could do together to support civil rights or press for a larger student voice in their school. I would explain that SDS was a membership organization, but I never pushed any student to pay the two-dollar membership fee and get their SDS card. I always emphasized, "What is most important is for you to start working with us, to be part of the movement and then later on, if you want to formally join SDS, you can."

For example, at Harvard I met David Loud, who was skeptical at first about SDS. David had just returned from a year in France. He wore a stylish cap, had a goatee, and seemed far more sophisticated than I ever could be. He was not sure SDS was left enough. I knew I would not get him to become a member right away, so I focused on the work that I knew he cared deeply about. "Don't worry about becoming a member," I would say. "Let's do the work." Soon he was engaged and went on to become a critical part of the Harvard SDS leadership and a lifelong friend.

Over the next year, small SDS chapters were formed on virtually every campus in New England. Many were helped along by Dave Smith or me but just as many started without any outside assistance.

In December of 1964, Amy and I went to New York City for our first national SDS meeting, the National Council. This gathering brought together SDS activists from all over the country. Attending were sixteen national officers, representatives of thirty-seven chapters, and almost 300 "observers" who did not have a vote but could participate in the discussions.[7] This made this four-day gathering much larger than the previous year's entire national convention. I was the official voting representative of Harvard-Radcliffe SDS.

The first day of the meeting was dedicated to speakers and panels, the second day to workshops, and the final two days to decision-making plenary sessions.

The first day began with welcoming speeches by Michael Harrington, the author of The Other America, the book that "discovered poverty" in America, and Paul Potter, the president of SDS. Then we swung into a panel on "Breakthroughs in Student Action" with Professor Staughton Lynd who had directed the Freedom Schools in Mississippi for Freedom Summer; Jesse Allen from Newark talking about the Newark Community Union Project, the SDS community organizing effort there; Eric Levine, a leader of SDS in Berkeley discussing the Free Speech Movement that had rocked the Bay Area; Peter Brandon of the Meat Cutters Union discussing a North Carolina Student Labor Project; and me, discussing the Day campaign and the ongoing organizing efforts that had emerged from the campaign.

I cannot remember what I said, only the excitement I felt at being part of this brilliant, passionate, moral group of young people. I thought I was mature and knew so much. I was young and knew so little. I liked everyone I met at the meeting. Yet the room was filled with tensions I did not understand, groups dividing, emotions, and arguments, like flashing schools of fish darting in the rapids, half seen. I could sense them but had no real understanding of what was happening or what was at stake.

SDS had grown out of the Student League for Industrial Democracy (SLID), the student arm of the League for Industrial Democracy, which traced its history back to its founding in 1905 by Jack London, Upton Sinclair, and Clarence Darrow.[8] SLID was generally associated with the Socialist Party and its anticommunist, social democratic politics. The Civil Rights Movement stirred young people across the country including those in SLID. The organization changed its name to Students for a Democratic Society, fortuitously planned a conference on Human Rights in the North, which was boosted by the first round of lunch counter sit-ins. With a grant from the UAW, SDS hired Al Haber, a University of Michigan grad student, as a full-time organizer. Haber cultivated a remarkable group of student leaders at Michigan, including Bob Ross, Dick Flacks, Tom Hayden, and Sharon Jeffrey. Then he began finding leaders at other campuses.

The first generation of SDS leaders were profoundly shaped by the Civil Rights Movement and began to conceive of the organization as the Northern, white analog to SNCC.

As ferment spread through young people, SDS was one of the few multi-issue organizations that transcended single-issue efforts. Throughout the early 1960s it steadily grew. By December 1964 it had chapters on a growing number of campuses, and it also had a significant number of leaders who had graduated from college.

At the December gathering, one clear grouping was made up of the organizers who had left the campuses and moved into poor communities. The year before, SDS had recruited one hundred young people to go into neighborhoods in Northern cities to organize an "interracial movement of the poor." These "ERAP" (Economic Research and Action Project) organizers were heavily influenced by SNCC and the twin concepts of grassroots organizing of the poor and creating "the beloved community." A concept embraced both by Dr. Martin Luther King, Jr., and SNCC, the beloved community was intended to describe and define both how the organizers and activists related to one another and what they sought to build "out there" in the world they sought to transform. Over time the beloved community in SNCC and then in SDS organizing came to mean decision making by consensus and nonhierarchical organizational forms where all were equal, and all were cherished, respected, and supported. It fed into the claim "there are no leaders here."

The young people of ERAP wanted to create a community of dedicated organizers who would entrench themselves in the poor neighborhoods of the North and Midwest. They hoped to bring low-income and working-class white people into "the movement." They lived together, worked together, grappling each day with issues of class and race and, without being as conscious of it, gender.

At the SDS National Council the ERAP organizers were led primarily by Tom Hayden. This was my first interaction with a person whose writings I had been reading and admiring for the last three years, especially his electrifying writing of travels to the front lines of Mississippi and Alabama where he had been savagely beaten. Now Tom was in Newark, New Jersey, with a group of ERAP organizers.

Throughout the meeting, Tom sat off slightly to the side or back, toothpick nonchalantly perched in the side of his mouth. Periodically he would rise, riveting the attention of the entire room and say, "Suppose we rush through the debate and 'decide' to do something by a vote of thirty-six to thirty-three. Will we really have decided anything?" Or "What if Robert's Rules of Order are really a capitalist conspiracy?" After each of these oracular, haiku-like questions he would slide back to his seat.

Always attuned to Amy, sitting in the chair next to me, I quickly realized she, along with many others in the room, was quite smitten with this charismatic figure. Instantly, I was seized with a silent determination to oppose whatever Tom supported and support whatever he did not. I would like to write that at my first national SDS meeting, I was driven by incisive strategy but in truth I was steered more by a carefully concealed jealousy. I was, for all my passionate dedication to the movement, only seventeen.

Another group of the SDS leadership led by Paul Booth and Todd Gitlin was more focused on politics and campaigns. They argued for launching a campaign on the fifth anniversary of the Sharpeville massacre in which the apartheid regime of South Africa fired on a peaceful protest killing or wounding over 200 people. They suggested we target the Chase Manhattan Bank given the institution's heavy investments there. Then, they audaciously proposed that SDS call for a first ever March on Washington to protest escalation in Vietnam. There was a subtle tension between these groups and even with other smaller subsets, which I could feel in the room but did not understand. It was all too exciting and new. In the end, the ERAP organizers largely went their own way but always remained part of SDS, as the "old guard."

Flowing into the organization were new undergraduates, like me, from an ever-increasing number of colleges, the vanguard of a massive wave that was soon to lift the organization into a totally new dimension and level of importance. We, the new folks, were in awe of the ERAP organizers; we were inspired by Freedom Summer, the courage and stalwart morality of the MFDP who had refused to accept a token compromise urged on them by the liberal leadership of the Democratic Party.

We were equally inspired by the Free Speech Movement in Berkeley that had given us the first glimpse of what mass student action could be. Returning from Freedom Summer, activists in the Bay Area had been determined to continue their work with a campaign to end discrimination at home. The university tried to stop them from recruiting on campus, activists were arrested, and the result was the first massive student uprising of the 1960s. Just before we met in New York for the SDS meeting, 4,000 students had demonstrated, sitting in at Berkeley's Sproul Hall. There, Free Speech leader Mario Savio, who would be one of the 800 arrested, gave a speech that captured the essence of how we all felt:

> we're a bunch of raw materials that don't mean to be . . . made into any product! Don't mean . . . to end up being bought by some clients of the University, be they the government, be they industry, be they organized labor, be they anyone! We're human beings! . . . There's a time when the operation of the machine becomes so odious—makes you so sick at heart—that you can't take part. You can't even passively take part. And you've got to put your bodies upon the gears and upon the wheels, upon the levers, upon all the apparatus and you've got to make it stop. And you've got to indicate to the people who run it, to the people who own it, that unless you're free, the machine will be prevented from working at all.[9]

We, the fresh-faced campus representatives who came to New York for that national SDS meeting, were ready to throw our bodies upon the gears and wheels. Even if at that meeting, we represented groups that numbered less than fifty, we felt the quickening pulse of a new movement. We felt that soon we would be marching, the walls shaking.

The debate over calling for a march against the war in Vietnam was heated. At first it failed to pass. Tom was opposed, so I was passionately in favor. The ERAP organizers feared such a march would take attention away from building the interracial movement of the poor. (In the long run, they were correct. The war and our opposition to it would overwhelm all other initiatives.) There was continued wrangling. The meeting was run with a conscientious adherence to Robert's Rules of Order. Bob Ross, who had voted against the resolution for the march, was persuaded to move reconsideration. In the end, we narrowly voted to call for the march in Washington in April to oppose the war. We also jumped at the chance to act against apartheid. We wanted a national movement, so we voted to have a national office for SDS—so long as it was not in New York where it would be in thrall to the "old left." We refused to continue the 1950s ritual of "cleansing" our organization by prohibiting communists from participating in the march and our other activities. While we had no love for communists, we were determined to break from the Cold War mentality with its rigid and to us, simplistic insistence that every conflict was part of the struggle against communism.

Our refusal immediately led to a rupture with the anticommunist left that had been the support and birthplace of SDS. It had been bad enough that SDS had not focused on unions as the instrument for change but our failure to embrace the anticommunist positioning of the Cold War American left was fatal in their eyes. Their rejection did not bother us at all. We were happy to be on our own. We knew we had everything to learn. At the same time, we were sure the stale old left in all its variety had nothing to teach us as we strode confidently, confusedly, onto the stage of American history.

On the fourth day of the conference a young Bob Dylan came by to shyly mingle and ask if he might volunteer at an ERAP project.

By then most of us had resonated to Dylan's words and music. "It'll soon shake your windows and rattle your walls, for the times they are a-changin'." When he sang, "come mothers and fathers throughout the land, don't criticize what you can't understand, your sons and your daughters are beyond your command," he was singing for us, "the old road was rapidly aging". Soon each of us could and would shout out: "please get out of the way of the new one if you can't lend a hand" because the times were certainly changing.

I would not be there to meet Dylan. I had received a message to call home right away. My father had experienced a massive heart attack. He was in the ICU, and it was not clear if he would live. My mother and seven-year-old brother needed me. Leaving Amy, I immediately took the bus for downtown Boston, hopped on a Green Line trolley to the Brigham Hospital and sought out my mother.

I went from the excitement of that meeting in New York to a hospital room where everything was flat and pale: the walls, the light, and my father's suddenly papery skin as he lay in that hospital bed.

My mother was uncharacteristically quiet. She explained that the doctors said it was touch and go and my father was in critical condition. She never asked me what I had been doing in New York, and I was happy not to discuss what seemed like a different world. We sat in silence, waiting for further word from the doctor.

My father would survive this attack. And over the next decade and a half, he would be back in the hospital again three more times, each time the outcome precarious. Whenever I was called back to the hospital, time seemed to slow. I would be yanked from my life of wild possibility back into the vortex of my immediate family, sliding into the inevitable waiting room where my mother, red-eyed, tired, smoking one cigarette and lighting the next before she finished the first; my brother wide-eyed, simultaneously bored and scared; and I would wait for the doctor's periodic pronouncements, *my father would live if he survived the next so many hours. . . . If the operation to take part of one vein and repair the aorta worked . . . if he made it through the night.*

The audacious decision to call for a national march against the war in Vietnam would transform SDS. While I had voted in favor of the resolution setting the date for the march as Saturday, April 17, 1965, coinciding with Easter college vacation, primarily out of jealously, I now threw myself enthusiastically into organizing for it. Throughout every college in New England, we were spreading the call. In March, President Lyndon B. Johnson had begun an unprecedented bombing campaign, Operation Rolling Thunder, dropping thousands of tons of explosives onto Vietnam every day. We had to make students feel the blasts of those bombs as they pursued their peaceful young lives on the idyllic campuses of America.

We had to explain the basic facts about Vietnam over and over. In leaflets that we would slide under every dorm room door. Over meals in dining halls. In small groups. After classes. Everywhere we could, we explained how Vietnam, after centuries as an independent country, had been colonized by the French, how then the Japanese had occupied the country during the Second World War, and how the United States had supported the resistance to the Japanese led by the communist Ho Chi Minh. Then after the defeat of the Japanese, the attempt by the French to reassert their colonial control, and the new war of independence once again led by the communists and Ho Chi Minh. The critical and misguided US support for the French all in the name of opposing communism. The 1954 Geneva Accords temporarily divided the country into north and south and promised internationally supervised free and fair national elections in a unified country in 1956. Those elections were never held because of US intervention. Over and over, we would use this quote from President Dwight D. Eisenhower in his memoir *Mandate for Change*:

> I have never talked or corresponded with a person knowledgeable in Indochinese affairs who did not agree that had elections been held as of the time of the fighting, possibly 80 per cent of the population would have voted for the Communist Ho Chi Minh as their leader.[10]

We relied on I. F. Stone, the crusading left journalist who published his own weekly newsletter and who consistently documented that the administration was lying about the history, lying about its policies, lying about the South Vietnamese government it was creating, lying about having been attacked in the Gulf of Tonkin.

FIGURE 5.   The SDS Vietnam protest in Washington, DC, April 15, 1965. Courtesy of the Associated Press.

We educated. We listened. We organized. We produced fact sheet after fact sheet, our hands stained purple from running leaflets on Gestetner machines, our clothes splotched, black from mimeo ink.

In the month before the march, the faculty and graduate students at the University of Michigan held the first "teach-in." Amazingly 3,000 students cycled through the prolonged event. Soon SDS and sympathetic younger faculty were organizing teach-ins at one hundred universities across the country. They were meant to be like a "sit-in," professors, teaching fellows, and students making presentations and speeches, one after the other, hour after hour. The crowded halls were filled with couples snuggling, antiwar activists recruiting the people in the next seat over, wide-eyed freshmen from conservative families wrestling with what they were hearing, a few members of Young Americans for Freedom at the doors denouncing the whole affair as a red conspiracy, and large numbers of reporters writing furious notes and doing interviews in the hallways outside. Of course, the teach-in organized at Berkeley was the largest. Over three days more than 30,000 young people participated. That spring, opposition to the war was taking root on America's campuses.

We expected a few thousand students to show up in Washington, DC, on April 17. Instead, 25,000 people marched that sunny day. I was thrilled that we brought 1,000 students from Boston, the men almost all in suit jackets and skinny ties, their hair short, many of the women in skirts, white socks, and ponytails. Most of the marchers were college students, but SNCC organizers marched alongside ministers and preachers. Roughly 10 percent of the march was made up of African Americans. The weather was warm and breezy. We listened to songs by Joan Baez, Judy Collins, and Phil Ochs. We listened to speeches from one of the two senators who had voted against the Tonkin Resolution; we were welcomed to Washington by a small, spectacled Izzy Stone. We were excited to hear from the legendary Bob Moses of SNCC up from Mississippi. The speech of our own SDS president Paul Potter, then twenty-six, gave voice to what we thought, what we had been saying in small groups but now was being said before 25,000 people.

As I sat on the grass on that wind-whipped April Saturday, I felt a direct connection with what Paul said.

> Most of us grew up thinking that the United States was a strong but humble nation, that involved itself in world affairs only reluctantly, that respected the integrity of other nations and other systems, and that engaged in wars only as a last resort . . . Vietnam has provided the razor, the terrifying sharp cutting edge that has finally severed the last vestige of illusion that morality and democracy are the guiding principles of American foreign policy.

Hearing that I nodded in agreement. That was exactly how I felt. I had genuinely believed in American exceptionalism, in the goodness of our nation.

Paul went on:

> We must accept the consequences that calling for an end of the war in Vietnam is in fact allowing for the likelihood that a Vietnam without war will be a self-styled Communist Vietnam . . . this country must come to understand that creation of a communist country in the world today is not an ultimate defeat.

Again, I felt a surge of assent as Paul continued:

> I do not believe that the president or Mr. Rusk or Mr. McNamara or even McGeorge Bundy are particularly evil men. If asked to throw napalm on the back of a ten-year-old child, they would shrink in horror—but their decisions have led to mutilation and death of thousands and thousands of people.
>
> What kind of system is it that allows good men to make those kinds of decisions? . . . What kind of system is it that disenfranchises people in the South, leaves millions upon millions of people throughout the

country impoverished and excluded from the mainstream and promise of American society, that creates faceless and terrible bureaucracies
and makes those the place where people spend their lives and do their
work, that consistently puts material values before human values-and
still persists in calling itself free and still persists in finding itself fit to
police the world?

We must name that system. We must name it, describe it, analyze
it, understand it and change it . . . How do you stop a war then? If the
war has its roots deep in the institutions of American society, how do
you stop it? Do you march to Washington? Is that enough? . . . I believe
that the administration is serious about expanding the war in Asia. The
question is whether the people here are as serious about ending it.

I thought about how serious I was about ending the war. On that April afternoon, as the sun started to go low in the Washington sky, I felt determined. I had
no idea that it would take us ten years—no idea of what that war would cost, not
just in Indochina but at home. No concept of what we were hurtling toward and
the role that march meant we would play in those next ten years. None.

The day after the March, President Johnson responded directly: "There is no
human power capable of forcing us from Vietnam. We will remain as long as necessary, with the might that is required, whatever the risk and whatever the cost."[11]

By the end of April 1965, American troops in Vietnam reached 46,500,[12]
headed to 184,000 by year's end.[13]

After the March on Washington, SDS emerged as the leading student organization opposing the war in Vietnam. As the war became the dominant issue on
American campuses, so SDS would become the dominant student movement
in opposition to the American government and its policies. SDS would become
a massive organization that grew faster than anyone could have expected and
would, briefly, carry many of the complex aspirations and dreams of a significant
part of my generation.

I had arrived at Harvard thinking I was part of birthing a New Left. It was to
have been a long-term project of building around values and vision. It was to
have been the political expression of a new generation, my generation, that would
slowly expand what was possible in American politics. I knew it would take years,
decades even, but I was filled with hope and expectations.

In fact, I had embarked on something quite different. I did not realize it at the
time, but I had started down a ten-year effort to do something that had never
happened before in American history: force our nation to stop a war.

My next decade would be consumed by that struggle. I would learn how
to organize sit-ins and marches and even riots. I would be part of a massive

movement not for a new vision of America but in opposition to the war in Vietnam. In that crucible of fevered resistance, we would sway the nation, topple a president, ultimately help end the war, and change the American campus forever. But at what cost? As the antiwar effort consumed us, we would lose the optimism and vision that animated us in 1964. And the incandescent heat of the experience would warp our souls.

CREATING ROOM FOR DISSENT

That first April 1965 march in Washington suddenly shaped SDS into the spearhead of the opposition to a war that, at that time, had the support of almost the entire nation. Editorial pages of the nation's leading newspapers supported the war. Virtually every single elected official in the land supported the war. Corporate leaders, cardinals, labor leaders, and university presidents all supported the war. We did not. Our first task was the difficult one of carving out space for dissent.

As Harvard let out for the summer, I returned home to live with my parents. Given their need for a financial contribution from me, I was immediately out rousting up jobs, reassembling my crew, climbing the ladders to paint the outsides of Brattle Street houses, all the time thinking about how to organize effectively against the war.

Unbeknownst to me that July, the FBI came to Harvard asking about me and others who had been active against the war. Mrs. Frances Osborn of the Harvard administration confirmed that I was indeed a student there and told them I had been granted sophomore standing in history and literature. The head of campus security promised the FBI that he and his men would keep a close eye on me and the other SDS members.[1]

At the same time that the FBI was checking up on us and inspired by the "teach-ins" that had swept the campuses that spring, we decided to organize a big teach-in at Harvard. To make ours unique, we planned an all-night affair. We would start at 8 p.m. and run the program into the early hours of the next morning when we would break into workshops and greet the sunrise.

On a hot July evening, large crowds of young people streamed into Sanders Theater, totally filling it. We opened up nearby Lowell Lecture Hall where we could pipe in the sound from Sanders and soon it too was totally packed. Over 2,000 people were eager to hear the lineup we had assembled. We had tried to secure a prowar speaker, inviting George Cabot Lodge, son of the US ambassador in Saigon. But no supporter of the war would agree to share the stage with an antiwar lineup that included I. F. Stone, Noam Chomsky, Howard Zinn, and Norman Mailer.

Things started uneventfully. The first speaker, Banks McDowell, a Boston University law professor, argued the illegality of the war. The second was Staughton Lynd, who had been in Mississippi for Freedom Summer, coordinating the Freedom Schools, and now was a professor at Yale. Lean and angular, normally a soft-spoken Quaker, Lynd launched into a vehement personal attack on President Lyndon B. Johnson, declared him unfit for office, called for his immediate removal and for civil disobedience at the White House. The audience cheered. Reporters scribbled. People flowed around the outside of both buildings trying to hear.

The next speaker was Mailer. Short, pugnacious, and intemperate, punctuating every other sentence with obscenities, he too attacked the president, calling him a "bully with an air force."

"The great fear that lies on America is not that Johnson is privately close to insanity, so much as he is the expression of the near insanity of most of us." Mailer went on, his thick short body tensed, straining, arms back, chest forward, looking as if he were about to punch somebody. He kept talking about Johnson's psychic need for action, any action, and how Americans lived for action; this was the American disease that Johnson suffered from. I found him puzzling but then, I thought, novelists are not organizers. Mailer was followed by the cosmopolitan scientist Sal Luria, an Italian-born biologist who got us back on a more focused track.

I was looking forward to our next speaker, Stone, but was stunned when he started to tell the audience that Mailer and Lynd were completely wrong. "You cannot oppose the war by going out to the American public and personally insulting and attacking their president! That will never work! That's just madness." Mailer stood up and yelled something at Stone that I could not make out. For a moment, the two of them were frozen, two bantams caught in a moment of fury.

Then Stone turned back to the audience, addressing the fallacies of American policy in Vietnam. I realized I had been holding my breath.

After Stone, the speakers became even more focused.

The program went on until 3 a.m. at which point the remaining several hundred students broke into workshops on the grass outside, staying until the summer sun finally rose in the Cambridge sky. I, however, had left at three to catch a few hours of sleep before gathering our crew to paint another house.

As experienced in that teach-in, even as early as 1965, the antiwar movement was fractious. It contained those who felt the need for more disruptive protests, some who saw the war in stark moral terms, others for whom the war was an expression of a larger cultural psychosis, others who felt it was driven by a system of power and logic that had to be confronted, and some who strove to be pragmatic and some who were preoccupied with organizing. For the moment, the movement, small but growing, was able to contain all of us.

In 1965 questioning the war was restricted to a tiny minority. Few Americans were even paying attention to what was happening in those distant lands. The vast majority had faith in our leaders, especially the military and the president. We passed out leaflets at Harvard showing that President Johnson had lied about the Gulf of Tonkin incident. Almost to a person the sophisticated students of Harvard responded by saying, "well you might, or might not, have a point about what is going on over there—but the president of the United States never lies!" It was indeed a different era, soon to be permanently swept away.

Unlike the rest of the country, we were increasingly preoccupied by the war.

At first, we thought Vietnam might be a mistake. Perhaps our government simply did not understand what it was doing. We felt a patriotic responsibility to speak up, to bring us back to our values, back to our senses.

In those days, the dominant metaphor in foreign policy was appeasement. The dominant framework was that of the Cold War. Both political parties agreed that the 1938 Munich appeasement of Adolf Hitler made the Second World War inevitable. Only by standing up to aggression early could greater disasters be averted. In the Cold War framework, the lesson of Munich was that the West must be strong in opposition to communist aggression. No appeasement. The domino theory was universally accepted—if we did not stop the march of communism in Vietnam, it would spread steadily, first to Cambodia, then to Indonesia, and then to the Philippines. In 1965, that foreign policy consensus appeared unbreakable.

To us that consensus discounted the history of Vietnam itself, reduced every conflict to a simplistic formula, insisted on monolithic communism and was profoundly ahistorical. Our job was to create room for debate and dissent, space for active opposition.

That fall of 1965, SDS became embroiled in national headlines. Among the most powerful newspaper columnists of the time, Rowland Evans and Robert Novak savaged SDS for what they said was a new plan to urge young men to resist the draft. The outrage gathered steam when Senator John Stennis denounced the

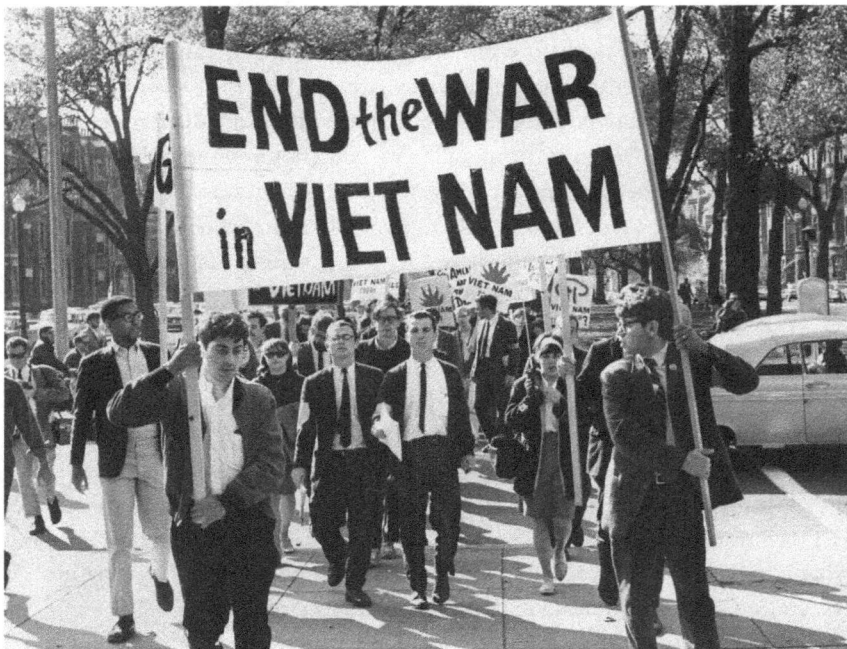

FIGURE 6.   Our first local march against the war, October 1965. Samuel B. Hammat, courtesy of the Boston Globe Library collection at Northeastern University Archives and Special Collections.

organization on the floor of the Senate, demanding that the government "immediately jerk this movement up by the roots and grind it into bits." Shortly following Stennis, Attorney General Nicholas Katzenbach and others held a press conference in Chicago attacking SDS and its plans for disruption of the draft.[2]

All of this perplexed us because the plans that everyone attacked were proposals that had been rejected by the September National Council. We were being accused of being traitors for planning draft resistance that we were not planning. Both the headlines and attacks only increased as we took to the streets in planned protest of the war in cities across the country.

The October sky has a fall rawness as I head to Cambridge Common for our march as part of the "International Days of Protest" of the war in Vietnam. I am excited and anxious. I feel better as more and more people trickle in. I count roughly 400 of us and am happy that we turned out the numbers we had set as a goal. We march down Mass Ave, a police car in front, another in back, a couple of motorcycle cops buzzing in and out. We march behind a large banner that simply says, "End the War in Vietnam." A few of us have hand-lettered signs: "Out Now!" and "Vietnam for the Vietnamese." One student carries a sign that says "My life is not your toy!" This is our first attempt at a large public protest on the streets of Cambridge and Boston.

The noise of the episodic police sirens, blending with our chants, pulls men out of the bars and taverns as we approach. Out onto the sidewalks spill men who fought in the Second World War, men who fought in Korea, men whose brothers fought, men who thought they ought to have fought, men who have always worked hard, paid their taxes, drank on Saturdays, and went to Mass on Sundays, men who would have given everything to have one of their kids attend Harvard, men who, when seeing our signs, were furious. Angry and well lubricated yells greet us: "Bomb Hanoi," "Victory in Vietnam," and even an occasional "Better dead than Red." "Why aren't you millionaires' kids over in Vietnam?" a middle-aged man in work clothes yells as we leave Central Square. Everywhere along the route we are met with jeers and hostile yells. I am ranging up and down the march encouraging people to stay tight, to not get into arguments, to keep marching. Not a single person we pass on the sidewalks utters a supportive word. Periodically we are charged by knots of men attempting to wrest away our homemade signs. Cambridge cops reluctantly push in and pull them off us.

We grimly march on, encouraged when our numbers swell to 600 as MIT students join us and then to 1,000 as Boston University, Boston College, and Northeastern feeder marches flow into us after we have crossed into Boston and march down the tree lined strip in the middle of Commonwealth Avenue. Arriving at the Parkman Bandstand on Boston Common, we realize we are not going to have an easy time of it. There are hundreds of counter demonstrators already on the Common. Some are passionate right-wing members of Young Americans for Freedom. Others are men who have emptied the nearby combat zone bars and are yelling, screaming, and swearing at us. They are enraged that any American would march against our leaders in times of war. "You are despicable," they yell. "Love America or leave it," some snarl. "Support our boys," they cry.

We have planned a small speaking program for the bandstand, but it is impossible. By the time Chomsky tries to speak, chants of "Bomb the Commies" and "Go Back to Hanoi" are too loud. On the outer edges, skirmishes flare, are broken up, and flare again. Numerically there are more of us than the counterprotestors, but anger and alcohol-fueled passion is in their favor. Soon, mounted police decide that the rally is over. We disburse, grimly determined that we have done what we wanted to—register that there are at least some people opposed to the war and willing to publicly protest. We take comfort in the fact that in eighty cities over two days, a total of 100,000 people protested. We disband and call it a day.

The next week, senator after senator took to the floor to denounce SDS. James Reston, the most prominent of liberal journalists, attacked the protestors.[3] Across the country SDS was constantly in the headlines. The result of those attacks, and of our protests, was a sudden jump in membership. As a special *SDS Bulletin* reported, "Our Harvard organizer reports that he walked into Harvard Yard with 30 membership cards and had to go back for more ½ hour later . . . He wasn't lying. We just received 50 new membership cards from him special delivery."[4] Many of those students whom we had urged to become active and not worry about formal membership now wanted their SDS cards. The surge in membership jumped the national membership from 3,000 $2-a-year dues paying members to 4,000. In the chapters we saw membership double.[5]

The attacks on the organization were unrelenting. The national office decided something needed to be done. Paul Booth, the national secretary, and Carl Oglesby, the president, flew to Washington and held a press conference at the National Press Club. There Paul read a statement reiterating our opposition to the war. He also called on the government to allow young people the choice of national service in Volunteers in Service to America (VISTA) and the Peace Corps rather than military service, saying "I predict that almost every member of my generation would choose to build, not to burn, to teach, not to torture, to help, not to kill." He concluded by saying that SDS would continue to urge young men to file for conscientious objector status not strategy. The statement became immediately known as Build Not Burn.

While it generated headlines around the country, it also ignited a firestorm within SDS. On the one hand, we had not decided on a path of urging men to file for conscientious objector (CO) status and resisting the draft. On the other, many of us, including myself, felt that the tone of the statement was too accommodating. The internal opposition to the statement undermined the authority of the national office and fed into the antiauthoritarian "we have no leaders here" mentality of SDS.

While I was not happy with the statement, I was not particularly upset about it. I felt we had too much work to do. I asked Paul to come speak to the Havard Radcliffe SDS chapter and give it a boost. He came up and spent the day with me. I took him for a long interview with the *Harvard Crimson*. Before the large meeting that evening, we had a chance to talk at length.

Paul, sharp featured, lean, close cropped, had a reasoned intensity and a wonderfully wry wit. He seemed always cheerful and unruffled. We talked about the organizing that I had been doing. I had a secret agenda for the conversation, however. It had recently come to my attention that two of the hardest working members of the chapter executive committee were members of the Communist Party (CP). This bothered me. I could not understand why anyone would be a member of the CP. I detested the old left.

I had studied the history of the American left enough to know its outlines and to feel strongly that the CP had surrendered its soul, and its autonomy, to the

Soviet Union. I was perplexed by the contortions that party members had put themselves through to be antifascists one day and then almost overnight switching to justify the Hitler–Stalin Pact. I knew that the CP had played a leading role in union organizing until it had been purged from the unions in the 1950s, and I was fascinated by the direct action it had spearheaded in the Depression to resist evictions. But that did little to lessen my contempt for the CP. Yet I also agreed with the SDS position of rejecting reflexive Cold War anticommunism. I liked the two members. I thought they did good work. As I tried to make sense of all this, I was confused, wondering over motives, and what was my responsibility now that I knew of their political affiliation.

Paul was sweetly patient. He pointed out that the two were probably born into CP families. And he asked me, if I was a young lefty wouldn't I want to be in SDS? After all, Paul said, the old joke about more than half the current members of the CP being FBI informers was probably true. But SDS was growing; SDS was vibrant and exciting. Wouldn't any lefty with half a brain want to be in it? Didn't I just say they were doing good work and helping us grow? I needed to keep focus on the organizing and not spend any time worrying about a few CP members in an SDS that was growing by leaps and bounds. Reassured by his calm advice, I felt my worry drop away.

Then we went to the largest chapter meeting we had ever had, and Paul excited everyone with his wide-ranging analysis of the war, American politics, and the importance of the New Left. I felt I gained a mentor, someone I could admire and ask for guidance.[6]

Late afternoon of November 2, 1965, employees pour out of the Pentagon, the command center of America's military might. With his one-year-old daughter by his side, Norman Morrison, a thirty-one-year-old Quaker pacifist, father of three, stands below the third-floor windows of Secretary of Defense Robert McNamara's office. He looks up at the windows, looks up at the Pentagon, looks up at McNamara's office, moves the baby to safety, takes several deep breaths, and with calm deliberation he pours kerosene all over himself. He sets himself on fire, immolates himself in protest of the war, like the Buddhist monks in Vietnam.[7]

I read the front-page stories, stared at the photo. Stunned. I cannot imagine killing myself. I cannot understand how anyone could burn themselves to death. It baffles me, disturbs me. And yet Morrison has done exactly that *because of the war*. A man of profound belief and morality. Still, to immolate oneself. I cannot understand. At another level that I try to shove aside, I think with foreboding, to end this war, we may have to be serious, take incredible risks, indeed risk all.

A few weeks later, we boarded buses once again for Washington. The November 27 march in Washington against the war had been called by more traditional liberal and peace organizations, in part as an attempt to recapture the leadership from us and our scandalous refusal to adopt standard Cold War anticommunism. In the end they were forced to ask for SDS support and to offer the president of SDS, Carl Oglesby, a speaking role, although they purposefully slotted him in at the very end of the rally. The crowd was larger than it had been in April. Oglesby's speech calling out liberals was electrifying and was the only speech that day to get a standing ovation. Our SDS contingents marched, a little reluctantly, but the need to oppose the war was more important than the games of these older people. We were part of 30,000 people marching. A little larger. Step by step.

Each time we marched, there was a reaction against us that opened room for discussion and debate. Each march, each bus ride to DC, each demonstration, forced students to choose—would they stay silent or would they act? Once you pinned on an antiwar button, once you passed out a leaflet, once you boarded the bus to DC, once you marched, you were committed and part of a new community of activists. Each time a student said to me "I think you are wrong to protest," I had the chance to make the case against this wrong war, to plant a seed of doubt, share facts, and offer an alternative framework.

In the long run, real-world events would prove decisive in building the opposition as the war was brought into living rooms through television in a way that no other war had been. But our organizing, educating, and constantly engaging with the young was required to create the room for dissent and build an organized antiwar movement.

While all this was happening, the bloody battle of the Ia Drang Valley was unfolding thousands of miles away. This was the first time American forces directly engaged North Vietnamese army units. Hundreds died. The American commanders and the Johnson administration fixated on the "body count," the number of enemies killed. No comfort to the families of the more than 300 Americans killed. This battle confirmed the American strategy of air mobile forces and a grinding war of attrition.[8]

The next month, I helped organize a two-day regional SDS gathering with 120 students from two dozen colleges. I argued that we needed to take our antiwar work beyond the confines of the campus.

The *Harvard Crimson* interviewed me about the meeting. My responses catch the naïve hope I still had that our leaders would understand the war was a mistake: "students want to get off the campus . . . They've had marches and teach-ins, and they're discouraged that the war hasn't ended . . . Johnson needs a huge anti-war movement so if he decides to end the war, it's politically safe for him to do it. The only way to get this movement going is to get out and talk to people."[9]

FIGURE 7. Search and destroy mission, November 14, 1965, during the Battle of Ia Drang, Vietnam. US Army Photo / Alamy Stock Photo.

We gathered a group of students for a foray into the meat-packing district wedged in between the expressway and the South End of Boston. The United Packing House Workers of America was a progressive union with a long history of interracial organizing. One of its leaders, Jesse Prosten, had been a supporter of the SDS's Economic Research and Action Project (ERAP) in Chicago. Knowing that history, I thought the union members might be open to hearing from us.

One afternoon, we walked through idling trucks, by cold storage units with animal carcasses swinging from overhead tracks, men carrying slabs of meat on their shoulders, men pushing the carcasses, knives and cleavers in their belts, many using wickedly sharp, curved meat hooks. Our small band of college students handed out leaflets explaining why the war was wrong and attempted to engage lounging workers on break.

Most of those workers were Eastern European immigrants and fervently anti-communist. They saw Vietnam through the prism of the "enslaved nations" of Eastern Europe. Heavily muscled, blood smearing their aprons, knives and cleavers still tucked in their belts, they were not interested in a bunch of privileged college students telling them the war was wrong. They had the urgent patriotism of immigrants and the sons of immigrants. Some started asking unpleasantly if we were communists. Soon small knots of men were yelling at us. There was a rising chorus, a mixture of Boston and Eastern European accents: "Get the fuck out of here, now!" "Take your commie propaganda and shove it up your ass." Some grabbed our leaflets and started burning them.

Suddenly the small team I had brought here was in the midst of an all too real nightmare. The possibility of physical violence rose; I felt it, physical and gut wrenching. The yelling men pushed closer, surrounding us. I started to panic. I was acutely aware of those knives and cleavers; my darting eyes kept landing on the bloodstains on once white aprons. I registered bleakly how many more of them there were than of us. I was at a complete loss.

Just then two African American men elbowed their way through the crowd, both glad-handing people and pushing them away. They were union stewards who barked at the men surrounding us to make room and directed us to follow them. They then hustled us, cowed and thankful, out of the cafeteria and out of the packing house complex. The stewards had saved us, but their last words were clear: get the fuck out of here and do not come back. I left with the dispirited group, embarrassed and gloomy. The whole day was a tough reminder of how far we had to go. Returning to Harvard, the best I could salvage from the day was that none of us had been injured.

I was depressed. These were members of a union with leftist leadership and a deep history of struggle. And they would not even listen. I came to see this small encounter as a vivid example of the divide that splintered the dominant Democratic coalition and reverberated through American politics for decades.

As I thought about the day, I was clear that the American "proletariat" was not going to be the engine for a movement capable of ending this war. Still, it was the sons of those guys in the meat-packing plants that were dying in Vietnam. The day left me more convinced than ever that it would be young people who would lead the assault on the tragic consensus of support for the war, not older people, not the unions. Yet I was worried. The burden felt heavy for our young shoulders.

It is easy to write about the demonstrations, the marches, the confrontations. They were dramatic and essential. However, they were only possible because of long hours of outreach, discussion, connecting. It was the mundane work of reaching out to students that occupied me, and the other SDS organizers and that made it possible for people to join the march, get on the bus, join the movement. Demonstrations not immediately followed by engagement, education, and organizing would do little to build the movement.

Evening after evening, I could be found in Harvard dorms or in small gatherings at nearby colleges talking about the war, about our lives, our dreams, our futures.

On a typical evening, I walk into Quincy House at Harvard. I had talked to several kids I knew who lived there, and they had pulled together a group of students in the common space. Some of the young men are still sporting the now increasingly out of fashion buzz cuts but others are beginning to let their hair grow long. One solid young man is a football player. Another gangly one is sporting a new, wispy, blond mustache just starting to grow out. Students slouch back in the chairs or flop on the floor. I am here to talk about the war and SDS. But I will not launch into a rant about the war.

I start by asking the football player how the prospects look for Saturday's game. I ask the kid with the new mustache how he is enjoying social studies, the major where all the radicals are congregating. Then I turn to the heart of why I am there.

"I don't know about you all," I say, "but I am still trying to figure out how the hell I am going to live my life given this damn war and given how fucked up everything is. What," I ask, "are you guys thinking about these days?" Hesitantly one of them says his parents expect him to become a doctor and he used to think he was set on that path. But now he is not so sure. How can he keep his deferment knowing that means other guys will be sent to Vietnam?

Another says he just doesn't know what his future will be. What if I get drafted? Can I, should I, serve and go to Nam?

He doesn't know.

Another says his parents expect him to go into business, but he is just not sure he can do it. "Why not?" I ask. He says, "Aww, I don't really know but sometimes I just think, you know, is chasing after money all that matters in life?"

"Yeah," I say, "of course that's what we are told—you are what you buy, you are what you own, accumulate, accumulate. That's what we are bombarded with every day and every week. But there is more to life than that. Think about the people in the Civil Rights Movement and what they are fighting for. Think about the poor kid that dies in Nam—he doesn't care what he owns, he doesn't care what kind of car he bought. Think about all those Vietnamese who are dying. We are being told that we must kill them to stop communism and it's true that many of them are led by communists, but they have been fighting the French, the Japanese, and then the French again and now us for the last thirty years."

Soon we are in a wide-ranging, freewheeling discussion about the war, about civil rights, about race, the university, about materialism, about commercialism and a culture of mass marketing, about human dignity, about what makes a life worth living, about all the things our classes do not include, and our professors cannot address. And then I am diving into the facts about the war because one student, or more, argues that this war is a necessary part of the struggle against communism. Soon we are discussing the history of the French in Indochina, the

Geneva Accords of 1954, the quote from Eisenhower . . . and on we go for an hour, two hours, or more. Everyone's talking. Everyone's making jokes but are also serious. This is our lives we are attempting to figure out. Being young men, we veer off into sex and relationships—is it possible to have an authentic relationship in this fucked-up world? Then back to the war. Then on to poor people and race and the war and who is dying and what are we willing to do about it, what do we think we can do about it. And finally, the discussion has run its course. I have never suggested anyone sign up for SDS. But I will see Pat and his slowly filling out mustache at the next SDS meeting. The intense Rob, tortured by his family's expectations for him, will finally decide months later, to get on that bus to Washington to protest the war. The football player will in a year turn in his bursar's card in solidarity with those of us sitting in against the Dow recruiter.

No one was changed in a single discussion. It took time and persistence. SDS distributed mimeographed leaflets in all the dorms once a week discussing the latest developments. SDS members talked, distributed newsletters, and talked more. Over and over again, we returned to the question of how we could manage to live a moral life in the face of mass consumer culture, racism, a stifling consensus in support of the corporate liberal state, and, above all else, an immoral war.

Increasingly we were fixated on the question of the "good Germans." We knew that there must have been hundreds of thousands of Germans who opposed the Nazis. Certainly, there was opposition early on by the German left. But what of the more middle-of-the-road, decent Germans who must have been appalled by the Nazis? Where were they in our history books? Nowhere, because they had acquiesced. We were determined not to acquiesce to a war that was growing bloodier by the month.

Despite our efforts, there seemed an unshakable consensus of the center. However, that center did not hold. In a remarkably short time, we rode a blood-dimmed tide. How little we understood. We should have studied our W. B. Yeats more.

Throughout the year 1966 we remained a clear, if vocal, minority. By the end of that year, American forces in Vietnam totaled 385,000 men, plus an additional 60,000 sailors stationed offshore.[10] More than 6,000 Americans were killed in that one year, and 30,000 wounded.[11] There are no numbers for the Vietnamese killed, wounded, driven from their homes. The bombs rained down.

In the fall, in New York City, more than 25,000 people marched in support of the war in Vietnam, calling for victory in Vietnam.

For my second year at Harvard, seven of us occupied two suites together on the third floor of Adams House. Harvard has a system of houses where students live after the first year. Adams House was known for attracting the artistic, creative, offbeat, and even rebellious. Its turn-of-the-century buildings, originally private housing for those students who could afford all the amenities, even included an elegant, small subterranean swimming pool that we could use at any hour of the day or night.

All seven of us were committed to SDS. Soon our rooms were an informal hub for SDS organizing.

We were learning that the war in Vietnam might not be a mistake, might instead be part of a larger pattern. In April 1965, 40,000 US troops had invaded the Dominican Republic.[12] Two years earlier, Juan Bosch had won the presidency in the first free elections in thirty years only to be overthrown by a military coup. Now the United States stopped a popular revolution seeking to return Bosch to power. That year also saw the start of a CIA-backed effort in Indonesia that ended up with the installation of a military dictatorship and the killing of one million communists and left-wing activists.[13] We avidly studied the recent history of American intervention, discovered the overthrow of the popularly elected Mohammad Mosaddegh in Iran, the overthrow of the popularly elected Jacobo Árbenz government in Guatemala. Vietnam, rather than a mistake, an aberration, started to fit a pattern of American intervention throughout the Third World. We began to conclude American foreign policy was motivated by making sure American businesses had access to oil, sugar cane, land, markets, and labor.

One late afternoon, as I was returning to our rooms, one of my roommates grabbed me in the first-floor entryway, saying, with an accusatory look, "There's a woman on your bed crying." I had no idea what he was talking about. I raced up the three flights to find, indeed, there on my narrow bed was a young woman, eyes red, my pillow wet with her tears. I did not recognize her.

As I come in, she sits up, haltingly says, "I am sorry. . . . I am sorry but I need to talk to someone . . . my friends told me about . . . My friends say you would be the right person to talk to . . . I just don't know; I just don't know." And her tears well up again. I am dumbfounded. A young woman, tall, open faced and sad, lying on my bed, asking for my help. I sit on my desk chair squeezed next to the bed and say "Okay. How can I help you?"

She says, "I'm Peggy. . . . look, I love my father, I really do. But I cannot do what he wants me to. I just cannot. I love him but I think he is so wrong, and he wants me to do something that I think is just wrong. But I love him. Is it so wrong to love someone who is doing something bad?"

I ask her to explain more. Hesitantly, she says, "My father, well, he has a bank. . . . I am his youngest. I have always been very close with him . . . Well, he has this bank, and he wants me to go with him to an opening for the newest branch and I just don't think I can do it. But he will be so disappointed . . . and it is so hard to explain . . . and he thinks he is doing good, but I don't think so . . . And I just cannot go."

I am confused. I gently press the question, "Why exactly don't you want to go with him?"

"The new branch is in Saigon. My father wants me to go with him to Vietnam. It will be a big deal. I agree with you, the war is wrong. My friends said you would understand. I just cannot go. But I do love him, is that so wrong?"

Peggy is tortured by the thought that her father is profiting from the war. Still, she does not want to disappoint him. She cannot go, symbolically blessing the war. She is tied into knots.

I confirm that it is possible to love someone, especially a parent, and still disagree with their views and their behavior. I say, "We do not get to choose our parents. But we do choose how we live our lives."

We talk about how bad the war is. I tell her I doubt her father sees the harm the bank causes, that he believes he is a good person. I stress that the structure of society shapes people's awareness and their lack of awareness. While we hold individuals responsible, we should always remember it is the system that drives what they do. And in that sense, they are not to be hated. It is important that we live by our principles. But our principles should include love and forgiveness.

We talk and talk, Peggy confirms that she will not go to Saigon. She seems to feel better about loving her father. I am quite taken with her. In truth I want nothing more than to give her a big hug, followed by a big kiss, and then an invitation to return to my bed. But I do nothing, indicate nothing, offer nothing beyond a sympathetic ear. We leave and I feel a bond and a possibility—but do nothing.

I have seen Peggy from time to time over the years. She has done remarkable things with her life. Repeatedly, she has figured out how to use her connections, her wealth, and her birth to benefit those who were not born powerful or wealthy. She has made a difference.

What Peggy was wrestling with in 1966 was common to many children of the elite. So many cabinet secretaries, senators, State Department officials, generals, and the masters of American industry and finance were finding it hard to have conversations around the dinner table when their daughters and sons came home on break from college. Their children might not join SDS, although many did, but increasingly they were being persuaded that the war was wrong. Increasingly they were seeing the war as being fought to defend the economic interests of their parents. Increasingly they were questioning the social and economic order that benefited them. Articulate, smart, brought up to be the next elite, they were tough to debate. Many a dinner table conversation ended in wrenching disagreements that shook America's elite families at their core. The best and the brightest, the masters of the universe, began to have a sinking feeling that they were losing their own daughters and sons. They were right. Over the years the children of such high-ranking administration figures as Secretary of Defense McNamara, Vice President Spiro Agnew, and Richard Nixon's key staff, H. R. Haldeman and John Erlichman, would join the antiwar movement.[14]

The day after I turned nineteen, LBJ announced the end to a five-week pause in the bombings; the air campaign intensified. That March, Senator Wayne Morse led an effort to repeal the Gulf of Tonkin Resolution, which had given Johnson total latitude to escalate and wage war in Vietnam. It failed by a vote of ninety-two to five.[15]

SDS and the National Coordinating Committee to End the War in Vietnam sponsored the Days of International Protest, March 25 to 26, 1966. Facing an escalating war that had near unanimous support in Congress, we were determined to turn out record numbers in opposition. About 25,000 marched in New York alone. We organized a faculty "speak out" with twenty-eight members of the Harvard faculty and then another local march.

With the memory of the debacle at the Parkman Bandstand still raw, we planned to hold the rally inside the Arlington Street Church. Once again, we marched behind a big banner demanding an end to the war. Our hand-lettered signs proclaimed "Immediate Withdrawal NOW!," "Peace Now," and "Stop the Bombing." We marched to regular chants of "What do we want? Peace! When do we want it? Now!" For the first time some chanted, "Hey, hey . . . LBJ . . . how many babies did you kill today?"

The march route, once again down Mass Ave through Cambridge, was met with even larger hostile crowds. Cops on motorcycles did their best to keep the peace, buzzing between us and the snarling patriots. As the march neared the Arlington Street Church, the 1,000 of us marching were more than equaled by the crowds against us. Around us were nonstop yells of "Kill the commies," "Down with Peaceniks," "Support our boys," "Go back to Russia." As we approached the church, fistfights flared up here and there. Then a can of soup hurtled into our march, bloodying a young man's face. Soon eggs and more cans and soda bottles and anything that could be thrown rained down on us; we rushed to get everyone into the church. I was too busy attempting to get everyone safely inside to feel any fear.

We had our rally against the war inside, sheltered in a church that had once housed the fiery meetings of abolitionists. I was certain we were acting in a great American moral tradition. Outside the crowd was just as certain that we were traitors. We waited for the police to clear the area before sending everyone home. No Boston newspaper decried the violence against us. They did not editorialize about free speech. Instead, they all called for supporting the troops and the president in a time of war. I tried to buoy spirits, pointing to the increase in our numbers, arguing against despair. However, I felt discouraged myself. It was so damn hard to make opposition to the war legitimate. But we had no choice, we had to keep on. The war was escalating. We could not stop. The isolation we felt engendered an even greater sense of responsibility. It was only us. It was up to us to find a way to stop the war. I felt that weight more and more, coloring each day.

At the end of the month a small group of young men burned their draft cards on the steps of the South Boston courthouse ushering in a new phase of resistance. Throughout the preceding months, there had been increasing discussion of draft resistance. In 1964 and 1965, 334,000 young men had been drafted. Their bodies were necessary for the war, and it was clear to us that many more would soon be needed.[16] We debated what was the most effective way to resist.

For some time, I had been in ever more frequent, intense, and troubled conversations about whether and how to evade the draft. Now those conversations had shifted into debates about how to best organize resistance to the draft. Among my close friends, there was a growing sentiment for people to refuse to be drafted or tear up or burn their draft cards in public acts of resistance, which almost certainly would mean jail. The Selective Service law that governed the draft was amended through HR1036 to specifically make it illegal to fail to carry your draft card with you at all times and a crime for anyone who "knowingly destroys, knowingly mutilates" their draft card.[17]

Many close SDS friends argued for active draft resistance. Others came to draft resistance from a religious background, influenced by the Catholic Worker Movement and brothers Daniel and Philip Berrigan, Catholic priests who became dedicated to stopping the war. I was not so interested in acts of moral witness. I believed only a mass movement could stop the war. I thought that the potential penalty of jail would prove to be too extreme for more than the most committed to risk. A hundred thousand young men flooding the jails might disrupt the country and could be enormously powerful. However, only 5,000 or 10,000 going to jail, while a strong symbolic act, would only rob the movement of the organizers and activists it needed. I was torn. In the end, I supported draft resistance organizing, but I was skeptical that draft card burning would become something hundreds of thousands of us would participate in—and I believed it would take hundreds of thousands of us, millions of us to bring the war to an end.

It is estimated that 25,000 Americans burned their draft cards, but only forty-six were actually indicted.[18]

SDS friends, including John Maher, Nick Eggleson, and Vernon Grizzard, among others, organized the Boston Draft Resistance Group (BDRG) aimed at reaching young working-class men, providing them options for resisting the draft. While draft card burning never reached the level of mass action, draft evasion certainly did. The BDRG would become a well-organized effort that assisted an ever-growing stream of draft eligible young men to know their rights and many to evade being drafted.

That spring, General Lewis Blaine Hershey, head of the Selective Service, proclaimed there would be a new test for one million male college students. The results of the three-hour test, along with college grades and class ranking, would be used by local draft boards to determine who kept their student deferment, and who lost it and would be sent to Vietnam. This literally was to be a life-or-death test. The new testing and ranking system required colleges and universities to work with the Selective Service to decide who stayed in school and who was sent to fight in Vietnam. Universities had to share their class ranks and a student's GPA with the government.

The reaction among students was swift and vehement. SDS organized, without much success, to demand that universities not participate. We decided to distribute our own test at as many test sites as possible. Our tests had our own questions with the answers included at the bottom. For example:

- If the US divided the money being spent on the war among everyone in South Vietnam, what would that amount be? Answer: $866 per person, making it the country with the highest per capita income in Asia
- What is the ratio of civilian deaths to Vietcong deaths? Answer: 2:1
- When the government of Indonesia launched a drive that killed 300,000 of its citizens, what was the US response? Answer: none[19]

We used humor, but our challenge was serious. We administered more than 350,000 tests. I was the regional coordinator for the exam in New England. "We can use hundreds of people on this," I told the *Harvard Crimson*. "There are test centers all over New England that have to be covered. Local campus chapters will handle operations at their own schools, but additional manpower will be needed to man campuses without chapters or centers that are not located at a specific college . . . I don't think there will be any violence here, but at places like the University of New Hampshire or the University of Maine, there's a possibility that some incidents will occur."[20]

The official test was received with dread. The American educational system had entered a new period of tracking: there was the college track, the vocational track, and the death track. University administrators were now an explicit arm of the Selective Service and the machinery of war.

Most historians, when writing about the antiwar movement, stress the draft as the motivating factor in student opposition. However, without the draft there still would have been an antiwar movement. Undoubtedly the fact that twenty-seven million American young men thought they could be sent to Vietnam made a broad swath of the population take notice of what was happening. There is no question that the threat of the draft made many young men, and their families, take a serious look at the war and helped build opposition.

Still women, not subject to the draft, and many men who had deferments, worked passionately against the war. It is wrong to think it was only fear of being drafted that impelled most of us to act against the war. The facts and nature of the war in Vietnam demanded we oppose it. Many of us were tortured by the privilege of a deferment. I certainly thought day after day about the young men who did not have a deferment and were paying such a high cost for a war that should never have been fought. Guilt drove me to work harder against the war.

The new tests, university cooperation, and the increasing numbers being drafted added to our sense of urgency. The war itself and our efforts were steadily convincing more and more American college students that they should oppose the war. The fact that their lives might depend on ending the war added an edge of urgency.

That late spring of 1966, I supported trying anything and everything that might expand the movement against the war. More marches—yes. Draft resistance—okay. Antiwar candidates for office—sure, give it a try. Give anything a try.

I accepted a job to be the lead organizer on the campaign of Thomas Boylston Adams, who was running in the Democratic Primary for the US Senate against former governor Endicott "Chub" Peabody and John Collins, the mayor of Boston.

Adams, every inch a Brahmin, the great-great-great-grandson of John Adams, the second president, always acutely conscious of his heritage, first announced his candidacy in February 1966. The campaign produced an insipid fifty-five–page platform that did not advocate an immediate withdrawal from Vietnam. Adams was going nowhere. In May, with the deadline looming, the campaign was unable to produce the 10,000 signatures needed to get on the ballot. Desperate to salvage the signature collecting, his campaign offered me a paid leadership position. I refused. Still, I was intrigued with what a statewide campaign could do to boost the antiwar movement. Adams had no chance of winning, but could his campaign demonstrate that the antiwar movement had spread beyond the campuses? I agreed to negotiate.

After a series of intense meetings, the campaign, with a remarkably hesitant candidate, changed its official positions to support a total withdrawal of all US forces from Vietnam, the desegregation fight in the Boston schools, and Mothers for Adequate Welfare. I agreed to be the senior person in charge of field, hired SDS organizers for the field staff, and recruited Abbie Hoffman to leave his "Friends of SNCC" store and become the coordinator for Worcester. All in a somewhat successful effort to jump start a stalled campaign. We scrambled and in record time secured the requisite number of signatures. The campaign, however, could never overcome a candidate ill-suited for the role of insurgent, a candidate who had a profound distrust of his new staff.

In the end Adams received 51,436 votes or 8 percent.[21] The candidate and the campaign were deeply flawed. The election had not proven to be a particularly successful way of opposing the war, unfortunately convincing many of my friends that electoral politics was a waste of time.

Despite the disappointment of the campaign, everything we had done for the last two years, the marches, the teach-ins, the protests, the organizing, and education, even the fact that Adams would run as an antiwar candidate at all, everything had indeed created room for dissent. There was now a powerful movement against the war. It was no longer fringe. It was growing. Now, we told ourselves, we needed to go "from protest to resistance." We needed to find a way to shatter the unity of the country, throw ourselves on the gears and make them pause in their relentless turning. We were ready for a new stage in our opposition to the war.

THE NOT-SO-RADICAL PERSONAL LIFE OF A SIXTIES RADICAL

I was swimming in the rushing waters of the youth revolt, a revolt challenging every norm and convention. All around me, my friends were experimenting, growing their hair long, inventing new music, experimenting with marijuana and even LSD. I was living through a profound sexual revolution.

I refused to indulge in any of it.

I remained focused on "the work." There were parties and friends and good times, but I was remarkably conventional in my personal life. I talked with other young people every day about the large issues confronting us, how to live a life of meaning, how not to be submerged in mass culture, how to be authentic, and I always strove to be flexible and understanding. Yet I was personally rigid and uptight when it came to my own choices.

A radical life in the 1960s: demonstrations, drugs, sex, and rock and roll. I certainly experienced the demonstrations. I certainly experienced the music, a constant soundtrack starting with blues, Chicago, Motown, and then finally embracing the Beatles, the Stones, the Doors. My eldest sister Martha went out with the guitarist of the Paul Butterfield Blues Band, and when they came to town, we partied with them. I loved our music.

But for me there was no adventuresome sex and no drugs. I was as strait laced as any fresh-faced Mormon missionary.

That is not to say that I did not think about women, long after them, silently fall in love with a myriad of fascinating women. But I refused to act on all that yearning. I stubbornly ignored all those baffling moments where afterward

I thought, perhaps something had been meant but was never sure, and certainly never took the next step to find out. Ignoring my endless desires, I doggedly and single mindedly pursued Amy, the first and only girl I had ever kissed. I was determined that she and I would marry.

Whenever the combination of SDS, classes, and jobs allowed, I would head down to Providence where Amy attended Pembroke, the women's college at Brown. I traveled on a small used moped—a bicycle with a tiny gas engine to boost performance that I had purchased for $25. I drove the fifty miles from Cambridge to Providence on the highway on my little sputtering moped, occasionally hitting twenty miles per hour on the downhill but peddling madly up steep hills. Rain or shine, hot or cold, I rode determinedly down the shoulder of the highway, cars whizzing by.

Amy was sometimes glad to see me. We explored Providence, we talked politics, I met her new friends. It was increasingly clear that she was a much more normal eighteen-year-old than me. She explored relationships with other men, dated, acted as most young college women did in those days. I was disappointed. I was surprised. I was hurt. Doggedly I kept on, unrelenting, determined.

I rejected all drugs, rarely consumed more than a beer, ignoring what was happening all around me. After giving a speech or leading a group discussion, I simply could not imagine that the women staying after to talk with me had any other interests than pursuing a discussion of strategy.

The social and sexual norms steadily changed around me. In my first years there, Harvard still had "parietals," rules that governed the hours and conditions under which women could visit our dorms. The rules were summed up as "an open door and one foot on the floor" at all times. And only during specific hours. These rules were increasingly being flouted.

Early one Sunday morning of my second year, I saw a friend emerging with his girlfriend. It was obvious she had spent the night. As we all walked out into the crisp sunshine, we met the longtime master of Adams House, Professor Reuben Brower. Brower, seeing the student and his girlfriend leaving Adams House, arm in arm, early on that Sunday, raised an eyebrow and said in a loud, arch voice, "On our way to church, are we?" and walked on. At that moment, all three of us understood that the parietals no longer would be enforced, at least at Adams House.

Sadly, there were no women walking out into the early morning sun with me.

Frequently my roommates and other friends wanted me to join them in getting high. I always refused as quietly as I could. I needed to be responsible, and stay focused on the work. I feared what I might discover if I ever let my emotions unbundle and spool out into the light.

My life the first two years at Harvard was dominated by SDS, organizing, paid jobs, and trips to Providence. Still I had room for friends who were not swept up in the heat of the movement. One, notably, was a fellow member of Adams House, Bill Weld, a tall, red-haired WASP, reeking of wealth and diffidence, descended from a signer of the Declaration of Independence, either the nineteenth or twentieth of the Welds to attend Harvard. Bill took nothing seriously. Several years older, he was the most apolitical person I spent any time with. I was drawn by his insouciant manner—such a contrast to my earnest and sincere passions. His natural peer group at Harvard was aghast to see him eating with the scruffy troublemaker they knew me to be. Several times his pals came by and openly upbraided him, ignoring me as if I were not there. "Bill, what are you doing? This guy isn't one of us. He is SDS and trouble. Why are you spending time with him?"

His response was direct: "But he is interesting and fun, way more interesting than you. So, who gives a damn!"

Bill and I had the same size feet even though he was much taller. He possessed numerous pairs of handcrafted shoes with fine-grained leather, English made. Tired of seeing me wearing the same cheap pair every day, offended by the hole visible in the sole and slowly enlarging, Bill handed me a pair of his shoes, saying simply, "Keep them. I have plenty and can buy as many as I want." (I would be shocked when years later Bill became the Republican governor of Massachusetts.)

Adams House and all of Cambridge was alive with creative energy. The poet Allen Ginsberg and his lover Peter Orlovsky spent a week in residence. The poet Denise Levertov became a passionate member of the antiwar effort. Bands were sprouting. Music ricocheted from every open window.

Political and social turmoil produced complex plays, attempts at creating new art, a new culture. I loved attending performances with young actors such as Stockard Channing, Maeve Kinkead, John Lithgow, and Tommy Lee Jones, all of whom went on after Harvard to have successful acting careers.

I was especially enamored of Kinkead. The first time I heard her name I was struck by its music. Then I met the slender young woman, her long hair cascading down her back, every gesture graceful and elegant. I could only stare and hope my hungry heart was not too obvious.

Tim Mayer, despite affecting a sybaritic diffidence accompanied by a constant cutting sarcasm, remarkable for both its verbal dexterity and casual cruelty, became a good friend. A senior, he decided to stage *The Threepenny Opera*. His research for the production, he thought, required studying contemporary radicals and that quickly took him to me.

Politics and culture were inseparably intertwined. I loved debating what John Ford's movie, *The Searchers*, said about the American character or if *The 400*

Blows was indeed ushering in a new cinema. I argued over *Mother Courage and Her Children*. I repeatedly went to see *The Threepenny Opera*, debating its staging with Tim. I silently longed for Kinkead. Played pinball at Tommy's Lunch late into the night with members of the J. Geils Band. Everywhere around me was a world of poets, actors, writers, musicians, and artists. I wanted to be one of them. But the war and politics always pulled me back to organizing.

I had a fierce need to be married and to be married to Amy. I felt a great, idealized, and idealistic love for her. Profoundly unaware of what drove me, I exerted every ounce of will into convincing Amy to marry me.

And in that spring of 1966, she agreed. We were both nineteen.

I had grown up with parents who preached the importance, the necessity, for tight-knit families. Yet I had felt a constant, inchoate ache, a sense that there was a hole in my family, a profound gap between what was said and what was real. Now I would finally have a family of my own, a chance for everything to be right. Amy succeeded in transferring to Brandeis for the fall semester

Other than the blur of the Adams campaign, I remember remarkably little from that summer. Amy and I lived with my parents in a house they had rented ten blocks from Harvard Square. For the fall we sublet a basement apartment at 1010 Mass Ave, opposite the Orson Welles Cinema.

I frequently took my nine-year-old brother Jim with me to the Adams campaign office. He loved to help in any way he could. Over the years he would attend a constant stream of demonstrations. Other than Amy, I felt most attached to and felt the most love for Jim.

Every few weeks that summer, Amy and I would meet with her parents in vain attempts to discuss our plans. Both her parents were frantically opposed to our getting married and simply refused to discuss it. As the summer ended, Amy and I informed them that we were going to get married in two weeks; it could either be in their house or at City Hall. They reluctantly agreed that we could get married at their house but insisted the guest list be kept very small. Her father then awkwardly informed me there would be no money from them—no money to pay for Amy's college tuition, no money for us to live on, not one dollar of support of any kind. I scoffed indignantly at the idea that we cared about his money. Our wedding took place in the Merrill home on the first block of Commonwealth Avenue. Beforehand, I went out to Jacob Wirth's restaurant with my six roommates and my two best friends from Commonwealth. We chose Jake Wirth's because the waiters were proud union members. We pooled all our money, piled it in the center of the round table, asked the waiter to bring as much of their wurst, red cabbage, warm potato salad, and beer as the small heap would cover. We paid no attention to time until someone pointed out that we were now late for the ceremony. Off we sprinted, running across the Common and the Public Gardens, arriving sweaty and late. The bride's mother wept throughout the ceremony; hers were not tears of joy. I did not care. I was married to Amy at last. I had a chance to form a family of my own. Despite having to borrow money for her tuition, and feeling an all too familiar financial pressure, I was delighted.

5

TAKING IT TO A NEW LEVEL: 1966–67

On the afternoon of November 7, 1966, I stand on the flat hood of a black car, next to Secretary of Defense Robert McNamara as he completely loses his composure, jabs his finger in my chest, shouts at me and the 800-student antiwar protestors surrounding us. Our protest will generate headlines at a time when the Johnson administration had sought to show that the war still had support on the campuses.[1] Their effort, sending McNamara to Harvard, boomerangs.

When the Harvard-Radcliffe SDS steering committee heard that the man overseeing the war was coming to our university, there was no question we would organize an appropriate reception. We were determined the university should not lend even tacit support to a criminal war.

We were so very young, earnest, and sincere. We took seriously the issue of freedom of speech. We did not take the position he could not come or could not speak. Instead, we insisted that if Harvard entertained McNamara, his visit must include an open public debate on the war. If we could force a debate, we would win. If McNamara refused the debate, we would stage a dramatic protest that would provoke more discussion of the war.

We circulated a petition demanding that McNamara debate Bob Scheer, the antiwar editor of *Ramparts*, who would be in Cambridge at the same time. Soon we had 1,600 signatures on the petition. McNamara and his Harvard handlers refused the debate. As part of the visit, McNamara would hold small discussions with selected students in Quincy House. His exit from those was our opportunity. We thought we could turn out enough students to surround the entire block. We would stop McNamara's car with our bodies, demanding he debate.

FIGURE 8.   McNamara and I on the hood of a car. HUPSF Student Life (471), olvwork369151. Harvard University Archives.

The day arrives. About 800 of us form a human chain around Quincy House while McNamara is inside. Prowar students have hung sheets out their windows "Welcome Mr. McNamara," "Kill for Peace," "Kill the Cong," "Back Mac," and "Napalm SDS" (along with another that reads "Black Day for Gordon Linen," the company unwittingly providing the sheets). Speakers blare "Mack the Knife" across the courtyard.

My job is overall coordination. I have a system of runners to keep me informed as the action gets underway. We ring the building. Attempting to help the secretary to evade us, decoy cars bolt out onto the street. In the ensuing confusion, we attempt to figure out which car is the right one. On the opposite side of the block, a car carrying the secretary attempts to leave at high speed. SDS members, heedless of risk, throw themselves down in front of the car, hoping it will stop.

As McNamara recounts thirty years later in his book *In Retrospect: The Tragedy and Lessons of Vietnam*, his driver wants to drive on and over the students and McNamara insists he stop before someone is killed.[2] Soon—according to McNamara's account—his car is surrounded by a milling, out of control, "mob" that rocks it and kicks it and threatens to overturn it.

I am on the other side of Quincy House from where the car is surrounded; a runner informs me that we have stopped the right car. We all rush to that side. Carrying a bullhorn, the badge of authority, I am passed through the tightly packed crowd, arriving to find that Hal Benenson, the captain of that portion of our line, has changed the plan. Hal had missed the final planning meeting. where we had all agreed that we would insist on a full public debate, peacefully blocking the car until he agreed. Now, Hal has reached an agreement with McNamara that he will take three questions and then we will let him go. The students around the car are sitting quietly in a circle three to four people deep. The rest of the 800 are pushing as close as they can, attempting to see what is happening. No one is kicking the car. No one is threatening McNamara. I am passed up onto the hood beside McNamara. I am totally flustered, not by being up on the car with the secretary of defense but by the sudden change in our plans. Standing on the car, holding the bull horn, looking out over the expectant crowd, I am unsure of what to do.

I decide to go with Hal's commitment. This seems the only honorable path. So up on the car alongside McNamara, with his trademark hair slicked back, his tie narrow, his suit dark, his glasses large, I announce that we will take three questions and that the secretary of defense has agreed to answer them. He seems to relax a little.

The next part of the event is totally absent from McNamara's book. I call on SDS members that I know I can count on. The first question is about the origins of the war and the Geneva Accords which promised free elections which the US never allowed. I repeat the question through the bull horn. McNamara responds, "It started in '54 to '55 when a million North Vietnamese flooded into South Vietnam." "Goin' home!" somebody shouts. He is tense and stiff. Despite the change in plans, I am starting to feel more in charge, and I call on another student whom I know will ask a good question.

He asks, "How many Vietnamese civilians are being killed and injured?"

I use the small bullhorn to repeat the question, so everyone can hear it. I turn to McNamara and ask him to share the statistics of Vietnamese civilian casualties. He answers abruptly that they are not known.

I ad lib, "Come on now, you are known for your command of numbers and statistics. Are you really saying you do not know how many civilians are being killed each day, each week, each month?"

Again, McNamara, the famed numbers wizard, answers, "I don't know."

I respond, "You do not know, or you do not care?"

At this point everything changes.

McNamara answers me by yelling to the crowd: "You know when I was at Berkeley, I spent four wonderful years and when I was a student, I did some of the things you are doing. . . . but there were two differences between you and me."

Now he turns to me, his hands trembling, and he shouts, "I was more courteous . . . and I was tougher."

To emphasize his point, he starts jabbing his forefinger at my chest, shouting, "I was tougher then and I am tougher now. I was tougher then and I am tougher now. I am tougher now!"

His spit flies in every direction, behind the glasses, his face wrinkles in either rage or fear or both. He jabs at my chest repeatedly, screaming, "Tougher then and tougher now!"

I am shocked, speechless in the face of the unexpected sight of one of the most powerful men in the world shrieking at us about how tough he is.

Everything seems to slow down. He pushes his finger again into my chest. He yells, his face contorted. It is as if standing before 800 of us, up on that car in the dull November Cambridge light, he is suddenly revealed as if naked, and we are all stunned at this shocking, intimate vision of a small man gone crazed and exposed. The finger jabs. The shrieking voice cracks. Later that evening, I will think, this is what demystification of the powerful looks like. But at that moment I am simply appalled. It's unnerving to see the man who commands the most powerful army in the world, a person who can summon bombers or release missiles with nuclear warheads, come so easily undone, completely losing the coolness that was his hallmark.

A wedge of policemen and his protection detail sweep through the crowd, over the crowd, over me. I am knocked to the ground and the trembling secretary of defense is rushed away, into the nearest doorway and down into the warren of underground steam tunnels to "safety." He will continue his visit to Harvard, recovering his composure and later attending a small dinner organized by the professors Richard Neustadt and Henry Kissinger, where they decided to launch the review and research project that would produce the Pentagon Papers.

The next day more than 2,000 Harvard students sign a letter to McNamara apologizing for his treatment. They excoriate us. On the surface, prowar sentiment seems dominant, and the conventional wisdom is that we had made a huge mistake. We are attacked in editorials across the state and the country as rude Cambridge rabble. The dean of the college, John Monro, sends a short but polite letter to the secretary of defense, apologizing on behalf of Harvard and ruing the lack of civility and rudeness of the protestors. He chooses not to discipline any of us, citing the need to protect freedom of speech and dissent. He and I talk about the demonstration and the logic that drove us. While he does not agree with me, the discussion is reasoned, empathetic, and substantial. Dean Monro, decent and moral, was the only administrator at Harvard during that period with whom we could have a substantive discussion. After this academic year, he will make the decision to leave his prestigious position at Harvard to go south and work at the historically Black Miles College. When he leaves, our last avenue to the Harvard administration leaves with him.

I do not share the common assessment that we have blundered. My more positive assessment is not based on stubbornness but because I see a process at work. The McNamara protest was a key step in organizing students against the war both at Harvard and across the country. Students on other campuses read the headlines and saw the national network TV coverage of what had happened when McNamara came to Harvard and knew they were not alone in their intense opposition to the war. It emboldened student protestors across the nation. Now, whenever any top administration figure attempts to visit a campus, they are met with intense protest.[3]

At Harvard, our actions provoked heated debate. While it seemed at first that the tide of that debate ran against us, we had an opening to discuss the war and why we opposed it with more students than ever. Again, to build the movement took more than protests. Every protest enabled more education, more engagement, more organizing.

For many students, their first step down an antiwar path started by saying "I do not agree with your actions, they were dead wrong. I wish you would choose different tactics, but I am worried about this war." That allowed us to explain why we felt we had to do what we had done. We did not yell at people who disagreed with us. We did not write them off when they said that we were wrong. Whenever possible we sought a discussion, confident that the facts were on our side. Even among some of those who most vociferously condemned us, seeds of doubt about the war were planted. Several years later, the facts of the war, the arrogance of the Johnson administration, the agony of so many Vietnamese civilians, the rising death toll of American soldiers, our constant outreach to them—all would drive many of those same students to occupy administration buildings, refuse the draft, and fill the streets with protest.

We had taken a significant step beyond marches into disruptive direct action. We had thrown our bodies in front of that car. We had shown we were willing to take serious risks to stop an immoral war.

Several months later, UN ambassador Arthur Goldberg came to visit Harvard. Once again, we demanded a debate. This time we got qualified support from Dean Monro, who, while deploring "our threats," decided that our request that the university encourage debate about such a controversial war was indeed right. Goldberg agreed to debate but insisted that it not be televised, nor open to anyone not part of the university community. We finally had our debate. The antiwar position was articulated by Professor Michael Walzer and my roommate and SDS leader David Loud. It was clear to us that we prevailed that night. Losing that debate and countless others across the nation had not the slightest impact on the administration's willingness to prosecute the war. We realized that our country was committed to a war that was a crime. It fell to us to stop it.

One ironic historical footnote to this whole episode: the graduate student in charge of McNamara's visit was Barney Frank. His mentors in the Harvard political science department planned for him to use the successful management

FIGURE 9. In 1966 images like this brought home the reality of the war. Larry Burrows/The LIFE Picture Collection/Shutterstock.

of the visit as springboard to a job in the Pentagon. We ruined that, and in later years I would remind Congressman Frank that we had saved his career. Despite the validity of that observation, he was never pleased.

The war intensified. Buddhists demonstrated. Political unrest rocked the American-supported South Vietnamese government. American forces increased to more than 385,000 soldiers. By the year's end, 6,000 Americans had died and another 30,000 had been wounded.[4] With each passing month, more and more Americans heard of someone who died or was wounded in the tall elephant grass, in the grim perimeter of Tan Son Nhut or other American outposts.

Those of us opposing the war now placed Vietnam in the sweep of recent US interventions where the government had lied to us: Iran, Guatemala, Indonesia, the Dominican Republic. We recognized that we were wading upstream in a river of lies.

One evening in the cold months of early 1967, my phone rang. A strange voice obviously from New York asked:

"Is this Michael Ansara?"

"Yes."

"This is Sol Stern from *Ramparts*. Bob Scheer says you are our man in Boston."

Rather surprised by this news, I respond hesitantly, "Well . . . okay."

"Listen I need you to do some work for us right away. I cannot tell you what it is about. I am calling you from a phone booth. Will you do it?"

"Well, what kind of work and are you willing to pay me for it?"

"It is research into two Boston based foundations. We will pay you $500."

That was a lot of money. I had no idea whatsoever how to research foundations, but I thought, what the hell, Amy and I could really use the money.

"Sure. What exactly do you want me to do?"

"I can't tell you anything more than that you should find everything you can about the Sidney & Esther Rabb Foundation and the Independence Foundation. They are based in Boston. I will call you in a few days. You cannot call me. You cannot tell anyone what you are doing. You cannot mention the name *Ramparts*. Can I count on you?"

"I guess so. Sure."

Ramparts, under the leadership of the flamboyant Warren Hinkle, was the principal popular publication of the New Left. Glossy, well designed, with a staff willing to tackle any subject, its circulation soon outstripped the staid *Nation* and *New Republic*. Bob Scheer, the editor, ran for Congress on an antiwar platform. I had met him at national antiwar conferences. He had been our choice to debate McNamara.

I had no idea what they were hoping I might find, nor how to look for it. Since foundations seemed to fall in the realm of professional fundraisers, I reached out to George Sommaripa, a Democratic fundraiser, who I had gotten to know during the Adams campaign. Tall, rail thin, and frail because of childhood polio, George had a burning intensity. He and David Bird had founded Bison Associates, a consulting company. David, short, compact, with a large head and bald dome, had grown up in the forty-room Bird family home in East Walpole. His father, Charles Sumner Bird, Jr., was the scion of Bird & Sons, a roofing and paper company founded in 1795.[5] Frequently when I went to see George, David would drop in and sing "The International" in five or six different languages, laughing at the end and making fun of me. At various times, David mentioned in a totally offhand fashion that he had worked for the CIA.

If I wanted to find information about foundations, George explained, I should go to the IRS and say I was working for him. I headed off to the IRS in the hideous federal office building next to Boston City Hall. I talked with a nameless clerk who was officious, rude, and adamant that I was entitled to no information.

When I reported my failure to George, he was furious. The regional IRS director was a Democratic appointee and an acquaintance. George immediately called and read him the Riot Act, starting with, "How can you treat one of my guys so poorly!" George sent me back with a letter on his firm's stationary. Upon arriving at the IRS offices, George's letter and call changed everything. I was politely ush-ered into a back room. Soon there was a knock on the door and the same harried clerk, who obviously had been yelled at, entered, and plopped down several large files and without a word, left me alone with them.

George had explained that only the top pages of form 990 were available to the public. Going through the folders, I quickly realized that they had given me the entire tax returns for the last three years for each of the foundations.

If I proceeded to look through the entire files, including the many pages that were not public, I would most likely be breaking federal law. I never hesitated.

The files revealed a clear pattern. Both foundations were vanilla family chari-ties with donations to very local organizations. Amid the many small grants, there were large grants that leapt off the pages, grants to national and interna-tional organizations. Most of the income came from the families that created the foundations, yet there were a series of nonfamily contributions that matched exactly the large donations to national and international organizations. A dona-tion of $50,000 would come in from a nonfamily source, and $50,000 would go out to one of the anomalous organizations—a rather obvious pass-through of the funds.

I quickly compiled a list of organizations that had received money and a list of sources for the passed-though amounts. Some of both were based in Mas-sachusetts. I went back to the front desk and asked for information on those. Not aware or not caring that he was giving me the entire files, the IRS clerk silently brought them to me. Again, there was a clear pattern of money being passed through. The list of organizations receiving the money kept growing: the National Student Association, the Asia Society, the International Student Confer-ence, the American Friends of Africa, American Friends of the Middle East, the Congress of Cultural Freedom, the American Fund for Free Jurists, the Indepen-dent Research Service, on and on. The money being passed through originated with a series of obscure foundations or funds run out of law offices around the country. The officers and directors for those originating funds were almost all lawyers. I needed to understand who they were.

In the quiet of the Boston Public Library, I pored over the Martindale and Hubbell directory listings for the law firms and the biographies of their many lawyers. I kept searching for something in common, some pattern. The only commonality among the law firms was that a founder or senior partner of each had served with the Office of Strategic Services (OSS) during World War II. The OSS was the direct predecessor to the CIA.

I realized I was looking at a massive money laundering scheme by the CIA to illegally fund numerous domestic and international organizations. I counted more than a dozen funding sources and one hundred nonprofit organizations receiving the funds. I was stunned—stunned at the scope and shocked that it should be this easy to unravel. I wanted to verify what I had uncovered before talking again to Sol, so I asked to meet with David, the only former CIA officer I knew.

He heard me out as I ran through a summary of what I had found and I asked if that seemed plausible to him. Then without saying anything to me, he picked up the phone, dialed, and proceeded to repeat the essence of what I had told him to someone at the end of the line. Hanging up the phone, David looked at me: "Yup, you have it absolutely right." I did not need to ask him who he had been talking to. I did not think about the probability that he had just warned the CIA about what I had uncovered.

I could barely wait for Sol's call. When he finally rang, I rattled on and on and he had to repeatedly ask me to slow down. I never explained exactly how I discovered all the information I was providing.

Sol said that he had been hoping that I would be able to confirm information *Ramparts* had received that the National Student Association (NSA) had been funded by the CIA for years. The funding started to counter Soviet-funded student groups active internationally. There were vicious ideological fights at international conferences of young leaders from around the world, many of whom would become the rulers of their countries. Soon the CIA was using the NSA's international programs to gather information on those future leaders and, where possible, recruit some of them. Over the years, the operation at the NSA expanded and became an important covert arm of the CIA. It was clear to me that this was only one part of a much larger pattern of funding, infiltration, and manipulation, all of which was illegal.

Soon I was in New York meeting with Hinkle, Sol, and Scheer, amazed to be staying at the famed Algonquin Hotel, uncomfortable that the waiters would not even let me pour my own beer. The *Ramparts* team drew the erroneous conclusion that they had found a crackerjack investigative reporter. I joined a team of researchers including my old SDS pal Lee Webb and a skilled, young reporter, Judith Colburn, who had been doing parallel research. They had deployed investigative skill, whereas I had relied on blind luck. Together we raced to follow up all the leads.

While I was buried in the details of research, a major drama was unfolding around the release of the information. To control the narrative, the CIA and the NSA thought they might be able to defang *Ramparts* by beating them to the punch. The NSA would hold a press conference announcing that there had been some funding in the past but that they had ended it. Once Hinkle and Scheer got wind of the possible NSA preemptive strike, they realized that *Ramparts* could not publish in time to beat the press conference. In those days, it took weeks to design, print, and distribute the magazine. Their way to break the story and get credit for it was to make a deal with the *New York Times*. *Ramparts* would get a full-page ad in the *Times* containing the NSA story, credit for breaking the larger story, and advance publicity about the upcoming issue. In exchange, *Ramparts* turned over all its research to the *Times*, including mine.

Following innumerable trails, pursuing ever expanding leads, I was only superficially aware of the "firestorm" that the *Ramparts* exposé unleashed. The crisis went all the way to the Oval Office, where top national security people and LBJ debated how to deal with the mess. An extensive US covert operation was mounted targeting *Ramparts*.[6] Soon there would be attempts to cut off funding, to get the IRS to strike at the magazine; there would be illegal "black bag" break-ins, and every effort made to discredit *Ramparts*, link it to Soviet espionage efforts, and undermine it in every possible way. One of the CIA agents assigned to destroy *Ramparts* is quoted decades later by Peter Richardson in his history of the magazine *A Bomb in Every Issue*, as saying, "I had all sorts of dirty tricks to hurt their circulation and financing. The people running *Ramparts* were vulnerable to blackmail. We had awful things in mind, some of which we carried off."[7] The campaign to end the magazine, or at least severely damage its credibility, however, did not stop *Ramparts* from continuing to publish.

The *Ramparts* stories set off a chain of discoveries and revelations. The investigative journalist Seymour (Sy) Hersh, of the My Lai massacre fame, was one of several reporters beginning to pry the cover off the massive web of secret operations that the CIA had been carrying out for years. Then came Watergate and more revelations of a different sort. All these revelations resulted in a Senate investigation led by the iconoclastic young senator Frank Church. The report of that committee still makes for chilling reading. For the first time, the overthrow of the elected prime minister, Mohammad Mosaddegh, in Iran and of the elected president, Jacobo Árbenz, of Guatemala, attempts to kill Fidel Castro, US involvement in the overthrow of the president of Chile, Salvador Allende, and more, were all officially confirmed as CIA operations. As well they documented years of domestic abuses including those of COINTELPRO, the FBI's effort to go after Black and antiwar leaders. The FBI and CIA had covertly opened the mail of Americans, illegally broken into homes, lied and smeared activists, and attempted to break up marriages. The agency experimented on Americans, including large numbers of prison inmates and military personnel, in an attempt to discover the key to mind control. One American, part of an experiment testing LSD, jumped out a window to his death. The Church Committee began revealing the national security state and some of its most closely kept secrets.[8]

Some spun the narrative of a rogue agency, an agency out of control. That was fiction. In 1976, a more critical draft congressional report, which was never officially released, stated, "All evidence in hand suggests that the CIA, far from being out of control, has been utterly responsive to the instructions of the President and the Assistant to the President for National Security Affairs."[9]

The national security state fought back. Using the assassination of the CIA station chief in Greece, whose name had never been released by the Church Committee, Donald Rumsfeld, then president Gerald Ford's chief of staff, and Dick Cheney, then deputy chief of staff, supported by the CIA director William Colby and Kissinger, mounted an assault on the committee.[10] They were able to preserve the CIA and its abilities to operate in the dark. Over time Congress returned to the habit of abrogating its responsibilities.

My new part-time position with *Ramparts* meant that Amy and I, for the first time, had a steady income. For thousands of young people reading it, this story confirmed that the government lied and lied and lied. It broke its own laws. All this provided even more context for understanding and opposing the American effort in Vietnam.

Over the next years ever more young people would realize that our government was lying to them. Soon millions of us would assume that anything our leaders said was a lie. Some would start to make the dangerous assumption that since our leaders were lying so often, they should trust the opposite of whatever they said.

The revelations of the CIA's covert funding scheme confirmed many young people's sense of betrayal and disillusionment. It also convinced me that unearthing the secrets of the government and elites was important to our movement building.

We are steadily being enveloped by the war; it is the ever-present fact of our lives. We go to parties. We dance. We make love. We study. We work on other issues. But always, clinging to us, a desperate awareness that bombs are dropping, people are dying. We seem to be the only people determined to stop the senseless violence. We understand now that our government is lying, every day, about what is happening. We understand that it is up to us to force the government to end the killing. Our support on colleges is increasing. So is our determination.

We have created room for dissent. Now we must do more. We call for a shift from protest to resistance. Resistance to us means upping the level of opposition. Seeking ways to throw ourselves onto the gears of the machine and actually stop it from functioning, if only briefly. We see the war machine's tentacles everywhere, even on our campuses, and we are determined to expose and find ways to stop them. Some of us will defy the draft. Some will focus on our schools. All of us will march and march and march. We are now determined to shatter the unity of the country.

The demonstration against McNamara produced headlines across the country and lead stories on the nightly TV news. Protests were held regularly now on most American campuses. Despite our increasing protests and revelations, the war machine rumbled on. There were now prisoners of war in North Vietnamese jails as some of our endless waves of bombers were shot down. The bombers kept flying, darkening the Asian sky. The bombs kept dropping. Six weeks after our protest with McNamara, the entire village of Cau Dat near Hanoi was leveled by our bombers.[11] The day after Christmas, 1966, McNamara's Department of Defense was forced to admit that civilians may have been inadvertently killed in our massive bombings of North Vietnam. That announcement was followed by an offensive the next day in the Mekong Delta in southernmost Vietnam, with hundreds of tons of bombs and fiery hurricanes of napalm.[12] The war, the bombing, the burning, the dying went on without end, without a break. The casualties mounted.

In late February, the United States launched the largest military offensive of the war so far. Operation Junction City involved twenty-two US and four South Vietnamese battalions. After almost three months of fighting, the United States announced the end of Junction City and the body count: 2,728 Vietcong killed and thirty-four captured. American losses were 282 killed and 1,576 wounded.[13] To us those were not numbers—they were once people who woke up with hopes, took showers, made love, made jokes, hoped to make families. Now they were dead. Now they were wounded, maimed. Their lives ended or splintered. Increasingly they inhabited both my waking and dreaming. If we do not do something, more will die. What do we do?

That spring of 1967, opposition to the war was increasing in quantum leaps. Quite different, if overlapping, strategies for opposing the war were emerging. Some were focused on campus organizing and campus demonstrations, others on national mobilization through ever larger national marches. Others were trying to figure out how to take the antiwar movement off campus. And there was the question of the 1968 elections. Could we run candidates? Should they run within the Democratic Party? New organizations were springing up such as one hundred clergy who had spoken out against the war and created a National Emergency Committee of Clergy and Laymen Concerned about Vietnam. A New Politics organization was formed to look at how to create an electoral expression of the antiwar and civil rights movements.

The Spring Mobilization in New York City on April 15 was by far the largest demonstration so far, as somewhere between 100,000 and 200,000 people flooded the streets. We brought thousands down from all the SDS chapters across New England. The snaking, chanting mass of people stretched from Central Park to the UN offices. Nearby seventy-five young men burned their draft cards. Simultaneously another 75,000 people marched in San Francisco.

At the UN, Martin Luther King, Jr., Dr. Benjamin Spock, and the Southern Christian Leadership Conference's (SCLC) James Bevel addressed the crowds. Bevel took everyone by surprise, even the other leaders of the Mobilization on the stage, when he announced that there would be an even bigger march in the fall in Washington. At that moment, the October 1967 March on the Pentagon was born.

Major changes were taking place in the Civil Rights Movement. Dr. King came out forcefully and eloquently against the war in Vietnam and participated in antiwar marches. He faced harsh criticism from liberals who thought he should restrict his focus to domestic civil rights issues. Instead, King spoke out against the war and also raised the challenge of economic inequality. SNCC's Stokely Carmichael called for Black Power, echoing Malcolm X by defining it as the coming together of Black people to fight for their liberation "by any means necessary." SNCC wanted to cast off its dependence on white people. In December of 1966 SNCC asked all white staff and volunteers to leave the organization. A quiet wave of dismay rolled its way up to me in Cambridge.

At a conference in New Haven, I sat outside with a SNCC organizer, Ivanhoe Donaldson whom I considered a friend. I asked him what the decision meant for white people like me who had long loved the organization. The idea that I no longer had a role in the fight alongside him was leaving me disoriented. I expected the usual: go organize white people. Instead, Ivanhoe took his time, looking at me obviously and carefully.

"Michael, have you looked in the mirror recently?" Long pause.

"Look at yourself. Kinky hair. Thick lips. Dark complexion. When are you going to stop hating yourself and accept that you are a brother? When are you going to stop trying to pass? C'mon my brother!"

We both burst out laughing. He gave me a slap on the shoulder. But underneath the jokes, I felt a growing gap, a new sense of loss, unsaid but real nonetheless. It would have been easy for me, raised to think of myself as Syrian Lebanese, to consider myself inextricably linked to the struggles of people of color. It would be nice to slide into thinking that somehow, I was indeed some sort of "brother." But I knew I had all the advantages of a second-generation American with white skin. My experience as a young teenager in the Civil Rights Movement had shaped me profoundly, enriched me, created a powerful identification with "the movement." Now the ebullient hope, the dream, of an interracial movement for social change, that had lifted me and so many others, sustained us, nourished us, was deflating.

H. Rap Brown became chairman of SNCC and, declaring "violence was as American as apple pie," renounced nonviolence. The Black Panthers of Oakland were getting national attention for openly carrying guns as they monitored the

FIGURE 10.   Detroit, July 25, 1967. The *Detroit News*. Keystone Press / Alamy Stock Photo.

Oakland police, a force long known for its racism. Then in the hot summer of 1967, America's cities exploded into riot and violence.

A Black cab driver is beaten by cops in Newark. Newark's Black community has had enough; things are supposed to be changing. Newark erupts. In Cairo, Illinois, Robert Hunt, a young Black serviceman home on leave is found dead in a cell. The police say suicide. The Black community in Cairo thinks otherwise. Things are supposed to be changing. Cairo erupts.[14] In Detroit, the police raid a welcome home party for three Black returning Vietnam vets at an illegal after-hours drinking spot known locally as a blind pig. Detroit explodes.[15]

In Boston, one hundred members of Mothers for Adequate Welfare, the organization that had grown out of Noel Day's Dudley Street Action Center, sit in at a state welfare office. The police clear them out and attempt to violently disburse the crowd outside, provoking a sustained riot.

In city after city across America, African Americans are fed up with the endemic unemployment, constant police brutality, unfulfilled promises, and dreams deferred too long. Refusing the heritage of thousands of lynchings, unafraid in their rage, tens of thousands take to the streets to vent their anger. The newspapers scream headlines about 159 "race riots." We see them as insurrections.

FIGURE 11.   Troops moving into Detroit, July 1967. Keystone Pictures USA/ Alamy Stock Photo.

While there is looting and arson, we see the explosions as uprisings, efforts to throw off white supremacy and the long heritage of slavery. The press and white politicians want to paint them as wanton, directionless and self-destructive. We want to see them as a rebellion. The National Guard and the Airborne occupy America's cities.

Like most white activists I feel relegated to the sidelines. There is no role for us. There is a sense that something profound is being lost. The bonds of hope that united us, Black and white, in the Civil Rights Movement are fraying. The beloved community is no longer the dream. Anger has replaced redemptive love.

At the same time the war in Vietnam dragged on. The war that Hunt in Cairo was on leave from. The war that three Black soldiers in Detroit had come home from, celebrating their safe return in that blind pig. The war that was killing Black soldiers more than white. The war that increasingly haunted us.

That spring, I was completing my senior year and thus, despite devoting all my time to stopping the war and occasional research for *Ramparts*, I had to write a thesis. I chose to write about the peasant revolt in England in 1381. I explored the role of culture and consciousness in shaping popular revolt. Why did the revolt break out when it did, since many of the conditions that underlay it had existed for years? I was sharply critical of traditional Marxist interpretations that I saw as overly deterministic. Distracted, I left the actual writing to the last minute. Although I knew it was not great, I thought I had produced a decent thesis. The new conservative head of the History and Literature Department was delighted to inform me that my effort had received the lowest grade in the history of Harvard College. I don't know if that was true, but it was clear that my grade was due as much to his and the two readers' dislike of my politics as to the quality of the thesis.

No matter—I was not bound for any career that Professor John L. Clive could take pleasure in ruining. I was to be a full-time organizer for the rest of my life. After two more perfunctory classes in the fall, I would graduate cum laude in general studies. I was eager to leave Harvard behind.

For weeks that spring, I had been participating in discussions with a small group of younger faculty members about where the antiwar movement should go next. I argued strenuously that just as we had organized students through education, leaflets, meeting in the dorms, and then campus-wide meetings leading to actions, now we needed to do the hard work of reaching out to communities. I knew the divide that I had experienced firsthand in the foray in the meat-packing plants was as strong as ever. However, in college communities and in the more educated suburbs, there were signs of growing disenchantment with the war. Perhaps we could organize in those neighborhoods now.

Gar Alperovitz, a former congressional staffer now at Harvard, was the moving force behind these discussions. He had started meeting with Marty Peretz, Michael Walzer, and Chester Hartman, all young faculty, around the idea of something he was calling a "teach-out," similar to a campus "teach-in" but for the public instead of students. They asked me to join their discussions, usually in Marty's small office.

I asked David and Hal to join the discussions with me. Finding the "teach-out" idea nebulous, we argued instead for a summer project modeled after the Mississippi Freedom Summer. We should set a goal to knock on a million doors that coming summer. After weeks of discussion, everyone agreed. We would try to recruit and train as many local organizers as possible and have them recruit as many local volunteers as possible. It would be left up to the local groups to decide exactly what their activities would be. They could do draft counseling, launch local referenda against the war, educate, circulate petitions, and organize. They could prepare for the elections. At the end of the summer, the project would end. We reasoned it would get the support of various organizations, including SDS, if it were not seen as a permanent and competing organization.

We persuaded National SDS to participate in what we now called "Vietnam Summer." SDS provided many, perhaps most, of the organizers and volunteers. Marty and Gar raised the funds. Rapidly other groups joined in: the National Committee for a Sane Nuclear Policy (SANE), SNCC, the American Friends Service Committee, and Clergy & Laymen. I recruited Lee Webb, the former SDS leader, to be the codirector.

Vietnam Summer was officially launched on April 23 with a press conference with Dr. King, Scheer, and Dr. Spock. After the press conference, King and his aide Andy Young met with us and there was discussion of a possible presidential run by King, although he and Young were highly skeptical. The next evening Dr. King spoke to an overflow crowd in Jordan Hall calling for an end to the war and urging volunteers to sign up for Vietnam Summer.

The fundraising efforts flourished. There were posters by significant artists. Benefit concerts. Vietnam Summer raised far more money than I had thought remotely possible.

The summer-long effort embodied the antiwar movement of that year: large, divided, diffuse, confused but determined and increasingly angry. Nevertheless, thousands of antiwar activists and students were trained how to knock on doors. Less than a year later, many of those staff and volunteers would be in New Hampshire knocking on doors for Gene McCarthy.

Vietnam Summer ended up with 700 paid staff members and over 20,000 volunteers working in hundreds of local projects across the country.[16] There were referenda campaigns, local rallies, community meetings, and hundreds of thousands of doors were knocked on. At the end of September, as agreed upon, Vietnam Summer shut its doors.

However, I missed all of it. I had decided to spend that summer taking up an invitation to join the *Ramparts* team in San Francisco. Neither Amy nor I had ever been to California. *Ramparts*, inaccurately believing I was a crackerjack researcher, offered me a good-paying job as associate editor. We desperately needed the money. I had borrowed from friends to pay for Amy's tuition at Brandeis and I needed to pay them back. Both of us were attracted to a break from the nonstop organizing and a change of location.

While 20,000 volunteers were knocking on doors across America, that summer of 1967 would come not to be known for their remarkable antiwar work. It would primarily be known as America's Long Hot Summer of riots. Also, that summer of '67 was the summer the "counterculture" burst into prominence and its epicenter was San Francisco's Haight Ashbury. Quite unintentionally Amy and I joined the thousands of young people making the trip to San Francisco for the "Summer of Love."

Soon after 100,000 young people descended on New York City for the "Mobilization," another 100,000 headed for San Francisco.[17] There was some overlap between the two groups; however, the counterculture explorers tended to eschew politics and organizing in favor of music, drugs, and sex. They were more drawn to "be-ins" than marches. In the media, all of us were conflated: the youth of America was in revolt and for many older Americans we were all rather revolting.

I loved being in San Francisco for that summer. Each morning, I would walk through Chinatown, down Jackson Street, often stopping for dim sum, food I had never previously encountered. Continuing to walk while eating a small pearl of a dumpling or a soft bun, I would pass by City Lights bookstore, where on my return trip I would stop and soak up being in the place where Jack Kerouac, Allen Ginsberg, Kenneth Rexroth, and Lawrence Ferlinghetti often stood.

Near City Lights was an astonishing Chinese restaurant that Amy and I frequented. It was our introduction to Peking duck and moo shu pork. At twenty, we felt grown up, so sophisticated. That feeling only increased when we went to Sunday brunch at Sam's of Tiburon, sitting on a long pier jutting out into the bay, a slight breeze riffing the water, the bright sun forcing us to wear sunglasses, drinking gin fizzes and having steak and eggs, people-watching, delighting when the tiny actress Julie Christie and her entourage sat only a few tables away. Early on, Amy's sister Catherine brought us to a concert on Mt. Tamalpais with Janis Joplin, barefoot, big voiced, wearing a large, floppy hat, singing on the small outdoor stage, the scent of pot wafting through sun splashed mountain fields.

We were young and feeling full of ourselves. We enjoyed the newness of everything that summer, the relief from the pressure of organizing, the chance to explore a strange city and each other, the smell of eucalyptus, the riot of color in the Berkeley rose garden, the foggy coast, the endless soundtrack of new music, the swirling political and journalistic scene centered on *Ramparts*. Each day, while Amy worked in a "head shop," I worked with Scheer and Hinkle in the *Rampart*'s office. Felt the menacing presence of Eldridge Cleaver. Talked with the young Jan Wenner about his dream of a magazine devoted to rock and roll.

Amy and I would head to Bill Graham's crowded Fillmore for sets by Eric Clapton and Cream, Jefferson Airplane, Quicksilver, or the Steve Miller band. We were amused at the antics of the hippies and intrigued by the anarchist collective of street theater actors and activists calling themselves the Diggers. We would wander wide-eyed through the crowds of stoned and tripping young people in the "be-ins" at Golden Gate Park, the ubiquitous bongo drumming cluster, the kite flyers, past couples furiously having sex under a ragged blanket, the smell of incense and pot mixing on the summer air. We would take in the street theater of the Mime Troupe with their intense political performances and radical sensibilities. We were surrounded by the sounds of countless musicians playing in the park, playing on street corners. Music, incense, young people everywhere. It was all a spectacle for us. We were not hippies. We were political activists, determined to change the country. While we felt a certain raw tribal kinship with those rebelling through dropping out, the countercultural path was not for us. But for that summer, instead of the constant medley of late-night meetings and endless organizing, we attended parties. One in Oakland was particularly memorable as we found ourselves dancing to recordings of Aretha Franklin singing "Respect" alongside the top leadership of the Black Panther Party.

The summer came to an end all too soon. The editors at *Ramparts* assumed I would stay. "No one leaves California," they would say. "No one leaves *Ramparts*, man—we are the most exciting magazine in the country, and you have a great future with us." But journalism was not my calling. Amy needed to get back to school and I needed to get back to opposing the war.

Throughout 1967, one hundred American soldiers a week were dying in Vietnam and more Vietnamese civilians than could be counted were being wounded, displaced, or killed. The United States kept pouring in more troops. That July as I was enjoying San Francisco, the US general William Westmoreland requested another 200,000 American boys in addition to the 475,000 already scheduled to be sent to Vietnam.[18]

I had helped conceive and plan Vietnam Summer and then I had skipped out to make money and have fun in San Francisco. My summer of love had been different from those of the thousands of flower children who had poured into that city, but it was no less self-indulgent.

I reached an agreement with *Ramparts* that I would continue to work part-time for them for what seemed to me an astronomical amount of money. That money would support us. I was eager to continue to organize against the war—a job that paid nothing.

While Vietnam Summer carried out its grassroots work, the attempts to create an insurgent politics, a "New Politics," moved forward haltingly. The exact nature of such a "New Politics" was vague and ill-defined.

While many of the new generation of SDS activists were not interested in electoral politics, I did not think that participating in elections needed to be at odds with local organizing or direct action. I saw them all as different aspects of our struggle. Lacking a coherent strategy, I was for anything that might work.

I doubted that the time was right for running a national presidential campaign, however. I thought it was a given in that summer of 1967 that the next year LBJ would be the incumbent nominee of the Democratic Party. I assumed he would be unassailable in the primaries. If we wanted a national antiwar ticket on the November ballot, it would have to be through a new third party, which struck me as an unrealistic prospect. Working in the *Ramparts* offices, staying in touch with Vietnam Summer and SDS leaders, I was in constant discussions about the possibility of a King/Spock ticket. I thought it would be more effective to select congressional districts where we could run insurgent candidates who had a chance of winning.

At the end of August, I flew with Scheer to attend the National Conference for a New Politics (NCNP). This was an ambitious effort to bring together Black organizations, the predominately white antiwar movement, the New Left, and liberal Democrats to create a new political expression that would encompass all of us. The steering committee included Paul Booth of SDS, Julian Bond of SNCC, SANE's Dr. Spock, and Simon Casady, the president of the powerful California Democratic Council.

Skeptical but intrigued, I joined the more than 2,000 delegates representing more than 200 different organizations in Chicago.[19] We met against a backdrop of insurrections in the urban heart of America. Cities were burning. SNCC leaders embraced Black Power. The Panthers had burst onto the national consciousness. White people who had supported the Civil Rights Movement were confused and hurt as they were asked to leave the organizations they had supported for so long. Still, in advance of the conference, Black leaders, including Bond, Fannie Lou Hamer, and Floyd McKissick had written an open letter calling for continued cooperation and political alliance between Black activists and white progressives.

The antiwar movement at this point was already an amorphous sprawling effort going in many different directions, from draft resistance to marches to local referenda to a very few insurgent candidates. There had only been a handful of attempts by the antiwar movement to enter the electoral arena. The robust but ultimately unsuccessful primary campaign of Scheer in the Bay Area in 1966 was one of the exceptions.

All the dysfunction of the movements of 1967 was on naked display as the conference rapidly splintered along racial lines. There was no agreement on direction, strategy, or tactics. Dr. King gave a rather disappointing keynote address. Bond appeared briefly and then vanished.

Early on, Black nationalist delegates walked out of the conference. Another group of remaining Black delegates formed an angry and aggrieved Black caucus and met separately. They framed the key issue of the moment as whether white people would finally accept Black leadership. They promulgated a thirteen-point list of "nonnegotiable demands" that had to be accepted before they would return to the conference. They demanded 50 percent of the votes at the conference, support for reparations, and condemnation of the "imperialist Zionist" Six Day War and Israel. They sent speakers into the main hall to denounce white liberals. There was a nasty undercurrent of criticism of the "Jewish" nature of so many of the white leaders. Jewish leaders who supported Israel—and even those who were critical of Israel—felt uncomfortable with what they saw as a growing anti-Semitism. Many Jews had been the very first to march with the Civil Rights Movement. Now they felt a stinging and very personal rejection.

Peretz played a major role in convening and funding the conference. He was furious with the Black caucus. This would be the start of a long journey that would leave Marty viciously opposed to those on the left and a fanatical defender of Israel. Peretz and Scheer hauled me aside. I was the perfect go-between. My mother came from a Jewish family and my father was Syrian Lebanese. I knew many of the leaders of the Black caucus. Yes, they told me, I was perfect. Scheer and Peretz charged me with negotiating with the Black caucus to find better language that could keep the conference from totally splintering.

I had absolutely no idea what to say or do. I told them so. They insisted. Soon I found myself shuttling back and forth between the Black caucus and the white leadership.

That sweltering summer in Chicago, I could no more bridge the gap at that dysfunctional conference than all the mediators over the years have done in the Middle East. I went back and forth. There were tweaks and modifications to this sentence and that paragraph. Many Jewish delegates felt pain and anger; Black leaders were confident of their perspective of internationalism, anti-imperialism, and Black Power. The breach could not be healed. Liberal and radical Jews now felt they were being cast aside after years of dedication to civil rights. Black leaders were not interested in being subordinated to the wishes of white people, even those who had marched with them.

In the end, amid chaos and confusion, the white delegates accepted the demands of the Black caucus. The conference led nowhere. Many Black delegates left convinced that the white left was attempting to use them. Many white delegates left angry, hurt, or determined to shed their "white skin privilege" and look to Black leaders for direction. I left confused but clear that no new national political formulation could emerge from this dysfunctional effort.

The NCNP conference would be seen over time as a farce. The failure it symbolized was a tragedy. The movements of the 1960s were unable to create an effective and lasting electoral political expression; that failure would cripple American politics for years. In a few short months, the presidential campaign of Senator Eugene McCarthy would build on the antiwar movement and directly on Vietnam Summer. It would not, however, draw the support of the Civil Rights Movement and of Black activists. Nor would it have the whole-hearted support of SDS and the bulk of the New Left.

The failure of the antiwar movement to be sophisticated enough to both embrace protest outside the electoral arena and at the same time insurgent candidates within it, would be a costly mistake.

Many of the most experienced antiwar and New Left organizers disdained the electoral arena. That would carry down the years as many of us became community organizers and stayed outside of elections. In those same years, many elections would be decided by such small margins that field organizing could have made the difference. Right-wing forces entrenched themselves in the National Rifle Association, evangelical and Catholic churches, right-to-life groups, small business associations, and conservative women's groups. They would use locally rooted organizations and cause-based groups to power their electoral efforts. On the left there would be nothing comparable. With the unions under constant attack and steadily declining, the right would often out organize the center left, winning close elections that could have been swung the other way, starting with the election of Richard Nixon in 1968.

The divisions between white progressives and Black radicals would hurt the efforts of both. That summer's conference could never have succeeded but the fault lines it revealed were tragic and long lasting. The nation was about to enter a period of unimaginable crisis and upheaval. And we were not preparing our movements to lead.

SITTING IN AND ARMIES OF THE NIGHT

Once Amy and I arrived back in Massachusetts, the immediate task was sign-
ing up people to go to Washington for what we hoped would be the biggest
demonstration yet against the war—the March on the Pentagon. That march
had its origin in James Bevel's surprise announcement in New York the previous
spring. The National Mobilization Committee to End the War in Vietnam, or
the "Mobe" as we called it, was a coalition of hundreds of groups. SDS had an
uneasy relationship with the coalition. While we would consistently participate
in the marches, turning out large numbers of students and young people, the
"Mobe" was mired in complicated coalitional politics that we had no patience
for. Pointless jockeying for position, protracted negotiations that would produce
silly, long lists of "demands" and slogans for each march, as if anyone cared what
was printed on the placards, what was chanted, or what was written in leaflets
that rarely got read. The march itself was what mattered. That sea of humanity
bursting out of the diurnal routine to say, "Stop this war or we will crack normality wide open."

American causalities were mounting. The future promised only greater and
greater violence, more troops, more bombs, more napalm, more tragedy. That fall
of 1967, the pace of protest picked up. October 16 we were back to the Arlington
Street Church, where an overflow crowd of close to 5,000 heard calls for draft
resistance by Dr. Benjamin Spock, Reverend Sloan Coffin and Michael Ferber,
a local Boston activist, and witnessed the burning of draft cards. This time the
counterprotestors were small in number and overwhelmed by our crowds.

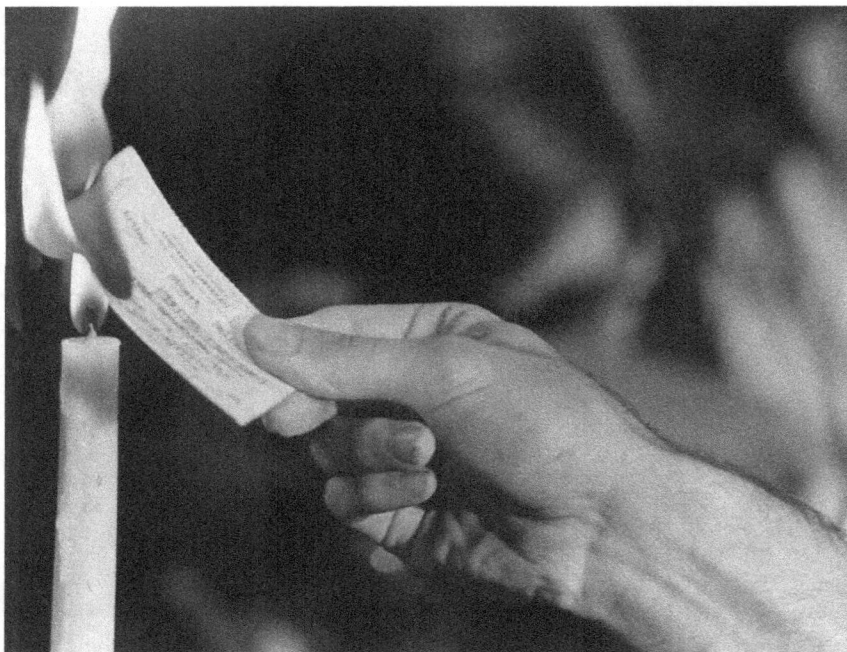

FIGURE 12.   Draft card being burned inside the Arlington Street Church, October 16, 1967. Courtesy of the *Boston Globe* Library collection at Northeastern University Archives and Special Collections.

Then it was on to Washington. All fall we had been renting buses, spending endless hours convincing people who were on the fence to get on the bus. We were overwhelmed by the last-minute rush of students who signed up. The tide was steadily shifting on campuses. That October 21 march brought 100,000 people to Washington to protest the war.[1] The chaotic mix of students, radicals, liberals, housewives (a common term in those years), pacifists, and clergy roiled down the streets of Washington, and snaked toward the Pentagon, the five-sided nerve center of the war itself.

While there was some Black participation, the protestors were overwhelmingly white—and young. Among us was a contingent of counterculture performers, writers, artists, and poets—Norman Mailer, Allen Ginsberg, the experimental rock band the Fugs—who planned a theater of the absurd to confront an absurd reality. They promised to levitate the Pentagon. The march also brought to prominence two acquaintances of mine: Jerry Rubin and Abbie Hoffman. Jerry was a leading activist in the Bay Area who had been at the center of many demonstrations, from the Free Speech Movement through intense and large antiwar protests. I had met him at a national SDS meeting and immediately disliked him, finding him self-promoting. Dave Dellinger and the other leaders of the "Mobe" had turned to Jerry to staff the October march. He joined forces with Abbie.

With the gift of a showman's shtick, Abbie was ten years older than me. I had first met him when he had been a SNCC supporter. He had studied with the political theorist Herbert Marcuse at Brandeis, then worked with SNCC and opened a small store in his hometown of Worcester, Massachusetts, to support civil rights work. I had hired him to be our lead Worcester organizer for the Adams campaign. Abbie had at some point connected with Peter Coyote and the Diggers. I chuckle now when I hear the sonorous voice of Coyote narrating documentaries, the Winter Olympics, or ads for Apple. Abbie quickly grasped the media opportunities that the Diggers' anarchist theater and radical performances could create. Soon he and Jerry would become a tandem leadership team for what they called the Youth International Party, an organization that did not exist. As "Yippies" they were soon garnering way more press coverage than our more prosaic and boring efforts.

Levitating the Pentagon was too frivolous for me. Nor was I drawn to the civil disobedience that resulted in over 500 arrests. I did not think our job was to make gestures. Our job was to build a movement too large to be denied.

Outside the Pentagon I had a glimpse of a troubling future. Many of my fellow SDS members from around the country, particularly those from the militant Columbia SDS chapter, seemed to think that the brief siege of the Department of Defense headquarters by tens of thousands of protestors was an exercise in guerilla warfare. They formed small groups, talked about a strategy of hit and run, and referred to the writings of the French intellectual Régis Debray who had been with Che Guevara in Bolivia. As I caught periodic glimpses of them outside of the massive building ringed with heavily armed soldiers, they seemed oddly out of touch with the reality of the moment. Engaging in child's play, revolutionary fantasies we could ill afford. We had a war to end.

Amy and I were part of the tens of thousands who marched on the Pentagon as it was protected by a stolid line of soldiers and military police from the 82nd Airborne. As some protestors in their small collectives looked for ways to breach the wall of soldiers, most of us milled around as young women, and a few young men, periodically approached unsmiling soldiers to insert a flower in the gun barrels, more often than not winning a brief, sheepish smile. Other protestors attempted to engage soldiers in discussion and dialogue. The usual few over amped and aggressive young men harangued the hapless GIs on the evils of the war and their duty to oppose it. As time passed, tensions lessened. Most of the thousands of protestors settled into conversations, chants, and songs. Inside the Pentagon, thousands of soldiers were held in reserve.[2]

FIGURE 13.   Outside the Pentagon, October 21, 1967. Everett Collection Historical / Alamy Stock Photo.

I was excited by the numbers—our largest turnout to date. We had gone from 25,000 in DC in April 1965 to 100,000 two and a half years later. Clearly, we were growing.

That night outside the Pentagon, the protestors still numbered in the tens of thousands. Skirmishes broke out. The self-conceived guerrillas mounted probes of the perimeter, found a few weak spots, and following their lead, crowds would surge in to be met by US Marshals determined to prevent anyone from breaching the outer walls of the war center itself. Those who committed civil disobedience were hauled off and protested that they were badly abused by the marshals. Later soldiers and marshals would recount tales of verbal and physical abuse: bottles and bags of shit hurled at them. I did not see any of the abuse on either side as by nightfall we were no longer on the front lines. Amy and I headed back to Cambridge, excited by the numbers and determined to find a way to keep up the momentum.

Despite massive coverage of the march, the war rolled on, a machine seemingly impervious to everything we did. The evening news and morning papers brought new and horrific images of towers of flame, hurricanes of fire—the destruction of napalm. Napalm became a searing image, symbol, and reality of the war.

Napalm was invented for use as a weapon in 1942 in a secret lab at Harvard and its first trial tests were held on the Harvard athletic fields.[3] It is jellied gasoline

FIGURE 14.   Napalm became a searing image of the war. Tango Images / Alamy Stock Photo.

that, when dropped from the air, explodes on impact, generating a storm system of flames. The winds generated reach seventy miles per hour.[4] The temperatures rise to 2,200 degrees Fahrenheit. It sticks, clings to skin and clothes, spreads, and burns. Around 388,000 tons of napalm were dropped on Indochina from 1963 to 1973.[5] Each barrel bore the stamp of the Dow Chemical Company.

On October 18 SDS led a peaceful sit in against a Dow recruiter at the University of Wisconsin. The protestors were violently attacked by police. Less than a week later, another recruiter was scheduled to visit Harvard. We were determined to not allow the university to welcome a company making an immoral weapon to fight an unjust war. Five hundred people rallied in Harvard Yard as we called for a picket line outside of the Dow recruiters' location when they arrived on campus.

On the morning of October 25—just four days after the Pentagon march— more than 200 of us first set up a picket line and then I led us inside to jam the narrow hall outside Room 233 in the Conant Chemistry Lab building where a small, neatly dressed recruiter from Dow is starting his interviews. We fill the narrow hallway making it difficult for anyone to get in or out. The deans arrive and chastise us for improper behavior and ask us to disperse. We politely refuse and continue to sit in the hall. At 10:30 when the first recruiter leaves, a second takes his place. It quickly dawns on us that the second recruiter was a decoy. No one is attempting to wade through us for an interview. Scouts fan out and soon locate the first Dow man, Fred Leavitt, continuing to interview in the building next door. We immediately move the entire demonstration next door and block access in and out of the room.

Now we have a gaggle of deans talking with us. We debate what to do. We know that the university will charge us with violating the rules. From the way the deans are talking to us, they will seek suspension or perhaps expulsion if we stay. But now we are committed and annoyed that the university was so committed to Dow recruiting that it had a decoy. It is time for us to stop the wheels of the war machine from turning even if it is just for this one day in this one minor way.

No one can get through us to see the recruiter. We agree that those who want to, will give me their "bursar's cards"—the way a student paid for meals and other services, and is identified by the university. I will hand them to a dean at the right time—a clear statement that we will take full responsibility for our actions. We know we are breaking university rules, and we are prepared to take the consequences for this civil disobedience.

University officials decide to try to move Leavitt once again. As they start stepping over and around seated students, a group of us stand up and link arms. We say no one is leaving until Leavitt signs a statement that says, "I agree to stop interviewing on the Harvard campus and not return for that purpose." There is then an exchange with Leavitt, who we rather rudely harangue about napalm and the war. Leavitt's response is that he did not know enough about the war or Dow's policies to answer our questions. He is a research scientist, not a policymaker and not management. One of us yells out that we should stop badgering the poor guy. We all feel chagrined. He is a symbol, the wrong person in the wrong place, with his thin tie and pencil protector. We do not want to mistreat him. Still, we hold fast—there will be no recruiting for Dow and since he has already tried the decoy once, he cannot leave unless he signs the pledge. Soon he returns into the room.

Now our numbers are growing. Word of what is happening is spreading. Leavitt is sitting bored with no one to interview. The hallway swarms with even more deans. I inform them that they can come and go but Leavitt can leave only when he signs the pledge to stop recruiting.

The deans are horrified. This is not the way the gentlemen and women of Harvard behave. Dean Fred Glimp reads out sections of the "Rules Relating to College," demanding that we stop "illegally incarcerating" Leavitt, and immediately stop disrupting the normal functioning of the university. If we do not, we will be subject to "severance of connection"—Harvard's language for expulsion. Glimp says we are not allowed to threaten another person by holding him hostage. That elicits a yelled, "Is that a threat?" Everyone, including Glimp, laughs.

I explain that we are nonviolent, but we will stay and passively block anyone from coming in to be interviewed or Leavitt from leaving. Glimp says the deans would like to talk individually to each of us. My response is that they must deal with us as a group—and I hand him 150 bursar's cards. We are taking full responsibility for our actions, I tell him. This war is immoral. He should know that. Napalm is immoral. How could they, Harvard, the deans, support either? Dropping napalm is a war crime. There can be no support for war crimes, no matter how indirect. Anyone with a conscience must take a stand. That means us. That meant the university. That means here. Now. If not us, who? If not now, when?

All afternoon deans, house masters, senior tutors, all the factotums of the university, come by. Word continues to spread about what is happening. Our numbers swell. More importantly, even students who could not join the sit-in send over their bursar's cards. Throughout the afternoon I periodically hand over another batch to the perplexed administrators. Increasingly non-SDS students turn in the cards as support spreads: the head of the Young Democrats turns in his card, the head of the official Undergraduate Council turns in his card. In the end more than 400 students turn in their cards.

The administration vacillates about what to do. They alert the Cambridge police who prepare 150 officers ready to dislodge us. We reiterate our determination to stay and our determination to be nonviolent and to accept the consequences of our actions. We provide lunch to the beleaguered Dow recruiter.

Finally, as afternoon turns into evening, we say we have accomplished what we had set out to accomplish. There was no recruiting that day, and Leavitt helpfully tells us he is not coming back. Glimp sternly reiterates that we are in deep trouble. We are feeling good. We decide to let Leavitt leave. We meet for our usual inefficient two hours' postaction evaluation and next step discussion, formulating a clear set of demands for the university. They are considering how to punish us. We demand that they change their policies on recruitment. After all, the CIA was scheduled to come recruit the following week.

In the next days, the university is in turmoil. The press blares the news of radical antiwar action at Harvard. Students and faculty at other Boston area colleges write letters supporting us. Debate rages. And whenever debate rages, even if it starts with the inappropriateness of our actions, people are forced to engage with the issue of the war. The more people engage the facts of the war, the more people steadily come over to our side.

The bursar's card strategy, an inspired improvisation, becomes a serious challenge for the deans and president Nathan Pusey. The 400-plus students who turned in their cards are saying, "If you punish them, you have to punish me." There is no question about our act of civil disobedience: by taking full and open responsibility for our actions we are clearly saying "Yes, we broke university rules, but we broke them following a greater moral imperative." It allows us to focus on why we broke the rules. We made no argument that the university could not punish us if they so choose. Instead, we argued that while we broke the rules, the university should stop being complicit in the manufacture of a terrible weapon being used in a hideous manner in an unjust and tragic war. We could see posted in the Office of Career Plans notices for recruitment interviews not just with Dow but also with dozens of companies making money from their essential participation in the war.

President Pusey, a gentleman tragically disconnected from his students and from the real passions and issues of the times, is firm in his insistence that the university must severely punish the demonstrators. Our actions have been to him a clear violation of the "freedom of expression or movement of others."[6] Following the McNamara demonstration, the deans felt that they had to make a stand.

They take the issue to a raucous faculty meeting. Many of the faculty could only see our actions through the lens of "McCarthyism of the Left." At the same time a significant group of the faculty was troubled by having to discipline so many students who clearly acted out of a moral passion. There is a growing number of professors who are now opposed to the war, George Wald, Hilary Putnam, Carl Sagan, Michael Walzer, and Jack Womack argue our case. The deans argue strenuously for selecting at least those students who blocked the doors. There was no question, for example, of my role or the role of other SDS leaders. Our pictures were there for all to see in the *Crimson*. In the end the faculty produced a shockingly moderate set of actions: seventy-four of us were placed on probation for the semester; the administration had pushed for "severance" and was unhappy with probation, but there was nothing they could do, having taken it to the faculty. All the others who turned in their bursar's cards were not punished in any way. Furthermore, the faculty voted to create a Student–Faculty Advisory Council to deal with the issues that we had raised, review campus recruitment policies, and the role of the university in the war.

In the coming weeks and months, on every campus where Dow sent a recruiter, students protested, often sitting in. We were excited by our success. We thought, as we framed it then, that we had started to move from protest into resistance.

In the run up to the March on the Pentagon, a group of prominent intellectuals, writers and clergy had issued a powerful "Call to Resist Illegitimate Authority," which made the case that the war was immoral, illegal, and unconstitutional.[7] All the signers pledged to do everything that they could to support those who resisted the draft and those in the military who refused to serve. We all began to debate what resistance meant. Resistance harked back to the famed French effort against German occupation. Resistance would mean our movement would directly seek to disrupt the processes necessary for the war: encourage resistance to the draft, force universities to disengage from all entanglements with the war, shut down recruitment for war companies, find increasingly serious ways to disrupt the everyday systems supporting the war, start exacting—through disruption—a real cost for continuing the war. We were both desperate and excited.

We conveniently forgot that the meeting to plan the Dow action had chosen a picket line and rejected a sit-in. We never discussed that I had led people into a direct action that had not been planned. Exciting direct action has its own dynamic.

While we would work on other issues, supporting the welfare mothers of MAW, against American support of apartheid in South Africa, for more student say in university decisions, assisting a union drive at a local hospital, even helping the Maverick Street Mothers protest airport expansion in East Boston, the war was inescapable. Always the war. It ground on without mercy or respite. We were convinced that now more than ever was the time moral people must fling themselves into the gears and onto the wheels to bring the machinery of war to a stop. From protest to resistance. But how, that was the question that bore down on us, how to bring those grinding wheels and gears of death to a halt?

Postscript: in November 1969, Dow declared that it would stop manufacturing napalm for the United States government. Dow's chairman of the board, Carl Gerstacker, explained, "We may have lost some recruits that we really would have wanted, we may have lost some sales that we otherwise would have had, we may have lost some stockholders that would otherwise have purchased our stock. The number of Dow shareholders dropped from 95,000 to 90,000 during the Napalm demonstrations although only a couple dozen stockholders specifically informed us that they were selling because of Napalm. We suspect a good many of the 5,000 we lost reacted at least in part to the Napalm stories, but we have no way of determining just how many."[8]

Late in 1967, Tom Hayden, and Rennie Davis came to town to drum up support for massive demonstrations in Chicago at the Democratic Convention the coming summer. As a dozen of us crowded into the small living room of a dingy Cambridgeport apartment, Tom and Rennie made the case that all eyes would be on Chicago for the coronation of Lyndon B. Johnson. We must not let the Democratic Party pretend there is no war, evade their responsibility for it. Vietnam was LBJ's war. There must be no business as usual, no politics as usual. We must not allow the war to remain remote, over there, only on the TV. We needed to make it real, felt, present in the streets of Chicago. We must bring 50,000 people to Chicago.

I was initially all in. We formed an organizing committee for New England. We all agreed: each day, the evening news brought the horrific nature of the war into our living rooms. We needed to summon the nation to protest. We planned to "bring the war home" to the streets of Chicago.

Over the next months, as I talked repeatedly with Tom and Rennie about the planning, I began to feel queasy about what might happen. I had a sense that they were willing to provoke an extreme police response. All my friends were itching for a battle. With blood being spilled every day 3,000 miles away, all of us felt desperate. We knew the reputation of the Chicago police. We knew that they too were itching for a fight. I was concerned because we were not being clear about the risks. We were recruiting people to participate in a peaceful protest that I worried would not stay peaceful if the Chicago police had anything to do with it. I was bothered enough that I tried to talk to Tom. He dismissed my worries and made it clear that we would bring the war to the streets of Chicago, the risks be damned, and there would be no change in our messaging.

I did not want to sabotage the effort. Still, I had pictures in my mind of peaceful demonstrators being set upon by police. I felt as if I would be deceiving people. I quietly disengaged from the planning group and stopped attending the meetings; decided not to go to Chicago. I would not recruit anyone to go. But I would not argue with anyone who wanted to go.

As winter lined the streets with dirty snow and 1967 drew to a close, it was undeniable that our antiwar movement had successfully grown larger and bolder. We could feel that we were slowly, steadily shaping opinion on America's campuses. We knew that the elites were worried about our influence. Still the war ground on, each day bringing more death. Each day we felt the pressure to do more. Increasingly antiwar leaders searched for strategies of resistance, whatever that actually meant, not mere protest. The interracial unity of the early civil rights days was frayed if not totally gone. Anger was growing. Anger throughout Black America. Anger among the young as well, a separate anger but no less real. Underneath our youthful exuberance, there was also a growing undercurrent of dread that we refused to put into words, perhaps something, some rough beast its hour come round at last, was slouching toward Bethlehem. We felt an unarticulated foreboding, but we did not yet realize the blood-dimmed tide that would be 1968.

1968

1968, one year which seems the length of ten. 1968, year of hope, year of blood, year of upheaval, year of historic inflection, year of firestorms, year of surprises, year of lost opportunities.

1968, a year in which history hinged, a year that rocked the foundations of societies around the world, from Paris to Prague, from Berlin to Mexico to Washington. We live it; we experience it. We think we are driving historic change when we are bobbing like small corks on the surface, driven furiously by the maelstrom.

The new year commenced with indictments. Dr. Benjamin Spock, the person so many of our mothers turned to for guidance; the reverend William Sloan Coffin, chaplain at Yale; Mitch Goodman, a writer; Marcus Raskin, one-time disarmament expert in the John F. Kennedy administration; and Michael Ferber, a friend from Boston draft resistance work, the "Boston Five," were indicted by a grand jury in Boston for urging young men to resist the draft, as many of us were doing every day.[1] Prison seemed increasingly possible for many of us.

On the twenty-first day of the new year, the nightly news started with coverage of the fighting at the encircled American air base at Khe Sanh. Lyndon B. Johnson, haunted by the catastrophic French defeat at Dien Bien Phu, told his generals, "I don't want any damn Dinbinfoo [*sic*]."[2]

On the thirtieth, Amy and I celebrated my twenty-first birthday.

At half past midnight on the last day of January, in Vietnam the Tet Offensive was launched; by 2:45 a.m. the US embassy in Saigon had been invaded and held for seven hours. There was fierce fighting, devastating fighting, door to door, in city after city. We all watched on television as the Vietcong, whom our military leaders had said were close to defeat, fought vicious battles. It went on and on, savage, bloody, remarkable, for days and then weeks. Cities devastated. Blood flowed in the streets, flowing into American living rooms on the nightly news.

Writing of the battle for Ben Tre, Peter Arnett of the Associated Press quoted an American officer's iconic lines that summed up so very much of the war: "It became necessary to destroy the town to save it."[3]

Less attention was paid to Czechoslovakia, where reformer Alexander Dubček was elected as the first secretary of the Communist Party.

Day after day, the entire globe increasingly seemed caught up in a struggle between the old and the young, between a tired, bloody present and a vastly different future. In Prague, the reformists challenged Soviet domination and orthodoxy. In New Hampshire, the antiwar senator Eugene McCarthy and a legion of young doorknockers challenged Johnson and suddenly, Vietnam was the most important issue in the Democratic primaries. On the right, Alabama's governor George Wallace, he of "Segregation now. Segregation tomorrow. And segregation forever," campaigned as an independent drawing large and very angry and very white crowds. The people turning out to cheer him were experiencing profound change and did not like it.

The first signs of spring arrived in Cambridge. The bulbs pushed up through the soil. We, too, experienced small shoots of hope, slender and tentative. Still, we could not shake the iron smell of blood. We kept replaying in our minds the Tet Offensive and the gruesome battle for Hue City that had gone on and on, the casualties horrific on all sides.

Undeniably though, spring was coming. LBJ's challenger, McCarthy, surged, along with antiwar sentiment, and almost won the New Hampshire primary. Robert F. Kennedy finally took the plunge and announced he would run for president. He campaigned against the war and for a vision of economic justice that appealed to both Black and white, working and poor families. Still, he and McCarthy were not radical enough for us.

Shockingly, President Johnson announced: "I do not believe that I should devote an hour or a day of my time to any personal partisan causes or to any duties other than the awesome duties of this office—the presidency of your country . . . Accordingly, I shall not seek, and I will not accept, the nomination of my party for another term as your president."[4]

We could hardly believe it. Johnson announced a unilateral reduction in the bombing of North Vietnam and called for peace negotiations. Perhaps the war would actually end. Hope flared, brief, a match struck in the dark.

Ramparts wanted me to write a book on the vast network of CIA funding. I assembled a small research team, including Jon Weiner in Cambridge and Danny Schechter, in London. When they proposed sending me to Europe to conduct research, I jumped at the chance, especially since it would allow me to connect with student leaders over there—and because Amy and I still needed the money.

I was done with Harvard. Even though my formal graduation ceremony would be with the rest of the class at the end of spring, I had completed all my course requirements.

My first time traveling to Europe was a whirlwind twenty-one days over March and early April. I did *Ramparts* research in the day and in the evenings met with student groups to explore how better to coordinate our activities. In those three weeks I hit London, Geneva, Bonn, Frankfurt, both East and West Berlin, Copenhagen, Oslo, and Helsinki. From there a quick stop in Paris, then back to London, and home. I visited no museums; I did no sightseeing. I spent each of the twenty-one days with Danny Schechter. Danny was insecure, boisterous, a consummate schmoozer, a complete charmer. His pudgy round face lit up when he was with people. He was completely self-centered but in such a fast-talking, humorous, charming manner that one could not help but forgive and enjoy him. We dashed from city to city. Decades later we would discover that James Angleton, the chief of the CIA's counterintelligence efforts, was receiving daily reports on our travels.

In London at the very start of the trip, Danny and I joined an anti–Vietnam War march with 25,000 people swelling into the streets heading to the American embassy in Grosvenor Square. Danny maneuvered us close behind Venessa Redgrave, tall, elegant with a symbolic bandage around her head, and British antiwar leader Tariq Ali, who presented a petition to the embassy. We left and only read later of intense fighting between police and protestors.

In Berlin, I found myself in a small apartment, filled with books, talking with a shaggy-haired leader of the German Socialist Student Union (whose German initials were conveniently SDS), Rudi Dutchke. I found him thoughtful, cogent, compelling. The German SDS was the student wing of the SDP, the Social Democratic Party. While from a far richer and different history than our SDS, it was very much a New Left student organization. Late afternoon light filled the apartment, accenting how devoid of color it was, except for the colors of the covers of books everywhere. I felt an instant kinship, a connection with both Rudi and his American-born wife Gretchen Klotz. Gretchen frequently left the discussion to check on their young son. Rudi and I talked about longer term strategy. The challenge to move from a student movement to something more permanent and powerful. We agreed on the overarching need to stop the war in Vietnam. "The American war in Vietnam," Rudi always called it. We talked about the shah of Iran and how protests of his rule had been important to the German students. We shared our concern that the concentration of power in fewer and fewer hands would only increase unless checked.

Rudi's face creased with concern, "We are worried especially about the concentration of the media. Here the Springer empire dominates news and has a profound impact on consciousness and politics. They are a powerful force."

Then he shifted: "Michael, we are only students for a short time. Here in Germany probably longer than you in the States. Our challenge is to see beyond a student movement to something larger."

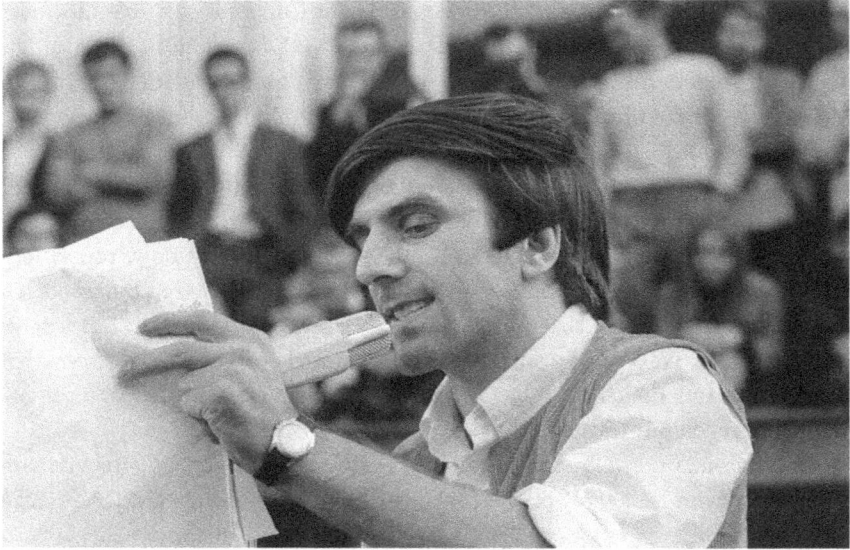

FIGURE 15. Rudi Dutschke, 1968. Photo by Dietmar Gottschall/Süddeutsche Zeitung Photo via Alamy.

He leaned back, looked at me, "We need a long march of our own. A long march through the institutions of society, yes?"

I nodded in agreement.

Rudi rocked forward, "We need to march through all the institutions, especially those that shape consciousness, schools, newspapers, television, but also all the institutions of everyday life." He went on to outline how our generation needed to transform the institutions that mattered or, if failing to do so, create new ones of our own.

Rudi then turned to more immediate challenges.

"We in SDS here take seriously the slogan: 'One, two, three Vietnams.' That means we in Germany must open another front against the war, lead a nonviolent campaign against the terrible power of America. If the Americans are to be stopped in Vietnam, it will be because of a global struggle against imperialism. We in Germany want to play our part."

"Yes," I responded, "but the real responsibility is ours, inside the US. We are in the center of it."

"You are," he says, "and we need you to be part of a global struggle."

I agreed and we talked briefly about promoting more communication between the German and American SDSs. I was excited to connect. I felt as if I could have talked with Rudi for a week and not be wasting time. But this trip did not allow for it. We exchanged addresses. Rudi and Gretchen loaded me down with literature, most of which was in German, which I could not read. But I took it. We promised to stay in touch. We hugged and I left.

The next day, I went by subway into East Berlin, under the border rather than through it. I was stopped, my bag searched by the East German police, who were shocked and irate that I carried German SDS literature. They acted as if the New Left was significantly more of a threat than NATO. They confiscated every pamphlet, every poster, every brochure. As an American I was sternly admonished and then set free to go on my way. It was clear that the old men who ruled the communist states and their many guards were part of the past we sought to overthrow.

Danny and I collected some useful research on CIA covert funding, but what I really took away from the trip was that I was part of a worldwide New Left of the young and that we were pitted against an elite of old men in a fight for our future, for decency, for democracy, and against barbarism. I felt confident as to the outcome. I was delighted to be part of the struggle.

On April 4, as I was concluding my dash through Europe, Martin Luther King, Jr., was shot dead on a Memphis motel balcony. He was there to aid the organizing of the garbage workers, to insist that economic rights were necessary for civil rights. The garbage workers were doing essential work but being paid wages they could not live on, treated miserably. They were on strike, and Dr. King, a fierce critic of poverty, of the war, of inequality, traveled to Memphis to support their struggle. Boulevards have been named after him. A holiday created in his honor. How many people remember why he went to Memphis?

From Frankfurt and Paris, I watched, angry, powerless as America's Black neighborhoods from Oakland to Boston erupted in sadness, in anger, in rage, and in frustration. The National Guard was called out. Washington burned. Detroit burned. Roxbury burned. Smoke and violence filled the air each spring day. I returned to a country on fire.

Back home, I was stunned again as exactly one week later, April 11, Rudi was shot in the head as he went to the drugstore for cold medicine for his child. It was unclear if he would live. (He lived for another decade before drowning in his bathtub from an epileptic fit brought on by the shooting.)[5] Around 2,000 students marched through Berlin to the offices of Springer Publishing. For months, the Springer media empire had mounted a savage, nonstop attack on SDS and especially on Rudi, its most charismatic leader. Springer papers repeatedly called on readers to act to "Stop the terror of the young reds now!" and "Eliminate the troublemakers." A reader had answered their call and shot "Red Rudi." The students marched. The police mobilized to defend the Springer buildings. The

FIGURE 16   April 4, 1968—after Rudi Dutschke was shot, "More than 20.000 policemen had trouble with student-demonstrators." Keystone Press / Alamy Stock Photo.

German student movement that had been surging, largely in opposition to the Vietnam War, now broke out into massive demonstrations. Tens of thousands took to the streets. All over Germany the young battled with the police. The country was rocked to its core.[6]

I was shocked. The Tet Offensive. Dr. King. Rudi. We were living in apocalyptic times. The unimaginable became each new day's headlines. The tide of blood was rising, rising.

Shortly after Rudi was shot, and student protests swept across West Germany, SDS and the Student Afro Society at Columbia University in New York mobilized over Columbia's ties to the Institute for Defense Analysis and the construction of a new gym opposed by the African American community surrounding Columbia. The leadership of Columbia SDS (declaring themselves the "Action Faction") was more militant than any other SDS group had been. They brought a new style and language to the organization that was rapidly taken up by newer SDS leaders across the country.

Hundreds of students occupied first one and then another and then another of the Columbia buildings. These were declared "free zones" producing a heady sense of rebellion and freedom.

Before dawn broke on April 30, the New York Police Department (NYPD) stormed the occupied buildings, liberally spread tear gas, and arrested over 700 students.[7] The following days there were more confrontations, and this time some of the students fought back. The protests continued into May with more police attacks and more arrests. The police savagely beat protestors. A massive student strike completely shut down Columbia for the rest of the academic year.

My high school friend Ron Carver had entered Columbia after several years organizing with SNCC in the South. In Mississippi he had been jailed, chased, and hunted, but, in the end, he escaped physically unharmed. He became the press person for the Columbia strike committee. During the second sweep of police, several Columbia deans recognized Ron and told him the police were looking for him in particular. The deans offered him safety in one of the unoccupied buildings. Only they were not offering him safety; they were intentionally sending him into a building where a squad of police waited to administer such a brutal beating with saps and blackjacks, that he was rushed to the hospital—a beating so savage, so thorough, that I literally could not recognize him when I visited him almost a week later. (He would eventually successfully sue the NYPD.)[8]

Anything, everything, seemed possible—from the worst of possibilities to wild soaring hope. Each week's news brought the improbable and unbelievable. Events were speeding up. History was all around us. First the massive demonstrations of the German students and then the battles of Columbia. On the heels of Columbia, the French students staged even larger demonstrations. In early May, authorities shut the University at Nanterre. The police occupied the Sorbonne. Twenty thousand students took to the streets of Paris. The police attacked; battles were joined all over the country. The result was a tidal wave of student strikes: college students went out on strike; soon high school students went out on strike; ever larger demonstrations were met by increasing police violence. Soon, unlike in Germany and in the United States, the movement spread beyond the schools and eleven million French workers went out on strike.[9] It made us think anything might be possible.

All Europe was ignited in protest and movement. Even in Eastern Europe, in Czechoslovakia, the Prague Spring led to the expulsion of the Soviet military forces and an experiment of "socialism with a human face." Hope was everywhere. So were tear gas, truncheons, and bullets.

In Mexico, in advance of the Olympic games, students there joined the worldwide explosion of protest. The student marches were met with government violence, which led to a country-wide student strike. Hope soared that decades of one-party rule might be effectively challenged. That hope was snuffed out in a bloody massacre that killed dozens of student protestors.[10]

FIGURE 17.   Students marching in Paris, May 1968. Photo by Fine Art Images/ Heritage Images via Alamy.

To us it seemed as if the whole world was caught up in struggle, protest, violence, and hope. I was riveted by each day's wild news, as were all my friends. Our moods would swing from hope to horror and back. Students around the world were reaching a new level of militancy and scale. The old men were determined to stop them, stop us, by any means, including naked violence. This was now more than protests. This was now more than a fight over one war. This was now a fight over everything. This was a fight for the future.

Somehow in the midst of the drama, the pain, the excitement, we failed to think carefully and strategically. Given how much was at stake, what could we actually win? How could we win it?

The tide of blood rolled on in Vietnam. Sustained battles. Tragedy piled on tragedy. I was convinced that we needed to keep the antiwar movement growing and militant. I was also convinced we needed to find a way to bridge the chasm between the movement and the people paying the highest price for the war. I started to focus on community colleges where returned Vietnam veterans were enrolling in large numbers. Many vets supported the war because otherwise their sacrifices, the deaths of their buddies, would have been in vain. But more and more of them in 1968 were already convinced that all that had been lost, all

FIGURE 18.   My Harvard commencement. Protesting, Amy is in the center.
Photo by Charles Dixon/The *Boston Globe* via Getty Images.

they had endured, was the result of terrible decisions made by feckless leaders.
Pain for them was turning to a bright, bitter anger.

That spring, I formally graduated from Harvard. I helped organize and signed a
letter that appeared in the *Crimson* with the names of 98 seniors, 112 juniors, 132
sophomores, and 100 freshmen. It stated simply:

> Our war in Vietnam is unjust and immoral. I believe that the United
> States should immediately withdraw from Vietnam and that no one
> should be drafted to fight in this war. As long as the United States is
> involved in this war I will not serve in the armed forces.[11]

The Harvard class of 1968 had invited Dr. King to be the class day speaker.
Now Coretta Scott King filled that role. More than half the class wore armbands
to show opposition to the war. Bizarrely, confirming precisely how tone deaf
the university was, Harvard's official choice for an honorary degree and commencement speaker was "His Imperial Majesty, Mohammed Reza Pahlavi, the
Shahanshah of Iran." The shah, installed by a CIA-backed coup, was a mod-
ernizing dictator whose secret police organization (SAVAK) was infamous for
throwing student protestors out of the upper-story windows of their towering

headquarters. Their record of torture and continuous violation of all basic standards of human rights was well known to anyone who cared to look. We and the Iranian Student Association protested. I was marching in a picket line during my own commencement. The *Crimson* reported, "Sargent Kennedy, secretary to the Corporation, said the Fellows were not upset by this demonstration. 'Any distinguished man,' Kennedy said, 'is bound to have some opposition.'"[12] I left Harvard convinced that its self-centered administration had no clue as to the maelstrom all around them. Thinking, mistakenly, that I was totally done with Harvard, I was glad to be gone.

The gulf between the old and the young was unbridgeable. Some of the elites were becoming fearful. They were losing their own children who came to oppose the war and some of whom condemned and denounced their parents as immoral. Even Robert McNamara's son Craig had turned the American flag on his bedroom wall upside down and stamped his letters with an upside-down flag.[13] The elites saw their private colleges riven and shut down. They saw the country seemingly spinning out of control and they feared what was coming. We did not fully sense their fears, missed the fissures opening in elite support for the war. Despite how large our protests had been, often we felt we were not making enough progress. We had made enormous strides. But we did not feel it. The war rolled on. We were desperate. We were hopeful. The future was the prize. We were determined to keep our eyes on the prize, keep on walking, keep on marching. Anything seemed possible.

That spring Amy and I heard that a trip was being organized for radicals to visit Cuba. Amy wanted to go. I had no interest in going myself, but it seemed a great opportunity for her. That summer she headed to Mexico City and then on to Cuba where the group traveled all over the island in a bus. She attended Fidel Castro's July 26 speech marking the anniversary of the revolution. Upon her return she told me about visiting a lot of artificial insemination facilities, finally earning the scorn of one of the guides when she hinted that they had seen enough cows, to which he replied, "Cows are the revolution." The group did agricultural work in the fields and met the only three women on the Central Committee. Soon there were regular groups of former SDS members and other activists going to Cuba to cut cane and fall in love with the Cuban Revolution.

That summer of 1968 continued wildly. There was no respite from savage news. Every week it seemed as if the world shook. What happened was beyond our wildest imaginings.

In June, Bobby Kennedy was shot dead on the night he won the California primary. While I was not a supporter of his, I had been impressed with his ability to connect with Black voters, suburban liberals, young people, and white working-class voters, the components that could be a Democratic majority. With his assassination that possibility was lost. Once again, the gun altered America's future. Moreover, his murder seemed one more example of the spreading violence that was engulfing us.

Also, in June four of the "Boston Five," including Dr. Spock, were found guilty and the next month sentenced to two years in federal prison. They would appeal and eventually win but that summer the message was clear: the government was coming for us.

In early August in Florida, Richard Nixon was nominated by the Republicans. On the night of August 20, 200,000 Soviet soldiers and 2,000 tanks invaded Czechoslovakia, crushing the Prague Spring and with it any chance of reform within the systems of Eastern European satellite countries.[14] I cursed the old men of Moscow and the old men of Miami Beach.

The very next week brought the Democratic Convention in Chicago. Antiwar protestors "bringing the war home" took to the streets of Chicago outside of the convention hall. The nation watched on television as the Chicago police force spun out of control, rioted, and beat anyone and everyone that they perceived as possibly the "other." It didn't matter—journalists, delegates, family of delegates, younger congressmen, they all were attacked by the rampaging cops, urged on, and unleashed by, the profane mayor, Boss Daley, kingmaker, Democrat. We were disgusted. The Democratic Party was torn apart. Hubert Humphrey became the nominee. I felt simultaneously vindicated in my judgment not to go or bring others to Chicago and guilty that I was not there.

Overall, I did not understand the profound change that was occurring. I knew we had more support than ever to end the war, but I did not grasp what it meant that a majority now opposed it. Perhaps that majority did not like us, but they had turned against the war. And I did not understand what it meant that the elites were deeply split. My friends and I never thought through what was entailed in shifting from a protesting minority to leading a movement with majoritarian aspirations. We certainly never entertained what we might do to swing the election to the woeful Democratic candidate Humphrey who, refusing to break with the war, emerged limping and dazed out of Chicago to mount a joyless campaign.

I had never seriously sat down to figure out exactly how we would end the war. There is a world of difference between *demands* and *strategy*. We knew our demands. We often debated tactics. But we rarely discussed exactly how the war could end. Would it be by electing a new president? No, the system was rotten and rigged. Would it be by cutting off funding for the war in Congress? That seemed simultaneously too mild and completely impossible. We would never get the votes. We elevated tactics to the level of strategy. We doubled down on what had worked for us when we were attempting to be a prophetic minority, when we were attempting desperately to carve out space for dissent. Now everything had shifted. But we did not grasp the meaning of that shift. We did not understand what was needed from us.

Working haphazardly on my CIA book for *Ramparts* paid our bills. The writing was not going all that well. My marriage was also not going that well. Amy was finishing up at Brandeis. While we often marched together, spent our nights together, much of the days we were apart. There were moments of shared joy, dismay, anger, and passion. However, for much of our days we remained separate, two young people thinking we were making a marriage, thinking we were shaping history, while being swept along by fierce currents, external and internal, that we could feel but did not understand.

In 1968, obviously, there was no internet. The cell phone did not yet exist. Fax machines had not been commercialized. Cable television was years in the future. There were three major commercial television networks and a new public broadcasting network, and there were daily newspapers. Most large metropolitan areas had two or more newspapers. In Boston we had the dominant *Boston Globe* with a morning and evening edition, and the *Herald Traveler*, as well as the *Boston Record American*.

In Boston we also had a new "free form" FM station, WBCN, that we increasingly claimed as our own. It was remarkable to have a station playing long sets of our music in a way no other radio station had before. Interspersed with the music, WBCN's disk jockeys, wild and exuberant, would promote our demonstrations. It was a powerful example of what media could do. I would regularly drop by the station to share our plans and found WBCN an important communication vehicle.

Increasingly we felt we also needed a way of communicating in print that was better and reached farther than our laboriously hand-cranked mimeo leaflets. I thought often of the conversation with Rudi about what to do if we could not seize the leadership of the institutions that shaped consciousness.

Contemplating a "long march through the institutions of America," we wanted to both transform existing institutions and create new, alternative ones of our own. We often repeated A. J. Liebling's saying: "Freedom of the press is guaranteed only to those who own one."[15]

In the early fall of 1968, I was spending more and more time on Brookline Street in Central Square, a rundown area that had once housed small manufacturing plants and wholesaling storefronts but now was in decline. While Harvard Square bustled with four bookstores, student hangouts, restaurants, and hip retailers, Central Square was a throwback to the old blue-collar Cambridge. If Harvard Square was all "gown," Central Square, only 1.2 miles away, was still an old-school "town."

Brookline Street was pockmarked with down-and-out, shabby, and often empty storefronts, and I was often in one, long vacant, that we had rented for next to nothing. It was the office for our new venture, our own newspaper. It sat directly across the street from the Brookline Lunch.

The Brookline Lunch looked unchanged since the year of my birth. Wooden booths down one side, and a long counter down the other, with round, anchored, padded bar stools. And always behind either the counter or the cash register was the owner, Mary. Big hearted, large breasted, her Irish face flushed with the heat of the griddle, framed by lank black hair streaked with gray, every day wearing what seemed like the same floral apron, Mary owned and ruled the Brookline Lunch. The place was, and had been for years, the breakfast and lunch stop for longtime neighborhood residents, cops, and fire fighters. Suddenly as the world swung wildly in that summer of 1968, it was now also the favorite hangout for our posse of radicals.

When we first showed up, there were some glares and quiet muttering. But Mary welcomed us and fed us home cooking at ridiculously low prices. We were her customers; that meant something. Mary had a small receipt pad for those awarded tabs. Once I realized I was among the favored, I ordered my meatloaf, gravy, and mashed potatoes even when I had no money in my pocket. Rarely did Mary let herself get drawn into a political conversation, even as she overheard us continuing our meetings from across the street. But on those few occasions when she did, she made it clear that while she did not agree with us on lots of things, she hated the war, and we were welcome.

On Brookline Street, we created a new underground newspaper, the *Old Mole*. We had no funds and even less experience. Somehow, we managed to publish forty-seven issues from the fall of 1968 to mid-1970. Sometimes once a month, sometimes more often as money and time allowed, we published a newspaper that covered movement activities, addressed critical issues of the time, and offered people a chance to be involved. Our journalism had no pretense of objectivity. It was raunchy, passionate, and always personal and political. We printed 10,000 copies, in a tabloid format, with a graphic image and bold, provocative, or witty headlines on the front page.

A free-flowing collective wrote the articles, laboriously laid out each issue on poorly constructed light tables, took it to a printer on the North Shore and organized a series of hawkers to sell it on street corners all over the city.

The Brookline Street storefront soon became more than the offices of the newspaper. It was the central spot for planning antiwar demonstrations, the place where new women's collectives met and got organized, where high school students showed up to ask for help fighting censorship in their schools and producing their own high school newspapers, the home of the Peace and Justice Coalition, and a place that nursing students used to form a "nurses against the war" group. It thrummed with activity eighteen hours a day every day of the week.

We were inspired by the counter cultural papers in California and New York. Whereas they focused more on music, sex, drugs, and culture, we wanted to create a newspaper that would be the paper of the movement. We wanted to be able to expose the lies, biases, and unnoticed ironies of the mainstream press. We wanted to cover what they would not cover. We wanted to write about events in a way that the mainstream reporters never dared to. We wanted a journalism of the committed.

Finding the right name was a challenge. After much debate and many suggestions, a graduate student, Jon Schwartz, suggested "the Old Mole" based on a quote from Karl Marx: "We recognize our old friend, our old mole, who knows so well how to work underground, suddenly to appear: the revolution."[16] We were so tired of searching for a name that we all agreed. It denoted underground, the revolution, and was enigmatic and unexpected—all good. The paper was rowdy, political, provocative, and funny.

The most popular page of the paper was called Zaps, very short ironic stories and quotes such as: "PEACE CORPS EXPELS 13 FOR ANTI-WAR ACTIVITY— A real live headline from the Washington Star." Another told the story of a court clerk in Kentucky who was supposed to intone at the start of each court session, "God save the Commonwealth and this honorable court." One day he scrambled his words, uttering what we thought was a hilarious truth: "God save the people from this honorable court."

Raffish, radical, unpredictable, crazy in a world gone mad. That was our spirit at the *Old Mole*.

Nixon, the Republican nominee, promised that he had a plan to end the war but would not announce it. He and Henry Kissinger secretly committed treason by interfering with the talks in Paris between America and the Vietnamese, making sure there was no breakthrough for peace. Nixon, even before entering the White House, subverted the law, prolonging the agony of the war.[17]

In the wake of the civil rights successes, Nixon adopted the first "Southern Strategy," which reshaped the Republican Party, and over time wiped out the once dominant Southern white Democrats, altering the direction of American politics for decades. His 1968 campaign started the Republican Party, the party of Abraham Lincoln, down its long march to become the party of white grievance and of Donald Trump. Seizing on the riots and continuous protests, Nixon ran "a law-and-order campaign." He proclaimed: "As we look at America, we see cities enveloped in smoke and flame. We hear sirens in the night . . . We see Americans hating each other; fighting each other; killing each other at home. And as we see and hear these things, millions of Americans cry out in anguish. Did we come all this way for this? Did American boys die in Normandy, and Korea, and in Valley Forge for this?"[18]

As America lurched toward election day, it became clear that this would be a remarkably close election. Humphrey had the entire Democratic establishment desperately working as hard as they could. They would not be enough in what turned out to be an election decided by less than one percentage point. Those of us in SDS saw Humphrey as profoundly corrupt, unredeemable, and tainted by his support for the war. We hated Nixon but we had no experience of what a right-wing government might do. We came of age, and to activism, in the years since 1960—so we only knew Kennedy and Johnson as presidents; we had experienced liberal domination of national politics and the policies we had protested were the policies of liberal Democrats.

In the fall of 1968, we experienced a great failure of political imagination.

We thought it would not matter if Nixon or Humphrey won. We thought the war would continue, exactly in the same deadly way, no matter who won. We could not imagine that the war would be expanded, that there would be a simultaneous policy of "Vietnamization," so that the American body count decreased, and escalation that would claim another million more Asian lives. We could not imagine the disaster that would befall Cambodia because of Nixon and Kissinger. We did not imagine the Christmas bombings of Hanoi and Haiphong. We did not see what was coming—at home, as well as internationally. We did not understand that soon Nixon would invite to the White House and celebrate the leaders of building trades unions who led violent attacks on antiwar protestors in New York. We thought the well of Black sadness could not get any deeper. We were wrong. We could not imagine what would be unleashed against Black leaders and the Black community.

We had no idea of the damage that would be done.

We could not conceive of the manipulative use of a "war on drugs" to go after Black communities and the antiwar movement. As cynical and as sophisticated as we thought ourselves to be, we could not conceive of policies that, years later, Nixon's top aide, John Ehrlichman would bluntly describe to Dan Baum of *Harper's Magazine*.

> The Nixon campaign in 1968, and the Nixon White House after that, had two enemies: the antiwar left and Black people . . . You understand what I'm saying? We knew we couldn't make it illegal to be either against

the war or black, but by getting the public to associate the hippies with marijuana and blacks with heroin, and then criminalizing both heavily, we could disrupt those communities. . . . We could arrest their leaders, raid their homes, break up their meetings, and vilify them night after night on the evening news. Did we know we were lying about the drugs? Of course, we did.[19]

Despite our growing dread, we did not imagine that protesting students would be gunned down at Kent State and Jackson State. That J. Edgar Hoover's FBI would get the green light to go after Nixon's "enemies" and unleash the full force of the FBI on Black organizations and the antiwar movement.

We, in SDS and the antiwar movement, had legions of young people with us. While the voting age was twenty-one and thus many of us could not have voted, there were enough of us over twenty-one that we could have played a pivotal role in the election. Most of us who built the antiwar movement, demonstration by demonstration, dorm meeting after dorm meeting, were so sickened by the corruption of American politics that we refused to participate. Real change, we thought, could only come from "outside" the system. The rules of the election game were rigged to favor the corporate elites. We were so habituated to being a prophetic minority that with a majority of the country turning against the war, we remained locked into the mindset of a minority. What strategy we possessed was simplistic and ill thought through: our job was to create so much disruption that the elites would somehow be forced to end the war. We completely failed to grasp that the war and our movement had already shattered the unity of the nation and that now our task was to reassemble a new majority. Instead, we were determined to keep shattering a status quo that was already splintered.

We boycotted the election. We organized street protests. Our slogan was "Vote with your feet, vote in the street." On election day we marched. We mocked. We did not organize young people twenty-one and older to vote in one of the closest elections in American history. We, in our anger and righteousness, said, "a plague on both your houses" and walked away. We said " the lessor of two evils is still evil. Don't vote." I had turned twenty-one in January. The following November, I did not bother to cast a vote.

Nixon won. There is no guarantee that we could have pressured Humphrey to end the war, but undoubtedly, we stood a much better chance of doing so with him in the White House than with Nixon. Humphrey certainly didn't help, as he refused to break from the war. We found it impossible to hold in our minds two possibly competing imperatives: stopping the war and stopping Nixon. And as always, the people of Indochina and Black people in America paid the price.

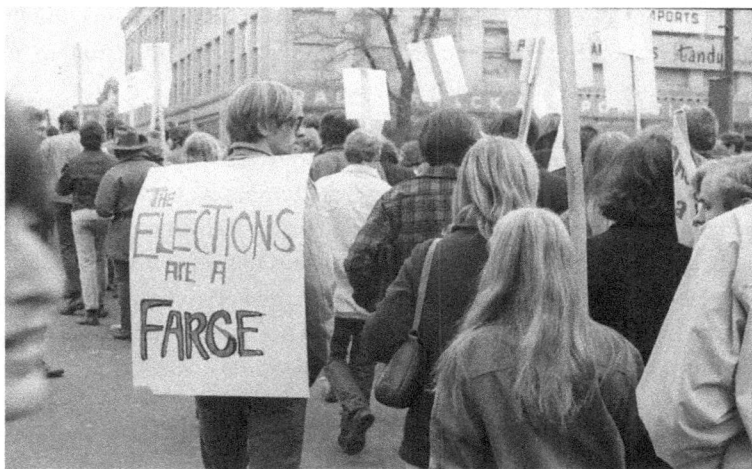

FIGURE 19.   In 1968 we organized thousands to protest on election day. Photo by Jeff Albertson, courtesy of the W. E. B. Du Bois Library, UMass Amherst.

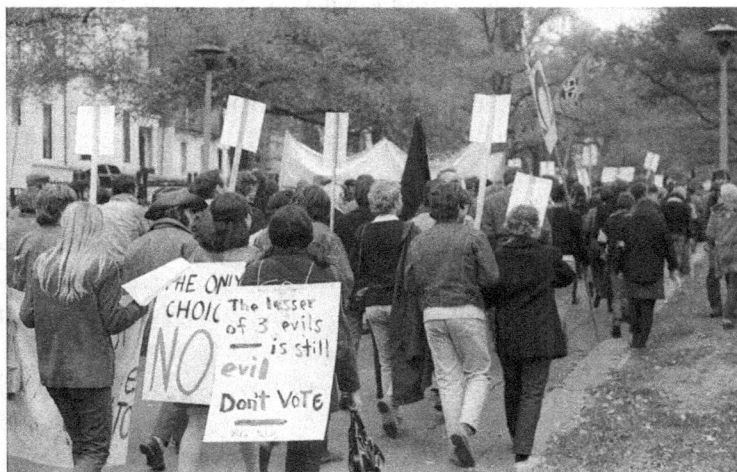

FIGURE 20.   Our signs said "Don't Vote." Photo by Jeff Albertson, courtesy of the W. E. B. Du Bois Library, UMass Amherst.

We started to dream of revolution at the very moment when we might have led a significant portion of the country. The young around the world were shaking the order of the old. SDS led hundreds of thousands of students. Our meetings that only a few years before had drawn a handful, now angrily fill the largest halls on hundreds of campuses. Given what had happened already in 1968, anything did seem possible.

Holding fast to our fantasies and nightmares, we could not imagine that in another twelve months SDS would be no more, blown apart by factions as foolish and dangerous as any of the old left we once despised.

Nineteen sixty-eight was the year of blood. The year of hope. A year in which history hinged. A year in which we thought we were winning and were in fact failing. We were not wrong in our assessments of Humphrey; we were wrong in our assessment of whether it matters if a corporate centrist liberal is elected over an insecure, unstable right-wing candidate who does not respect the Constitution. We failed to understand Nixon and what was at stake. We allowed him to start a right-wing counterreformation that would hold power and warp American politics for much of the next four decades. We allowed our embrace of militancy to replace strategy.

We would continue to march. Hundreds of thousands of us continued to protest the war. We shut down campuses. We organized sit-ins. We organized returning veterans to join the fight against the war. Millions would still participate in 1969 and 1970. The moratorium in the next year would be a massive outpouring of opposition to the war reaching into cities and towns across the huge expanse that is America. The antiwar movement would put a brake on some of Nixon's worst schemes for the war. Many long-term, enduring changes in the country have their roots, at least partially, in our efforts. None of that alters the fact that in 1968 we made serious mistakes and failed to meet the moment.

The record player blares Motown. Most of us are dancing. The day has been spent turning out young people to protest the war and the election. The night is for letting it all out. Dancers pack the room, most in pairs but some alone and seemingly oblivious. Inside a circle of men and women pressed as tight as possible, a small group of women dances with other women, shyly at first and then the exuberance of the room ripples through them as well. Women, and for some reason it is only the women, sing the words of the songs as loud as they can; they shake their heads, they shimmy. They are young, they are strong, they are exuberant. The men in the room feel their presence acutely, the gravitational pull strong for all the men, all that is except for the small, scattered group somehow not at ease, even among their friends, seemingly impervious to the waves of sexual desire radiating around the room. Or are they covertly responding to a very different set of desires?

Another small group is smoking dope on the back porch, discreetly, as it is illegal. Over in the front hall, by a keg of beer, a very few serious ones are didactically debating what they think is political strategy; they too, but for different reasons, are impervious to the raw animalism of the room. They live in their heads. Out on the dance floor a pudgy young man with a wispy beard and sweat-stained curls breaks out into some surprising moves, with a special grace of movement for one whose middle is so significant. Behind him two women start to dance within the circle of other women. The men draw near and one suddenly ducks in to dance with both women, head back, eyes wide, energy pumping up, palpable, and felt.

We are proud, we are young, and we are so certain. We will never be so certain again. We are swimming in the river of history, and we know it. For these few hours we are shrugging off the weight of the war. We are diving into the exuberance of our age. Just for these few hours we don't think about napalm, the war, the dead, King, Kennedy, the election. We are feeling so alive. We have no idea of the future and for these few hours we really don't give a good god damn. For this evening, we just want to be young. Slowly there is some filtering and pairs form and begin to hope for connection. Over in a shadow one couple cannot resist kissing. For everyone, the pull is there, yearning comes in waves and in its own way is delicious. The beat picks up. A line forms, and soon most people are dancing one behind the other.

And now suddenly the years open up. I am looking back. I am there in the dance line. I can see myself, dark haired, awkward; Amy, slender, is swaying in front of me. I feel a sudden wave of immense sadness not just for the loss of youth and all that inevitably brings, but for the loss of so many people I once loved and for the hopes we had. I see Sara singing, head tilted back, curls shaking, and no idea that within five years she will be dead of breast cancer. Right behind her is Hal who will end up twenty-five years later throwing himself out of a forty-story window. Pat is dancing with no concept that in the very next year he will be killed in a tractor accident doing community service in Africa. There, in the dark corner, I imagine one of the gentlest intellectuals I knew. He is shy and sweet. He will end up in the Weather Underground, will participate in a robbery that goes terribly bad, people will die, and he will spend decades, the rest of his life, most of his life, in prison.

Students will die in Mexico. Tanks roll across Prague. Students will die at Kent State and Jackson State. More Black leaders will be shot dead. The tectonic plates of our politics will shift but not as we are imagining. Then the old men seemed destined to fail and fall. They will eventually die but be replaced often by those conservative students we despised and thought irrelevant, those right-wing students who were such an embittered minority, the awkward and mean-spirited, close-cropped students who hated our protests, hated our politics, hated our rebellious spirit, hated our excesses and our values—those students will grow up to rule America causing endless pain and damage. They will become the old men of today.

We didn't think enough about the 65 percent of our peers who were not in college. Many of them will leave the inchoate rebellion of youth to embrace a raw conservatism as they age.

The long ripples of our movements will change how America understands itself. Those ripples will crest again in waves of feminism, environmentalism, and gay rights. The young old men of the right will battle against them, perplexed that even as they seem to have won politically, the country continues to change.

Some of us will stay in the fight for a lifetime. Others drop away. That is all in the future. This night we are dancing; this night we think we are winning; this night we think anything is possible. We dance into the night.

SHUTTING DOWN HARVARD

One April day in 1969, the phone rang in our small house in an alleyway near Harvard Square. Mark Dyen, one of the SDS leaders two years behind me at Harvard was breathless, his voice agitated.

"Michael, we need you. Can you possibly come to the meeting tonight?"

I had stayed away from Harvard, focusing my work on state and community colleges, and while I felt a strong attachment to Mark and the other younger SDS leaders there, I was not enthusiastic.

"What meeting?" I asked somewhat distractedly.

"We are getting somewhere on getting rid of ROTC, but I'm worried that the PL people will ruin everything. You know how they are. Always attacking anyone in SDS who isn't part of their faction. And tone deaf. They are trying to force a seizure of a building. We're for that but only when we have broad support for it. We are gaining support for doing away with ROTC but if we aren't careful, PL will blow it. We need you. People still look to you here. Not the PL people of course. But can you come tonight?"

"I would rather not. I haven't been doing anything at Harvard for months. "

"Come on. We need you. Don't leave us in the lurch. We are going to have a huge crowd at the meeting tonight, maybe eight hundred or a thousand. Come and if we need you, be prepared to speak. If we don't need you, you don't have to say anything."

Since I lived a five-minute walk from the meeting and did not have anything pressing to do that evening, I reluctantly agreed. I would show up, sit in the back, and be there if they needed me.

The number of supporters for SDS at Harvard had grown to well over a thousand students, and a much larger number opposed the war.

In the last couple of years, the Progressive Labor Party (PL) had gained increasing support within SDS. The Progressive Labor Party was formed after several of its leaders were expelled from the Communist Party. Early on, its opposition to the war attracted a number of younger activists. When its own youth organization was rapidly outpaced by the growth of SDS, PL started organizing within SDS. There it argued for a "Worker Student Alliance." The very success of SDS brought Marxist grouplets like PL rushing to it. Because of our rejection of reflexive anticommunism, SDS was peculiarly ill equipped to deal with these parasitic organizations.

Like all Leninist organizations, PL was disciplined, well-organized, and constantly organizing in opposition to "misleaders," those who disagreed with them. Most of the Harvard students who joined PL and its "Worker Student Alliance" were very decent young people who in their anguish and anger embraced a strident and reductionist politics. I had known and liked many of them, although now they detested me. Desperate to make sense of endlessly head-spinning news, they were attracted to the simplistic politics of this bizarre, self-proclaimed Maoist organization. The organization made its biggest inroads into SDS in the most elite schools. By April of 1969 PL and its Worker Student Alliance had won a majority on the Harvard-Radcliffe SDS executive committee even though they represented a minority of the total SDS membership on campus.

Those not sympathetic with PL had loosely organized under the banner of the New Left Caucus. The New Left leaders were the most active, most committed SDS members who did not share PL's fantasies. They were focused on ending the war, supporting Mothers for Adequate Welfare, and challenging the university to be an authentic center for critical thought and debate. The PL people were focused on attacking anyone who was not loyal to their group. The New Left activists were simply not emotionally equipped to wage a fierce sectarian battle. They were too honest, too sincere, too open, too willing to struggle with complexity. They played fair. They knew that they represented the larger group of students who cared about ending the war. But they were not adept at packing meetings, exercising iron discipline, or keeping their supporters in their seats no matter how late into the night the meeting went.

On that evening of April 8, the large public SDS meeting was to decide the next steps in the ongoing SDS campaign to get the Reserve Officer Training Corps (ROTC) program shut down at Harvard.

The hundreds of students packed into the large hall ratified the proposed demands: the university should abolish the ROTC program, provide alternative scholarships for the kids in it, freeze or lower rents in Harvard-owned off-campus buildings, and make a pledge not to demolish residential buildings in the Harvard Medical area. The demands mirrored the demands at Columbia the year before.

SDS had been campaigning against any form of university support for the war effort in Vietnam. The ROTC program was an obvious target. Our position was gaining strength. The previous December, one hundred SDS students, angered by not being allowed to sit in on faculty meetings on the status of ROTC, held a sit-in at Paine Hall. Fifty-seven were eventually placed on probation.[1] As the *Harvard Crimson* editorialized: "ROTC is based on the notion that the country's universities should serve the needs of the warfare state" and the "over-expansion of the American military machine has become perhaps the greatest threat of all."[2]

At this meeting, the PL faction pushed hard to get a vote to seize a building right away. The New Left people attempted to get authorization for the executive committee to be able to seize a building in the future, much like a union's vote to authorize a strike if negotiations break down. Michael Kazin, the New Left SDS leader chairing the meeting, took multiple votes, trying to get to a majority vote for authorization. Finally, he got what they wanted. No building seizure immediately but authorization for it if the university failed to negotiate.

The meeting ended; 300 students marched to Harvard's president Nathan Pusey's residence to tack their demands on his door. I went home, happily thinking everything was on an even course, and that I was not needed.

I was quite surprised when I received another call the next morning asking me to rush back to Harvard.

Early that morning, hearing that the PL faction of SDS was massing at University Hall, New Left leaders rushed there to find Jared Israel, the PL leader, haranguing a small but growing crowd on a bullhorn. He argued for the necessity of seizing the building now. The New Left students started a chant—"Vote, vote, vote." This demand for another vote infuriated Jared, who had no interest, as he readily proclaimed, in "bourgeoise democratic norms." The chant grew in volume until Jared seemingly relented and called for a vote. As it had the night before, the majority rejected the immediate seizure. Jared snarled through his bullhorn, "Great, now you have had your bullshit vote and now we are seizing this building." A small squad of students supporting Jared—perhaps with visions of the 1917 Bolshevik storming of the Winter Palace—marched into University Hall determined to occupy it.

University Hall sits in the middle of Harvard Yard, its gray stone surrounded by trees, grass, and the older brick buildings of the freshman dorms. It contains a large room with rugs on the floor, sculpted busts of famous professors and great intellectuals scattered around, and walls adorned with gilt framed paintings. A room of quiet and opulence, history, and classical echoes, a room that could have been in the Enlightenment, or held the great antebellum debates of the 1840s and 1850s. A room removed from the present, distant from the grubby realities of the everyday life of most Americans, now or ever. A room of the cloistered elite.

University Hall also housed the college deans, the middle management of Harvard, loyal and narrowly focused. Some were born to be at Harvard. Some had made themselves into Harvard men and Harvard had made them. As the students marched into University Hall, they confronted deans totally unprepared, despite having repeatedly discussed this possibility. Since the Columbia uprising, they had undertaken studies and debated the proper responses. One could reasonably have expected them to be ready. But they were not and could not be. Their world view simply did not allow for this. As the students rushed in and manhandled the deans out of the building, two parallel universes collided.

The dean Robert Watson was a product of St. Mark's and Harvard ('37). In World War II, as executive officer on a destroyer, he survived five hours in the cold waters of the North Atlantic. He told his children that his St. Mark's letterman sweater had saved his life. Watson returned to Harvard in 1946, spending the next decades as the associate dean and then dean of students.[3] In 1963 when there was a debate over parietal rules, Watson proclaimed, "It is not appropriate for a Harvard student to entertain a girl in his own room. It's our positive duty to deal with fornication just as we do with thievery, lying and cheating, by taking severe disciplinary measures against the offenders."[4]

The dean Skiddy von Stade was also in every way a perfect Harvard gentleman. While a student there (also class of 1937), he played on two championship polo teams.[5] As reported by the *Harvard Crimson*, he had this to say about women and Harvard:

> When I see the bright, well-educated, but relatively dull housewives who attended the Seven Sisters, I honestly shudder at the thought of changing the balance of males versus females at Harvard. Quite simply, I do not see highly educated women making startling strides in contributing to our society in the foreseeable future. They are not, in my opinion, going to stop getting married and/or having children. They will fail in their present role as women if they do.[6]

As the PL squad rushed to evict the deans, Archie Epps, the first African American dean of students and my boss from the 1963 March on Washington, was the most physically resistant. The students hustled the deans out, pushing them, shoving them, physically forcing them from the building, the stupidest thing they could have done. Compared to what was happening in Vietnam that day, this behavior should never have registered on any accurate scale as violent. However, the "violence" of the morning burned the events of the entire strike into the minds of the deans and most of the faculty as the days when the "mob" attacked Harvard. Forty years later, Harvard faculty members still referred to the events of that April as the "Harvard riots of 1969."

My friends were fuming at PL for ignoring both votes against seizing the building. Once the building was taken, however, they were in a bind. If they left them alone, the PL faction would become isolated, behaving in ways that would most probably bail the administration out of having to deal with the demands around ROTC just as SDS was winning a majority of the students and a sizeable portion of the faculty to their position. So, they made the bitter decision to occupy University Hall and urge other students to join them. They fanned out and, using the relationships built over the last years of steady antiwar organizing, soon had several hundred students occupying University Hall. Then they called me.

When I arrived, solemn-faced students "guarded" the entrances. A few of the doors had been chained, but the rest remained open as dozens of students flowed in and out, checking out what was going on. Outside hundreds of students milled around the Yard. Some chanted slogans against SDS. Some offered support. Many were simply curious to see what would happen.

In University Hall itself, there was chaos, as the PL kids focused on guarding the entrances and failed to organize anything inside.

Many of the students sitting in disliked the PL leadership, but they hated the war more and wanted to see the university step decisively away from anything that either symbolically or materially supported it. Without thought or discussion, I easily slid into a familiar leadership role. Quickly I worked with the younger SDS leaders to organize inside and outside of University Hall.

We assumed that there would be an inevitable call to the Cambridge police to clear the building. Some SDS members, especially those already on probation from earlier actions, were detailed to avoid arrest and, after the expected mass arrest, to help organize a university wide meeting.

In the large room the light filters in through the big windows. Two hundred students are debating tactics, strategy, and issues germane and issues that come out of some haze. There is a sense of impending catastrophe as well as a sense of desperate purpose. There is no euphoria, at least not yet. A small group has forced this on us. I do not want to be there. But I have friends to support. Harvard being Harvard, whatever happens will be big news and could help the antiwar cause—or hurt it.

Members of the *Old Mole* team arrive. We secure select offices, claiming that we do not want there to be any vandalism that could discredit us and distract from the demands. In the sealed-off offices, a team of close friends goes to work conducting a thorough search of the files of the administration. All the file cabinets are locked. One graduate student brings an electric drill so we can drill out

FIGURE 21.   Inside occupied University Hall. Michael Kazin is in the middle. Photo by Timothy Carlson.

the locks, but we discover that a simple, bare metal book end, turned sideways, held with one hand and whacked hard with the other, quickly pops the locks. Soon we are working to a muffled beat, *whack pop*, *whack pop*, as we systematically go through the private university files taking any file folder that was marked CIA, Department of Defense, ROTC, and the like. These files are surreptitiously wrapped in jackets, some handed to Danny Schechter, my former traveling companion, who walks out with them; others are passed out a back window to runners to take them off campus.

I am surprised at how easy it is to gather definitive documentation that the Harvard administration has been lying. They have been saying the university is not doing work for the war effort or for the CIA. They have been lying to the faculty and working to undermine any faculty decision against ROTC. It's all there spelled out in their files, letters, and contracts. It never occurred to the administration that we would pop the locks on their filing cabinets and steal their documents. We carefully replaced file folders without the critical documents that we had stolen and pushed in the locks so that whenever the administration regained control of the building, it would not be immediately obvious what we had done. We know we are committing a crime. We feel strongly that our greater purpose more than justifies it. The fact that the administration lied so frequently makes us feel even more confident that it is our duty to expose the truth.

We work in haste as we expect the Harvard administration to retake its building at any moment. But hours go by. The dean Franklin Ford orders everyone to leave. No one does. The day slowly passes. Inside I think my mission is to make sure that this move by the PL people does not result in disaster. We have everyone discuss whether they are willing to get arrested. At the first sign of the police, those who do not want to get arrested, and do not want to risk getting kicked out of Harvard, are to leave. We stress the need for nonviolence.

All day interested students come and go. Endless debates about the nature of the war, the nature of the university, and the strategy for the movement swirl inside. Outside there are endless arguments between supporters and opponents. The whole campus tenses. Everyone knows something will happen, but no one knows what or when.

If the university simply had let us stew in place, it would have been a disaster for SDS. A majority of Harvard University students, undergraduates and graduates, teaching fellows, and even many professors had come to oppose the war. In that sense the majority are sympathetic to the demands of the demonstrators. Still as night settles on Cambridge, the great majority are against this actual occupation. The "manhandling" of the deans is thoroughly opposed—indeed even by a majority of those of us occupying University Hall. If President Pusey had simply sat back, issued a statement condemning our tactics, and argued there were better ways to press the demands, support would most likely have petered out, students would slowly have left to attend classes, take their tests, visit their loved ones, and eat dinner. Over several days with a diehard group endlessly debating each other and getting smaller by the hour, the occupation would have come to an end.

However, the Harvard task force that studied the Columbia revolt concluded that the mistake made by the administration there was waiting too long. Instead of waiting us out, Pusey and the Harvard Corporation reverted to the only alternative response, violence. I am sure they did not see unleashing police as initiating violence; instead, they saw it as restoring the rightful order of things. They certainly should have foreseen the inevitable consequences of their decision. We did.

We expect violence. We expect that the violence that we believe lay just under the surface, the violence that rages every day in faraway Asia and in the nearby ghettos, the ever-present violence of America, will finally be made manifest, even on this most serene, cloistered, pampered, elite campus. Violence we think was the only way the old men who run Harvard and the world can maintain their crumbling order.

Many of the police summoned to Harvard Yard early in the predawn hours of that April morning simmered with rage—rage at Harvard, rage at its elite, rage at the privileged students. It enraged many of them that protesting students were "throwing away" a chance, a privilege, that so many cops would have died to give their own kids. Some of them have fought in Vietnam and their sacrifices require that the war be necessary. All of them have friends from their blue-collar neighborhoods who were killed or maimed in the war. Many of them have grand-parents who had seen the signs "no Irish need apply." Everything about Harvard reeks to them of affluence, elitism, and privilege—and they are not wrong. Now the elite masters of the universe cannot even take care of their own fucking cam-pus! Many of those police marching into Harvard Yard that morning, march in with generations of well-earned resentments merging with new angers at us, the privileged antiwar students. The job they are assigned that day gives them a once in a lifetime opportunity to let loose for one paroxysm of officially sanctioned violence.

At 3:00 a.m., the police march into Harvard Yard to confront 500 sleepy, scared students, standing in bunched rows in every entrance to University Hall, arms locked, fearful but determined to resist nonviolently. The police do what they have been trained to do, but with a vehemence and a rage that should not really have surprised anyone.

As I link arms with students on either side of me, I cannot really see what is happening. The hall is crowded. We pack ourselves as tightly as we can; we know the onslaught is about to hit us. State police, black boots polished to the proper sheen, visors obscuring their faces, break through the line of students in front of me. They are furious. They swing their nightsticks, and you can hear the *thunk* as they land on skulls and shoulders. They want to break the lines of students, and they want to break some heads. As they hit us one after another, we reflexively reach up to bloody hair and as we do, police grab us, yank us forward, and the line breaks. The police haul students, toss them and drag them down the stairs onto the moist spring ground.

My turn comes. I hear the crack of the club on my head, and then it is hard to see because the blood pours down into my eyes. My head does not hurt as much as I was expecting as I am hurled down the stairs and given an angry choice: I can walk to the police wagon or I can be hauled and beaten to the police wagon. I walk. It is all happening too fast to have any coherent thoughts. Everywhere kids are bleeding. A dozen of us are jammed into each police wagon—normally called the "paddy wagon" in derision of the Irish that used to be the ones being hauled away. We are taken to the police station in Central Square and packed into crowded cells, our adrenaline-fueled energy bleeding away, leaving us dazed, exhausted.

After clearing the building, the police indiscriminately lay into any student they encounter. Sleepy but excited freshmen pour from their dorms into the Yard to see what is happening. The police club and punch any of them they can catch. Students from nearby Harvard houses, hearing the noise, rush to the Yard to

FIGURE 22.   Police beating a student in Harvard Yard, early morning, April 10, 1969. Bettman via Getty Images.

witness an early morning scene of chaos and blue-coated violence totally outside their realm of experience. Policemen do not beat people, especially young, white people. Yet here are hundreds of police doing exactly that with lights strobing the early morning gray light, screams and cries and blood and shock everywhere. Even the students who had been screaming at SDS as unpatriotic only hours before suddenly find themselves subject to a police attack.

No one seeing the sight of the police rampaging across Harvard Yard can believe it, nor believe this is the right way to handle the protests. Shock soon gives way to anger. Those watching, those caught up in it, and then those hearing about it are outraged. All the anxiety about the war, about their future, about their lives, is crystallized into anger. There is no question that now the Harvard community is ready to rise up against Pusey and against the war brought so visibly home to Harvard Yard. The leaders of Harvard will wring their hands over the manhandling of the deans. Harvard students are pushed over the edge by the violence they experience firsthand, a police ferocity sanctioned by Harvard. All the organizing of the past five years, the demonstrations, the dorm meetings, the flyers, the teach-ins, the sit-ins, the marches, the discussions, all suddenly make sense. Thousands of Harvard students, both undergraduate and graduate, are furious, fed up with the war and appalled at the leadership of their university.

As the police withdrew, having restored control of University Hall, and early dawn begins to break, dozens of stunned students gravitate to the long, wide steps of Widener Library. There the PL leadership has one more chance to kill the brewing revolt and almost succeeds. One PL person has brought a bullhorn. He rants about the police violence and the need to fight back and then declares that the assembled students should join him and burn down the colonial house inhabited by President Pusey. "Burn it to the ground now!" he declares. His demand for more violence in the aftermath of what has happened produces an uneasy silence. The crowd of students is ready to walk away.

Kazin, steps forward. His thick, dark hair is matted with blood. Blood drips down his face. He grabs the bull horn and starts to talk about what everyone has just seen. No matter what, he says, we all now have to stick together. All of us must work together to answer the violence of the administration. All of us must stick together to say no to the war, no to ROTC, no to police violence. He outlines the beginning of a plan to arouse all of Harvard and regroup in a mass meeting of everyone, not just SDS, in Memorial Church. The crowd comes back. They feel their anger transform into determination. The Harvard Strike of 1969 commences.

Meanwhile those of us arrested are sitting in cells. Included in our ranks are at least two reporters. Chris Wallace, then an undergraduate, has been reporting for the Harvard radio station from inside University Hall, as has my friend Parker Donham, who works for the *Boston Globe*. When Parker is spotted by the mayor of Cambridge, Al Vellucci, he asks the notoriously anti-Harvard mayor to get him released so he can file his story. Vellucci orders his release. The rest of us sit sleepily in our cells for several more hours.

Finally, we are booked, arraigned on trespassing charges, and released. We make our way back to Harvard to catch the tail end of the mass meeting in Memorial Church. At that meeting the call goes out for a university wide strike. A committee is created to lead the strike with representatives of both SDS and the "moderate" non-SDS students. I make a plea for an inclusive and democratic strike committee: there should be an elected representative for any Harvard House, any academic department, any graduate school, and any reasonable group that votes to go on strike and support our demands. Somehow, I am chosen to be the chair of the strike committee, even though I am no longer an official student.

House after house, department after department, have mass meetings and vote overwhelmingly to go on strike. The Med School. The Design School. The Law School. The Ed School. Teaching fellows. And as each group votes to go on strike, they select their own leaders to sit on the strike committee. Many of these new leaders had not even thought about going on strike before the events in Harvard Yard. The self-described "moderates" play a large role. Many are new

FIGURE 23.   Thousands of members of the Harvard community rally in the stadium. Leonard Mccombe/The LIFE Picture Collection, Shutterstock.

to activism, against the war, and fed up with the Harvard administration. Now, along with SDS, they are leading a massive and complete shutdown of the oldest and most famous university in America.

Harvard's Black students, under the banner of Harvard Afro, demand an African American studies department and stage their own demonstrations. Many faculty and the administration believe a totally fallacious rumor that Harvard Afro was planning to take over Widener Library and destroy its books. Nothing of the sort was ever discussed. Over the objections of the PL folks, for whom race is always a "distraction from the class struggle," the strike committee adds a new demand: that the university institute a full-fledged Department of African American Studies.

A few days later, the strike has taken hold. A crowd of over 10,000 students from every part of the university marches into the ivy-covered stadium. Waves of undergraduates, medical students in their scrubs, grad students from labs in their white coats, design and architectural students with gorgeous posters, and somber law school students, all march into the stadium. It is an awesome display

FIGURE 24.   I (second from right) was among those ratifying strike demands in Harvard Stadium. Leonard Mccombe/The LIFE Picture Collection, Shutterstock.

of the entire student community of Harvard rising up in opposition to President Pusey, the deans, and the war.

For SDS this rally is a moment of triumph and joy. We are making headlines around the world. This gathering of the Harvard community yells as loudly as possible to ratify the core demands. The opposition to the war has broadened and become the dominant force on campus. This level of mass movement is incomprehensible for the PL leaders. For them, attacking those closest to them is not a tactic—it is core to their politics. So as the overwhelming majority of Harvard rises up against the Harvard Corporation, all they can do is intensify their attacks on the misleaders—their fellow SDS members and now the "moderates." Speaking to 10,000 people in Harvard Stadium, they denounce the crowd, accuse them all of selling out because not every single one of their demands is incorporated in the unified strike committee's demands. Luckily, most of the crowd is not even listening.

For the Harvard faculty and administration, the strike of 1969 is a tragedy that will haunt them for decades. They have lost control of their university. Students suddenly stop obeying them and stop following the rules. President Pusey, Dean Ford, the various other deans, and the elite Harvard Corporation have lost all legitimacy. The strike was heady and hopeful as is any peaceful revolution where people create their own leaders, their own new rules, their own fresh forums, and governing councils. Classes are held outside of the regular classrooms with new subjects created by younger faculty and students. Students study the economy of the military state. The poetry of protest. Creative artwork blossoms all over campus. For a short while Harvard is completely engulfed in debate and discussion of the very real and powerful issues of the day: the war in Indochina, the role of the university in society, the legacy of America's original sin of slavery, how the university should interact with the community around it, how students could live lives that were moral and meaningful. As with any upheaval the thinking is passionate and sometimes sloppy, sometimes insightful, occasionally brilliant, often foolish.

There is one poster that above all else captures the mood of those spring days. The silkscreened poster has the red fist of the youth revolt. Imposed over it are these words written by a young aspiring novelist, Jay Cantor:

> Strike for the eight demands
> Strike because you hate cops
> Strike because your roommate was clubbed
> Strike to stop expansion
> Strike to seize control of your life
> Strike to become more human
> Strike to return Paine Hall scholarships
> Strike because there is no poetry in your lectures
> Strike because classes are a bore
> Strike for power
> Strike to smash the corporation
> Strike to abolish ROTC
> Strike because they are trying to squeeze the life out of you.
> Strike

This seemed like nonsense to Pusey and the old men who ran Harvard. It seemed foolish to a few students like Eliot Abrams who would become Republicans and lead America into new wars. But for six weeks in the spring of 1969, there were thousands of students at Harvard who understood exactly what that poster said and were doing their best to live its lines.

I was consumed with making sure the strike committee was democratic and fully represented every segment of the Harvard community on strike. I went from one small group to another, and then another, in the Harvard Houses, in all departments and graduate schools, urging them on and encouraging their imagination and creativity.

In the Harvard Design School silk screened posters were everywhere. There were t-shirts with red fists worn by kids who only weeks before never imagined that they would be on strike. Music blared from open windows. Harvard Yard was dotted with small groups holding alternative classes. Teaching fellows felt liberated to offer the courses they had always fantasized about. The spring flowers bloomed and with them a heady excitement and a sense that for a moment, we

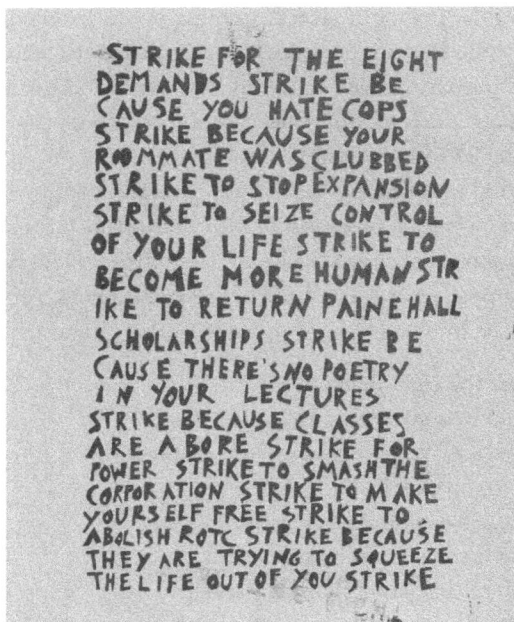

FIGURE 25. Harvard strike poster. HUA 969.100.2 (50), olvwork449770. Harvard University Archives.

were winning, that this most elite of institutions has been seized by the young, that the old men were in retreat. Classes and final exams were canceled or transformed. The strike was total.

The *Old Mole* came out with a Strike Special, "Reading the Mail of the Ruling Class," with the university's private documents splashed across its pages, documents showing CIA contracts with the university when the university had sworn there were no such contracts. The faculty was horrified to read in the *Old Mole* that Dean Ford and President Pusey had been lying to them and were working on ways to circumvent any decision they might make to curtail the ROTC program. Whatever the faculty thought of us, they could not forgive Pusey and Ford's dismissal of them. Under enormous stress, Dean Ford was hospitalized and finally resigned.

In the end the strike committee negotiated a successful conclusion with the Harvard Corporation. It was a stunning victory for us and an astonishing capitulation by them. The ROTC program was abolished. The scholarships for ROTC members were retained. The ROTC building became a day care center. An African American studies department was created. Harvard committed to better treatment of the community around it.

Because it was Harvard, these events generated enormous media coverage. Both *Time* and *Life* devoted their covers to the strike. Because it was Harvard, segments of the Harvard faculty and the entire administration thought the events of that spring were a historic tragedy. Because it was Harvard, the elites were shocked, stunned.

With its unbounded creativity, amazing posters and t-shirts, slogans of poetry and humor, the unbounded debates, forums, discussions, and changed classes, the strike was a brief, marvelous moment. However, it is important to see the larger context. What happened for those weeks in the spring of 1969 at Harvard was simply one small part of what was happening on campus after campus. The war galvanized students to action. Campus administrations reacted predictably, stupidly, and with a heavy hand, turning the majority of their students and younger faculty against them. African American students, feeling part of the Black liberation struggle, took up their own demands, occupied their own buildings with rumors of guns being stockpiled (usually false), and fought for Black studies programs and for increased numbers of students and professors of color. While the war and racism had been at the heart of the struggle, over the following years university life would be changed in other ways we never anticipated, best symbolized by coed dorms and salad bars.

At Harvard, over the next years the vindictive administration would "expunge" and "separate" many of the most militant students, mostly supporters of the Progressive Labor Movement. For a number of those students who evicted the deans, a hand on the shoulder, a push in the back became violent assault, and at Harvard's request they were tried, convicted, and a few sent to prison. Others were "banned" from ever setting foot on the campus, and one, who innocently returned to visit friends, was jailed for trespassing.

I, however, was long gone and glad to finally be rid of Harvard.

For years, the faculty and the administration relitigated the events of April 1969, always focusing on the "mob" of radical students, always referring to those events as the "Harvard Riots," and never focusing on the behavior of the police and the men who unleashed them. Harvard could never see itself as other than special and different. For a few heady weeks in the spring of 1969, it was swept by the movement that had spread to campuses from one end of America to the other and burst forth in Paris, Mexico City, Prague, and Berlin, a movement sparked first and foremost by the American disaster in Vietnam, that then turned into a hopeful explosion of youth, of rebellion against elites, against the grinding wheels of materialism, against the realities of violence, and barbarism. For one brief moment, the men and women of Harvard stood in solidarity with the young of America and the young of the world in opposition to the war and in favor of hope, democracy, and an attempt to stop the life being squeezed out of all of us.

STRANGE DAYS: 1969–70

In the coming years, the weight of that damn war sits heavy on our young shoulders. It ratchets up each day, each week, each long month. Year after year. We carry it with us. We do not experience the savage horrors of those who fight in it. The dark tunnels we fight in are often the tunnels of our mind. The responsibility to end it rests uncomfortably. Images, facts, lies replay in our minds, in our dreams, waking, sleeping. Incessant. Urgent. Over and over. They weigh us down.

A silent monk in flames. American boys dying in tall elephant grass. A naked girl running from inferno towers of napalm, mouth open, arms extended, exposed skin, silently screaming save us, save us . . . a man being shot in the head . . . 300 still bodies sprawled in the ditch by the road at My Lai. A war measured in nightly "body counts." Endless deceit, deceit in the Tonkin Gulf. Deceit in each day's press conference. Lies. Death. A friend's first cousin from Ohio, a first lieutenant dead in the Ia Drang Valley. Napalm, jellied flame, jellied death. The incessant lies. Escalation. Always escalation.

Willie Pete—white phosphorus that burns to the bone, burns even in water, burns unchecked when exposed to the very air we all breathe. Christmas bombing, mining of Hanoi and Haiphong harbors. Agent Orange. Deforestation. Pacification. Endless words. Endless fictions. Endless waves of B-52s dropping seven million tons of bombs on Vietnam, Laos, and Cambodia—more than twice the bombs dropped altogether on all of Europe and Asia in World War II; endless explosions; endless death. The invasion of Cambodia. Uncounted villages destroyed. Uncounted dead "Gooks" who are in reality mothers, daughters, sons, brothers, fathers, and grandfathers. Bodies deemed unimportant.

FIGURE 26.   Image that haunted us. The South Vietnamese National Police chief executes a suspected Vietcong officer, February 1, 1968. Associated Press / Hal Buell.

One million, two million, three million dead. How to count so many dead? Numbers that sit heavy on us. Wake us up. Torment us. Not numbers. People. People who should have lived, loved, seen the glory of another sunrise. The uncounted dead form mountains in the mind. Weigh upon us. Prey upon us.

Where there should be the exuberant joy of youth, there is a sense of death all around: in Vietnam, in Cambodia, killing fields, staggering numbers of dead that haunt our days and nights. The dead of this decade are not just in distant Asia. Medgar Evers gunned down in his driveway. Schwerner, Goodman and Chaney pulled dead from the mud of a Mississippi dam. Malcolm dead in a Harlem ballroom. Martin Luther King dead on a motel balcony in Memphis. Bobby Kennedy, dying on a California hotel kitchen floor. Fred Hampton dead as he slept, shot by Chicago police in his own bed. Jeffrey Miller, Allison Krause, William Schroeder, and Sandra Lee Scheuer shot dead on the campus of Kent State. Phillip Lafayette Gibbs and James Earl Green shot dead at Jackson State.

The weight of the war wraps around us, wraps our every day, warps our minds. Guilt boils under the surface. Guilt at not going; guilt knowing someone else goes; guilt at not stopping them from going; guilt at not being able to stop this abomination, so wrong, so unnecessary.

FIGURE 27. The iconic picture of a young girl and others fleeing a napalm attack, 1972. Associated Press.

We are determined to stop it all. We are desperate to stop it all. Until it stops, we cannot stop. We will not stop. We march, we educate, we protest, we sit in, we surround cars, we march again, we will try everything, we will do anything. Desperation and despair battle with hope. Some days we think we will win. Some nights we feel as if we are suffocating in failure. The weight presses down, burns us like Willie Pete; the very air we breathe burns our souls.

Those days and nights of 1969 and 1970 are strange, surreal. Amy and I walk out into the slanting, gold filtered light of an early Cambridge evening, heading to the movies. As usual, Amy walks faster, head down, three feet ahead of me. I am lost looking at her, the stacked heels she wears accentuating the shape of her legs, her A-line skirt drawing me to her slender waist, the setting sun catching reddish tints in her long hair as it falls down her back. Suddenly an unmarked police car cuts us off, its tires squeal; doors fly open, and Detective Dominick Scalese runs up to us, gun in hand, pushes me against a wall, and says, yes, "Up against the wall, motherfucker." Amy stands silent nearby as he presses the blued barrel against my temple, and growls, "One of these days, maggot, one of these days, I am going to find you in a dark alley, and I will blow out your motherfucking brains." I say nothing; there is nothing to say. Detective Scalese glares with all the menace he can summon. I remind myself he is not going to do anything, here in public view, not now, not this time, so I smile.

Both Boston and Cambridge police thought it great sport to occasionally throw me up against a wall and put a gun to my head. We sensed the pressure mounting. We felt the threat from the state with its sanctioned monopoly on force and violence. While unaware of it, I had been placed on multiple FBI registries: the Security Index,[1] and the Rabble Rouser Index,[2] which in 1968 was renamed the Agitator Index.[3] These were lists of the people that the FBI considered dangerous and who, if the president invoked the Emergency Detention Program, would be immediately imprisoned.

The Nixon administration was obsessed with the antiwar movement. Vice President Spiro Agnew continued his campaign role of hatchet man attacking antiwar protestors as an "effete corps of impudent snobs."[4] More ominously, the attorney general, John N. Mitchell, made sure a grand jury in Chicago indicted Tom Hayden and seven others for the demonstrations at the Chicago Democratic Convention. I knew all the defendants. Beyond Tom and Rennie Davis and the Panthers' Bobby Seale, they seemed chosen almost randomly, sending the clear message that the government could indict any of us. We understood the message, felt the threat.

The Los Angeles police department with support from Washington formed the nation's first SWAT team—the Special Weapons and Tactics team—and violently raided the local Panthers.[5]

Though we didn't know it at the time, Nixon gave J. Edgar Hoover carte blanche to escalate the FBI's Counterintelligence Program (COINTELPRO) targeting the antiwar movement and Black militants. COINTELPRO was secret and illegal. As usual, the people who paid the steepest price were Black activists, a number of whom would be killed in the coming months.

Along with all my friends, I had a growing sense that the government was increasing its surveillance, its disruption, and making plans to lock some of us up. We debated this from time to time: was it our paranoia or a realistic assessment of the inevitable corollary to a policy of pursuing a war that, like some distant voracious beast, devoured lives without any sign of stopping?

Nixon and his administration did everything they could to paint the antiwar movement as unpatriotic. They developed the trope of the silent majority. When, in May of 1970, 400 construction workers rampaged in New York, beating up antiwar high school and college students,[6] their leaders were conspicuously honored by Nixon with a reception at the White House.[7]

In May of 1969, Dick Flacks, a founder of SDS, now a professor at the University of Chicago, was attacked in his office, beaten so badly he almost died.[8] The

FIGURE 28.   Hard Hats rally in New York to support the war, just before attacking antiwar high school and college students. Photo by Stuart Lutz/Gado via Alamy.

attack most likely was the work of the "Legion of Justice," a right-wing group with ties to the Chicago police and possibly the FBI.[9] Even though we didn't know who was responsible, the attack seemed part of a growing effort to intimidate and destroy our movements.

We could feel the pressure building. Who would be attacked next? Which people in our meeting were undercover agents? Paranoia was increasing. Who would be indicted next? I could not help but wonder if that dark night might come when the threats of Scalese and other cops became more than words.

One blustery spring day, crossing Harvard Square, I saw the familiar figure of John Maher, tall and lanky, passing out leaflets. I had known and admired John for many years. He was one of the older graduate students who had taken me under their wing when I was still in high school. I had attended John's wedding. He and Frinde, his wife, had thrown a party for Amy and me after we had gotten married. He had loaned us money to help pay Amy's tuition. I considered him a good friend even if I had been seeing less of him in recent months. I had heard that he was getting close to the Progressive Labor Party (PL), but I did not take it seriously.

As I walked up to him, I heard him saying in his soft Texas drawl, "Read about how the CIA is destroying the movement. Join the fight against the misleaders of the people."

He avoided looking at me. I stopped and took a leaflet from another member of the small group passing them out.

I was stunned to read "Ansara, misleader of the people . . . Ansara, CIA agent."

I looked at Johnny in disbelief.

Walking up to him, I made a point of looking him directly in the eye. "I can understand you might disagree with me on strategy and what we should be doing," I said, "but how can you possibly accuse me of being an agent of the CIA? Johnny, you know me. We've been friends. You know I am no CIA agent. Come on man, how can you do this?"

John, my friend of six years, never missed a beat. Without any hesitation, he replied, "You may not actually be paid or directed by the CIA, but since you are doing what they would want you to do, *objectively* you are the same as their agent! And so, the leaflet is right on."

I stood dumbfounded, dismayed. I felt a pain behind my temples. I was used to attacks by various crazies. But this was John, a good friend. He knew me. I felt a deep chill, sensed a future where many of the most active members of SDS would veer off the rails into a series of bizarre, alternative realities. I shook my head, not wanting to believe it, and walked away without saying another word.

I am in an ornate wood paneled room of the US Senate, facing the chief investigator for the Senate Subcommittee on Internal Security. Alongside him, staring off into the distance, is Senator Strom Thurmond, he who famously filibustered against the Civil Rights Act of 1957. Now he says absolutely nothing. Down the length of the table is a stenographer taking notes. Beside me is my friend David Landau and our two lawyers. We are there in response to a subpoena, part of an ongoing investigation into the antiwar movement and New Left.

Jules Sourwine, the chief investigator, turns directly to me, his narrow face almost resolving into one thin line. "Have you brought all the records?" he demands. "Are you prepared to hand them over to us?" Senator Thurmond continues to stare into the distance, uninterested.

"Yes," I say.

The chief investigator looks around, casting around for the boxes of materials he is expecting.

I produce one plastic check register. He takes it, holding it as if it was potentially toxic and asks, "Where are the rest of the records?"

"You asked for all the records we possess," I say. "Here they are."

"We want every document and record in your possession." He is clearly annoyed.

"I understand. I am responding completely. This checkbook is the only document I have in my possession."

He looks perplexed and angry.

I have a hard time not laughing.

Sourwine icily points out that if they find we have withheld documents from them, they will find us in contempt of Congress, and we will face jail. Again, I assure him we have complied completely and voluntarily.

He tells us we can now leave. Senator Thurmond does not stand as we leave. He continues to stare off into the distance.

The Senate investigators have been focusing on a unique fundraising entity I created the year before.[10] Ralph Hoagland was a cofounder of CVS, the massive drug store chain. Having made incredible amounts of money, he and his wife became immersed in the counterculture zeitgeist. They operated an art theater in Cambridge, the Orson Welles Cinema. Ralph also was very committed to the Civil Rights Movement and then to Black liberation. He met Amy in Roxbury and from their conversation, he asked to meet with me. I was rather surprised when Ralph, thin, awkward, wearing thick, black glasses, without any small talk or preamble, asked me what would happen if he donated significant money to us. Would it be used to purchase guns for the Panthers? While I was unclear what answer Ralph hoped for, I explained no, we were not interested in purchasing guns for anyone. We were interested in raising money for all the organizing efforts and alternative media. We talked about creating a "movement center."

Ralph pledged $100,000, a shockingly large amount. He had only one condition: his donation must be in the form of an investment in a for-profit company that would make no money so that he could use it as a tax offset. That amount of money with no other strings attached was too enticing for us to turn down.

Sitting in my kitchen a group of us kicked around possible names for the new entity, a for-profit business that would lose money by giving it all to the movement. We wanted something ironic and euphonic. We almost went with names of Cambridge streets, Putnam, Pearl & Kinnaird. That had some music to it but lacked irony. We wanted something with an ironic "heavy industry" connotation. Laughing, we settled on "Cambridge Iron & Steel."

Receiving the first check for $25,000, we quickly wrote checks to the *Old Mole*, the Liberation News Service, the Boston Draft Resistance Group, SDS and Sgt. Brown's Memorial Necktie, an antiwar café. It would be $25,000 in and $25,000 out. Immediately the PL pounced on this the proof, at last, that we were agents of either the government or the ruling class, or both.

Once the PL leaflets came to the attention of the *Boston Globe*, the story was too good to pass up. On page 2 of the paper for Saturday, July 12, 1969, there was a long piece by Richard Connolly, headlined "Businessman, Dummy Firm Funds Boston SDS."[11] The article, accompanied by a photograph of the small house that Amy and I rented, "The office of Cambridge Iron & Steel," quotes PL's bizarre conspiracy theories and our response.

Soon FBI agents visited Ralph Hoagland. Subpoenas were issued by the Senate's Internal Security Subcommittee. This was all too much for poor Ralph; there would be no additional payments. He was forced off the board of CVS for his donation to us.[12]

In 1969 and 1970 both the House and the Senate mounted full-scale investigations of the New Left. I felt flattered when one government agency produced a poster of the "100 Most Dangerous Radicals in America" with thumbnail photos, and I made the list. I was somewhere down around #80, but still I was there, my picture showing a bearded, scowling face. A two-volume Senate report on the threat from the New Left and antiwar movements in Massachusetts was published complete with extensive undercover surveillance photos of me. Riddled with factual mistakes, we thought the report hilarious. But still there was a chill down the back of my neck realizing all the times the government had been tracking every move, recruiting informants for every meeting, taking photos of us, without my ever having noticed. And logic said they were continuing their efforts to watch us, disrupt us, and possibly indict us.

While some of us were beginning to lose our way, others, the women among us, were finding their voice. The rise of a new feminist movement would empower women and at the same time become a source of new pressure and even pain for many men.

I was sitting in the S & S Deli in Inman Square, Cambridge, having lunch with five SDS women. All of them were women I had worked closely with, all of whom I trusted. They had asked to get together with me for what I thought was a social gathering. After we ordered, one said:

"Michael, we have an important message for you. We need you to listen carefully."

"Okay," I replied, not sure what this was about.

"Look," the next one said, "we need you to change your chauvinist ways. We think you can change but you need to work at it."

I stopped eating my sandwich. I was not sure what we were talking about, but I felt suddenly uneasy.

"Okay," I said, "what exactly do I need to change?"

"You need to stop seeing women only as sexual objects, and you must stop sleeping with so many different women. You male leaders are all alike. You profess your support for feminism and yet the only use you have for women is for your sexual pleasure. Michael, you need to stop it."

I was speechless.

I thought, "These women know me, they know me. We have worked closely together in SDS, in the antiwar movement and at the *Old Mole*. They know me. . . . How can they think this . . . ."

I started to say, "But I don't—"

Several of them cut me off. "Don't try to make excuses for yourself. Listen to us. We like you. We want you to change. But you cannot make excuses."

I could not bring myself to break in and confess that my entire lifetime sexual experience had been limited to two women, one of whom was my wife of the last four years and the other a one-night encounter while traveling in Europe. I tried to suggest I was not the person they thought I was.

They would have none of my fumbling responses. I was not listening to them, and I needed to. They concluded with an ultimatum: I must stop my chauvinist ways and stop sleeping with so many women if I was to stay part of the movement.

This meeting was only one of many, as the wave of women's liberation swept through the movement, through our lives. It had been a long time building.

Within SDS there were many strong women leaders, but repeatedly they were treated as secondary to men. One illustrative story was told by Barbara Haber, married to Al Haber, both a key part of the small group that founded SDS. They were at an SDS national meeting in the mid-sixties and the group was outside discussing something. As it got colder, Barbara suggested that they all move inside. No response. The intense political discussion continued. Then she made her suggestion again. Again, no response. Her husband Al, leaned over to her and whispered, "Watch this." Al made the same suggestion to move inside. The group picked up their chairs and moved inside.[13]

Early attempts by women to meet, to discuss their roles in the movement, and the roles of women in the larger society often produced derision and hostility. Defensive and patronizing male leaders in SNCC and SDS could not understand what women were talking about.

Many of the most charismatic male leaders were indeed predatory when it came to sex. They expected that wherever they traveled, after every speech, there would be willing young women ready to sleep with them.

When national SDS leaders came to Boston, I was often tasked with planning the details of their visits. There were many who never asked me to find them women but there were a number who did. At first, I simply did not understand what they were asking of me. Then, when it became clear, I quickly changed the subject and pretended it had not happened. Not once did I call them out. Not once did I confront them. In that way, I was like all the rest of the men in the movement, tolerating the oppressive treatment of women, while waxing eloquently about the need to stand with the oppressed of the world.

SDS was dominated by articulate, arrogant men, men who led by their verbal dexterity, men who felt little need to make space for those less confident or less verbal, men who paid little attention to formal structures of accountability, men who spent no time thinking about how to make sure women were heard—and I was certainly one of them.

Radcliffe admissions were carefully controlled to never exceed 25 percent of the male Harvard class size. Yet, women made up a significantly greater percentage of the SDS activists. However, far fewer were in leadership positions. In fact, the Harvard strike committee in 1969 was initially composed of all men until we made sure to add two women.

It took women organizing themselves to change things. Women active in civil rights and SDS played a pivotal role in creating a new feminism.

As early as 1964, Mary King and Casey Hayden, two white women in SNCC wrote, "The average white person doesn't realize that he assumes he is superior. So too the average SNCC worker finds it difficult to discuss the woman problem because of the assumption of male superiority. Assumptions of male superiority are as widespread and deep-rooted and as crippling to the woman as the assumptions of white supremacy are to the Negro."[14]

King and Hayden would later write "A Kind of Memo" elaborating on their earlier thoughts and raising a specific critique of movement culture and behavior. Who gets named project director? Who sweeps the office floor? Who takes the minutes? Who speaks to the press?[15] They mailed this to a larger group of women active in the antiwar movement.

At the 1966 national SDS conference in Urbana-Champaign, women in SDS took up the memo and its ideas. Marilyn Salzman, Vivien Rothstein, and Heather Booth, all talented organizers, all women I knew and admired, experienced resistance from the men in SDS. Soon they made the decision to work outside of the organization. Heather and Vivien formed the first women's liberation organization in Chicago. Marilyn did the same in Washington, DC.[16]

Within SDS, feminism faced significant initial resistance either framed in terms of "you are splitting the movement" or "first we need to win our other fights and then we can turn to this issue." In other words, wait, wait.

Vibrant women's caucuses formed despite, or perhaps because of, the skepticism and resistance of men. Amy started attending women-only "consciousness raising" groups. She had to navigate the burden of being married to me, one of the most prominent of male leaders. The *Old Mole* had a strong women's group. By 1969 there was a full-blown women's movement in Boston. Amy and most of the women I knew enthusiastically attended a conference of 500 women at Emmanuel College. Bread and Roses, a new organization of New Left women formed and took on the responsibility of confronting male leaders. And I was one. They would hold hundreds of "consciousness raising" sessions for women. They seized a building and created a new women's center. Another offshoot was the famed publication *"Our Bodies, Ourselves."*

The Boston group was part of a much larger women's movement that would profoundly alter America, changing expectations, roles, and possibilities.

Those first women in SNCC and SDS and the waves of women who came after changed what is possible for women and thus what is possible for men as well. It was not easy.

I, of course, thought I was different from the other male leaders. Many of the women did not think so. If I was different, it was only in degree.

While internal SDS factionalism grew, and women found their voices, I wrestled with a profound exhaustion. Years of leadership, of always being on, of always pretending I knew just what to do, combined with relentless personal attacks, were exacting a toll. All around me, young men were being told to report for their draft physicals. The increasing numbers of young men being fed into the war by the draft ratcheted up the pressure. We had to save them. I had to save them. And I was not good enough.

There was no pause in the violence. The newly installed Nixon administration publicly promised "Peace with Honor" and secretly launched a covert, massive bombing of Cambodia.[17] I knew our work was essential, but I felt I was failing.

The ground war pounded on with an illogic all its own. Over ten days American soldiers were flung again and again in frontal assaults on Hill 937—an insignificant hill that our grunts named Hamburger Hill—where seventy-two of them died and more than 300 were wounded for no strategic reason.[18]

US forces in Vietnam peaked at 543,400.[19] The war was a massive, complex, logistical machine, a deadly marvel, a monument to our nation's unmatched ability to move, supply, equip, feed, and arm hundreds of thousands of soldiers halfway around the world. From 1964 through February of 1973, 2,709,918 Americans served in uniform in Vietnam.[20] The Selective Service system was essential to that war effort. During the war, 1,857,304 American men were drafted. In 1969 alone, 283,586 young men received the call from the Selective Service, passed their preinduction physicals and were forced into the armed forces.[21] An equal number enlisted.

Every young man I knew worried about what to do when ordered to report for their preinduction physical. For me, because of my mysterious joint disease, there was no way I would ever pass the physical. But that knowledge added more guilt, thinking about all those others who would be going, in a sense, in my stead. That guilt lay like a heavy fog, the backdrop to every day, every event. A birthday celebration inevitably led me to think of all those who would never celebrate another birthday.

FIGURE 29.   Injured paratroopers of the 101st Airborne make their way down "Hamburger Hill." Photo by Bettmann via Getty Images.

For others, fear was a more pressing emotion. Should they apply for conscientious objector status? The law specified that only members of formally recognized religions could receive that status. Should they evade the draft by not reporting and hiding for years? Head to Canada? Or by intentionally failing the physical?

One widely shared, perhaps apocryphal, story of an SDS member at his physical comes to mind: when he got to the question "Are you homosexual or have you had sex with another man?" purposefully he checked it, erased, checked it, erased it, repeating that process until the page was visibly almost worn through. When the doctors asked him, "Are you a homosexual?" he paused, looked panicked, and wide-eyed shook his head no. He had not lied. He was rejected.

In the end more than 500,000 young Americans refused to register for the draft or refused to report for their physical.[22] About 200,000 were charged with some sort of evasion.[23] Between 30,000 and 40,000 fled to Canada; thousands fled to other countries.[24]

Who knows how many elite families pulled strings to get their sons out of the war, into safe jobs with the National Guard, or managed to convince doctors to provide false medical conditions? Out of the 1,200 men who graduated from Harvard in the class of 1970, just two went on to serve in Vietnam. Only twelve Harvard men died in Vietnam out of the 12,595 men who graduated from Harvard College between 1962 and 1972. Compare that to the twenty-five South

Boston men who died in the war out of a total draft eligible population of only 2,000.[25]

Thirty of us gathered in the early morning outside the local draft board in Coolidge Corner, near where I had first stepped into that Woolworth's picket line nine years earlier. No longer a student, I had been called for my preinduction physical. I brought leaflets that opposed the war, informed draftees of their rights, and listed the number for the Boston Draft Resistance Group (BDRG). All of us boarded a bus for the army base, and I began distributing my leaflets. Many of the men sat, slouched and forlorn. There was little talk. As the bus bounced and lurched, I tried to engage guys in discussion. There were terse responses that, sure, the war sucked, the war was wrong. But the general sense, as articulated by a lanky, especially young-looking man in the back, was "We are all so fucked!" A gritty resignation was evident in the slope of everyone's shoulders, eyes downcast, heads bent, not in prayer but certainly hoping for some unlikely salvation.

Soon enough the bus entered the South Boston army base, the one whose proximity had sparked my resistance to duck and cover what seemed like a lifetime ago. Inside the processing room, reminiscent of a factory floor, vast open spaces were broken up by a few private exam rooms. I could not help feeling I had entered a sausage factory. A flutter of anxiety pulsed through me as I continued to distribute leaflets. A small, neatly creased and pressed sergeant immediately approached. I realized this was Sergeant Brown, so notorious for his drill sergeant attitude that the BDRG named its antidraft café Sgt. Brown's Necktie. Here he was, in person, confronting me, calling for a team of military police and yelling, "You cannot pass out leaflets here. Who do you think you are? Stop that right now. You are resisting the draft. That is illegal. Stop or I will have you arrested right now."

Knowing full well that I would fail any physical, I responded very formally, "Sergeant, I am here for my physical, I am prepared to serve my country, but that doesn't mean I have to stop opposing this war."

The sergeant, his uniform perfect in every detail, stared at me in surprise. "What do you mean? Aren't you refusing the physical? Aren't you refusing to be drafted?"

"No sir," I responded, evenly and without rancor. "I am here to serve. I am a good, loyal American. I love my country and our Constitution, which is why I have reported here as ordered and why I am exercising my constitutional rights." I went on to expound a little on the Constitution and my rights and to point out that I was not yet in the Army.

Sheer bluster on my part. Much to my surprise he backed down, turning to two MPs. "You take this guy and lead him through all the stations. I want him done, through, and out of here as fast as possible. Do it. Now!"

Escorted by two silent MPs, I was led to the head of each line, leapfrogging dozens of young men who had been slowly shuffling forward a step at a time. Soon many of them were yelling at me "Who the hell do you think you are, cutting ahead of us? Get back in line!"

I shrugged, "Hey guys, the MPs are forcing me to cut ahead because of these," and held up my leaflets. "Want some?"

The immediate response from half a dozen guys: "Hey, gimme some of those leaflets." Soon a growing number were passing out my leaflets. The two baffled MPs sent for the colonel, who, stern and serious, looked over my leaflets.

"Look," he said, "you cannot distribute these here."

"Sir," I responded, "I respectfully disagree." Once again, I politely but firmly stated my case, referred to the Constitution, reminded him that he had sworn an oath to uphold it, stated my willingness to serve, and pointed out that I was not yet sworn into the Army. Then I said: "But aren't you ashamed to oversee this whole thing, sending American men to serve in a war that is a disastrous mistake?"

He reacted as if slapped, his eyes bulging in surprise. I continued: "Look, this is the wrong war. We should never have been fighting it to begin with and now we need to end it."

"No," he responds, his voice steadily getting louder. "We have to stop the communists. Come on. We cannot stand by while they overrun one country after another. We need—"

I cut in, "Do you know anything about the history of Vietnam? How they threw out the French? That the Geneva Accords said there were to be free elections, but those elections were canceled because of us? Even President Eisenhower said if those elections had been held, eighty percent of the population would have voted for the communist Ho Chi Minh—and that's a quote."

The colonel started to yell: "That's wrong. You don't know what you are talking about!"

I remained calm, measured. I had debated this war endlessly for the last five years, with facts and figures, logic, and emotion all at my fingertips. I patiently instructed him as if he was a student who had failed his exam.

After three or four more minutes of back and forth, our voices steadily getting louder, his face red, veins now visible, he screamed:

"You don't understand! If we don't stop the reds in Vietnam, soon we will be fighting commies in the Philippines and then in Hawaii and then before you know it, we are gonna be fighting them on Boston Common, for Christ sake, fighting commies on Boston Common! Do you want that? On Boston Common!"

He screamed at me at the top of his lungs. Suddenly there was silence. I looked around. The stations right around us processing young men for the army had come to a complete stop, everyone riveted on our debate. The doctors and nurses and assistants had stopped doing anything and were watching us. The young men in their long lines were staring at us, following the debate with amazement. Along one side of the room there was a line of guys standing bare assed with their pants around their ankles, waiting the inevitable order to bend over and cough. Behind them were a few doctors and nurses, rubber gloved hands stopped in midair, the whole tableau frozen as they listened to us. No one moving. The entire place gone silent.

In the minute of silence, the colonel took this in. He turned back to me.

"Well, you may have your rights, but this is my base, and I decide who is allowed on it and you are not allowed to be here anymore."

I responded, "Hey I am here prepared to go through my physical. I am here to serve my country."

He glared at me, still red in the face, his neck seeming to push against the tight knot of his military tie, outrage stamped on his features.

"You are not fit for the Army. Get off my base and do not call us again and do not step foot here ever again."

Turning to the MPs and Sergeant Brown, he ordered "Get this guy off my base now!"

I was hustled out of the base and walked to South Station. As I walked through South Boston, I was not sure how I felt, how I should feel. I certainly felt relieved that my draft was over. But I thought about all the guys I left behind, being processed. I wanted to laugh at the memory of all the skinny legs and bare asses lined up while the colonel and I debated. I wanted to take some satisfaction in even a tiny momentary disruption of the war machine's gears and spindles grinding away. But I could not. I walked through South Boston thinking about all those Southie boys either drafted or enlisted, who would continue to die while I was able to take the Red Line home to Cambridge.

Despite remaining 1A, I never heard from the Army again.

There is a pervasive narrative about how badly Vietnam veterans were treated upon their return. Antiwar activists spat upon them, called them "murderer" and "baby killer," heaping abuse on returning soldiers in airports and on the streets.[26] This narrative has been an important conservative characterization of the antiwar movement. While I cannot say it never happened, I never witnessed anything like that, nor would we have supported such behavior.

My friends and I certainly chanted "Hey, hey, LBJ, how many kids did you kill today?" We viewed the top political leadership and the top generals to be criminals and to have blood on their hands. And we certainly grew to hate them. And certainly, we grew to hate the police.

That hatred, however, was never directed at the men who were forced to fight the war. They were every bit as much victims as the Vietnamese. Increasingly I met Vietnam veterans on the campuses and on street corners and in taverns. I felt empathy and respect for them whether they were against the war or not. I met veteran after veteran who had re-upped for a second tour in Nam, not because they supported the war but because they had lost a best friend, the buddy beside them. When I talked with them, they were not waving the flag and denouncing us.

Most of the vets I encountered, especially those who had experienced hard combat, were looking for a way of putting it all behind them, attempting to reconstruct their lives. Many had deep wellsprings of anger. Many felt that the war had to be supported if they were to honor those who died beside them. However, an increasing number—small but growing—felt that the best way to honor those sacrifices was to join us in opposing the war.

We reached out very delicately to Gold Star families—the families who had lost a son in the war. Overwhelmingly the Gold Star families supported the war. It was simply too painful to think they had lost a child to a war that should never have been fought. However, a small group of parents did oppose that war, and worked to stop it before it took the lives of any more sons. Ruth and Harry Gottschalk were the first Gold Star parents I knew who took a stand after their son Billy, a marine lieutenant and helicopter pilot, was killed in Vietnam. I met Ruth when she joined Gold Star Mothers for Peace and worked with us against the war. Ruth and Harry were determined to oppose the war and later became supporters of our community organizing efforts.[27]

I was occasionally invited to visit American Legion and Veterans of Foreign Wars posts to talk about the war. Usually, I was invited by a younger veteran who had returned from Vietnam. Usually, the older vets disagreed with what I said— but almost always politely and respectfully. That would not have been the case even two years earlier. But now the great majority of Americans either opposed the war or had profound misgivings about it.[28]

That summer of 1969, the war raged on. Nixon announced the withdrawal of 25,000 troops and escalated the bombing.[29] Muhammad Ali went on trial for refusing to fight in Vietnam.[30] That summer of 1969 the factionalism that had been poisoning our ranks burst forward into a spectacular display of surreal lunacy.

On June 18, 1969, I joined 2,000 young people packed into the dirty, ratty Chicago Coliseum for what became the last SDS convention. For four days I wandered the vast hall, feeling lost, repulsed as two factions waged a bizarre war against each other. I had only contempt for the crazed sectarian PL group with their warmed over old left Marxism-Leninism. But I found myself appalled at the behavior of the current SDS national officers and leaders from around the country who had formed what they called the Revolutionary Youth Movement (RYM).

Sitting high up in the stands I watched with disbelief as hundreds of RYM people waved the little red books of Mao Zedong, waved them in unison, chanting slogans from China, one upping the would-be Maoists of PL.[31]

The national SDS leadership brought in leaders from the Black Panthers and the Hispanic Young Lords to denounce "white skin privilege"—and to attack PL, which put class above race. During a diatribe attacking PL as armchair Marxists and racists who refused to follow Black leadership, Chaka Walls, the Panther speaker, veered off into an attack on feminism as "pussy power."[32] I felt physically ill.

All four days, I felt trapped in a nightmare with no way out. What had happened to the organization I had loved? What had become of our audacious vision of a New Left? This was a sick parody of everything I despised in the old left.

There were occasional fistfights. The convention site was fittingly gray and ugly. The debate was ugly and bizarre. There was nothing inspirational, only a vicious desperation. Everyone except the PL group walked out and held a separate convention. I could not find a place within either faction.

SDS was no longer my home.

When I joined SDS, the organization sought a new left rooted in American realities. We were contemptuous of the bankrupt old left. Now SDS was dominated by factions, each one bizarre, worshiping at the altar of cartoon Marxism.

I was totally perplexed how so many of my friends in SDS could spin off into weird cults. The Maoists of the PL and their "Student Worker Alliance," which never had any workers in it, had a certain appeal for the sons and daughters of the elite. I, for one, never took them seriously. My mistake.

At Harvard, the PL's chief organizer, Jared Israel was an unhappy, paranoid person. Arrogantly, I was confident that people would see the ridiculousness of his positions. Decades later, Jared's paranoid politics led him to become cochairman of the International Committee to Defend Slobodan Milošević, the former Serbian leader war criminal,[33] and to claim that the September 11 attacks were the product of a conspiracy involving the CIA.[34] In 1969, his politics were no less paranoid and fantastic. Yet, with all the turmoil, dismay and confusion abounding, the reductionist certainty of PL, for all its ludicrousness, attracted otherwise smart and decent young people.

Grouplets and cults abounded. Some young people fled into faux religion, shaved their heads, and chanted Hare Krishna in the airports and on street corners. Others became Trotskyites, Leninists, Maoists. Others were drawn like the proverbial moth to the flame of violence. The overwhelming majority of the student movement remained young and confused and as decently passionate as ever. However, among the most committed, the most active, there was a growing inability to differentiate fears and dreams from reality. The most committed and the most passionate were driving themselves into delusion in a world seemingly gone mad.

Unknown to us, the FBI had 120 undercover informants working inside SDS. Many of them were in Chicago stoking the fires of conflict and craziness. Hoover ordered them to support the national office because he was frightened of the disciplined and familiar Leninist approach of PL. Ironically, that meant FBI agents worked hard to support the weirdness that became Weatherman.[35]

For the next year I felt I was fighting for souls—and all too often losing—as one after another, decent young activists entered the dark world of end-of-SDS weirdness.

I had always thought that the "movement" made people better. For the first time I thought that people who struggled in the raw caldron of political passions and fought injustice could emerge changed, but maybe not for the better. I read and reread a poem by Bertolt Brecht, "To Posterity" that ends:[36]

> For we knew only too well:
> Even the hatred of squalor
> Makes the brow grow stern.
> Even anger against injustice
> Makes the voice grow harsh. Alas, we
> Who wished to lay the foundations of kindness
> Could not ourselves be kind.
> But you, when at last it comes to pass
> That man can help his fellow man,
> Do not judge us
> Too harshly.

I now had nagging doubts, not about the justice of our cause, not about the goals we fought for but about who we were becoming as we fought for them.

My abstemious nature continued to drive my closest friends wild. My refusal to get high was most infuriating to them. David, my old roommate from Adams House, insisted on the two of us making a special trip to the abandoned granite quarry in Milford just over the border of New Hampshire, which had become a place of episodic sanctuary. To get to it, we had to sneak through private property adding a smidge of outlaw quality to the adventure. On hot summer evenings when we wanted to escape, we gathered a small crowd, piled into several cars, drove to sleepy Milford, careful not to attract any undue attention from the local police, parked at the end of a dirt road, and made our way quietly past several homes, down an abandoned dirt track to the quarry. The solitude, the cool waters, the star filled clear night sky, the ripple of the moon reflected in the strokes of a naked body swimming through the dark water became our favorite respite from the war, from organizing, from the news, from the pressure.

Once in the water, we were muted and hushed, enveloped by a sense of the sacred we felt lying back in that coolness and looking up at the inverted bowl of brilliant stars.

On this night, it was just the two of us. David brought pot-laced sugar cookies. We were hushed and reverent as we stared up at the summer night sky. The cookies were almost inedible, burnt, gritty, terrible tasting. We choked some down and afterward, every fifteen minutes or so, we asked each other "Feel anything?" or "You buzzed yet?" shaking our heads, no, nothing happening.

David brought out his saxophone. Later, I realized that I had played it for over an hour. I had never picked up a sax before. Not only had I played it, but David and I also agreed that I had played it beautifully, gorgeous tones rising into the night air above the quarry, lingering in small echoes perched in the steep clean cuts of the sheer granite walls.

It was a brief disconnected moment of beauty and grace. And then it was gone. I would not experiment further in this time of epic experimentation. I told myself that I had work to do, wars to stop, cops to face down, racism to confront, a nation to change.

The morning of December 4, 1969, dawned clear and cold. The cold had settled down on us and every day, even a clear day, seemed gray and unrelenting. The phone rang early. The caller on the other end of the line sounded frantic, almost incoherent.

"The pigs killed Fred Hampton last night. Shot him dead while he slept. Fucking pigs! Happened early this morning. He is dead. This is fucking war."

I was speechless. The spiral of death and violence was spinning ever faster. Fred Hampton had seemed special, a powerful, young Black leader who was militant and spoke articulately of the need to rebuild a multiracial movement. Hampton was the young leader of the Black Panthers in Chicago. He was particularly close with SDS. Just twenty-one, he was a year younger than me.

Slowly over the next days, we learned some of what happened. As Fred slept in his bed, before dawn, the Chicago police and the FBI raided the apartment that also served as the headquarters for the Panthers in Chicago. There was no warning, no request for surrender. The police fired more than eighty rounds into the apartment, through the walls of his bedroom, killing Fred while he slept and also murdering Mark Clark, another Panther. The police described what happened as a shootout, but they could offer no proof that the Panthers in the apartment had actually fired at them. We were clear: the government had murdered one of the most promising young Black leaders in the land. Indeed, years later documents would establish that Fred's personal bodyguard was an FBI informant who provided detailed plans of the apartment and had slipped Fred a sleeping potion. His killing was a cold-blooded, state-sponsored assassination.[37]

The murders of Fred and other prominent Black Panthers confirmed for us that the state was willing to sanction extrajudicial execution, at least for Black leaders. The trial of the Chicago Eight confirmed that the state was willing to use the force of the legal machine to jail antiwar activists. Local police were more than eager to bash heads. All contributed to the sense that we had entered a stage of conflict more violent, more potentially deadly than before. It felt as if the war had indeed come home.

And thus, the year ended as it had begun—bleak, violent, and bloodstained.

DAYS OF RAGE

I would prefer not to remember those days, weeks, months, the year following the disintegration of SDS. Those were dark days, days of craziness, days of rage. While much of the country had turned against the war, still the killing ground on. We had done everything we thought we knew how to do. We had marched, held teach-ins, debated, won debates, and had even organized mass fasts against the war. We had told ourselves to make the leap from protest to resistance. We had organized sit-ins, occupied buildings, shut down colleges. We had organized draft card burnings and large-scale draft resistance. And still the bombs fell, still the blood flowed, now not just in Asia but also at home.

I would prefer not to recall my role in those days. I, too, experienced some of the craziness that seemed to flood the synapses of so many of us who had worked so hard to end a war that showed no signs of ending.

I lived a split life. On the one hand I was trying to learn to organize beyond the campus, reaching out to young people in Dorchester, working with returning Vietnam veterans, mobilizing large numbers of people to join peaceful marches. On the other hand, I was part of a team that kept up a frenetic pace of demonstrations that were more and more militant, leading to ever more violent clashes with police, to near riots and then actual riots. We and the police were in constant conflict. We hated them. They hated us. The violence in Asia was nonstop. The conflict at home was equally without pause and intensifying every month. We needed thoughtful strategy. All we had was rage.

FIGURE 30. Marching on MIT's iLabs. Photo by Timothy Carlson.

FIGURE 31. By 1970 we usually marched with National Liberation Front flags. Marmaduke St. John/Alamy Stock Photo.

SDS no longer existed as a functioning national organization, torn apart by sectarian warfare. The faction known as Weatherman (from their major statement quoting Bob Dylan, "You don't need a weatherman to know which way the wind blows") had embraced violence and formed into collectives to organize "the revolutionary youth." Weather collectives parading with National Liberation Front (NLF) flags fought with kids on beaches and outside high schools, somehow thinking that showing toughness was a prerequisite to gaining respect. I thought they were simply stupid crazy.

Weatherman announced the "October Days of Rage." They were going to Chicago to fight the Chicago police. They told everyone to bring helmets and gas masks and boots. I spent a good part of that August and September of 1969 desperately attempting to talk people out of this madness. I continued to feel a sense of personal failure and growing despair as I "lost" friends to Weatherman: Mike Spiegel, Mike Kazin, Bo Burlingham, Mark Dyen. The list grew depressingly long. Bizarrely it seemed to be the gentlest, the most intellectual of my friends who succumbed to the Weatherman cult.

Mark arrived at Harvard in 1966 looking for SDS. There was no need to recruit him. He had grown up in New Haven, the son of Isidore Dyen, a brilliant, rigorous "linguistic scientist" who taught at Yale for forty years. Mark was one of the smartest younger people to join SDS. Once at Harvard he threw himself completely and passionately into "the movement." Years later, looking back at his trajectory, seeing him jolted out of a natural path that would have led him most likely to become a professor and a public intellectual, I felt occasional guilt.

I was horrified as I watched this decent intellectual, squeezed by the demands of stopping the war, furious at the murder of Black people, ground down by the unrelenting attacks of the Progressive Labor Party (PL) people, turn increasingly angry and violent. Soon Mark was pledging to "renounce his white skin privilege," join the struggle of Third World people against the United States and loudly committing to use "any means necessary." Soon he was proudly discussing getting into fistfights with high school students as a strategy for building a revolutionary youth movement. I was baffled. He was so damn smart. And now seemed crazed.

I would try to reason with Mark that violence was a strategic and moral disaster. I was unpersuasive. Increasingly he was drawn into Weatherman, as were other young activists that I had led. Well, I was their leader no longer. I could not talk them out of a path that seemed to me obviously stupid. Contemptuous of my lack of commitment, my unwillingness to take the final steps, Mark soon stopped talking to me. Then he was gone, joining a collective whose secrets I did not want to know. Baffled, I felt I had let him down. I had failed him. I had lost him and too many others. His embrace of craziness seemed to me to be, at least in part,

FIGURE 32. *New York Daily News* front page, August 26, 1969. Headline: "SIR, MY MEN REFUSE TO GO!" Photo by: *New York Daily News* via Getty Images.

a result of my poor leadership. (Mark would come back to political sanity faster than many others. By the winter of 1973, we would be working together again and would do so for many years, remaining lifelong friends.)

Feeling the need to create an alternative that could keep people out of Weatherman and keep up pressure to end the war, I helped organize the November Action Coalition (NAC) planning a week of actions for that November. The *Old Mole* office on Brookline Street was the hub for everything we did. Despite the splintering of SDS, the office hummed with constant activity.

Opposition to the war had spread so far that active-duty military marched and signed petitions calling for an end to the war. There was now an antiwar movement within the military.[1] Soldiers had begun refusing to fight. The August 1969 *New York Daily News* front-page headline was: "SIR MY MEN REFUSE TO GO!—Weary Viet GIs Defy Order."

My friends Ron Carver and Robert Zevin were part of an extensive effort to organize antiwar coffeehouses near military bases and support GI antiwar newspapers and organizing. The antiwar movement was no longer restricted to campuses. It was an inchoate, sprawling social movement that reached into every institution and zip code of the country.

Despite the ongoing growth of opposition to the war, with Richard Nixon in the White House, my mood was not one of hope but of grinding desperation. The forces opposed to us were loud and angry. The power of the state was poised to strike us. The tension constant.

October 15, 1969, brought the biggest demonstrations against the war yet.[2] Originally the Vietnam Moratorium was to be a one-day strike—everyone stopping what they were doing to oppose the war. It spread across the country, into every city, onto every campus, and into countless small cities and rural towns. Across America people stood up to be counted as opposed to the war. It would prove to be a powerful brake on Nixon and Henry Kissinger as they considered extreme escalations.

In Cambridge, Amy and I were part of 15,000 people who assembled on Cambridge Common and marched once again into Boston. So different from those first marches. This time no one heckled us. There were no visible opponents. This time the march was led by a contingent of Vietnam veterans. So much had changed in just a few short years. As we marched across the Mass Ave bridge, a great cheer rose up as a sky writing plane created a giant peace sign in the air high above us. On Boston Common 100,000 of us thronged to hear Senator George McGovern remind everyone of what the New York Mets baseball pitcher Tom Seaver had said: "If the Mets can win the world series, we can get out of Vietnam." My old leader, Reverend Jim Breeden also spoke to the enormous and festive crowd. The entire city seemed overrun with those who opposed the war.[3]

I worked hard to bring thousands out for the moratorium. I was thrilled at the scale of it. Still, in part as an alternative to Weatherman, and in part, because I had bought into the path of "increasing the cost to continue the war by increasing disruption," the November Action Coalition offered a much more militant follow up. We targeted MIT, declaring: "MIT isn't a center for scientific and social research to serve humanity. It's a part of the US war machine. Into MIT flow over $100 million a year in Pentagon research and development funds, making it the tenth largest Defense Department R&D contractor in the country."

Michael Albert, the elected MIT student body president, was the coleader of the Coalition. Michael could have been one of the most successful theoretical physicists in the world. Faced with the war, he became the leader of the Rosa Luxemburg SDS chapter at MIT (named for the famed and doomed German revolutionary). The Coalition brought together students from twenty-five colleges, as well as high schools, nursing schools, and new anti–Vietnam War local groups. We promised to shut down the war machine at MIT. For three days in November, Cambridge police and State Police fought to prevent thousands of

FIGURE 33.   October 15, 1969, the moratorium on the Common. Photo by Spencer Grant.

students from occupying the labs where the defense work was done. MIT went to court to get an injunction prohibiting us from "employing force or violence . . . damaging or defacing facilities . . . converting documents to their own use . . . congregating within buildings to disrupt or interfere with normal functions conducted by M.I.T. . . . [and] inciting or counseling others to do any of these acts."[4] While our lawyers went to court in an unsuccessful attempt to get the injunction lifted, we simply ignored it.

At the iLabs, snipers, their rifles and scopes visible to us, were placed on top of nearby buildings. Behind the lines of police, with their usual riot control truncheons, walked special police with rifles at the ready. It was obvious that serious violence could break out at any moment. Still thousands of us surged toward the buildings undeterred by the obvious escalation of force being marshaled to defend them. There were running battles in the narrow streets around MIT. The cops always won the day, but for the first time, they were paying a price. It was not just the protestors who were bleeding as night fell.

That October, 150,000 workers at General Electric (GE) walked out in the first national strike in twenty-three years. Their contract had expired, and management was refusing to bargain in good faith. NAC decided to support the striking workers. When GE's CEO came to Boston University during Thanksgiving break, a group of us, perhaps fifty, showed up to picket. Most students were away. The area on Commonwealth Avenue where we were picketing was empty of its normal swirl of busy students, and now held only street cleaners and a few vendors tending their food carts. There was a chill in the air and an eerie quiet on the street.

After fifteen minutes, I was surprised to see the man behind the cart selling sausage and onions taking out a blackjack, the street cleaners dropping their brooms and charging toward us. Spilling out of the building came an array of plain-clothed and uniformed officers. The police outnumbered the protestors. Even though that day we were peacefully picketing, the police charged into us, laying about with their clubs and blackjacks.

The next morning the *Boston Globe* had a dramatic picture on its front page alongside the headline "4 Officers Injured in BU Melee."[5] A policeman has pulled my jacket over my head and is getting ready to whale into me. A slender, young Miles Rapoport along with the curly headed Vietnam veteran Mike O'Connor appear to be punching him squarely in the jaw. Also helping is Ivy Leichman, another of our activist crew. Had it not been for Miles, Mike, and Ivy I would have been beaten and arrested. As it was, thanks to them, I pulled away, and we all scattered as fast as we could. Twenty-four of us were arrested, and we had to concede that the well-planned police ambush was a victory for them. It only increased our anger, hardening our resolve not to be intimidated by the police.

All that fall, the trial of those indicted for the protests at the Democratic Convention, known as the Chicago Eight, proceeded, intensely, grotesquely. Bobby Seale, the lone Black defendant, was ordered chained and gagged by Judge Julius Hoffman, who made no effort to hide his hatred of the defendants. We thought it clear that this trial was meant to intimidate all of us. It was imperative that we respond in a forceful way to make the point that we would not be deterred by this or any other attempts at repression by the state.

Our response in Boston was organized under the banner of "The Day After" (TDA). Since we had no idea when the verdict would come, we organized to bring people out into the streets within twenty-four hours of any verdict that was not total exoneration. It was hard to organize an event with no fixed date. Still, we hoped we could put 5,000 protestors into the streets on such short notice.

While organizing for TDA, I received a worried call from one of our activists. Her relative, a member of the US attorney's team in Boston, wanted her to know that there had been a secret grand jury convened to investigate us. That grand jury had, he claimed, handed down conspiracy indictments for a small group of us. He did not have the whole list—just the first name on the indictment, mine. He wanted us to know that they were waiting for the next out of control demonstration after which they would announce the indictments and arrest us.

We had no way of knowing whether he was telling the truth. It certainly seemed plausible. All of us agreed that we should do our best to turn out the largest number of people possible for TDA and hope we deterred any move to indict us. We never considered toning down our militancy.

The verdict finding five of the Chicago defendants guilty was issued on February 18, 1970. David Dellinger, Rennie Davis, Tom Hayden, Abbie Hoffman, and Jerry Rubin faced maximum sentences of five years in prison. (Seale had been separated for a trial of his own.) Judge Hoffman did not set a date for sentencing. Declaring, "I find the men in this trial too dangerous to be at large," Hoffman denied bail for the five.[6]

We immediately announced our march for the next day declaring that the demonstration would be "disciplined and orderly. We will not initiate violence." However, our press statement went on to say, "We will not let ourselves be attacked and mauled without appropriate defense."

The news of our planned demonstration brought a strong reaction from the Boston cop Richard G. MacEachern, president of the National Patrolman's Association, who called on policemen "to meet force with force. . . . All patrolmen in the United States should take this as an outright challenge and threat to not only themselves but the very basic idea of freedom in America. . . . If the group that is attempting to coerce the basic concept of law and order—with regard to the trials in Chicago—assumes they will succeed, let them know they will receive as much force as they wish to exert."[7]

On February 19 we turned out 10,000 people marching through downtown Boston. After the march, thousands of protestors battled with charging police who eagerly attempted to clear the streets. It was unclear who wanted those clashes more—our folks or the cops. The numbers we turned out on such short notice exceeded our goals. There were no arrests. Officially twelve were injured, including three policemen.

We never found out if the rumored indictments had been real, but none were forthcoming. However, the demonstrations kept coming without a break, each more tension filled than the one before it. In March 1970 we supported the first women's liberation march on International Women's Day.

Then at a demonstration at Northeastern, we took the offensive. S. I. Hayakawa, the conservative head of San Francisco State University, was locked in a battle with Black students and SDS leading to a protracted student strike. He came to give a major speech at Northeastern. We were determined to protest. We and the police were itching for another fight; both sides felt the time had come. I was totally caught up in an intense spiral: we would protest, the police would respond with unnecessary force, which produced not only more protests but also more militancy, which led to even more vigorous assault by the cops. We called them pigs. They called us maggots. Dehumanization was expansive on both sides.

FIGURE 34. Ten thousand marched the day after the Chicago verdict was announced. Photo by Jeff Albertson, courtesy of the W. E. B. Du Bois Library, UMass Amherst.

Outside of Northeastern, a police car, its sirens blaring, its lights flashing, came quickly down the side street where I was part of knots of protestors who had fled after the police had charged the march, billy clubs flailing. The sun was going down; shadows played on the street as I pried a brick loose. The cop car kept coming. I thought of the times I had been thrown up against a wall, a gun pressed to my head. I thought of the times I had been hit by the men in blue, the number of times they had beaten my friends.

Fuck you, I thought, and heaved the brick as hard as I could toward the oncoming police car. It sailed in the evening sky. I watched it fly as if it was moving in slow motion. I followed its arc, seeing it turning over as it flew. I was sure I could never actually reach the police car. But there it was flying, tumbling, true. I saw the windshield shatter, I saw the car swerve suddenly to the left, slow, swerve repeatedly, like a parody of a drunk walking, and finally come to a rest on the sidewalk. I stood transfixed. I wanted to throw up.

"Come on," urged one of my team. "Come on, run." I couldn't move. I felt sick. Physically sick. Sick in the soul.

One of my group shook my shoulder, "Come on, Michael—great shot, run now. God dammit, run!"

I ran.

And as I ran, I kept imagining two policemen, men with families, men who wanted to serve, men whom I probably disagreed with on everything but who were most likely decent people, sitting in that car covered in blood and their families at home, worrying, waiting.

FIGURE 35. Photographer's caption was "Police attack demonstrators," Northeastern, 1970. Photo by Spencer Grant.

As I ran down the street, I swore to myself that I would never throw another brick in my life.

I never did.

Still, I pushed on organizing ever-escalating demonstrations, our goal to keep maximum pressure to end the war. I had totally bought into the "strategy" of "bringing the war home," bringing it onto the streets of America.

On the first of April, indicative of how widespread opposition to the war was, the Massachusetts legislature passed the "Shea Act," challenging the legality of the Vietnam War. The act declared that no one from Massachusetts "shall be required to serve" abroad in an armed hostility that had not been declared a war by Congress.[8]

Two weeks later we again turned out large numbers for more peaceful massive protests called by the moratorium and the Mobe. After the huge rally on Boston Common, 10,000 people marched back to Cambridge, Amy and I in the lead group. Entering Cambridge, we saw more and more police, including state troopers. Every cop had removed their badge; each was now anonymous, unaccountable for whatever actions they might take as darkness fell. Every cop had a gas mask.

FIGURE 36.   Injured police at Northeastern, 1970. Photo by Spencer Grant.

FIGURE 37.   Harvard Square as night fell. Photo by Spencer Grant.

A little after 7 p.m., we rallied on the Cambridge Common. Soon groups of protestors were blocking traffic in Harvard Square. The chants echoed in the spring evening air.

"Free Bobby Seale!"

"One, two, three, four, we don't want your fucking war!"

FIGURE 38.   Caption by photographer: "Massachusetts State Troopers in riot gear assault a protestor at an anti–Vietnam War demonstration in Harvard Square." Marmaduke St. John / Alamy Stock Photo.

"The streets belong to the people!"

Some sat down on the street. Some set fire in trash cans. Some climbed onto the news kiosk in the middle of the square. We chanted, "the streets are ours." The police thought otherwise.

Suddenly all the streetlights went off. In the darkness, hundreds of state troopers and local police moved forward. We let them. Our strategy, planned and carefully communicated in the weeks leading up to that night, was to break into small groups and stay on the streets for hours, playing cat and mouse, hit and run. Soon plate-glass bank windows came crashing down, and tear gas cannisters started flying. Fires were set but whenever possible our teams ran to put them out. The fighting spread from Harvard Square down Mass Ave into side streets and into Central Square. Cops charged. Kids ran away, gathered again, and heaved taunts and bricks toward the tired police who charged again. The police began beating anyone young, even if they were not part of the protests. Young reporters showed their press credentials to no avail. The fighting took a toll. By early morning

FIGURE 39.   Full-blown riot in Cambridge. Marmaduke St. John / Alamy Stock Photo.

more than 300 people were hurt. We thought the action a success as the headlines across the country reinforced the sense that there was an insurrection continuing from coast to coast.

As we skirmished with police in Cambridge, desperate fighting of a much deadlier nature was taking place in the A Shau Valley of Vietnam. Soon, the Cambodian prince Norodom Sihanouk was deposed by the pro-US general Lon Nol, and Nixon launched the Cambodian bombing and incursions. In response, there were enormous student strikes across the country, the largest wave yet of student protests. Virtually every single college and university in America was shut down. Then came the killings at Kent State and Jackson State. The nation teetered on the edge of coming unhinged.

Amid our ever-escalating battles with police, on March 6 a Greenwich Village townhouse exploded, killing Ted Gold, Diana Oughton, and Terry Robbins, members of Weatherman—all of whom I had known in SDS. I was horrified, saddened, and shocked. People I knew had blown themselves up making a powerful bomb. I had no idea what they had planned to bomb, but whatever plans they had were most likely terrible. While some of the remaining Weatherman leaders would deny it in later years, they had been making bombs to blow up a dance at Fort Dix in New Jersey.[9] Fort Dix had become a focal point of antiwar efforts in New York and New Jersey. Had they succeeded, it is probable that scores would have been killed and hundreds injured. My former comrades in Weatherman had totally lost their way.

I had heard about the Weatherman "war council," where Bernadine Dohrn told the group that now we need to be "crazy motherfuckers and [scare] the shit out of honky America," and went on to talk about the Manson murders as if they were somehow political. "Dig it! First, they killed those pigs, then they ate dinner in the same room with them. They even shoved a fork into the victim's stomach! Wild!"[10]

Hearing this I thought, *How sick! How demented!*

As Weatherman planned to go underground and prepare for violent insurrection, they met with the Vietnamese, who were horrified and argued for more peaceful protests against the war. They met with the Black Panthers who also had argued that this path would be disastrous. The leaders of Weatherman simply lied, claimed the blessings of both, and proceeded with their plans.[11] The Weather collectives vanished. Over the next years, they would explode a dozen bombs, whose only effect was to damage the movement. They were delusional and morally bankrupt. They believed they were part of a revolutionary movement in a revolutionary moment. Neither was true.

Bizarrely, Nixon and his inner circle were the only other people who believed that the country was on the brink of serious urban guerrilla warfare. Nixon, personally, along with his top law enforcement officials, became convinced that they were in an existential struggle with an incipient urban guerrilla force.[12] Indeed, the FBI reported 2,500 domestic bombings over eighteen months in 1971 and 1972.[13] However, almost all of these were carried out by isolated, uncoordinated, random radicals—what happens when a movement listens only to itself, feels intense frustration, and has decided that the state no longer possesses any legitimate authority.

Nixon directed the FBI to increase their illegal wiretapping without warrants. He sanctioned scores of illegal "black bag" break-ins. The FBI, at the request of the White House, enthusiastically broke law after law.[14] Still the Weatherman collectives eluded them.

One day in June there was knocking on our door. Opening the door, Amy and I saw a man and woman so pale it was as if they had not seen sunlight in months. I was delighted to see that it was Bo Burlingham, who then introduced the young woman as Lisa Meisel.

They said little except that they had left Weatherman and had no place to go. I don't know why they chose to land on our doorstep, but we were delighted to see them and insisted they stay with us. We asked no questions, the bruised circles under their eyes deep enough to testify to experiences we did not want to hear.

I had felt great affection for Bo. My friend Ron had introduced me to a small group of organizers who mounted the first efforts to reach out to those in active military service and organize them against the war. One of them was Arlo Jacobs. Arlo was everything I was not: slender, blond, Robert Redford handsome, with a sweet innate charm and graciousness.

Sometime later, I met "Arlo" again, except this time he was not Arlo but Bo. For some time, I was not sure which was his real name and which his nom de guerre. Each time I encountered him, by whichever name, I liked him more.

As SDS crumbled, I saw Bo only occasionally, hearing about a trip to Cuba and then about him slipping away into the orbit of Weatherman. I was heartbroken.

I had not met Lisa before, but she had been on the Ohio SDS regional organizing team with Terry Robbins, had been active in the first Kent State demonstrations, and at a very young age began organizing for SDS throughout Ohio and Wisconsin.

That summer Bo and Lisa stayed with us, and we could see their true gentle and decent natures revive. Quickly Bo and Lisa married. Bo asked for assistance finding a job. I was eager to help and grilled him on what jobs he had held so far. As an undergraduate he had hosted a popular blues radio program on Princeton's student radio station. That made me think of approaching WBCN. In recent years, as I regularly stopped into the station to let them know about plans for upcoming demonstrations, DJ Charles Laquidara, an especially enthusiastic supporter, kept talking to me about helping the station start a news program. "Come on man, why don't you become our first director of news?" But I was an organizer, not a radio newscaster. Now I thought Bo might be the right choice for the job. Charles took to Bo immediately, and he was hired to be the director of news for WBCN. I helped him assemble a small team of volunteer researchers to support him.

Bo's natural charm quickly won over everyone at the station. Then on his fourth day, July 23, as Bo was rushing to prepare the noon news, he saw a story come clickety clacking over the AP teletype machine: *12 radicals indicted by federal grand jury in Detroit.* Bo ripped off the story, in a rush to start the newscast. As he read it, he was stunned to see that one of the last names on the list of those indicted was his.

In a panic that the FBI would immediately arrest him, Bo first called Lisa and then me. I had a stable of lawyers who regularly defended us, almost always pro bono, and one, who had good relations with the US Marshals, said Bo should go somewhere where he would be inconspicuous, while the lawyer figured out what was going on.

I took Bo to the movies and we watched the newly released *Cotton Comes to Harlem*; two tense white boys in a three-fourths–empty downtown movie theater in the middle of the afternoon, trying not to talk or think about a massive dragnet combing the nation for Bo and the other fugitives, talking instead about Chester Himes and Grave Digger Jones and Coffin Ed, and calling the lawyers from pay phones every so often.

Finally, the lawyers arranged that Bo could surrender without punitive bail. It turned out that the FBI had absolutely no clue where he had been or that he was even living in Massachusetts. With a trial likely a year or two away, Bo and I attempted to save his job at WBCN.

We met with the owner, Ray Riepen, who, while remarkably patient and sympathetic, kept coming back to the problem of the Federal Communications Commission (FCC). He feared that keeping an indicted Weatherman on the air would be the tipping point given all the other controversial things the WBCN team was constantly doing. I argued passionately, "Ray, you can't throw Bo out onto the street; he just got married, he just started here, he has no money, now he has legal bills. I know you are not heartless. You won't throw him to the wolves. You must have a job for him somewhere, somehow."

Remarkably, Ray proposed a solution. His weekly newspaper, *Boston after Dark*, would hire Bo with the same salary, same benefits, no break in income. Ray was pleased; he had managed to do the right thing and avoid the wrath of the FCC. Bo was pleased; he had a job and an income. Quickly Danny Schechter, one of the volunteers we had organized to support Bo, stepped in and became "the news dissector" to modest fame in Greater Boston.[15]

Bo began a career in journalism that would carry over the decades. It would be a journey from *Boston after Dark* to editor at *Ramparts* and then into a long and distinguished career in business writing that led to *Inc. Magazine* and numerous acclaimed books including, *Small Giant, Finish Big, Street Smarts* (with Norm Brodsky), and *The Great Game of Business* (with Jack Stack).

Eventually, the indictment in Detroit would be dismissed because it was revealed that the government had illegally wiretapped phones and broken into people's homes.[16] In the end, it was the FBI officials and agents who would be indicted.[17]

Like Bo and Lisa, most of those who as young people participated in Weatherman, or PL, or other forms of late-sixties sectarian militancy and weirdness, have gone on to live full lives complete with many contributions to civic life, education, and the arts. Most have become sweet and loving parents and grandparents.

Still, I would prefer not to remember those dismal days when so many friends edged into craziness at the very moment when our leadership was so urgently needed. I would prefer not to think of my own lack of strategy. I was searching for a way forward. I wanted to keep the pressure on to end the war. I wanted to "increase the cost" of continuing the war through ever more disruption. At the same time, I wanted to find a way to organize blue-collar communities. I wanted to reach out to returning veterans. And I still harbored the dream of a long march through the institutions of America, a long march that could produce a new democratic consciousness. Anxious and often miserable, still I thought I was leading. More often than not, I was floundering.

A MARCH IN LOWELL

The Lowell Police Station seems particularly small this spring evening. The police break out a few shotguns. Outside waves of young people, hopped up on speed, acid, and booze, or simply the energy of the crowd, bay for blood, every ten or fifteen minutes charging the steps of the station. Repeatedly the cops sally out into the crowd, freely swinging their clubs, determined to deter the kids from storming the police station. Amy and I sit rigidly alert on the hard, wooden visitors' benches somewhat relieved, but enormously uncomfortable and embarrassed. The front sitting area bustles with cops coming and going. Soon a noisy group of clean-shaven, close-cropped men, thick-waisted and wide-shouldered, come through the door laughing, backslapping, enjoying every moment. After a quick double take upon seeing us, they start in with gleeful banter: "What are you doing here? Hey, is that your wife? Hmm . . . Jack does that look like the woman we saw Mike with last time. Nope totally different. Hey last time I was on him he was with some babe of a blonde. . . . Really at MIT, I saw him with a gorgeous red head. . . . Which is his real wife? . . . Hey Mike saw all the gang tonight. What a night. Ira and Miles and Moofy, Josh, Debbie, and Danny and . . ." making manifest that they know every organizer I work with. These are the State Police assigned to the antiwar movement and radicals—the "red squad."

Police drag in a kid from the crowds on the streets. As we sit in the waiting room, silent, embarrassed, we hear the cops work over the kid in the back, hear the impact of fists, boots, the angry yells of pain, rage, rebellion. And we sit there, attempting to make sense of what has happened. Sit there as "dangerous radicals" purposefully remaining in that police station. Sit there because originally those mobs of kids outside, now fighting police and threatening to storm the station, had been howling for our blood.

There are the occasional epiphanies: moments of sudden clarity, sometimes revealing truths that should have been blindingly obvious. My road to Damascus ran straight through Lowell in the spring of 1970.

The organizing group in Lowell was led by Ira Arlook. Handsome, small, intense, persuasive, Ira had been an antiwar leader at Stanford. He then moved to Boston and became an organizer of draft resistance. I grew increasingly close to him and thought of him as one of our best organizers and strategists. Neither of us had the slightest interest in any of the sectarian craziness that tore SDS to shreds. When Ira moved to Lowell to lead a small organizing group, I had little doubt that there would soon be a thriving community-based antiwar organization there. Indeed, the Lowell organizers steadily built a base of committed activists and many more supporters.

By 1970, Lowell was a hollow shell of the vibrant mill town that brought the industrial revolution to North America and sustained a strong textile industry for a hundred years. The massive brick mill buildings, beautiful and mighty, stood vacant, stripped of the machinery that had been moved to the American South before continuing on to Central America and Asia. The economy sagged, then cratered. Unemployment soared to 12 percent. The population was falling, the city failing. Neglect clawed the streets, the closed mill buildings, the boarded storefronts. Only the bars and taverns were full at ten in the morning and ten at night.

By the late sixties, the streets of Lowell would still be filled with young people, even as they longed to leave. Downtown was no longer vibrant, but it would be jammed, especially on Thursday—pay day, shopping night, drug-buying night. The culture was its own form of Wild West; young men challenging each other for no reason, for every reason, for the slightest reason, to fist fights on street corners, at gas stations, outside bars, inside bars. The Golden Glove regional boxing tournament was the annual talk of the town. Youth culture, few jobs, angry music, and a rolling river of despair powered a thriving drug market that was visible on downtown Market Street once the sun set. On a Thursday night, Ira and his team would be out on Market Street, talking with the long-haired, bell-bottomed men and the young women in their bell-bottoms, miniskirts, and short shorts. It was never hard to start up a conversation about the war.

"What do you think of the war in Vietnam?"

"Oh man, it sucks. Everyone knows that."

"Do you have friends who are over there?"

"Yeah, my cousin is a marine in Nam right now."

"We are working to get him home before he gets killed," the organizer would tell them. "The politicians and the generals don't care about your cousin; they don't care about all the guys who get drafted. And you know it's not their sons over there. It's the guys from Lowell who are cannon fodder."

Soon enough there would be a tight knot of young people intensely debating, most with serious faces, some stoned. Sometimes it would be a group of young women who had boyfriends and cousins facing the draft. Someone might bring up "We have to fight the commies," and there would be a discussion of the history of the war. But usually, the real question was not whether the war was right or wrong, but would a kid be willing to do something out of the ordinary, would they join a march; would they take our flyers and pass them out?

While the young of Lowell seemed open to opposing the war, many of their parents were still firmly in the camp of "America, right or wrong."

After months of these conversations, on street corners, in bars, outside of schools, the Lowell organizing team decided it was time for a march to show that the antiwar movement had come to Lowell. Flyers were handed out across the city, throughout downtown, at Lowell State and the community college and at the high school. The whole city seemed to be buzzing about the march and debating the war. Just what we had hoped for. The organizers thought they would turn out 500 people for this first march.

Two days before the march was scheduled, I talked with Ira who was somewhat concerned.

"Michael," he said, "I am not sure what exactly is happening but in the last days, a lot of kids who had said they were marching with us are now saying they cannot. One kid in particular, I know he is with us, I know it. But now he keeps saying to me that he just can't do it but he won't tell me why."

"Well often people get cold feet," I said, "but I am guessing once the march happens, they will join in."

"No," Ira responded, "something is up, I am just not sure what. So, it will be good to have you and the rest of the organizers from other cities up here with us. Meet us early in front of City Hall."

I thought nothing of this conversation at the time. So often we had seen people wrestle with the decision to take a first public step against the war.

Amy and I arrived early, meeting Ira and the other organizers who explained the plans for the March. We would start at City Hall and march through downtown Lowell. The lead contingent would be made up entirely of returned Vietnam veterans. A modest number of student antiwar activists from outside of Lowell showed up. We expected hundreds of Lowell young people to join us, but Ira said the numbers were definitely going to be lower than we had hoped for.

The late afternoon April light seemed harsh and flat as Amy and I made our way from our car toward City Hall, past Merrimack and Market Streets—the streets filled with even more young people than usual. The crowds large, roiling, talking, anxious, eager. Men were spilling out of bars, already juiced. As we walked by the crowds of young people, we could sense excitement. All around us were people nervously bouncing, talking heatedly. We could not make out the conversations. Perhaps, I thought, Ira is wrong, and this march is going to be larger than we thought.

While we made our way toward the assembly spot for the march, unknown to us, another group was getting ready, the regulars at the Celtic Club, a drinking spot above the Lull and Hartford Sporting Goods, a place often referred to as a "tough joint." Some days before, the Massachusetts State Police Red Squad, accompanied by local police, had dropped into the bar, searching out some of the toughest young men in the city, some of whom ran and enforced the street-level drug selling, ex-jocks, bouncers, leg breakers, and street corner toughs. Days after the march we were told about what had transpired in the Celtic Club. Decades later, most of what we had been told was confirmed in an article in the *Lowell Sun* with the exception that the meeting with the police might have been the day of the march.[1] The conversation in the Celtic Club went something along these lines:

"Let us buy a round," said the cops, to the surprise of the guys in the bar.

"Look," the lead cop said, "you are All American boys, you love our country, right?"

"Sure do," replied Gouch Gauthier, the de facto leader of the Celtic regulars.

"Look," the cop went on, "you know about this planned march. Well, this march is not really about the war at all. It's a ploy by a group of commies. They are getting big money from Fidel Castro and the Cubans. Listen these guys' real aim is to take over your streets, your turf. . . . If you care about Lowell, if you love America, you need to get out there and kick the shit out of these outsiders. They don't belong in Lowell. And they want to take over."

The cops stood several more rounds. As everyone drank, the "Staties" passed around some pictures. "See this one—that's Ira Arlook; he is one of the leaders. See this guy with the mustache? That's Ansara. He is coming up for the march from Boston."

Photos of the other organizers were shared, identities explained.

As the last round was drunk and one of the cops actually paid the barkeep, one of the lead Staties concluded: "Look. No guns. We don't want you to kill anyone. Just kick their asses, show them what Lowell men are made of. Do your patriotic job. Protect your turf. The Lowell police will look the other way. Just run these commie maggots out of town."

The Celtic crew was more than willing.

As Amy and I arrived at the march starting point, there were remarkably few policemen on the streets. Perhaps 200 marchers assembled. There were eight or nine Vietnam vets, most wearing their fatigue jackets. A group of thirty students and a few professors from UMass Lowell showed up. Some high school students. Our organizers from around the state. A group of women from Cambridge arrived, many wearing army surplus, several with head bands, carrying flags of the National Liberation Front. Several marchers showed up with "Free Bobby Seale" posters. Almost all the marchers were white except for a small contingent from Lowell public housing. Their leader pulled Ira aside.

"Look man, I've heard there is serious trouble coming. I think I better run home and get my piece."

"No. Look we have to keep things peaceful. Please don't do that."

"Okay, man, but I am telling you there is big-time trouble coming our way."

Ira announced that we would start marching.

"Stay together," he said. "Watch out for trouble. Stick close and be careful. We have marshals to guide us, please follow their lead."

The Vietnam vets took their place at the head of the march. The small brigade of women swung in behind, the rest of the marchers following.

No sooner had the march begun than it became clear we were in for more trouble than we could possibly handle. The sidewalks were jammed with far more people than were marching; they pressed forward to get a good look at us. I had the distinct sense that the dense jostling crowds were eager, excited, and expectant, not actively hostile but not supportive. Every few minutes, the crowds would part, and a wedge of young men swinging two-by-fours would charge into the march, rapidly breaking it up. Soon we were ducking, trying to avoid a brick hurled from the back of the crowd. Suddenly a battered metal garbage can soared out of the back of the crowds and into the march, landing with a jarring clang and spilling its rotting contents onto the street. A beer bottle arced high, hit a woman in the head and she dropped, bloodied, and hurt. More beer bottles came flying. The worst damage, however, was done by the brawling guys with two-by-fours who kept sprinting into the march swinging wildly. I was jarred by the sound of wood hitting backs, the smash of bottles breaking on the street, the growing number of injured and bloody marchers.

The march quickly dissolved into a frightened and disorganized mess. It was clear that attempting to continue would result in serious injuries. The vets wanted to keep going. Ira said, "No, stop and head home." We started breaking people into clusters and shepherding them away in different directions as quickly as we could. We knew the only safety lay in splitting the marchers into so many different groups that those intent on attacking us could not follow everyone. Still, we wanted our people to stay in large enough groups that the size offered some protection. Skirmishes broke out all over the place as the protestors headed to cars and vans. Soon the marchers had all gone. But the crowds of kids swelled and remained.

Amy and I finished successfully escorting one group to their cars and decided to head for our car and beat a retreat. Stupidly, we were alone. We had to walk back across Merrimack Street and the downtown to get to our car. Taking off our antiwar buttons, we hoped no one would know who we were. We were wrong. Crossing Merrimack Street, a small group of young men spotted us and yelled to each other, "There's one of the cocksuckers!"

I was now quite worried.

I told Amy, "Okay let's walk, not run, quickly in the other direction."

The small pack of men walked briskly parallel to us on the other side of the street taunting and yelling.

"Don't pay any attention," I said to Amy. "Just keep walking."

She put her head down and strode on purposefully. Everything slowed down and then sped into a blur of motion as Gauthier and his Celtic crew sprinted across the street, charging into us. Amy went flying, ending up wrapped around a parking meter. In a fraction of a second, Gauthier confronted me. I thought nothing, reacted not at all, as he suddenly swung a practiced right to the jaw followed by a quick combination from the left.

I felt the impact, a quick blow on one side of the jaw followed by the blow on the other side. The adrenaline was pumping. I couldn't think straight. I was worried about Amy. I wanted to get us out of there but had no idea how. I just stood there. Hands down. He looked at me in surprise. I was still standing. Later he would tell our organizers that he was certain he had broken my jaw and was expecting me to fall. For a minute we just stood there looking at each other.

A passing group of older men, seeing a young couple in obvious distress and not knowing, perhaps not caring, who we were, came across the street and yelled at the younger guys to knock it off. Amy stood up, bruised but not seriously hurt. We huddled close together. As the guys who had attacked us followed, the older men escorted us around the corner, telling us we should be okay now and veered off. We walked down the street as quickly as we could without running. Suddenly, ahead of us, we could see a much larger crowd of kids, screaming, laughing, running, throwing things randomly at windows, totally out of control and coming directly at us. At this point the smaller group behind us picked up their pace. We were caught in the middle. The crowd in front at full charge. The small group behind us running to catch up.

As we realized how much trouble we were in, we also realized why the older "good Samaritans" had suggested we would be okay. We sprinted for the only open doorway that offered safety—the front door of the Lowell Police Station.

We rushed in and sat down. Outside the young crowds were in an uproar. The violence against the march was quickly replaced by a joyful explosion of youthful revolt against authority as the crowd began to attempt to storm the police station. We were forgotten in a surge of rebellion directed at the police. Worried police broke out black helmets and chest protectors and—looking ominously anonymous and slightly robotic—charged past us to protect the front of the station. Shortly a few cops went into the back room and came out with shotguns. As the lethal violence of the state was made manifest, we sat there, silent, unsettled, attempting to pull ourselves back together.

Everyone was too busy to pay attention to us.

We watched, pained and miserable, as two of the police in riot gear dragged in a young man, one pulling him by the arms, the other alternating between pushing him and beating him with his baton. The young man, in bell-bottom jeans, brown hair down to his shoulders, his band-emblazoned tee shirt now torn, screamed at the cops as he was dragged along the floor, "Get off me you fucking pigs!" Each yell occasioned more beating. They dragged him past us and into the back to the cells. Amy and I found it hard to sit there, to do nothing. But the alternative seemed to be to leave, and outside the crowd was raging. We sat, silent, ashamed.

Every few minutes, policemen would return from out front, dragging another young man from the crowd outside. Soon we could hear screams coming from the cells in the back as furious police vented their anger on the rebellious kids. Slowly the crowds were beaten back from the front of the police station. More prisoners were dragged swearing and screaming into the station and some were worked over in the back.

The State Police Red Squad, smiling, obviously quite pleased with the results of their work, strolled in and started to mock us.

A young distant cousin snuck in to check if we were all right. We were physically bruised, but what hurt was sitting in that police station watching kids being worked over. We continued to sit. And as we sat, saying nothing, I thought, *This is upside down. The young people of Lowell are in revolt, are being beaten by angry cops, and they want to kick the shit out of us.*

The momentary youth revolt burned out, doused in part by the arrests. Slowly calm settled. We could no longer hear the noise of angry crowds outside. Still, we continued to sit. After a time, a small trickle of young men and a few young women made their way into the station hoping to get friends released.

Soon we were joined on our bench by a group of men in their mid-twenties, there to collect their friends. They did not know who we were and assumed we were there for the same reason.

The one sitting closest to me asked in a friendly tone: "Have you heard when the cops are going to release people or are they actually holding them for processing?"

"I am not here for a friend. Nope I haven't heard anything about timing. Who are you here for?"

"We're here for some of the guys we work with. All of us work together."

"Oh," I asked, "were you and your friends breaking up the antiwar march? Was that why your pals were arrested?"

He laughed and gestured toward the rest of his group down the bench.

"No. We thought the march was all fucked up, but we don't like the war either. We were just watching what was going on but when the cops tried to arrest some of us, well, then it was all in. You know. We don't let anyone push us around."

I asked where they all worked.

"We all work at the GE plant," he said.

I asked about how that work was and what they thought of their union. Good jobs, they said. Decent pay and bennies. Decent union.

"Well," I said, "my wife here—Amy—and I helped organize the march tonight."

"Shit you don't say!"

"Yes, we are dead opposed to the war. I hate that so many guys from Lowell have to go fight that war and you know the sons of the rich don't go. I think the war is wrong and I don't want to see another American die over there for no reason at all."

"Amen brother," came the response.

"You know," he said, bringing the rest of his buddies into the conversation, "we all served in Nam. We don't support the fucking war. We know what's going on."

"So why did you hate the march?" I asked.

They listed their reasons in rapid and compelling order: "You marched under the flag of the Vietcong who killed our buddies. We actually respect the Vietcong; they're tough motherfuckers but it disrespects our dead, our fight, and us to march under that flag."

There was nothing I could say. I thought about all the years of hating the war and then hating the government that prosecuted it. I thought of how we had steadily slipped into a rage and in that rage, it seemed that we wanted to take the most extreme position of opposition that we could. How could I explain my path from loving the Declaration of Independence and believing in American exceptionalism to marching with National Liberation Front (NLF) flags? I didn't bring them or wave them. I didn't chant "Ho Ho Ho Chi Minh, NLF is gonna win." But I had been totally comfortable marching with my pals who did. How could I explain any of that to these guys? How could I make sense of it myself?

They went on: "You had a group of women all march together and taunt us. What is that about? Trying to make us feel as if we are not men. Trying to provoke us? Well, you succeeded. And then some of the women were waving the Vietcong flag and waving posters of Ho. What the fuck was all that about? That was fucking insulting us, insulting our sacrifices and mocking our lives that was what that was all about."

Again, I had no response. I felt sick to my stomach. I liked these guys.

Then, one of them stated with finality, "And you don't come from here."

"Well," I said, "it's true we don't live here now, but my father was born right on Fletcher Street in the Acre and grew up here."

That seemed to make me and by extension Amy somewhat less foreign. Also it was as if the act of listening respectfully while they explained what we had done wrong, had created a bond at least for that moment on that strange spring night.

I smiled at them and said, "I hear you. We respect you and we respect your sacrifices. Really, we do. We want to make sure that no one else has to go over there. You know we have spent so much time opposing this damn war, that sometimes we just get carried away. But I hear you. We should have been marching under the American flag. I hear you. We love our country, but we hate this fucking war—and we hate the people who sent you over there. The ones who sit in their nice offices and send others off to kill and die."

As we sat on that hard wooden bench in the Lowell Police Station, waiting for their friends to be released, we relaxed into talking about everything; did we like the Stones; what did we think could stop Richard Nixon; we all agreed he was no good. Amy asked more about their experiences in Nam, and they shared stories, some funny, some frightening. We made the point that many Vietnam veterans were joining the antiwar movement. They weren't sure that they could do that since they didn't want to dishonor the sacrifices of their friends who had died there. But they were against the war so maybe. But what about those damn flags and the women?

Amy tried to talk about why women were marching together and how it was time for the roles of women to change. Their response to that was at best skeptical. Then we asked about their experiences with the police and that produced an outburst of profanity and more stories. We listened more than we talked.

After their friends were finally released, many battered, they introduced them to us. As we all got up to leave, they made a point of protectively walking us to our car to ensure that we did not get into any more trouble. Both Amy and I felt totally thrown off-kilter. The embarrassment and the irony of being in that police station was intense. The idea that the police had protected us from young Americans who also opposed the war but were insulted by us was profoundly upsetting.

I recognized their truths. How would I feel if my closest friend had been killed in Vietnam? I would hate the war that killed him. But I would not respond to anyone marching under the flag of the enemy. I understood how disrespectful and challenging we seemed. As much of a feminist as I thought myself, I also understood that there was a discussion and a process needed to get American men to change. Confronting men with chanting brigades of women just might not be the best way to get that discussion started. We needed to listen as much as we talked. More than anything else we needed to be respectful of the people we wanted to reach and organize—and we were going about it in the wrong way. I felt I had just seen how much I had to learn. I liked and respected those young men who sat on the bench next to us that night. I felt despair that the student and antiwar movements would ever be able to change enough to reach them. I also felt new hope that they could be reached. I was determined to learn a better way to organize.

Ira and the other organizers went out onto the streets of downtown Lowell the next day. Their audacity so impressed the group that had broken up the march, that a meeting was set up. Slowly trust was built. Gauthier and his guys realized that they had been played. They promised to protect the next antiwar march in Lowell, and they did. No one had the audacity to explain that with them on our side, there would be no one to protect the march from.

DORCHESTER AND THE PEOPLE FIRST

The halting pathway to becoming a better organizer had already begun prior to the march in Lowell. Throughout 1969 my bifurcated life had spun on. I was organizing and participating in ever more militant protests, and at the same time, I continued to seek ways to spread the antiwar movement into the communities whose families were paying the steepest price, the blue-collar and low-income neighborhoods that continued to send their young men into the machine of war.

I had helped convince teams of student activists to move to the blue-collar cities of Lowell, Lynn, Worcester, and Fall River. That was how Ira and his team had gone to Lowell. Miles Rapoport led a team to Lynn where, in one of the more humorous moments of those bleak years, they passed out leaflets to high school students reprinting an R. Crumb comic. They were arrested and charged with sedition (under a law dating back to the early 1800s) and corrupting the morals of minors. The case was thrown out by an angry judge who declared it should never have been brought, and they continued to organize both high school students and local college students.

Overall, the strategy of focusing on state and community colleges began to pay off. When I wasn't leading demonstrations and the occasional riot, I was meeting with students, especially returning Vietnam vets, at Boston State, the new U Mass Boston, Quincy Community College, and Quinsigamond Community College. I had been hopeful that students in these colleges would lead us back to their working-class neighborhoods and indeed, that began to happen. Soon I was in taverns and on street corners, talking about the war and how to exist in this fucked-up world. Now those conversations were with people who had never dreamed of attending Harvard or, often, any college at all.

One muggy August evening in 1969, I stood on a corner of Ronan Park in Dorchester. The park was on the top of a hill, from which one could see all the way to the harbor. Around me were a group of young and restless residents of the neighborhood.

They felt the rebelliousness that had seized so many under the age of twenty-five. Joints were passed around; the smoke hung in the hot evening air. A raw energy pulsed through the group. The conversation jumped all around, music and dope and the war and the "fucking cops." Buddy O'Connor, talking fast, always moving, jiggling, his narrow face framed by long, wispy brown hair and his younger brother Mikey, golden handsome in leather jacket and goatee, wanted to know if I was free that weekend. They were getting a group of friends together for what they had heard was going to be a "freakin' great" free concert in Woodstock, New York. "Come with us," urged Buddy. "All the bands are going to be there. A whole group of us are going to go right after work and convoy all night. Come on. It's going to be a trip."

I passed. I liked the music, but I didn't have the time to go traipsing around to a concert in New York. I had more organizing to do.

This group had reached out to us through Seamus Glynn, a Dorchester student at UMass Boston. Seamus, a river of red hair down to his waist, skin as white as lace, whip smart, had been active against the war. He heard of the endless conflict with the police going on in Ronan Park and talked with acquaintances there, telling them about us.

Since then, I had been dropping by regularly to talk with the Ronan Park kids. Their fathers were electricians, plumbers, butchers in supermarket meat departments, construction workers, and welders. Their mothers were nurses or telephone operators. They all came from large families and were always introducing me to siblings. The guys habitually wore leather jackets and bell-bottoms. Many had short beards, some ponytails. The girls also wore bell-bottoms, or short shorts and often psychedelic swirled t-shirts. Their world revolved around music, their friends, and dope.

They were furious that a few cops were forever chasing them from the park and from their street corners. They hated the war. Some were vets. Some were just released from "juvie." Most still lived in their parents' homes, feeling cramped, stultified. There was a constant, repressed anger. They were determined that they would not become their parents.

Soon they came with me to the *Old Mole* offices on Brookline Street where they produced a leaflet calling on kids to stand up to the cops, to fight police harassment. I helped them produce the leaflet but insisted that they write the

FIGURE 40.   Younger kids hanging at Ronan Park. ©Michael Dobo/Dobophoto.com

content. "It needs to be yours, your words." Then we discussed how they could organize, how they could be part of the rebellious movement rocking the country. They thought it sounded cool but first they had a concert in Woodstock.

A year later, Amy and I had moved to Dorchester to live and organize.

Dorchester was the largest neighborhood in Boston proper, home to a solid core of working-class families, living in the traditional three-deckers that predominated. It was as tribal as the rest of Boston in those days, with distinct neighborhoods. One was unlikely to say, "I come from Dorchester." White working-class families would more often say they came from St. Peter's, or St. Mark's, or one of the other Catholic parishes that had been the core of their lives for decades. Or if you were not Catholic, you might describe yourself as living in Uphams Corner, Savin Hill, Fields Corner, Meetinghouse Hill, Mount Bowdoin, Neponset, or any one of the fifteen neighborhoods in Dorchester.

In 1969 Dorchester was experiencing rapid change. The areas around Franklin Park that had been a predominately Jewish neighborhood for the last sixty years were now being emptied of white families as African American families moved in. Real money could be made by turning the neighborhood over, with older residents being frightened into white flight by real estate brokers, bankers, and speculators so that they would reduce the selling price of their homes, and Black families being charged a premium to buy them.

Throughout Dorchester, white families were thinking the unthinkable: picking up and moving south to Quincy, Weymouth, Brockton and Abbington. The Catholic parishes, still strong, were losing their appeal for younger people. The old order that had held sway for decades was fraying. Older white working-class families had grown up in Dorchester with a set of certainties. They would vote for the candidates that the local Democratic Party ward leaders told them to vote for—and they could expect to be taken care of. They could expect that their sons would get jobs in the police or fire departments, other city positions, or the utility or phone company; or in the building trades, at the post office, at Gillette, or one of the insurance companies downtown, jobs with pensions and benefits. Their daughters could expect to become teachers, secretaries, nurses, and directory assistance operators—and mothers.

Now everything was changing. Their sons were coming back from a war that they did not understand, coming home with an unusual bitterness. The political machine was declining and, while still asking for their votes, was not providing access to solid jobs. The economy was uncertain. Recent mayors seemed more interested in urban renewal and placating downtown business interests than in the politics embodied for so long by James Curley, under whom, as my friend Marty Hanley once said, "It was one for the people and one for James Michael—and that was one more than the people have ever gotten before or since!"

In many parks and street corners, each weekend brought running skirmishes between kids who just wanted to be left alone to party with their friends, drink beer, smoke joints, and listen to music, and a segment of cops who felt it was their duty to rigidly enforce laws against underage drinking, public drinking, and dope smoking. An increasing number of the police who patrolled Dorchester had moved to the suburbs, coming back to what they derogatorily referred to as "the jungle" (even the white parts of the city). In past decades, the men who patrolled the streets of Dorchester had lived in Dorchester, were part of the parish, were rooted in the community. It used to be that when a Dorchester cop saw a Dorchester kid causing trouble, he would first haul them home to their parents. Now most of the cops didn't know the kid's family and simply hauled him to jail.

The young people of Ronan Park continued to clash repeatedly with the police. They were furious at the continual harassment, especially from one clueless motorcycle cop, Vinnie, who they took great delight in taunting, as well as claiming that his brother was a "mobbed-up arsonist." They and Seamus Glynn, who had first brought us to Dorchester, were the heart of our initial efforts. Buddy, the eldest of three brothers, was fast talking and rebellious. He understood class and lack of opportunity. He was torn between a desire to simply smoke and sell dope and a desire to make change. Seamus and Buddy rapidly helped us launch a new organization that we named The People First (TPF), ironically the same initials as the Boston Police Tactical Patrol Force, the toughest of the cops.

Our little band of organizers spent time hanging with kids on street corners, talking with vets outside variety stores, talking about the war in veterans' posts, knocking on doors, sitting in people's kitchens. We had no set organizing methodology. But we did attract a growing and eclectic group. Soon we had a headquarters on Bowdoin Street, once the thriving commercial heart of Meeting House Hill and St. Peter's parish, now with only a few active stores and many boarded up vacant storefronts.

Amy and I first moved into a house on Bloomfield Street and started a commune. It was not long before it was a disaster. We had our group of organizers living communally and soon some of the most dysfunctional young people joined us, often stoned and occasionally violent. Amy and I left that ill-fated experiment to move into a triple-decker just down the street from Ronan Park. I took a job working the late shift, pumping gas at an all-night Sunoco station on Gallivan Boulevard. My real job, of course, continued to be organizing in Dorchester and with the larger antiwar effort.

As we talked with people in the neighborhood, we realized that the lack of a real grocery store was an issue. Why couldn't we create our own food distribution system, one that rejected profit and instead was a co-op? Such ventures were starting up in affluent counter cultural enclaves. Why not in a blue-collar neighborhood?

We started a small, fast-growing food cooperative. Each week we would get up to be at the Chelsea wholesale vegetable market by 5 a.m.; drive back to Dorchester loaded with fresh vegetables, bread, and other staples; and lay them out in the storefront. Co-op members came and purchased their food at drastic discounts. Everyone had to contribute a portion of one day a month as a volunteer. Soon we had young mothers and older women coming into the storefront for the food and to debate ideas and politics with us. Parochial schoolgirls from St. Peter's in their plaid skirt school uniforms regularly helped out. Welfare mothers started to depend on the co-op and on us. Soon Donna Finn, petite in body but large in presence with a personality matching her fiery red hair, was a fixture in the store front. A group of women who had husbands, sons and loved ones in prison, began a discussion group, often led by Donna. In another corner, by long loaves of Italian bread, you might find an argument going on about how to best end the war. In the back a group of tenants would be composing a leaflet targeting an absentee landlord who refused to fix up their property. Dusty Maguire, a recently returned Vietnam vet would race up on his ever-present bicycle in cutoff shorts, bearing the news of the most recent outrages, determined to organize against the war. Soon Dusty had formed a local group of Vietnam Veterans Against the War.

The storefront hummed and buzzed, and soon those less marginal, older, and deeply curious residents could not stop themselves from dropping by to check out the strange happenings in the recently vacant but now busy storefront.

TPF had no real structure. It had no formal members. We published a sporadic newspaper of the same name. We brought Dorchester residents to antiwar demonstrations.

We were denounced by the established community leadership. Over time some of them began to open up to us even as others were convinced that we represented everything that was going wrong with the country and the neighborhood.

Ira Arlook, relocating from Lowell, worked with two well-established leaders from the Savin Hill neighborhood, Jim Canny and Peg Moran, to organize a community meeting about the war with Howard Zinn, a well-known Boston University antiwar professor, as the speaker. Many in the packed hall supported the war, but they were willing to listen in part because of the respect so many had for Jim and Peg. Jim was the head of the local neighborhood association and Peg was the driving force behind the local health clinic. Both had turned against the war. Peg and her son participated in antiwar protests where her husband, a Boston police detective, would be working the other side.

In less than two years, TPF became part of the political and social landscape of the community, albeit somewhat of an outlier. Ira and Donna Finn were part of the first task force formed by UMass Boston as it worked with the community to plan the new campus on Columbia Point. The group of women with loved ones in prison formed a prison support group that would outlast TPF. The storefront became a meeting place for kids and the rebellious of all ages.

I was particularly drawn to the returning veterans and was welcomed into their community. We often met at taverns to discuss the war, their experiences, the challenges of adjusting to being back, or sometimes just to drink beer, talk about sports and music and their wives and girlfriends. Many times, they wanted to know about the antiwar movement, why I did what I did, and if I had been in the military. They often thought the story of my predraft physical was hilarious; after all they knew that scene all too well; they remembered the day they reported to their physical in the same South Boston army base. Sometimes they wanted to have deep metaphysical discussions, what it meant for America not to win a war, how to think about what they had been a part of, how to honor the sacrifices of so many of their best friends.

The evening is blustery, dark, and cold. The few of us out walking are blown like sail boats being driven onto a reef. I am walking across Columbia Road in Upham's Corner to keep an appointment arranged on a street corner several days before. I can see the neon lights twinkling in the small window of my destination calling me to warmth and light—and a meeting with a small group of vets who all work together at the local utility company. This tavern is where they are to be found most evenings—and it is a tavern not a bar. Bars serve women and men. Taverns, including ones like Reilly's, which is attached to a bar, are exclusively for men. I pass O'Brien's Liquors, pass the closed Strand Theatre, and arrive at my destination. As I open the door the light spills out onto the darkened street. Framed in the brightness is a large man standing inside the open door, his right hand pulled back into a fist ready to punch me. I stand silently and look at him. I realize the whole tavern is quiet, watching what is happening. The man facing me lowers his fist, turns around, and the whole establishment breaks out into catcalls and laughter as he slowly walks over to the bar, puts his head down onto his folded left arm and with the other, starts slowly pounding the polished wood, repeating in a despairing voice, "Just my fucking luck, just my dumb fucking luck. . . ."

I say nothing. I have no idea what is happening. The place is an uproar. I locate the guys I am to see, who are also roaring with laughter. They quickly rise from their round table in the corner to offer me congratulatory whacks on the back and tell me the guy sitting despondent at the bar, head in his hands, will stand me a beer.

They quickly fill me in. The guy at the door had taken a $5 bet that he would slug the next guy who came through the door regardless of who it was. I was the next guy. In a remarkable miscalculation, he decided that I—the large, husky, young man standing framed in the dark, wearing a leather jacket—was too tough to mess with. Ironically, I was probably the only person to walk through that door that evening whom he could have hit with complete impunity. But appearances count, and I looked as tough and as serious as these young guys who fought in Vietnam, who now make a place for me in their circle at their habitual table in the tavern, welcoming me into their battle-tested company.

Jimmy Kelly was typical of the best of the returned veterans I met in Dorchester. Smart, loyal, fearless, and abused by the country's leaders over and over again. I met Jimmy one evening outside of the Geneva Street Spa. He was sitting on a milk carton. Jimmy had jet-black hair and startling blue eyes. He sees me passing out a leaflet about the war and stands up, says, "Sure, man" and then reels off a string of initials and words that I can barely decipher as they come tumbling out. "FTA coup qualified Dinky dau FUBAR BOHICA, yeah FTA!" I understood that FTA meant "Fuck the Army" and sat down to chat with him. His story was not atypical. I hope I remember it accurately: into the marines right after high school, enlisted with his best friend, long tour of duty in Nam. His best friend was the radio man and like so many radio men was killed, dying beside Jimmy.

So, Jimmy re-ups for a second tour and insists on being the radio man. Humps his way through battle after battle. Finally begins to ask what this is all for and for that, gets disciplined. Ends up serving time in the brig. Hates the politicians that sent him and his friends to fight the wrong war in the wrong place in the wrong way. Now home, married, expecting a kid, and starting work at UPS, he would join our efforts and the Vietnam Veterans Against the War. I always think of Jimmy when I think of the best Americans. Honest, direct, courageous.

As impressed as I was by so many of these smart young Dorchester men and women, I also encountered many who bounced along on the edge of violence and a rage that would inevitably destroy them. I would come home stunned at the waste, the unbelievable waste, of so much promise. Tragedies abounded. For example, there were two young men from Meetinghouse Hill who had been peripherally involved in TPF, both strong, vibrant, and fucked up. They were the closest of buddies, inseparable. Both fathers were butchers at a Stop & Shop, and they fully expected to follow in their footsteps. One night they are playing cards and tripping on some powerful hallucinogenic cocktail washed down with copious alcohol. One thinks the other is cheating. The argument sends them to more drugs and more alcohol and stokes more hallucinatory anger. One grabs a shotgun from behind a closet door and "blew the other way." In the morning, the survivor not only had to face a lifetime in prison but also the overwhelming guilt of murdering his best friend and for no reason at all.

So many people, so much talent, so many unrealized dreams, locked in a desperate struggle to just get through the day, through the week. It was not surprising that so many young people, especially the ones drawn to us, wanted a way out, wanted a different life. Feisty, creative, spirited, they were willing to march against the war, drop everything and head for the summer mud fields of Woodstock, and get up early to drive to Chelsea's wholesale food depot. They were excited about learning how to put out their own newspaper and spreading it all over Dorchester. They engaged in numerous small acts of disobedience and confrontation. When the police insisted that they leave a park, more often than not they refused. They were wild and rebellious, and TPF was their way to express exactly how far they were willing to go.

Steadily more Dorchester folks, especially young ones joined in with TPF. Their parents told them not to go near us. The cops warned them. Still, they came and helped mount campaigns against high utility rates, and tackled absentee slum landlords. They worked with us to organize forums and marches against the war. But in a surprise to me and the other organizers, the real heart of what we did became the risky campaign to take on Jerome Troy, the chief justice of the Dorchester District Court. And that was driven completely by the young of Dorchester who refused to surrender to either fear or complacency.

I had never heard of Judge Troy before moving to Dorchester. Then we encountered kids who had been hauled before him and been shaken down by the bondsman in cahoots with the judge. We even heard from a few of the police who were furious that violent offenders could buy their way back to the streets. It was common knowledge that if you secured the services of the right bail bondsman, paid him the amount quoted, you could walk free. The word on the street was that murder cost "twenty-five big ones." For minor offenses you might have to provide a service for the judge. Troy thought nothing of forcing construction workers to do work on his home. As he came in to work, he would stop in at the stores near the courthouse in Codman Square, without paying, taking whatever pastry or product struck his fancy, as if he were the king of Dorchester.

Often a mother receiving welfare appeared before him; perhaps her child was truant, perhaps she was in a legal dispute with a landlord. Judge Troy frequently demanded that the mother tell him the name and location of the father of her child. He would then issue a bench warrant for his arrest for nonsupport. If the mother refused, or did not know where the father was living, it was not unusual for Judge Troy to cite the woman for contempt of court and have her fined or locked up for several days, the consequences for her young children be damned.

As the *Boston Globe* would headline in 1973: "From a poor beginning, he progressed to two houses, yacht, Cadillac and frequent vacations in 10 years on the bench."[1]

For the young in Dorchester, Troy stood for all authority—corrupt, arbitrary, and not worthy of their respect. At a series of meetings, Buddy and his wilder, youngest brother Mikey argued for launching a campaign.

"C'mon," Buddy argued, "Troy sucks. He is everything we are opposed to. We have to take him on."

A few others quietly voiced their fears.

"Troy can send any of us away and no one will stop him."

"He is too powerful. He has the cops in his pocket. We aren't strong enough."

Buddy, Seamus, and Donna Finn were not persuaded. "We need to put him on trial. Okay, we cannot try him in a court of law, but we can try him in the people's court."

"We cannot let him scare us. That's what is so fucked up. Everyone being scared by Troy and his buddies. It's way past time for a change."

After several chaotic meetings, it was clear that most of our folks were willing to tackle Troy. Once the decision was made, the news that we dared to take on Troy spread rapidly, crackling through the community.

When we first launched our campaign against Troy, we did not understand that in the 180-year history of the Commonwealth of Massachusetts, no judge had ever been removed by a popular campaign. In Massachusetts a judge could be impeached by the House and convicted by the Senate—and with Troy being a product of the Democratic cabal that controlled the legislature, that was not going to happen. The governor could remove a judge but that required the consent of the Governor's Council, and the members of the council were all old cronies of Troy's.

Still the young people of Dorchester were determined to do something. We passed out literature. At first everyone was amazed at our audacity. They fully expected that Judge Troy would have us all hauled before him and sent away. When that did not happen, we began to gather significant support.

One day as I was arranging tomatoes, lettuce, and cantaloupes for the food co-op, two middle-aged men in fedoras, suits, and heavy overcoats came into our dingy storefront, looking like noir detectives out of the 1940s. The smaller of the two never said a word. The other, heavily muscled, chewed on a toothpick and asked questions. No names were given. He wanted to know how seriously we wanted to get Troy. I explained that I thought Troy was the embodiment of the corruption of American justice. Suddenly he turned on me: "You think you know Jerry Troy? You don't know nothing!"

I was slightly taken aback and replied, "Okay, I am willing to learn more. How would I learn more?"

"You sure you have the balls to take him on? Will you stick with it or when it starts to involve important people, will you cut and run?"

I answered, "I don't care who his pals are. I have never backed down from a fight in my life, and I am sure as hell not doing so now. We're going to get him, and if you're a friend of his, it's too bad."

That produced a loud emphatic snort. "You really don't know shit, do you? I know all there is to know about Jerry Troy, that fucker. You want to learn more, you meet me at ten p.m. at the Venetian Gardens two nights from now, and I will tell you about Jerry Troy. Be there."

And with that the two of them left.

The Venetian Gardens was a dive of a bar between Upham's Corner and the South End near the old meat-packing area. Seedy and dimly lit, it stayed open late. I was a little concerned at first. Was this some sort of setup?

But in the end my curiosity was too much. I learned the story of how Troy became a judge, and I made the most unlikely ally and friend I could ever have imagined.

Martin J. Hanley was a remarkable man. He had started out in politics with Mayor James Michael Curley, whom he idolized with a clear eye. In 1958 when John Thompson, the "Iron Duke" from Ludlow in Western Mass, became the speaker, Marty was his "bag man," the one collecting the bribes and payoffs. He was given the position of commissioner of small loans.

In 1962, as Marty told it, the Yankee establishment, determined to roll back the rising tide of Irish political power, created the Massachusetts Crime Commission. One of their major targets was Thompson, and the best route to get him was through Marty. They indicted Marty on forty-seven counts of bribery and conspiracy. (Marty would say to me, "I have committed many crimes, just not the ones they charged me with.") They also indicted Thompson, forcing his resignation in 1964.[2] Thompson died before coming to trial. Attorney General Edward Brooke, who would ride the Crime Commission all the way to the US Senate, continued to press Hanley to strike a deal. In 1966, Marty proposed that he would testify before the grand jury if, and only if, he would be allowed to share everything he knew including about those in the Massachusetts Senate. A document was written up codifying this agreement and placed in a safety deposit box at the US Trust Company. Hanley's attorney, Robert Muse, was given one key and the assistant attorney general Herbert Travers the other.[3] The box could only be opened with both keys.

When Marty went before the grand jury, he was betrayed. No testimony was allowed about those in the Senate. Furious, Marty repudiated his testimony knowing that he would face many years in prison. He defended himself in what became the longest lasting court proceedings in the history of Massachusetts. Marty became a committed truth teller determined to wreak vengeance or seek redemption; I was never clear which.

Of course, I knew none of that when I met him in the smoky, dank Venetian. The lights were low and the place almost empty as I greeted the two men from the storefront. I still was completely uncertain as to who they were and what to expect.

We walked to the back of the bar and sat at a grungy table. Marty, shedding his coat and taking off a hat to reveal his shiny, shaven head, ordered a whiskey and a beer chaser, and then immediately launched into a long soliloquy, posing questions and then answering them at great length. I didn't need to say much.

"How did Jerry Troy get to be a judge? He bought his judgeship by paying twenty-five thousand dollars to Sonny McDonough who controlled the Governor's Council. Outgoing governor Volpe appointed Troy with four minutes left in his term as part of a deal engineered by 'Sonny.' How do I know this? Simple, I arranged it. I set the amount and negotiated the deal for Jerry Troy, that ungrateful son of a bitch." The shadows played across Marty's large head as he reared back and said, "You want to know about Jerry Troy? I will tell you about Jerry Troy."

Marty then went on at length about Troy's corruption. It became clear that he had been a pal of Troy, but somewhere during Marty's trials and tribulations, Troy had proved an ungrateful and disloyal friend. Now Marty would do everything he could to bring the man down.

Armed with information from Marty, we released a special edition of TPF, our episodic newspaper, blaring the scandal that was Troy from the very first day he became a judge. The response was raucous. Our audacity amazed many and inspired more to join the campaign.

The lawyers of the Boston Legal Assistance Project (BLAP) were critical to unseating Troy. Several would go on to become judges. At that time, they were young, idealistic, dedicated to serving the poor. We formed relationships with two BLAP offices. The first was the Fields Corner office, where a young, dynamic lawyer named Paula Gold was at work and the secretary was Ruth Gottschalk. The other BLAP office was in Grove Hall, where Michael Feldman and other young attorneys represented many welfare mothers in front of Judge Troy. They were appalled at his treatment of them.

We knew we could never get the legislature to remove Troy; he frequently took long vacations with groups of reps and senators. The judicial system had no internal way to remove a judge. However, we learned that if we could get Troy disbarred, he could not remain a judge.

The activists of TPF spread out across Dorchester, knocking on doors, standing in front of supermarkets, reaching out to their friends on street corners, in taverns and in the parks, even talking with their parents. The message was clear: it was time to get rid of Troy. They convinced 10,000 people to sign a petition asking for Troy's removal.

A TPF delegation went to the governor's office to demand that he act. He said his hands were tied. We brazenly picketed the courthouse. We held an Anti-Troy Day on Town Field in Fields Corner, with live bands, food, and a mock trial. Dorchester was abuzz; there was a sense that the young people of TPF were daring fate. Still more and more people agreed that Troy should go.

On September 30, 1971, lawyers from the BLAP representing TPF of Dorchester filed a petition with Chief Justice Franklin N. Flaschner of the Mass Supreme Court, a well-known reformer, alleging serious illegalities in Judge Troy's courtroom conduct. They submitted numerous affidavits from those victimized by Troy. In response Justice Flaschner launched an investigation. On April 20, 1972, Justice Flaschner released a damning report, substantiating the many charges we had made. Flaschner asked the Supreme Judicial Court (SJC) to act. The SJC replied it was up to Flashner. Judge Flaschner replied he did not have the authority to remove a judge. The SJC responded that he could reassign Troy, which he did, sending him to five different courts.[4] Encouraged, we were still determined to get Troy off the bench entirely.

The *Boston Globe* ran a series of exposés of Troy. Finally, under pressure from us and the SJC itself, the Massachusetts Bar Association took up Troy's disbarment. Defending Troy was Lawrence F. O'Donnell, a pugnacious lawyer

FIGURE 41. Gathering signatures to demand the judge Jerome Troy be removed. Courtesy of University Archives and Special Collections, Joseph P. Healey Library, University of Massachusetts Boston: Ann Raszmann Brown community organizations photographs.

famous through Boston for his aggressive defense of many cases that no one else would take. (His son of the same name would go on to become a progressive cable television news personality.)

Opposing him, the Bar Association brought in their own heavyweight, James St. Clair, the famed Hale and Dorr lawyer who first gained attention assisting Joe Welch in taking on Joe McCarthy in the Army McCarthy hearings. St. Clair came to this proceeding fresh off the defense of Richard Nixon in the Watergate mess. His choice was a clear message that the Bar Association found this whole affair an embarrassment and wanted it over quickly. Events moved with remarkable speed.

Troy was disbarred and forced off the bench. The governor nominated Paula Gold, the young crusading BLAP lawyer, to replace Troy. That was too much for Sonny McDonough, he who had sold Troy his judgeship and who still controlled the antiquated Governor's Council that had a veto over judicial appointments.

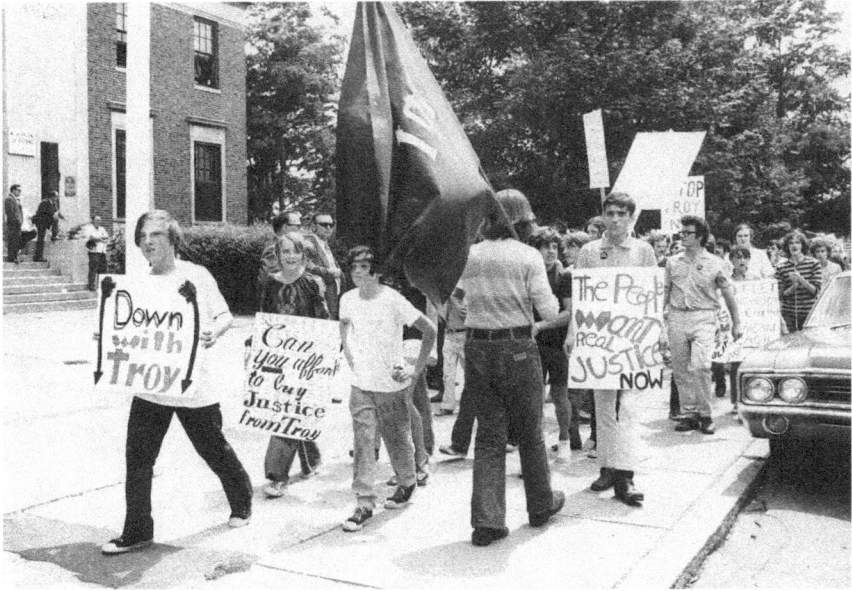

FIGURE 42. The People First (TPF) protesting Judge Troy. Photo by Sam Masotta/The Boston Globe via Getty Images.

He killed her appointment. In the end another BLAP lawyer, Jim Dolan, took Troy's place on the bench, and was a humane, fair, and honest judge.

TPF had done what had never been done before—launched a grassroots campaign that ended up unseating a Massachusetts judge.

Ironically TPF did not last to reap the benefits. While we were skilled at campaigns, we had not done the careful work of building the organization. While we were shedding some of the baggage of our student movement days, we still were confused about leadership and structure. We did not build organizational structures that developed leaders, tested them, and held them accountable. Instead of carefully cultivating leaders who had a base, who could turn out others to volunteer, to protest, to vote, we advanced anyone who was passionate. The young people most involved in TPF, for all their passion and courage, were frequently mercurial. In the end our campaigns, despite their creativity, were built on sandcastles that regularly washed away.

I realized, painfully, that I lacked the craft needed to build a deep, stable, community-based organization. Many of the Dorchester folks active with TPF stayed active in the community and politics for many years to come. But the actual organization was not sustainable.

HOW DOES A WAR END?

These are the times that try men's souls. The summer soldier and the sunshine patriot will, in this crisis, shrink from the service of their country; but he that stands by it now, deserves the love and thanks of man and woman.

—Thomas Paine

April 30, 1975, was a warm day in Boston. Spring was everywhere. The lilacs were blooming in the arboretum; tulips bursting in the public garden. The whole day was drenched in bright sun. I never stepped outside. I could not separate myself from the images on the television. For the last weeks, I had watched, in disbelief, as North Vietnamese forces rolled forward toward Saigon and toward the end of a war that had killed over 2,000,000 Vietnamese and 58,000 Americans and had dominated my life for so many years. I watched the crowded helicopters taking off from Saigon, frantic Vietnamese attempting to hang on to them. The jettisoning of those helicopters pushed into the South China Sea from the decks of American ships too crowded to keep them was a symbolic coda to a tragedy of waste: wasted lives, wasted treasure, wasted years.

All this was happening ten years since the first SDS March on Washington against that war. And for all those ten long years, there was rarely a day that I had not thought about what was unfolding in Vietnam, Cambodia, and Laos: the bombs, the napalm, the deaths, and more deaths. The damage done had been catastrophic. Millions dead, maimed, displaced. Damage to America. The country cleaved. The old Democratic coalition shattered. Lives disrupted. Hundreds of thousands of soldiers returned bitter. A generation of America's young frustrated and cynical.

Now that war was finally coming to an end, my main reaction was not so much relief as disbelief. Could this really, finally, be the end of the nightmare? I felt no elation, only sadness at all that had been lost. I could not even summon

FIGURE 43. Pushing a US helicopter into the sea after the fall of Saigon. CPA Media Pte Ltd / Alamy Stock Photo.

up any pride that I was a member of that group of Americans who had fought to the very end against the war, who had stayed the course.

Even as I worked with TPF in Dorchester, I had kept up organizing against the war. After that dramatic march in Lowell, I was determined to change how we were opposing the war. We once again embraced nonviolence. Instead of working to further divide the country, we sought to achieve a moral clarity that could unify the country in opposition to Richard Nixon's continuation of the war.

Our efforts, and my sanity, were helped along by the emergence of the Vietnam Veterans Against the War (VVAW). They had a credibility and a creativity that no one else could match. They had served. They had seen. They had wounds and medals. They knew how to deploy their experiences in a dramatic way, repeatedly creating powerful political theater.

In 1971 they staged a dramatic three-day march from Lexington and Concord to Bunker Hill, the reverse of Paul Revere's storied ride. Wearing remnants of their uniforms, often with their medals visible, they talked of the "winter soldiers," those whose commitment ran deepest, and invoked an American patriotism with long roots in the country's history. There was no question that these were patriots. Their very presence was a powerful statement. Later in Washington, when Vietnam vets from across the country assembled and physically returned their medals, symbols of sacrifice, service, and courage, it was a stunning act of bitter grace, a powerful indictment of the war and those who continued to prosecute

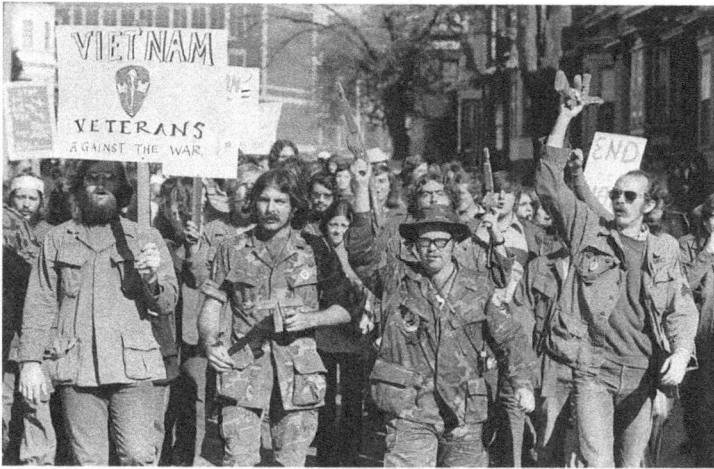

FIGURE 44.   Vietnam Veterans Against the War marching in East Boston, 1971. ©Michael Dobo/Dobophoto.com.

it. They would go on to hold a "Winter Soldier Investigation" documenting war crimes. Everything VVAW did was credible, dramatic, and effective. Always they were careful to evoke patriotism and American history, even as they made powerful and damaging charges against the prosecution of the war.

I had first met two New England organizers for VVAW in the offices of Mass Pax. Jerry Grossman was one of the great progressive leaders in Massachusetts. He had convinced H. Stuart Hughes to run and maintained Mass Pax after the campaign ended. He recruited Father Robert Drinan to run a successful antiwar campaign for Congress. He had been a driving force behind the creation of the Vietnam Moratorium. Jerry had also funded the Legal In-Service Project (LISP), which operated out of a back room of the PAX offices in Harvard Square. The LISP provided legal support and counseling to those in the military who wanted to speak out against the war, file for conscientious objector status, or defend their right to dissent. He had hired two young veterans to staff it, Bestor Cram and Art Johnson. They soon became the New England organizers for VVAW. Deeply impressed by them, I did what I could to connect them with the veterans I had met in Dorchester and elsewhere. I got to know the core of the local VVAW well, Art, Bestor, Chris Gregory, and Lenni Rottman. I was impressed with a young naval vet that they introduced me to, John Kerry. John was tall, patrician, and articulate. His role was to give moving speeches which he did superbly, and to convince wealthy donors to support VVAW. It was clear even then that John possessed a sense of personal destiny. No one was a more powerful speaker against the war than John.

FIGURE 45. VVAW. From left to right: Al Hubbard, John Kerry, Bestor Cram, Art Johnson. Photo by Ted Polumbaum/Freedom Forum's Newseum Collection.

These vets were the perfect antidote to our failings that were so visible that shocking night in Lowell. I was heartened by them and, even as we organized in Dorchester developing the campaign against Judge Troy, I was determined to keep the pressure on to end the war.

Nixon reduced opposition through a strategy of drawing down American troops, even as he increased bombing and invested even more heavily in pro–United States Vietnamese military forces. However, the invasion of Cambodia in the spring of 1970 provoked the largest antiwar demonstrations to date. A year later, more than half a million protestors flooded Washington. That massive April demonstration was then followed by "May Day" demonstrations that brought tens of thousands of protestors blocking roads and bridges throughout Washington.

The following year I helped organize a massive act of civil disobedience: a nonviolent sit-in at the federal building in Boston. On May 6, 1971, a sea of people marched through downtown Boston. Flooding into the plaza in front of City Hall, more than 5,000 of us surrounded the building. Those of us willing to be arrested sat down in the front. After the requisite demand that we disburse, the police began arresting people, dragging limp bodies into the building. At first, they were restrained but as time went on, they grew frustrated and began pulling protestors by the hair.

We had a tight system of our own marshals patrolling the crowd, making sure there would be no incitement by provocateurs, or from homegrown crazies. Small bands of cops had been instructed to find the leaders and arrest us as quickly as possible, hoping that might break the spirit of the crowd. I kept moving attempting to evade them. However, as our marshals kept coming to me to report, I was easy to spot.

Announcing that I was under arrest for trespassing, a policeman towered over me as I sat inside a small circle of friends. He lifted me up off the ground entirely by my nose, fingers in my nostrils, thumb pressed hard on top. I heard a soft crunch, a little pain, and ever since my nose has had a pronounced curve.

Arms pinioned behind, I was hustled through the crowd and into the lobby of the Federal building where commanders, the Boston Tactical Police Force, and the State Police "Red Squad" had a command station. My arrest sparked a small celebration, and congratulations were offered to the arresting officer, who was directed to turn me over to two members of the Tac Squad. Handcuffed, I was taken to the elevator to go down into the basement where the paddy wagons were taking those arrested on the very short ride to the nearby station for booking.

Once in the elevator, as we descended, one of the cops flipped off the elevator switch, stopping it between floors. I was suddenly aware how big these two policemen were.

"So, maggot, you like it when our boys get killed in Vietnam? In fact you want them to be killed, don't you, you fucking maggot?"

"No sir," was my polite reply.

"Yes, you do. You have no respect for our soldiers; you have no respect for our country; you want to burn our flag. You fucking maggot. You traitor."

"No sir. That's not right."

"You maggot. You're un-American. You love it when our boys die. You are a fucking disgrace."

"No sir. I am against the war but . . ."

Before I could finish, my jacket was pulled up over my head, and the two cops started to beat on me. The jacket over my head meant that when they did strike my head, no mark was left. Mainly they hit me where they were less likely to leave any telltale marks, and they did a good job. For days, I was quite sore but unmarked. Seeing me you would never have known I had received a beating.

After a couple of minutes, the elevator was turned on, and I was silently escorted down to the wagon and off to jail. All in all, not as bad as it could have been. The judges, faced with so many arrested protestors, issued continuances. If we were not arrested again within six months, all the charges would be dropped.

FIGURE 46. Police dragging protestor at federal building sit-in, May 11, 1972. Courtesy of the *Boston Globe* Library collection at Northeastern University Archives and Special Collections.

FIGURE 47. Frustrated police pulling those sitting in by their hair, May 11, 1972. Courtesy of the *Boston Globe* Library collection at Northeastern University Archives and Special Collections.

In our after-demonstration evaluation, there was one extremely upset participant whom I had not met before. Trim, clean cut, he kept talking about the shocking police violence. I tried to make the point that I thought given everything, the police had been relatively restrained. It was challenging to arrest hundreds of us, especially as many of us had gone limp, forcing them to drag or carry us inside the building. I got nowhere. I assumed the agitated man was a professor and that this was his first demonstration. It was always shocking to see for the first time young, white, middle-class kids getting arrested and being treated roughly by police. After the meeting broke up, I asked if anyone knew his name. Someone said, "Yeah—that is Dan Ellsberg. He used to work for the government."

The name meant nothing to me then. In a little over a month all America would know of him as the *New York Times* began publishing the Pentagon Papers provided by Dan. I would puzzle over how someone who had been to Vietnam, as he had, could be so shocked by the police actions at the sit-in. More importantly, I would feel enormous gratitude to him for stealing the internal Department of Defense study of the war that showed definitively that our government had lied and lied and lied about the war. His release of the Pentagon Papers, and the newspapers' willingness to publish them, became another critical turning point in the struggle to end the war.

Nixon resumed bombing of North Vietnam, and we were back again for another sit-in at the federal building on May 8, 1972. This time our numbers were even larger, as many as 10,000 protestors. Again, small teams of police combed the crowd looking to arrest the leaders before arresting others. However, this time, my experience was completely different—all because of one Boston cop whom I will call Billy C.

Billy C. was born and bred in Dorchester, one of ten brothers, remarkably all of whom served in Vietnam. Upon his return, he joined the Boston police. Unlike many other policemen he continued to live in Dorchester. He took seriously that he was a cop to serve and protect. I first heard about him when rumors circulated that there had been a fight between cops in the Fields Corner Precinct House and that Billy had taken on several cops now living in suburbia because of their contempt for Dorchester people. Over time I met him and every now and then, when he was off duty, we would have long talks about the war, Dorchester, and Judge Troy. He exuded a down-to-earth dignity. He could see that I was patriotic and cared about the guys who were forced to fight in Nam. He was reticent about his personal experiences over there, but it was clear they had affected him deeply. While Billy was quite short, taut, and wire thin, you could tell he was someone you would be making a huge mistake to tangle with. We were never close, but I developed a great deal of respect for him.

Now outside of the Federal Building, in the midst of the huge throng sitting in, I saw Billy C. in uniform approaching me. He whispered into my ear,

"Mike I will return in a few minutes to arrest you; you gotta trust me. Okay?"

I nodded okay.

"Listen when I grab you, I want you to squeal like a stuck pig, okay? And then keep yelling at me as I take you inside, okay? You gotta trust me. There are some Tac Squad guys who have plans to do you worse than last year. So just let me take you in. Okay? You got it?"

"Yup."

In a few minutes he came back, yelled something at me, grabbed me, and told me I was under arrest. Despite the obvious commotion we made, he was exceedingly gentle in his handling of me. As we started to enter the federal building itself, he held my arms more tightly behind my back and started to rant at me in a loud voice. Once again, the Tac Squad, the commanders, and the Red Squad were all there to congratulate him. Two of them told Billy he had done a great job, and they would take it from there.

At which Billy, the top of his head barely reaching to their shoulders yelled at them: "Do you think I served two tours in Nam, had my best friend blown away next to me, so that I could turn this maggot over to you. Fuck you! This one is mine, all mine. I arrested him, and I get to take him downstairs. This maggot is all mine!"

His vehemence brooked no response and swearing away at me, he dragged me to the elevator. Once inside with the doors closed, Billy politely stood me up and released me saying,

"Hey sorry if I twisted your arms a little. You okay?"

I assured him I was and that I greatly appreciated him taking care of me.

Downstairs, his performance was repeated with the cops processing arrested protestors, and I rode alone in a wagon with Billy there to ensure that no harm came to me. Billy did not represent a large segment of police in Boston in 1971 and 1972, but he was not completely alone in his sentiments.

Over the next three years, even as I increasingly focused on other issues, I continued to work against the war, always with Ira Arlook. Ira had an intensity to match my own. We made a good team. We refused to forget about the war even as American casualties dropped, the draft was ended, and dramatic headlines decreased.

Dropping American casualties did deflate much of the movement against the war. In 1973 Nixon signed an agreement to withdraw most US troops but continued to pour millions into supporting the newest South Vietnamese dictatorship.

With the draft ended, and large numbers of US troops brought home, most Americans wanted to forget the war and get on with life. There would continue to be significant demonstrations, but those were less frequent and drew fewer people. Still the war was not over.

There were only two ways for American military involvement in Indochina to end. First, the commander-in-chief, the president, could make the decision to withdraw all remaining forces, order a permanent end to the bombing, and end the war. The chances of Nixon and Henry Kissinger doing that seemed dim at best.

The second option was that Congress could exercise the power of the purse, cutting off the required funding for US military actions and for the South Vietnamese military. A large majority of the country was weary of the war. With Democrats controlling both the House and Senate, cutting off the funding for the war effort seemed the most rational path forward.

Ira was now working closely with Tom Hayden and Jane Fonda and a network of activists throughout the country to drum up support for ending funding for the war. Jane had created an antiwar tour of actors and musicians, FTA ("fuck the army"), that played to many GIs and returned military. They built on this to develop a barnstorming political and musical tour that drew huge crowds wherever they went. Those crowds then produced an outpouring of volunteers to lobby Congress and conduct voter education. We hired Larry Levin to work full-time lobbying Congress—something unthinkable for us even a few years earlier.

I worked with Ira on what became the Indochina Peace Campaign (IPC). We used the *Old Mole* space once again as our office. Our biggest contribution may have been carefully written educational pieces that went out to hundreds of thousands of voters. We were careful to jettison all the rhetoric that had characterized our efforts in 1968 and 1969. These large brochures made our case with fact-based argument, and were even footnoted, using information from the Pentagon Papers. They were distributed across the country in targeted congressional districts. They documented the millions of dollars going to prop up a dictatorship and support torture and murder of political opponents. They argued for Congress to cut off funding and finally, end the war for good.

Nixon won reelection overwhelmingly in 1972. We continued with our efforts. IPC conducted grassroots lobbying campaigns in key districts, setting up replicas of the fearsome Tiger Cages used to hold prisoners in South Vietnam. Soon Watergate would unspool American politics. With Nixon's political collapse, the Democratic Congress did steadily throttle down the funding of the war.

The war in Vietnam finally ended. Crowded helicopters took thousands of Vietnamese to the waiting ships in the South China Sea but left tens of thousands behind. On April 29, two young marines—Darwin Lee Judge and Charles

McMahon—became the last Americans to be killed in the war.[1] Both had been in the country less than two months. As in so much of this tragic war, the removal of their bodies was botched, and they would not come home for a year. When Saigon fell, waves of South Vietnamese fled.

Many of us who opposed the war had been guilty of romanticizing the National Liberation Front (NLF, the Vietcong to the rest of America), myself sometimes included. But we felt no satisfaction at their victory. A country defoliated with chemical weapons, the economy devastated, millions displaced, a culture corrupted and with hardline communists coming to power, Vietnam was in for hard times. With the war over I felt nothing but grief.

We knew that the war had been in part a civil war (one that would have been over quickly without US intervention). There would be hundreds of thousands of Vietnamese who had thrown in their lot with the Americans and now with the end of the war, faced "reeducation" camps and worse. We did, however, also read stories of trusted translators, guides, and drivers who turned out, after the war, to be working for the NLF all along.

While the war ended, the tragedy for Vietnamese continued. The refugee "boat people" of Vietnam poured out of their country, ignored, and abandoned by most Americans, including most of us in the antiwar movement.

In 1975 and in the years that followed, we, the people who had been the antiwar movement, should have been fighting for our country to do more to take care of those people. Thousands would make their way to the United States over time, but many would have a horrendous journey before arriving on our shores. We who opposed the war had the moral obligation to care about these victims of the war, as well as about the tens of thousands of Americans who were attempting to return to a normal life after the searing disruption of combat in Vietnam.

Our country, however, divided and scarred by the war, the protests, Nixon, and Watergate, wanted desperately to return to a normality of some sort, to move on. America had lost its first war, and most thought it would be better to forget it. Of course, that was impossible. There would be no return to the "normalcy" of the fifties. The divisions would fester and be a powerful undercurrent in American politics for decades.

With a few exceptions, those of us who fought against the war were also eager to move on. I certainly was.

TO BE AN ORGANIZER

After Lowell and my time with TPF in Dorchester, I wrestled with what changes I would have to make to be a more effective organizer.

As I thought about it, there was a major difference between being a *mobilizer* and someone who built effective organizations. The mobilizer gathers those who share a position, excites, energizes, and motivates them to spring into action and, hopefully, finds ways to sustain them throughout the actions and beyond.

The organizer, of course, builds organizations. I increasingly came to believe that an organizer should also be focused on changing people through the experience of collective action and organization.

Going back to my early experiences with the Boston Action Group, I thought people needed to realize that the problems that plague their lives, the problems that they have always believed were their fault, or were inevitable, or theirs and theirs alone, are, in fact, shared problems. Once they begin to realize their problems are not unique but shared, they can begin to look at how the source of those problems is not to be found in the stars, or within, or because of the "other," but are rooted in structures of power and wealth. That realization can then lead to the belief that the solution to these problems lies in collective organization and action.

I wanted to become an organizer who could build large organizations that would contest for power, change policies, win structural reforms, and *at the same time* become great schools of democracy.

As I looked back over the years of antiwar organizing, there were some things that I had done well. I had always tried to reach out to students who did not agree

FIGURE 48.   Me in 1972. ©Michael Dobo/Dobophoto.com.

with me. I had been empathetic, resonating to their doubts and fears. I had not, at least most of the time, been dismissive of those who disagreed with me.

I understood that if I wanted to be an effective organizer, I needed to be able to listen. I realized I had to have a deep-seated respect for those I wanted to organize, including those who initially disagreed with me.

That respect had to be expressed in a myriad of small ways. Off came the beard. I decided that clothes were only a costume. And those costumes are always chosen, unconsciously or deliberately, to communicate a message: difference, defiance, group membership, provocation, reassurance.

The changes I needed to go through, however, were far deeper than the external changes of clothes and haircut. I had to be able to go into an American Legion post with a deep appreciation for the lives and wisdom of men whose first instinct was to support the war. I needed to be able to sit in the home of a white family that might start a conversation about what was happening to their chang-ing neighborhood by blaming the newly arrived people of color. While I could never agree with their position and would never accede to derogatory language, my job was not to pick a fight with them—that would only confirm stereotypes. Instead, I had to understand what led them to think Black people were causing their problems and find a way, respectfully and empathetically, to engage them in a manner that opened up the discussion rather than closing it down.

The more I worked to become an effective organizer, the more I realized I had to push myself out of my comfort zone and leave behind my "safe space." Instead, I needed to listen, to learn, to see through the eyes of others. If you want to change people, you have no chance if you do not love them and respect them.

The challenge was to lose arrogance without losing passion and principle, to learn to hear without losing the vision of profound change, to become a radical who changed minds and created new possibilities.

There is nothing safe about being an organizer. There is nothing easy. There is nothing more challenging. And other than being a parent, there is nothing I have done in my life that was more rewarding.

Amy went to nursing school and became a licensed practical nurse working in hospitals and eventually neighborhood health clinics. She participated in organizing nurses against the war and in union organizing drives, as well as participating in the Dorchester work. We lived on the third floor of a classic triple-decker on Holmes Avenue in Dorchester, a few blocks down the hill from Ronan Park. Mark Dyen and Beth Reisen moved into the first floor. Mark had resurfaced after a stint doing things that I have never asked him about. He first returned to graduate school but then organizing drew him away from the university once again. Beth was an early SDS member who had organized with the Newark Emergency Economic Research and Action Project (ERAP). Now they were living together, soon to be married.

When I first arrived in Dorchester, all the "corners" along Geneva and Bowdoin had "spas" (small convenience stores). Outside of each a group of young men sat passing the time. They were all white. Most had served in Vietnam. Now they were back and having a hard time adjusting.

In a span of twenty-five years those very same corners would have a new set of young men and young women hanging out on the same streets, sitting on the same overturned milk crates, but they would be entirely Black and brown.

When we moved to Holmes Avenue that transition was just beginning. While we lived there the first Black family moved in. We had a stern conversation with the white kids that we knew, discussing how they would respond—or rather not respond. Otherwise, their first impulse would be to drive that family out of "their neighborhood." Our TPF engendered credibility was enough to prevent that.

Life for me was more settled than it had ever been. Late in the summer of 1973, Amy asked what I thought about us having children. I was ambivalent. Were we ready? Would movement work allow us to be good parents? How would our unsteady marriage make it through? We went off to a vacation in Cape Breton, Nova Scotia, hiked the trails, and camped on a beach with a waterfall cascading onto the sands, the waves trilling in. While I wondered if we would ever be ready, we tiptoed around the question of a baby.

Eight weeks after we returned to Dorchester, Amy announced she was pregnant. Our entire universe was altered. Those nine months were, for me, the best months of our marriage. I was convinced we were finally achieving what I had ached for all my life: I could not wait for the baby. Amy and I agreed that we would rent a cottage on an island off the coast of Maine and escape for the entire summer once the baby was born. I was in love with the thought of a family with a new baby—and had no clue as to the reality of newborns and the frequent condition of mothers of newborn babies. I had never thought about postpartum depression. I had not thought about sleep deprivation.

The birth went well. We named her Emma, perhaps for Jane Austen's Emma, perhaps for famed revolutionary Emma Goldman. Now with a child, Amy and I wanted a "real home." We found a gorgeous Victorian house on Melville Avenue at the midpoint between Codman Square and Fields Corner in a community composed of remarkable one- and two-family homes. Each of the homes had wonderful detailing, intricate wood paneling, built-in cabinetry, and wide yards. In the 1920s with the construction of the Dorchester District Court House on Washington Street, the neighborhood became home to up-and-coming lawyers, judges, union leaders, and other successful second-generation Dorchester families. By the 1960s the homes were now proudly owned by large blue-collar families (such as those of Donnie and Mark Wahlberg and Jordan and Jonathan Knight, who would go on to form New Kids on the Block).

We teamed up with Tom Davidson and Lillian Shirley to buy the two-family house at 41 Melville Avenue. We had met Tom and Lillian through antiwar work. They too had just had their first child, Sean.

Without realizing it, we were part of a process that would bring change to urban centers across the country—gentrification. When we purchased our house, many of the longtime white residents thought we were crazy as they expected the neighborhood to become a totally African American area over the next five to ten years. They told us property values would plummet. We were part of a steady influx of young, middle-class families who drove up property values.

Groups of citizen activists were springing up all over the city and around the state, fighting highways, airport expansion, advocating tenants' rights. The examples of the Civil Rights and antiwar movements had suggested a model for fighting for change even to people who disagreed with the goals of those movements.

A group of us created the Massachusetts Community Center and the Boston Community School, located in the old leather district near South Station. The school provided a wide range of classes for activists and leaders. The Massachusetts Community Center was what would now be called an "incubator." We supported new organizations just starting out.

For the first time, I got serious about raising money. I was able to find some remarkably generous donors, particularly several wealthy Cambridge women, who supported the center. We paid people, including me, minimal but real salaries.

Among the more successful initiatives was an organizing effort of women clerical workers launched by Karen Nussbaum and Ellen Cassedy.[1] They had been antiwar activists who supported their activism by getting clerical jobs at Harvard. They quickly recognized that women office workers were underpaid, treated poorly, and, with feminism percolating everywhere, ready to organize. Fusing their feminist insights and their movement activism into a successful organizing effort, they created 9 to 5, which advocated for equal pay, more promotion opportunities, better working conditions, and an end to harassment at the workplace.

With energy prices surging, the center helped launch CAP-Energy, a coalition of low-income organizations, community groups and newly formed consumer groups which campaigned for lower utility rates. Mark became its director.

Miles Rapoport, another SDS veteran who had gone to Lynn as part of an effort to organize in blue-collar communities, now went to Chicago to work in a neighborhood organization that was part of a network started by Saul Alinsky. Alinsky was a brilliant former union organizer who had applied the skills of union organizing to community organizing. He trained dozens of organizers who built deeply rooted, carefully structured community organizations with an emphasis on leadership development and creative tactics. One of those organizations was a city-wide effort in Chicago, CAP, that had attracted Paul Booth, the former SDS national leader. If it was something Paul wanted to do, I wanted to learn about it. I started studying Alinsky's strategies and the series of competing networks that evolved from his inspiration. Alinsky had died in 1972, so I met with his lieutenants and found them to be too arrogant and set in their ways. They dismissed me as a former student leader who had no real sense of how to organize. Despite that, I read everything I could about Alinsky's work and started to follow what the organizers he had trained were doing. Miles periodically filled me in on his organizing work in Chicago's Logan Square neighborhood.

I also connected with Heather Booth, Paul's wife, who had started a new training center for organizers in Chicago. Two years older than me, her life had often paralleled mine. While in high school she had joined the Congress of Racial

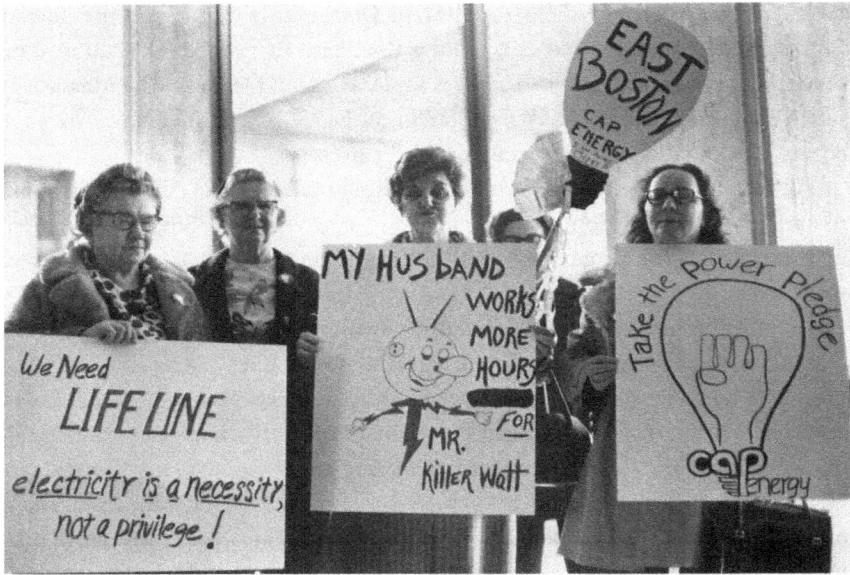

FIGURE 49. CAP-Energy protest. Photo by Bob Stanton/Courtesy of University Archives and Special Collections, Joseph P. Healey Library, University of Massachusetts Boston: Ann Raszmann Brown community organizations photographs.

Equality and then when she went to the University of Chicago, had thrown herself into the Friends of SNCC. At nineteen she had gone to Mississippi for the Freedom Summer. Back at college she was active in civil rights and SDS. She and Paul met when he dropped into a sit-in at the University of Chicago against the draft. Heather became a leading feminist and organized the Jane Collective, clandestinely assisting women to access abortions.[2]

In 1973, as I was starting to organize the Massachusetts Community Center, Heather founded the Midwest Academy to train organizers. As I felt my way forward toward a new kind of organizing, she and I connected, and I felt immediately I had found a kindred soul. Over the next years we would send organizers to study with Heather and her team at the academy, share thoughts on strategy, and help each other. Our friendship and mutual support have lasted all these years.

With support and leadership from a special group of Catholic priests, we began to explore what it would take to organize a city-wide, neighborhood-based organization in Boston. They were a new kind of priest, focused on social justice. They had come of age during the Civil Rights Movement. They went into parishes in

Roxbury, the South End, East Boston, and Charlestown and immediately participated in efforts such as stopping the proposed mega highway known as the inner belt which would have meant the bulldozing of thousands of homes and slicing up neighborhoods. They worked hard for more affordable housing.

Miles was confirming that we had a great deal to learn from the organizing that Alinsky organizers were doing. I also spent a significant amount of time, looking at the successes and failures of SNCC, SDS, and the antiwar movement. In that process I discovered an essay called "The Tyranny of Structurelessness" by Jo Freeman, a feminist and civil rights veteran, that clicked right away with me. While it was written initially about early women's organizations and consciousness-raising groups, it was clearly descriptive of my experience in SDS and the movement generally. So often I had been able to be a leader, unaccountable to any democratic forms, just by dint of being articulate. We claimed that "we have no leaders here." Yet we clearly had leaders—I had been one of them. We had few clear structures and rarely elected anyone to a position of leadership and thus could not replace them (or me). As Freeman wrote, "This apparent lack of structure too often disguised an informal, unacknowledged and unaccountable leadership that was all the more pernicious because its very existence was denied."[3] Her article went on to discuss the "star system" and elitism, then laid out principles of democratic structuring. I started sharing it with everyone I knew.

Three days a week I would bring Emma to my office where I had a "pack and play" set up. Soon it was normal to see me at work changing a diaper or quieting everyone during nap times. In May of 1975 the *Boston Globe* ran a long profile of me titled "The Evolution of a Revolutionary," complete with a picture of me and Emma at the Mass Community Center.

That article was soon followed by an invitation to have lunch with Tom Winship, the longtime editor of the *Globe* and Charlie Whipple, the editorial page editor. After discussing politics for a while, Winship asked if I would write a column every other week. Surprised, I blurted out, "But Tom, you know I am still a radical!" His reply was immediate: "Michael, you may be a goddamn radical, but you are our radical." By which he meant I was a *Harvard* radical. I wrote twenty columns before the pull of organizing drew me away.

The work progressed, 9 to 5 grew. With fuel prices high, CAP-Energy was gaining traction. I was meeting new people in Boston who were willing to help us build a large citizen's organization rooted in neighborhoods. Miles was willing to return from Chicago to head up the organizing.

Then the city spiraled into the crisis of forced desegregation and the busing of children to new schools. Under a court order, Boston was busing white and Black students to integrate schools. That meant that Black students were for the first time attending schools in South Boston and Hyde Park and West Roxbury, then totally white communities. Louise Day Hicks, leading resistance to any desegregation of the schools, founded an organization to stop "forced busing." Later that organization took on the name "Restore Our Alienated Rights," or ROAR.

ROAR's leadership included women from Boston's white working-class neighborhoods. Among the most prominent was Elvira "Pixie" Palladino from East Boston, who thought nothing of cursing out a monseigneur or attempting to punch Senator Ted Kennedy. Slightly more restrained in manner, but no less fierce in commitment, was Fran Johene, from Hyde Park. While racism was front and center, these mothers articulated a powerful sense of class grievance. Why was it that the students from blue-collar and poor neighborhoods would be bused, while the affluent suburbs sat by and paid no cost?

The city was riven along racial lines, but we thought there were issues that could unite across those divides—if there were organizers and a creative strategy. We worked even harder to create the foundation for a new organization in Boston to do exactly that.

There were secret attempts to bring together these militant white mothers and African American leaders. I was part of four meetings with the ROAR mothers and the Black mothers who had fought for desegregation and created the voluntary metropolitan busing program (METCO) taking kids from Roxbury to attend affluent schools in the suburbs. The center of attention was always Mel King, a social worker activist at the South End Settlement House who I knew from the old BAG days.[4] Mel attended these meetings wearing denim overalls, the uniform of a SNCC organizer. Tall, strong, head shaved, bearded, the effect he had on the ROAR mothers, especially Pixie, was bizarre. She and the others literally could not keep their hands off him. They would sit next to him, lean on him, put their hand on his arm, put their arm around his shoulders, gravitate around him. Mel just smiled and made the case for protecting children. Nothing came out of these meetings. I would later see Pixie and Fran speaking at public meetings, railing against Black leaders, and wish I had a video to show of them with Mel.

The busing crises went on, ugly and divisive, white mobs hurling stones and racist epithets at small children in school buses. There were physical attacks on Black people in numerous settings. The deeper the crisis became, the more convinced we were that we needed to create a new organization that could bring together white and Black families from the neighborhoods across the city. We hoped to make that part of a statewide effort. Using CAP-Energy, we would build statewide populist action around utility rates and other economic justice issues. In Boston we would dig deep into the blue-collar and low-income neighborhoods, mixing neighborhood issues and issues of economic justice. We put together a broad sponsoring committee, made up of existing neighborhood leaders and parish priests. Father Tom Corrigan of Holy Redeemer Church in East Boston quickly assumed a leadership role. Father Corrigan looked every bit a prototypical Boston Irish Catholic priest: thin to the point of almost haggard, his Roman collar too large for his narrow neck, his face habitually creased with concern. He had an immediate and innate sense of organizing and became passionate about our efforts.

Father Corrigan steered us to the Campaign for Human Development (CHD), a unique social justice arm of the US Conference of Catholic Bishops. The spirit of Vatican II was still sweeping through the Catholic church. Liberation theology from Latin America resonated with some of the clergy in North America. CHD was funding organizations that sought to empower the poor, organizing for social and economic justice. Their funds came from a national collection in every Catholic church across the country on the Sunday before Thanksgiving. That collection produced millions of dollars that could go to address poverty and injustice.

We submitted a proposal to CHD to support our Boston Organizing Project. We did not know that they had also received a proposal from a group of former welfare rights organizers in Massachusetts.

Those organizers were part of a new effort, the Movement for Economic Justice, whose strategy was to find economic issues where the very poor and blue-collar families had a shared interest.[5]

The very first project of the Movement for Economic Justice was in Chelsea. Nestled across the Mystic River, cut off from Boston, dominated by the shadows of the huge Tobin Bridge, Chelsea has been one of the gateway cities for new immigrants entering Massachusetts for one hundred years. It has also consistently been one of, if not the, poorest community in the state. Lee Staples, Mark Splain, and Barbara Bowen Splain, all former welfare rights organizers, moved there to start Chelsea Fair Share. They were deeply committed to fighting for the needs of the poorest families.

They built a remarkable group of local Chelsea leaders. They won an end to the tolls for Chelsea residents on the Tobin Bridge, built in, over, and through Chelsea, that every Chelsea resident had to pay along with other drivers to get into the city of Boston. Realizing that Chelsea was too small to support three organizers, they expanded into nearby East Boston and the city of Waltham to the west of Boston, declaring the three chapters part of Massachusetts Fair Share.

The name "Fair Share" was inspired. It appealed to people who had always obeyed the rules, done what was asked of them, and paid their fair share—and had not received their fair share in return. It went quickly to the heart of economic justice but was not leftist lingo. Appealing to a basic American impulse toward fairness, it allowed the organization to attack those who did not pay their fair share.

With the organization growing, they added a brilliant young lawyer, Jim Katz, to do issue research and campaign strategy. To increase their support and expand further, they—as we had done—submitted a proposal to CHD.

Confronted with two proposals that seemed so much alike, CHD did something remarkable—they reached out to both groups of organizers and said, if you merge into one organizing effort, bringing the Boston Organizing Project, Mass Fair Share, and CAP-Energy into one single organization, we will fund you with a commitment of $100,000 per year for two years or more. If you do not, we will not fund either proposal.

The two organizing groups were unfamiliar with each other. While our strategies seemed to converge, the welfare rights organizers were skeptical about our commitment to the poorest of the poor. They were humble and dedicated. When they looked at us, they saw former campus radicals, people who had been part of the New Left with an appetite for, and a daring to do things on a large scale, that attracted them but that they distrusted. Yet our strategies converged. Our plans were compatible.

We brought the capacity to organize throughout the neighborhoods of Boston and through CAP-Energy, the possibility for statewide efforts around spiking energy costs. Following the Organization of Petroleum Exporting Countries (OPEC) embargo of 1973, the price of oil more than quadrupled in less than twelve months and kept rising.[6] That oil shock rolled on through the economy, boosting the price of gas at the pump, jumping up the price of home heating oil, and sending electricity prices shooting upward. This was producing significant pain, especially for the poor and anyone on fixed incomes.

There were weeks of difficult meetings. More funding for organizing than we had ever imagined was too strong a carrot to be resisted. Both groups of organizers wanted to merge. Discussions edged into negotiations. We agreed on many details. We would keep the name Mass Fair Share. Mark Dyen would become statewide coordinator of energy work. Miles would direct the organizing in Boston. Staples would direct the organizing in the ring of cities surrounding Boston. Katz would be research director.

The remaining issue was who would be the executive director of the merged effort. Mark Splain, sounding profoundly uncomfortable, asked to meet with me privately. He told me the merger could only happen if he was the executive director. I immediately agreed. I would be in charge of fundraising and play a role in the statewide campaigns.

Certainly, I had wanted to be the executive director. I was still young and cocky. However, the chance to build an organization fighting for economic justice that was both deep and statewide was too important to throw away over who was the executive director.

With this shotgun wedding, Mass Fair Share was created and launched.

One of the earliest campaigns was around electric rates. Mark Dyen and his team produced a detailed analysis of what was driving up costs, proving that among other factors, new construction of electric plants now produced no gains in efficiency. We demonstrated that building to meet peak demand meant that there was unused, extremely costly capacity sitting idle so that the electric producers could respond to periodic demands of the largest users. But the costs of this were not reflected in the rates for larger users. We pushed for pricing that guaranteed a low price for the minimum usage most families needed and provided strong incentives for conservation.

We discovered that the Department of Public Utilities (DPU) had a rule that a family could dispute their bill and until the dispute was resolved, the electric company could not turn off the power. That allowed us to organize people to refuse to pay their electric bills, disputing the charges and sending the payments to us. Over 10,000 people sent their payments to Fair Share creating a powerful boycott of the electric companies and forcing the DPU to act.

As the campaign ramped up, we encountered a serious strategic dispute. Mark Splain insisted that, since the legislature was unlikely to pass our proposals, the best path forward was a referendum campaign to pass our radical proposal for flat rates which would have made large users pay their fair share. He argued that since there was going to be another attempt to pass a graduated income tax by referendum, pairing the two would make sense. Mark Dyen and I felt strongly that we would lose both referenda. We were not ready, and taking our proposal into a referendum campaign was likely to unite the entire business community, as well as all large users of electricity, including the media, hospitals, and universities. We were unable to persuade Mark Splain, and so we launched referendum campaigns pushing for flat rate electric rates and the graduated income tax.

Both went down to crushing defeats, losing by over a million votes.[7] In the closing weeks of the campaign, there was a massive advertising blitz against us. Then hundreds of thousands of workers received a notice in their paycheck envelopes saying that if our electric rate proposal, Question 7, passed, they would receive their layoff notice. (This was back when employees received a paper paycheck.) Hospitals, universities, even churches, all major users of electricity with huge discounts, urged a no vote on Question 7. The *Boston Globe* urged its

FIGURE 50. Fair Share leaders at the State House filing petitions for the referendum. Courtesy of University Archives and Special Collections, Joseph P. Healey Library, University of Massachusetts Boston: Ann Raszmann Brown community organizations photographs.

readers to vote yes on referendum questions one through six but at all costs, to vote no on Question 7. We did not just lose: we lost two to one.

That loss taught us important lessons about what would be needed to pass a referendum, lessons we would use a few years later to win on tax issues. Still, it was a significant setback.

Many of our other organizing efforts went very well, however. We launched the Boston organizing effort with a press conference where twelve Catholic and Protestant clergy, along with fourteen neighborhood leaders, announced support for the new organizing effort. Mel King of the South End joined John Regan of South Boston. Frank Manning, the most well-known senior activist in the state, urged seniors to join the new effort. Anna De Fronzo, the leader of the East Boston Maverick Street Mothers who had campaigned against the expansion of Logan Airport, spoke and said, "Just imagine if all the neighborhoods got together, there isn't anything we can't win."

There had been nothing like what we were proposing: a city-wide effort that was rooted in all the neighborhoods and that was not beholden to any politician. The changes besetting so many neighborhoods made it imperative that residents find ways to have their voices heard, their needs considered. The rage and violence of the antibusing movement had confirmed that not only was racism virulently alive in Boston but also that the city was in fundamental ways broken. The proposed new organization offered a path forward.

Under the guidance of Miles, organizers in Boston were trained and assigned to most blue-collar and low-income neighborhoods. Under Lee and Barbara, organizers were placed in a growing list of communities across the state. We hired young people, most of whom had been active as students and now wanted to learn the "profession of organizing." Each day they came into the office for seminar style training on how to think about the neighborhoods they would be organizing, how to meet one on one with community leaders, and how to think about the stages of building an organization. They would role play door knocking and one-on-one meetings until they were confident. We stressed repeatedly that they were not selling, that they needed to listen and engage.

We had a clear organizing methodology. We borrowed a lot from the farm worker organizing in California. Fred Ross, trained by Alinsky, had gone to California to build an organization for farm workers. Out of his work would emerge Cesar Chavez and the farmworkers union. The key to his organizing process was the house meeting that allowed an organizer to train and test potential leaders. People who could bring ten to twenty people to their home and lead a discussion were good candidates to become leaders.

Miles would walk people through how to analyze a neighborhood. He would challenge them: "Okay I want you to chart out the institutions and leadership in your neighborhood." The organizers would then make a list of the churches, the existing neighborhood associations, sometimes unions, small business associations, veterans' organizations, local papers, sports leagues, and parent organizations. Miles would push them to look deeper, to explore more. "Go work on this and come back at our next session with the names of the actual leaders filled in and a plan for you to visit with them."

In the next session, each organizer would share their analysis of the neighborhood and the names of the leaders that they were going to visit. Miles would patiently push and educate. "Okay you have the parish priest but who are the lay leaders in the parish? Who are the people who make bingo nights so successful? Look not just for the formal leaders but look for those people who are making things happen. Who is the head of the local parents' organization but also who are the ones that make the bake sales really happen?"

Then the organizers would work through the process of visits to established leaders. Then they would discuss the need to do door knocking to discover new people who could be cultivated into leadership.

Miles would walk them through how all of this would lead to the creation of an organizing committee. "Look," he would say, "we don't want to immediately lock in a formal leadership structure. First, we need to test people, to see who the real leaders are by seeing who can actually bring people to a house meeting or to a first action. You often know the top person, say the lay leader in a parish, but they are too busy with what they are already committed to and so won't make an effective leader for Fair Share. And often the guy who talks great and you think that's my guy, will turn out to have no follow through. So, you have to go slow and be flexible at first. The organizing committee allows you to test people and see who can really produce. Your job right now is to learn and listen. Learn who the leaders are. Learn the issues that people really care about. Discover both the issues and the people that will build the organization."

After the discussions, every day the organizers would be out in the afternoon and evening, knocking on doors, meeting people face to face, holding their "one on ones," and setting up house meetings. Later in the night, they would all get together for a debrief and then head to a local bar to drink and talk and talk. The days were long. The camaraderie was immediate and strong.

Despite the great divisions tearing at the city from the fight over school busing, the organizers specifically said that people in these diverse neighborhoods had more in common than what divided them.

The leadership of the antibusing campaign vehemently opposed our efforts, but some of their supporters became involved. New Fair Share chapters formed in neighborhood after neighborhood. The organizers followed a careful approach: first meet and learn from the existing leaders in a community, listen to them, find the people who may not be in the most prominent leadership positions but still were of real substance, the quiet woman who holds together the parish activities including the bingo nights, the welfare mother who has also been talking about the state of housing, the neighborhood leader who is concerned about redlining. Then go door to door, whenever possible with local leaders, talking to people, learning about them and their issues, as well as talking about the issues others have raised. Find people who will agree to host a house meeting in their home. Work with them to see who is able to turn out twelve to twenty-five friends and neighbors. After a dozen or more house meetings and several hundred conversations, build an organizing committee, at every point testing to see who can actually lead people. Don't be fooled by the people who talk the best game. Look for the people who deliver. Don't lock in leaders too early—leave room at the table for the people who emerge. Offer training sessions in leadership, issues, skills, and strategy. Take several direct actions around the issues that excited the most people. Collect memberships and dues to produce local ownership and financing of the organizing drive. Finally, there would be a founding chapter meeting of one to two hundred residents. After that the organizers and the organizing committee would keep reaching out, keep starting new campaigns, with each campaign having its own leadership committee. Over time there would be chapter elections for local leaders and then of statewide leaders.

Across the city and the state Fair Share chapters blossomed and thrived. Organizers built teams of volunteers. In each neighborhood dozens of house meetings brought in several hundred active members. Soon the local group was engaging the city on community issues, as well as working on statewide issues. The community issues could be as narrow as winning a stop sign or stop lights at an intersection where there had been repeated accidents. Or working to get more foot patrols in an area where the residents were feeling fearful. Or getting the city to repair a rundown school or clean up a neglected park. Soon the issues were taking up larger economic issues of taxes, insurance, and utility rates. There would be meetings of 300 to 400 people. Elected officials were invited and found themselves suddenly confronted with well-prepared local residents who made demands of them and held up a big score card to grade their response— "Yes, No, and Waffle." Rapidly Fair Share was becoming known and popular in almost every neighborhood in Boston and in dozens of neighborhoods across the state.

In Dorchester, Lew Finfer who had organized the Dorchester Community Action Council (DCAC) became convinced that Fair Share offered a rare opportunity. Lew convinced the leaders of the DCAC to merge into Dorchester Fair Share, immediately increasing the size and depth of the organization.[8]

In South Boston, however, our organizers were totally unsuccessful. Even though they were brought into South Boston by John Regan, a longtime community leader and head of the South Boston Small Business Council, as well as several South Boston priests and even though two dozen local residents responded enthusiastically to forming a South Boston Fair Share chapter, Jimmy Kelly, then the leader of the South Boston Marshals, the well-organized antibusing group, made it clear that there would be no organizing in South Boston by those "n----- lovers." Kelly would go on to a long political career as a twenty-year city councilor. In those days, however, he was coming out of the Sheet Metal Workers Union and the conservative building trades. Even though we had the active support of Joe Joyce, the president of the Sheet Metal Workers Union, we could not dissuade Kelly. He and the antibusing South Boston Marshals delivered a clear message: there would be no founding meeting of Fair Share in South Boston. I wanted to proceed but all our South Boston people dropped away when it became clear that Kelly had been delivering a message from the mobster Whitey Bulger. Everyone in South Boston knew that if Whitey Bulger said that he was not allowing a meeting to happen or an organization to form, that threat would be backed up by whatever level of violence was needed to stop it. As much as they wanted a Fair Share chapter, they wanted to live more.

At the same time that the organizing in Boston was proceeding, across the state Fair Share organizers, following the same approaches, started chapters in neighborhoods in Worcester, Lowell, Lynn, Revere, Malden, Somerville, Fall River, New Bedford, Springfield, Holyoke, and Chicopee.

Our first year had been a wild ride. By the end of 1976, we felt a little battered, but we could see the potential of the organizing. We had not yet broken through, but it seemed possible. Then Mark Splain once again asked to meet with me privately.

He looked uncomfortable. To my surprise he asked me to become the executive director, saying he was far better at training organizers than leading the whole organization. He would stay as director of organizing if I took the job. I was delighted.

MASSACHUSETTS FAIR SHARE

It is a hot late June evening in Revere. A town meeting with the governor is to take place at the Lincoln Public School auditorium that seats 400 people. It is two months before the 1978 Democratic primary in which Governor Michael Dukakis is being challenged by the conservative, stiff-jawed Ed King. Dukakis is confident he will win. His advance people turn out their usual eighty to a hundred people. We turn out 3,000 people. Soon the auditorium is jammed—the Dukakis supporters and the curious, scattered among 300 Fair Share members. Buses roll up and out come people from Fall River and Lynn and Worcester and Chelsea and the various neighborhoods of Boston to form a picket line surrounding the school.

I pace around outside, getting reports from various organizers as to the numbers they have brought. Unlike so many demonstrations I have led, in this one, it's Fair Share leaders who are in charge. Occasionally one of them checks in with me, but generally I am content to watch the action unfold.

We are there to demand that Dukakis support tax reform, which he adamantly opposes. He argues that the Commonwealth does not need the Fair Share "circuit breaker" bill, limiting property tax payments to a percentage of household income. Dukakis is determined that the $150,000,000 state surplus should go to local cities and towns to beef up their spending. None of it should go to the circuit breaker. He is an earnest, thoughtful liberal who wants to see more public sector spending—and is convinced he knows best.

The problem on this night is that we have brought 3,000 people who are struggling economically, who know there is a government surplus, who have seen their fuel costs skyrocket; their wages stay flat, and their taxes increase. They want tax reform and tax relief.

It starts to drizzle. The Red Sox are playing the hated Yankees. Yet there are thousands marching around the Lincoln School. Outside, we lead chants and confer with police to make sure nothing gets out of hand. Inside, while the audience fans themselves with Fair Share factsheets, Dukakis duels with Carolyn Lucas, a Boston "housewife" who had become an articulate Fair Share leader. The chants from outside keep penetrating the town meeting: "Sign our bill or get off the Hill." "Tax relief now." The people both outside and inside the school do not look anything like what protestors were thought to be. Most have never protested before. They are factory workers, housewives, senior citizens, store clerks, office workers, mothers on welfare. And they are mad.

I had been to California and seen what was happening with the right-wing tax revolt embodied in Proposition 13 that put caps on taxes, giving relief to businesses and the wealthy, as well as those hard pressed to pay their bills. That tax revolt will choke the public sector, and the wealthiest will get the most relief. Still for many low-income Massachusetts families, property taxes are too high and threaten their ability to hang on to their homes. We are determined to win progressive tax reform in Massachusetts. Only a progressive alternative will stop the wave of right-wing tax revolts from sweeping over our state next.

At the legislative hearings on our circuit breaker weeks before the Revere town hall, Mike Regan, a Fair Share leader from Chelsea, had testified before state legislators. Mike, a small, profoundly moral, longtime worker at the Shraft's candy plant, warned, "Before we leave, we want you to know something. We want you to know . . . that we are just about ready to blow . . . our tops. . . . We are going to blow a fuse." Then drawing himself up to his full height of 5'5", he strode directly up to the chairman of the committee. As security guards moved forward, he reached into his pocket, placing two blown fuses on the table, followed by a procession of 200 other Fair Share activists who each deposited a fuse as the television lights glared and the cameras rolled.

To everyone's surprise, we managed to get the circuit breaker into the budget that was passed by the House. But Dukakis still refused to support it. We demanded that he meet with a delegation to discuss tax reform. He refused.

Now, inside the school, the argument with Dukakis gets heated. Fair Share members shout at him. The governor lectures them. He knows what is best. He flatly refuses to discuss a circuit breaker or to meet with Fair Share leaders to negotiate.

Carolyn calls for all in the audience who support the circuit breaker to stand up and walk out. Eighty percent of the audience heads for the door. Someone starts a chant, "We put you in, we can put you out." The crowd outside gets briefed by Carolyn and becomes angry. Everywhere cameras whirl; everywhere reporters are interviewing people, surprised by how much they know about the state budget, about the circuit breaker bill, about how unfair the tax system is. Reporters don't expect protestors to be regular blue-collar folks, and to be so well informed. Dukakis quietly exits through a back door to avoid the crowd. He is angry. In the next few days, he makes huge political gaffes by publicly dismissing the need for tax reform. When asked about a California Prop 13–style threat to Massachusetts, he is quoted as saying that Massachusetts taxpayers are not stupid enough to support lower taxes. The press coverage of the town meeting and his statements about taxes dramatically hurt his campaign. King trounces him in the primary. "We put you in, we can put you out" becomes prophetic.

Starting in 1975, I devoted myself to Mass Fair Share. Brilliant campaigns and systematic organizing built an organization with greater name recognition and greater support than any organization or politician at that time in Massachusetts.

Mass Fair Share was everything I wanted to be doing. It mattered. It made a difference both in the lives of specific families but also in society at large. It had the potential to alter the politics of Massachusetts in a profound way. It was a large school of democracy, giving people the tools that they needed to become effective citizens and giving them a taste of what democratic action could accomplish when they combined and organized.

As executive director I spent my days in a myriad of ways: working on strategy for the organization, doing leadership training, raising money, hiring staff, managing senior staff, attending statewide leadership and issue meetings, raising more money. I was working ten- and twelve-hour days. I was getting paid a real salary, $35,000 a year. My days were a rush of meeting after meeting, punctuated by nonstop phone calls. Three or four evenings a week I would be out at a meeting in one part of the state or another. Often, I was in Worcester, a central location, for a meeting of one of the campaign committees, or a leadership training session or an executive committee meeting. I would try to drop into neighborhood meetings from time to time. I could not keep up with the Fair Share meetings—they were so numerous and constant. Each day was challenging and exciting, working to build an organization that was taking off, becoming a populist force.

Neighborhoods were changing. The economy was changing. The blue-collar manufacturing jobs of the last forty years were leaving. Energy prices were spiking. The old urban Democratic political machines were steadily withering. Women were no longer willing or able to stay at home and out of the work force. Still, for most people the mid-1970s was not a time when they felt compelled to step out of their day-to-day lives and take action at all costs. Fair Share was not riding a wave of social movement. Yet it was a remarkable example of how

FIGURE 51. As executive director of Mass Fair Share. Photo by Barbara Alper/ Getty Images.

progressive populism could resonate with Americans. How creative strategy could win tangible victories against entrenched special interests. How deep and systematic organizing could build power and transform lives. How organizers and emerging leaders could build a powerful organization.

All these years later, it is a challenge to convey exactly how popular, how large, how creative, and how successful Fair Share was. A quick search of the *Boston Globe* archives for the words "Mass Fair Share" for the time period 1975 to 1983 produces story after story, headline after headline, often as many as a dozen major news stories in a single month. That level of coverage was true for television and the other daily newspapers in the cities across the state. Stories about large public meetings, about creative protests, the release of muckraking reports, regulatory challenges to rate hikes, legislation filed, and legislation passed. Continuous reports of confrontations with elected officials, with regulators, with corporate CEOs. An endless stream of neighborhood issues. Victories, large and small: rate hikes stopped, rebates and tax abatements in the millions of dollars sent to working and low-income families, the release of previously secret information. Stop lights won. Parks cleaned up. Action to fix up abandoned buildings.

The scale of the organization was significant. By 1979, over 110,000 families in Massachusetts—10 percent of the households in the state—were members, paying dues of at least $15 per year and receiving the monthly newspaper, the *Fair*

Fighter. By that year, other than on major holidays, each day of the year, all year long, somewhere in Massachusetts, there was a Fair Share meeting of between ten and 500 people.

The genius of Mass Fair Share was in combining deep, systematic, constant organizing with creative campaign strategies. There were concurrent or sequential campaigns on energy, taxes, insurance, toxic waste sites, plant closings, telephone rates and policies, banking, redlining, youth jobs, as well as continuous neighborhood-specific issues. Each campaign was carefully designed and meticulously researched. Always we were looking for who had authority that was not being used, what loophole could we find to give us leverage, how could popular power change the outcome. Each campaign used symbols that could capture the imagination: blown fuses, pennies, brown bag lunches, and the empty chair on the stage. There were always catchy names: the Dirty Dozen for tax delinquents, Lifeline Rates, Circuit Breaker, and of course, always the name Fair Share. Coming up with creative strategies took time, resources, and effort. We built a research and campaign team of the smartest people we could find. Jim Katz and Barry Margolin led a research team, while Mark Dyen led a campaign staff. They spent hours studying the issues that were being raised in the neighborhoods or that we thought might also be significant.

The research and campaign teams identified both long-term significant reforms, and potential smaller victories that we might achieve. We designed campaigns with local, municipal, and statewide "handles," as we called them. We wanted campaigns where we could organize and win initial victories that would build confidence and strength.

While not an intentional part of our organizing methodology, repeatedly women stepped forward to lead the local organizations. Some were very poor, receiving welfare. Others were from solidly middle-income, blue-collar families. What they shared was intelligence and a passion for justice.

Both men and women leaders would over time confront and challenge the elites of business and politics. Our people would need to know more than the CEOs, elected officials, and bureaucrats that they were going up against. We invested heavily and continuously in leadership training. We taught organizing skills, how to lead productive meetings, how to think about strategy, and in-depth training on every issue the organization took on.

Many local leaders at first lacked the confidence that they could challenge those in authority. From their earliest days in school, in their families, in their churches, on sports teams, in the military, and for women, all too often, in their marriages, they had been trained to do what authority figures told them to do. It took courage for the "little people," as they thought of themselves, to demand answers. When Fair Share leaders took on the elites, they discovered that often

CEOs and elected officials didn't have good answers, were less well informed than they were and were frequently caught lying. In those moments Fair Share leaders realized that they were just as smart as those in authority. Out of that experience came a new confidence. Ordinary people who had been deferential all their lives began to see that through organization and collective action, they could win victories. They could be part of something larger than themselves; they could fight for justice, fight for a fair share.

We were constantly blending outreach with "actions." Actions could be as simple as a group meeting with a politician, a regulator, a bureaucrat, a landlord, or a corporate executive. While the meeting would always be respectful, the demands and questions would be formulated precisely, and the answers recorded and shared publicly. The decision makers were always put in a position where they had to answer the hard questions. Sometimes the action would be confronting one of the elites at their place of work or in their wealthy suburban neighborhood or even at their country club. Another action might be meeting with state legislators with hundreds of their voters back in the districts. It could be swamping a normally sparsely attended "public" hearing by the City of Lynn Water and Sewer Commission. Or it could be showing up in large numbers at a mayor's office or at some obscure regulatory hearing that no one ever attended.

These actions and confrontations were always part of a careful effort to build campaigns, create a broader base of support, and win initial victories. Ongoing outreach was essential and continuous. The early victories often were winning release of information that had been kept secret. For example, information about large delinquent taxpayers or about a toxic waste site in a neighborhood. Forcing the release of information was a victory that fueled the next phase of the campaign.

We wanted campaigns to build to a peak, then subside, then build again. Wherever possible, we wanted to build from the local to the citywide to statewide, and then back into the local neighborhood. We looked for ways to attack where we were not expected and to go outside of the rules of the game whenever possible. We looked for ways that we could split the opposition (usually the business community).

Even when we lost, we regrouped and looked for new direction for the campaigns. Despite the flat rate referendum loss in 1976, we kept fighting. We took the fight directly to the utility companies. One day 300 Fair Share members showed up at the Boston Edison stockholders meeting—as stockholders. George Pillsbury, the crusading heir to part of the Pillsbury fortune, donated 300 shares of Boston Edison stock. We forced the normally routine shareholders meeting to be moved from the Edison cafeteria to Hynes Auditorium down the street. The Fair Share members dominated the meeting arguing for a drastic change in the rate structure.

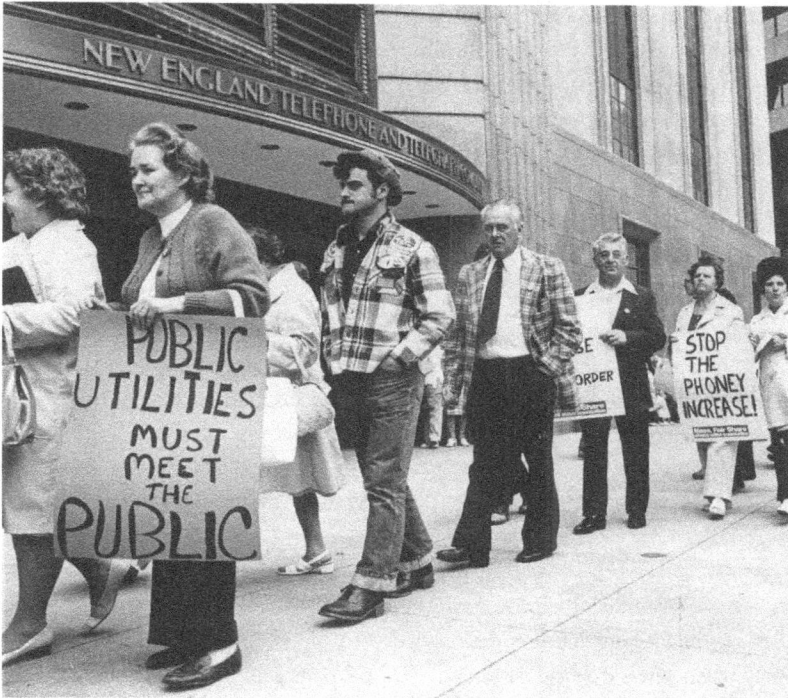

FIGURE 52.   Mass Fair Share picketing the phone company. Courtesy of University Archives and Special Collections, Joseph P. Healey Library, University of Massachusetts Boston: Ann Raszmann Brown community organizations photographs.

We exposed that the utility companies had collected $32 million from customers for federal income taxes that the companies had never paid because of tax loopholes. We won. We stopped new rate hikes. Each battle brought new people into the organization and broadened our support. Each new report demonstrated that the energy companies were not to be trusted, and that the people who were supposed to regulate them were not doing their jobs. In the long run, the Department of Public Utilities put in place most of what we fought for but kept insisting that they were not doing what we had demanded. One result was a first-in-the-nation residential conservation program that has lasted over forty years. To this day Massachusetts spends more each year on retrofitting structures and promoting conservation than does the much larger conservation-oriented state of California.

One of the best examples of Fair Share's many campaigns was our effort around tax reform. We designed a long-term, multifaceted campaign strategy that ultimately centered on the notion that not all tax cuts were the same. We posed two simple questions: Who pays? Who benefits?

The average family in Boston had experienced increases in their property taxes of 11 percent annually over the previous ten years, more than doubling. That was unsustainable. The average family making $10,500 (the median family income in 1975) paid over 14 percent of their income just on property taxes. Counting all local and state taxes, that figure rose to 19.3 percent—almost a fifth of the total family income. Wealthier people paid a diminishing percentage of their income on state and local taxes.

In certain neighborhoods we discovered that homeowners had been significantly over assessed. We researched the appeal and abatement process that existed but was rarely used. We organized large-scale group abatement filings. In those meetings we confronted city officials with compelling data and large numbers of irate homeowners. In 1975, Boston Fair Share filed 800 tax abatements and 675 were approved, returning $122,000 to those homeowners (over $700,000 in today's dollars).

The next year the campaign increased. About 1,500 people attended meetings across Dorchester alone, and 1,400 filled out abatement forms. A group of Boston Fair Share leaders descended on City Hall demanding to meet with Robert Ryan, the associate city tax assessor. The group brought enlarged photos. One photo was of Harvard Stadium. As Boston Fair Share leader, Al Mickiewicz explained, "See this photo? Harvard with all its property and its huge endowment, what does it pay in taxes? Nothing." Then, pointing to another enlarged photograph, this one of a traditional three-decker, he said, "See this home in Dorchester? This home is assessed at forty percent of its market value. Now look at this"—another Fair Share member held up a large photo of the First National Bank Headquarters—"See this bank building? Guess what it is assessed at. Ten percent of its market value. Ten percent! No wonder our taxes are so high. Or look at this." Another photo was held aloft, this time of an airplane taking off at Logan Airport. Al continued, "Logan Airport, Mass Port. They refuse to pay six million dollars in taxes. So, we the homeowners, have to pay more because these special interests don't pay their fair share. We are sick and tired of it. This has to stop." The TV lights illuminated the whole scene as reporters eagerly made sure that each photo was caught on camera as was the sweating Mr. Ryan who tried to explain that there were reasons that Harvard, First National, and Logan Airport paid or didn't pay what Fair Share said.

There was increased urgency when, in 1976, Boston announced a 20 percent increase in the property tax as did other cities. Fair Share unleashed campaigns against large delinquent taxpayers, often slumlords and corporations, and against special loopholes and tax breaks.

Typical of the meetings held across the state was the one at St. Ambrose in Dorchester. It was a hot August evening. I came to observe and see the progress of the local chapter. These were the same streets where I had worked against the war and to dump Jerry Troy only a few years earlier. Then my organizing was seen as threatening and marginal by many of the longtime residents. Now 600 residents, many homeowners who had lived their entire lives in Dorchester, packed the parish hall to confront the city treasurer James Young. We released an eight-page fact sheet documenting who paid and who didn't pay property taxes. The meeting started with a twenty-minute slideshow walking through the city's tax structure and focusing on the abatement routinely doled out to businesses, especially the large ones. Irate taxpayers wanted to know why the Prudential Company was receiving a $100,000 abatement. Why other downtown commercial buildings were getting tax breaks. How much was being handed out and to whom. The Fair Share leaders demanded the city start closing loopholes. One after another, homeowners spoke up, saying, "I want to stay here, stay in my house, but with these tax increases, you are forcing me out of my home." "Let's go out and fight. Let's not pay our taxes—they can't put us all in jail," said another.

The Fair Share leaders made specific demands on the treasurer and on the city assessor. Under pressure they agreed that within thirty days the city would release to Fair Share a list of all tax abatements of $10,000 or more made in the last three years, a complete list of all delinquent property owners who owed over $5,000 for six months or longer, and the terms of preconstruction tax agreements with developers. After the meeting the homeowners streamed out into the hot night, determined that once Fair Share got that information, they would press the fight.

Once released, the list of large delinquent taxpayers was explosive. In Boston, there were some marvelous names on the list, including the famous attorney F. Lee Bailey, the Catholic Archdiocese, a deputy mayor, and several major businesses. We then released lists of the "Dirty Dozen," the most notorious delinquents in cities across the state. With great ceremony the organization delivered citizen tax bills to them with a deadline for them to pay up. The press went wild. New England Life paid $110,000 just before our "deadline" passed and notified us of that fact by hand-delivered letter. Action was producing results. Those on the list who did not pay before the deadline found themselves subject to repeated demonstrations—even at their country clubs—and an unrelenting barrage of public shaming.

In the Allston Brighton neighborhood Fair Share picketed the offices of Allyn Levy and Gerald Feinberg, two landlords who were delinquent on the taxes for seven large apartment buildings. Fair Share revealed that not only had they not paid their property taxes, but they also had used the increased taxes that they had not paid as the legal justification for a significant rent increase that their tenants had been paying. Fair Share held tenants' meetings in homes and church halls across the community. With the base built and outrage growing, the local leaders acted. Fair Share protestors marched in front of the real estate office, the TV cameras whirred, and reporters asked for interviews. The protestors were clear: "There is no place in this community for landlords like you." "Pay your fair share." "Levy and Feinberg are tax cheats and swindlers!" The Fair Share protestors tried to go inside but were barred at the doors. A message was sent out: you can meet tomorrow with our lawyers. The next day the local leaders and the lawyers met. The lawyers proposed that the back taxes would be paid immediately, and the tenants would be sent checks totaling the $6,000 in rent increases so long as Fair Share agreed to call off the picketing. The agreement was reached. The taxes were paid. The tenants received their checks and joined Fair Share.

Across the state, Fair Share mounted campaigns targeting large tax delinquents. In Lynn we sued and finally won a court order that said the information on who was delinquent was public information and had to be turned over to us. Until then, mayors had resisted. In Revere, the requests for the list of delinquents produced a fight between the mayor and the tax collector, as the mayor tried to make the collector the fall guy. The mayor then proposed a shakeup that would consolidate all tax issues under the office of the city treasurer. The collector, Joe DiCarlo, then leaked that the mayor, William Reinstein, owed $4,000 in unpaid taxes. Betsy Tuttle, a local Fair Share leader, led a delegation to see the mayor and showed him the article in the local paper detailing the back taxes owed on his Sweeney Avenue home.[1] The mayor "was so surprised his eyeballs were popping out," Tuttle later reported. "He went storming down to DiCarlo's office." It took winning the court case and successful pressure on the state tax collector Owen Clark, before we won access to the lists. The fight in Revere, as in so many other cities, was so intense that the local newspaper, the *Revere Journal*, reported on Tuttle being elected to the statewide Fair Share executive board, as well as the progress made on the campaign to get the lists released.[2]

When we found a nursing home chain on the delinquent list in both Boston and Worcester, we worked with their employees who were seeking a union and decent wages. Across the state, Fair Share campaigns about tax breaks, delinquent slum landlords, overassessed neighborhoods, and underassessed commercial property built a strong base for tax reform.

That base was then mobilized around two statewide issues. The first was direct property tax relief through the circuit breaker, which created a rebate program based upon the percentage of income that was paid in property taxes. The second was a fight to deal with a court order for 100 percent revaluation, which would have shifted $265 million in tax burden from business and commercial property onto residential taxpayers—a bonanza for business interests.[3]

Local meetings pushing for the circuit breaker were held with state legislators, drawing anywhere from one hundred to 500 people in over eighty locations
across the state. The legislature began to feel the pressure of angry taxpayers,
including many who made up their electoral base and some who were their
campaign volunteers. The circuit breaker would need to be part of the annual
budget, always a fraught and complicated legislative process and almost always
conducted behind closed doors.

The budget was being passed in the context of the heated primary between
Governor Dukakis and King, a probusiness, prolife Catholic, supportive of offshore oil drilling, and in favor of cutting back regulation. King had run Mass
Port, and our East Boston leaders had fought him over airport expansion. We
had no love for King.

Dukakis, however, was out of touch with the economic pain of a significant
portion of the Democratic vote. Winning the governor's office had reinforced a
certain arrogance that he knew what was best for people, even when they were
telling him something quite different.

In the House, the chair of ways and means, John J. Finnegan, made his opposition to the circuit breaker known early. His counterpart in the Senate, the ways
and means chair Jim Kelly, was also an old-line Democratic leader who occasionally lined his own pockets. (Kelly would eventually be charged and convicted of
extorting payment for state contracts.)[4] Plump, dressed in gray suits, Kelly always
seemed like the middle-aged former certified public accountant from the small
town of Oxford, Massachusetts, that he was. Surprisingly, Kelly became a partner
with us working to pass the circuit breaker.

On May 5, 1978, the Massachusetts House went into a marathon session on the
budget starting at 10 a.m. The galleries were packed with Fair Share members. In
the halls, small groups of Fair Share members chased down their state representatives as they took breaks from the heated debate on the House floor. The key issue
holding up the budget was what to do with a $150 million surplus. We wanted
most of that to pay for the circuit breaker. Finnegan, urged on by Kelly, agreed
to offer a token $10 million for a pilot circuit breaker in a $4.78 billion budget.
We rejected it and fought for a $130 million line item to fund the circuit breaker.
Under our plan there would be rebates of up to $500 for any household with
incomes of less than $30,000 and property taxes of more than 8 percent of their
income. For those who rented, tenants could count 25 percent of their rent as tax
payments and the same formula applied. Dukakis, Speaker Thomas McGee, and
the Senate president, Kevin B. Harrington, all made it clear they opposed us.

The debate on the house floor went on, hour after hour, as Finnegan kept
counting votes and making deals. The hours dragged on. The Fair Share members stayed. They continued to buttonhole reps and remind them of the meetings

that they had attended back in the districts. Dinner came and went. Still the budget was not brought to a final vote. It was clear something unusual was happening. Finnegan and Speaker McGee were twisting arms but were having trouble getting everyone in line. Ten p.m. came and went without a budget. The tired Fair Share members crowding the balcony galleries refused to leave. Midnight came. Finally, Finnegan and McGee allowed a vote on the amendment allocating the $130 million for the circuit breaker. Shockingly it passed 139 to 84.[5] The Fair Share members in the galleries stood, hollered, cheered, high-fived, and hugged. Even many of the reps clapped and cheered. Everyone was stunned.

Our victory was short lived. Senate President Harrington made it crystal clear that he would only allow the circuit breaker to be in the Senate version of the budget if we secured support from Dukakis. That led to Revere.

In the end Senator Kelly did manage to enact a small "pilot" circuit breaker that is still in effect for seniors in Massachusetts.

We had hopes that in future years we could expand the pilot. But there was a more urgent issue facing us: the tax burden in Massachusetts was about to become even more unfair. A court had issued an order that would have resulted in even larger increases in residential property taxes and reductions for industrial and commercial property. Fair Share responded by proposing a referendum campaign that would allow municipalities to set different tax rates according to the classification of the property by use: residential, commercial, agricultural.

We had learned the lesson from the failed flat electric rate referendum. There the progressive forces were isolated and faced an extremely broad, united coalition of the wealthy, corporations, and small businesses. We needed to change that dynamic. To pass our classification referendum, we wanted to build a broad coalition of cities, public sector unions, human service groups, churches, and others. The key to that coalition was first to get the cities to join us. The key to the cities was the mercurial mayor of Boston, Kevin White. If White could be persuaded, other mayors would jump in. While it was clearly in the interest of the city to join us, there was a real question as to whether we could convince the mayor to cooperate with the very organization that his operatives were fighting month after month in Boston.

Fair Share had battled his administration on everything from its failure to place stop signs at dangerous locations to forcing rebates for over-assessed neighborhoods. White saw us as a constant threat. Repeatedly delegations of angry Fair Share members made it to the mayor's outer office in City Hall. There they would always be told that the mayor was not in. Many times, the harried and furious aide sent out to deflect the protest was none other than my old adversary from the Robert McNamara demonstration at Harvard, Barney Frank. Out he would come, rumpled and disheveled, disbelieving that once again protestors were challenging the decisions of his boss. We took aim at White in other ways as well. One spring evening, even as we were preparing for the referendum campaign, White held a $1,000 a couple fundraising event, a poorly named "Salute to the Neighborhoods" held in a downtown citadel of elite power, the First National Bank Building. Outside Carolyn Lucas led hundreds of protestors unhappy with White's policies on bank closings and tax concessions to the banks. The Fair Share members all had paper plates and bags of peanuts for their "peanut-a-plate" dinner—all they could afford in contrast with the fat cats dining inside.

As we fought and competed with them, we got to know White's people. Frank was always furious with us, and we were glad to see him leave City Hall for the State Legislature and the start of a career as an elected official that would, over time, take him to Congress and a powerful national role. With others on White's team, mutual respect, and even, occasionally, friendship, slowly evolved. I had gotten personally close with fellow Dorchester resident Kirk O'Donnell, one of White's top political people. Fred Salvucci had worked closely with the Maverick Street Mothers in opposition to the airport and then had become a member of White's team. Perhaps the closest to the mayor was a young Cuban American woman, Micho Spring, who was open to our arguments about classification.[6] We went to see each of them and laid out our case.

White agreed to meet but only with me and only in secret. I was summoned to a late-night meeting with the mayor at the Parkman House, the nineteenth-century National Historic Landmark townhouse on Beacon Hill. I was carefully instructed not to come to the front door, but instead to ring the bell at the back door in the small alley. In this meeting and those that followed, it was always just the two of us, always very late at night, always at the Parkman House, always through the alley.

I found it hard to follow a lot of what the mayor said. His mind seemed to slip and jump. Yet it was clear that White was remarkably shrewd. And that he was deeply enamored of conspiracy and secrecy.

He took great delight in explaining to me how politics in Massachusetts really worked.

"So," he said, "you failed to get the circuit breaker. If you had come to me, I could have told you how to pass that bill. You shoulda come to me."

"What would you have told me?"

"Well, I would've told you that to pass a bill you need to have the support of a guy who is not in the legislature. Not Tommy and not Kevin and not Bill. For Chrissakes, you gotta know the guy you need to call. Do you know the guy you gotta call?"

It was obvious that I didn't, so I said nothing.

"Well, you need to call my good buddy Bobby Crane. You know why?"

White stopped, he cocked his head to the side, grinned and paused.

I knew Crane was the state treasurer. I didn't know, however, that he was close with White. And I had no idea where White was going with this.

"You need to call Bob because then he calls Tommy, he calls Kevin, see. And they want to help Bob. Right? And you know why they want to help Bob? The jobs, it's all about the jobs. You know—cousins, nephews, friends. Jobs. The jobs. You understand?"

Again, it was obvious to both of us that I knew nothing.

"Come on, Bob has the jobs. You are a rep and you want to be able to get your people jobs. It's about jobs. Bob controls more non–civil service patronage positions than anyone else in Massachusetts. The lottery. You know. The lottery. You want to get something done, let me call Bob. That's how it works. I can call him right now if you want."

Of course, White was right. Crane hired huge numbers of friends and family members of the legislators to work for the lottery and as a result, the legislature for years gave Crane what he asked for.

White finally decided he was all in on the classification campaign. The city needed to win on the issue. White and his team became an important part of the coalition we were building. With his support, other mayors signed on. The public sector unions joined. On the local level we organized churches to join. The human services agencies all jumped in, then private sector unions. We thought it would be diplomatic to have someone outside of Fair Share as the coalition campaign manager. We hired John Sasso, a young staffer for Congressman Gerry Studds.

For the classification referendum, we developed reinforcing messages delivered by people voters trusted. Stop a massive tax increase. For once let business pay its fair share. Classification is fair and works. They would hear from their mayor, and their local priest or clergy, and then from Fair Share—each saying how important it was to pass classification. We had enough money to hire political message experts like Dan Payne and John Martilla. Fair Share was spearheading its usual grassroots efforts and now because of the coalition that we had assembled, we could buy ads and send persuasion mail. We even had a barnstorming train that toured the state holding rallies at every stop.[7] Despite the best efforts of the business community to defeat it, the referendum won with 66 percent of the votes.[8]

(As important as the classification victory was, without the circuit breaker we could not stop the conservative tax cap referendum that came a few years later. Furious about rising taxes that outpaced stagnant incomes, many Democratic voters were hearing the appeals of a right-wing campaign that argued not to shift the burden of taxes but simply to cut them across the board, providing large windfalls for the wealthy and the corporations and strangling public revenues.)

One day a few months after the referendum victory, I received a call from Dukakis, asking to meet with me. Heartbroken by his loss to King, he wanted advice in advance of an attempt to run again. As soon as he sat down in my office on Boylston Street in Boston's Back Bay, he launched immediately into why he had come. "Yes, I know. I was wrong about the way I handled tax reform. But I think it reflected a larger problem. I didn't understand that I needed to build a coalition of constituencies. I wasn't in touch enough. Talk to me about what you saw as our mistakes."

At the end of an hour-long discussion, he asked me, "If I want to hire one person to help me put together the coalition that I will need to reclaim the governor's office, who would you suggest?"

Without hesitation I responded, "You can do no better than to hire John Sasso, he would be perfect."

Dukakis hired Sasso, and for years John was his essential partner guiding Dukakis through his successful reelection to the governor's office, then throughout his two terms, and finally, almost making it to the White House.

Fair Share won significant campaign after campaign.

The phone company attempted to raise rates. We countered with a proposal for "Lifeline Phone Rates" where the initial small amount of usage was less expensive and then as usage increased, the rates increased. We fought and won to keep payphones, used disproportionally by the poor, to a dime—pricing that would stand for more than thirty years.

The organization fought for and won massive changes in how auto insurance rates were set, and equally massive rebate checks. In 1977 insurance companies were given the ability to set their own rates. Auto insurance companies set rates in part based on the overall accident rates in communities—not the performance of the individual driver. Then they overlaid community rates with personal rates using gender, age, and marital status. The result was that drivers in urban areas were paying dramatically inflated insurance bills. In dense places like East Boston, with all the traffic going to and from the airport, it was not uncommon for a family to pay more than $2,000 a year to insure one old car. At the same time, the companies abused the "high risk pool," placing sound drivers with good records in a pool designed for drivers with a history of poor driving. Fair Share swung into action, pressuring the governor, the insurance commissioner, and the legislature. As a result of that first Fair Share insurance campaign, the legislature passed a bill ordering the companies to refund $55 million to 800,000 motorists.[9]

The legislation also gave the insurance commissioner new, broader powers to determine how rates were set. Commissioner Jim Stone, extraordinarily smart and progressive, was delighted to have Fair Share pressure him to make drastic

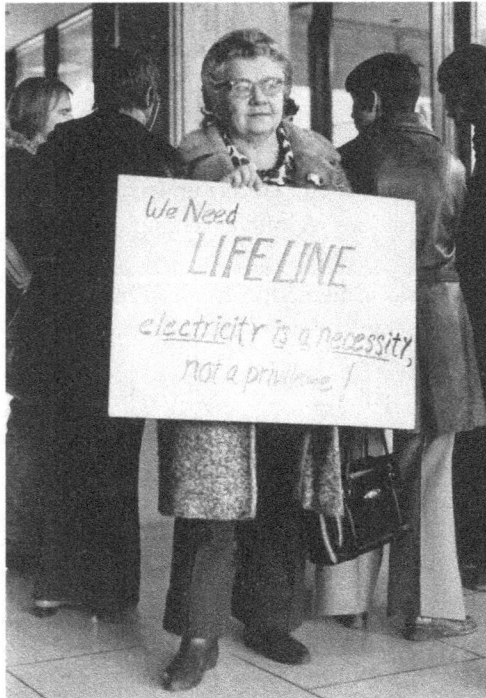

FIGURE 53. Typical Fair Share member. Courtesy of University Archives and Special Collections, Joseph P. Healey Library, University of Massachusetts Boston: Ann Raszmann Brown community organizations photographs.

changes in how insurance companies set rates. Under public pressure from Fair Share, Stone ruled that there would be one uniform rate setting for all companies. Several days after Christmas, 1978, Stone announced a statewide drop in rates of 12 percent and in urban areas two and three times that.[10] It was clear that the decrease came from the Fair Share campaign.

There is nothing like winning to boost support for an organization. Thousands of people received checks from our campaigns. We joked that the only thing that could have been better was if the checks had said on them "Brought to you by Mass Fair Share." Still, it was clear to most recipients why they had gotten the money and reductions in rates, and loyalty to Fair Share grew dramatically.

One evening I was again in Worcester, this time for a meeting of our statewide leadership team working on the auto insurance campaign. In reaction, really overreaction, to the wild ideological excesses of the late sixties (in a moment of complete foolishness I had once told a *Boston Globe* reporter in 1969 that I was a "democratic communist"), now I focused firmly on "self-interest." We wanted the organization's appeal to be "specific, immediate, realizable and rooted in self-interest." However, I was beginning to sense that we were selling our leaders short and failing to articulate the values that motivated them.

After the meeting, several leaders approached me, needing rides to get home as they had come with organizers who had left early for another meeting. In getting rides sorted out, I realized that several leaders such as the indefatigable Mike Regan did not own a car.

Surprised, I asked, "You don't own a car? Then why are you here working on auto insurance reform?"

Mike answered simply, "Because I want justice." I turned to the other people still in the room.

"Why are you here?"

Answer: "I want fair play."

These and so many Fair Share leaders gave of their time not primarily out of a narrowly defined self-interest; they were in it for justice, for fairness. Even though they would never have used the words, they believed in social solidarity. I left the meeting convinced that the organization needed to start using more explicit exploration of values in our leadership development and training programs. From then on, we wove values and vision into the work. We still focused on victories that would benefit people, but we edged away from a narrative based on a narrow definition of self-interest.

The list of campaigns and successes stretched on and on. Of course there were defeats. Still, each year, Fair Share members and the public could see the impact of the organization, the impact of direct citizen action. Sometimes those victories were highly local neighborhood issues. For example, the Chelsea Street Bridge, an old drawbridge that was one of two connecting East Boston to Chelsea, was opened for a tanker and became stuck in the upright position. Traffic became snarled, accidents common. Yet the bridge went unfixed for months, with the residents of East Boston getting more and more furious. There was federal money for new bridge construction but not for repair of old ones. More months went by. Then East Boston Fair Share took it on, targeting Congressional House speaker Tip O'Neill, he of the famous quote "all politics is local." His district included East Boston. Marches and protests demanding that O'Neill free up funds resulted quickly in the bridge finally being fixed.

To fully understand Mass Fair Share and its impact, repeat that story over and over again in sixty low-income neighborhoods across the state. Instead of a broken bridge, it might be a missing stop light. A dangerous abandoned building. A vacant lot infested with garbage and rats. A toxic waste dump. A park that needed cleaning up. The last bank leaving a neighborhood. A rash of uninvestigated arson. Redlining. Block busting. Story after story of citizens demanding that the government work for them for a change and making sure it did.

At Fair Share we were committed to an old dream: an interracial movement. It was not easy in Boston, where the virulent racist populism of the antibusing movement was prevalent in the white working-class neighborhoods. We insisted on a direct approach to residents in those neighborhoods. Our message was: "We are not asking that you love Black folk, but we are asking that you work together to win on issues that matter to you and to them. There is no way you or they will win economic justice if you allow the elites to divide you. Their game is all divide and conquer. Our response must be to work together and win."

We didn't shy away from hard campaigns. We tackled issues of redlining and block busting. We stressed building a multiracial effort. The failure to focus exclusively on organizing around specific needs of Black people as Black people, caused unrelenting criticism from Black leaders like Chuck Turner and even sometimes from my old friend Mel King. How could we think an organization led by white people could seriously organize in Black communities? How could we think it was proper to mobilize around common issues when Black people had been oppressed so severely and specifically for hundreds of years?

While the attacks from the antibusing leaders were strident, attacks from Black leaders in Boston were more painful. Mostly we were running up against a different strategy from thoughtful leaders. They saw the need to organize Black people around their identity as Black people and to press for demands that were unique to them.

We did not oppose that strategy. We felt something else was needed as well—our multiracial populism. In those days, Boston was a very white city. Black families made up only 16 percent of the city.[11] We felt the need for a multiracial populism precisely because of the power of the antibusing movement and its racist populism, the extreme tribalism, and segregation that plagued the city.

The response to Fair Share from Black families, particularly Black women, was enthusiastic. They wanted to be part of an organization that fought for economic justice and fought for their neighborhood.

We did struggle to hire and train Black organizers. There were precious few talented younger Black people who wanted to take up organizing with Fair Share. In part that was because new corporate and professional opportunities were opening up quickly for well-educated, talented young members of the first generation to benefit from the civil rights gains. It was hard for us to compete with banks, law schools, investment companies, and so many other better-paying employers wooing the "best and brightest" of Black college graduates. And those who were looking for a different path were often leery of coming into an organization whose staff was overwhelmingly white. We were determined to recruit young Black organizers to train, and to search across the country to find Black senior staff.

Our search finally turned up an unlikely pair who brought exactly what we needed. I got a call from a Bill Thompson who said that he had heard that we were looking for senior organizers. He had heard of Fair Share and was interested. He and a close friend, Richard Montgomery, would be open to coming up to Boston from Pennsylvania to interview us to see if we fit what they were looking for. I asked about his organizing experience and was impressed by the long list of organizations he had worked with.

Bill and Richard soon arrived, and we spent the next several days in nonstop conversation. Bill was not a large man in physical size, but he felt large, large in spirit, large in generosity, large in humor, poetry, and song, always filling the room. After talking with him at length, I thought Bill was as close to a Black analog to me as was possible within the mirror of the American racial divide. He came from blue-collar Pennsylvania, had been fired up with hope by the Civil Rights Movement, plunged into it, then radicalized by the war and Richard Nixon, worked against the war, joined the Black Panthers, and was as militant as anyone. However, he came to see the failings in his militancy and slowly found his way back to a belief in serious grassroots organizing. He thought Fair Share was the model for what he wanted to build. He wanted to play a senior role with us and then some day, return to Pennsylvania and build a similar organization based in Reading and Allentown, where he had grown up.

He was accompanied by his close friend Richard, who had been a serious basketball prospect before becoming radicalized and converting to Islam. Richard exuded passion and a warm heart with a clear affinity for the verbal patter of Muhammad Ali. The two made a formidable pair. I was thrilled to hire them.

For two years, they led our organizing efforts in Boston's Black communities and started training younger organizers. All seemed to be going well. Bill and I took to working out together at the rather seedy gym down the street from our offices. One day he stayed after I returned to the Fair Share office. I received a frantic call from the gym: Bill had collapsed from some kind of stroke. He was rushed to the hospital. I immediately went there, and the first reports were promising; the stroke was not that serious and was treatable. He and I talked; he was eager to recover and get back to work. Later that night he suffered a horrible reaction to the medicine given to him, a reaction that was confined to an exceedingly small percentage of patients, all African American. And he was gone. Then a long, numbingly sad ride on the train to Pennsylvania to bring his body back to his grieving family. That experience shook me. On that ride to Pennsylvania, as I sat and listened to the steady rhythm of the train on the tracks, I heard the blood beating in my veins in a way I never had before.

In some ways we never recovered from Bill's death. Richard stayed on but was not the same without Bill. We managed to keep some of the organizers they were training and even attract a few more talented young Black trainees who became good organizers. But we never found that senior replacement to fill Bill's shoes. Our young white organizers were always welcomed on Black blocks, but we had wanted to build senior organizing leadership of color. We failed to do that.

Despite that failure, we did build an interracial organization in Boston and in other cities around the state. We built deep organizations in the Black neighborhoods of Boston. While two African American men, Art Shephard and George Huggins, rose to be statewide leaders, on the ground in those neighborhoods, it was amazing Black women who took the lead. Women like Vernice Gabriel, Bernice Smith, Cheryl Harris, Inez Wilkins, Dottie Sellman, and so many more, who had deep networks, devoted themselves to caring for their families, friends, and community. They were active in their churches, active on their blocks and could move others to action.

In one campaign, Boston Fair Share took on bus transportation, specifically in the Black neighborhoods. Fair Share charged the Massachusetts Bay Transportation Authority (MBTA) with clear racial discrimination for maintaining inferior service, a poorly maintained Dudley Station, a lack of bus shelters on routes serving the Black community, and poor scheduling. The *Boston Globe* headlined: "Citizen Group Charges Racial Bias in T Service."[12] The chapters in the other white neighborhoods joined in and supported the African American Fair Share leaders who won changes in bus services, bus shelters, and investment in improved maintenance.

In 1980 at the annual convention of several thousand Fair Share members, Art Shephard lead an effort to pass a resolution condemning racism and endorsing the Fair Share "Covenant of Racial Justice and Harmony." The motion passed unanimously. Sitting in the hall and voting for it were some white Fair Share members who had supported the antibusing movement only six years earlier.

This certainly did not mean that Fair Share successfully drove out racism. It was always there, simmering, and real. But we were able to witness changes in some white families who had supported the antibusing movement but through the experience of working in a multiracial organization, grew out of their virulent racism. As had the great union organizing drives of the 1930s, the experience of being in Fair Share, in fighting alongside Black families changed those white working-class families.

Fair Share was in some ways two organizations. There were the chapters based in the blue-collar and low-income major urban neighborhoods, as well as in the smaller cities across the state. The chapters were organizer intensive. At our height there were close to one hundred paid staff, including full-time organizers, trainees, interns, and paid Volunteers in Service to America (VISTA) working in the chapter areas.

In addition to the neighborhood organizers, Fair Share employed a new form of outreach staff—paid door-to-door canvassers.

In the year before the merger, the original Fair Share team had contracted with Marc Anderson to run a door-to-door canvassing operation. Marc was a Vietnam vet and passionate environmentalist. In Chicago he founded Citizens for a Better Environment, hiring young people to go door to door, asking people to sign a petition, and to make a donation. It worked. Marc was willing to bring his operation to Massachusetts for Fair Share and to other organizations around the country.

From the start, the canvass was successful. However, having it run from long distance proved problematic. We decided the arrangement with Marc was unsustainable. I was delegated the job of breaking the contract and bringing the canvass under our control with all of its staff becoming Mass Fair Share employees. Marc was remarkably accommodating and generous.

We ran our own canvass at a time when there were no other door-to-door efforts in the state. Every year we knocked on more than 400,000 doors. In the summers, the canvassing staff grew to over 300 boisterous, excited, idealistic college students. In the winter, it kept going with a smaller number of college graduates and dropouts. The canvass raised funds, while it also allowed us to garner statewide support. It produced a flow of lawsuits as wealthy towns attempted to keep us out (we always won). While successful, the canvass was never extremely profitable, as most of the funds went to pay the salaries of the canvassers, their trainers, and managers. Still, in the early years it netted 10 to 15 percent and was a powerful outreach effort that brought Fair Share to the doors of thousands of people each month.

Twice a year I insisted that every staff member go out with the canvass teams to experience the work they were doing. That, of course, meant I had to do it as well. There was a lot of pressure on me to do well. The first time, I drove with a team of canvassers to the North Shore, was dropped off on a street with very large and well-appointed homes. The first several houses I visited, I came up empty and was starting to worry. It would be embarrassing if I failed to meet the quota we asked every canvasser to raise. I rang the doorbell of the next home. I could see lights on, so I knew someone was there. No one came to the door. I rang again. Finally, a disheveled young woman, who looked to me to be in her late teens, opened the door, standing there among toys strewn about. She was attempting to quickly button her untucked blouse. I had the distinct impression I was interrupting something, but since she did not ask me to leave, I explained why I was there. She told me to wait. After a few minutes, an even more unkempt middle-aged man, appeared at the door, obviously flustered. I started my pitch and he cut me off: "Yes, yes Fair Share, yes. . . . Here take this and please go away." He emptied his wallet of cash, and I walked away with $140. That meant I was already over quota for the night and still had two hours to go. The fact that I beat quota by so much enhanced my reputation with the canvassers. I refrained from explaining to anyone that I thought that I probably caught a father having illicit sex with the babysitter.

Many organizers, especially those working in low-income communities, feel conflicted about asking for money. When I first organized in Dorchester with TPF, I thought the people there were too strapped to be asked to contribute anything. In our storefront, someone, most definitely not one of the organizers, put out a huge blue water bottle and attached a hand-lettered sign: Support TPF—Remove Troy. People started dropping change and dollar bills into it. As time went on people would stop in at the storefront just to drop a few dollars into that big blue bottle.

One time I mentioned my initial reluctance to ask for donations. The response was unequivocal: "What, you don't think we would want to pay our own way? Hell, nothing in this world is free. For Chrissake if you don't allow some of us to make contributions, you're blocking us from participating. I thought you were here to help us participate more!"

At Fair Share, I was all about raising money to scale up the organization. Since money was essential to organizing, we developed a multifaceted fundraising program. Membership dues were $15 per year. We had membership drives in the neighborhoods. The canvass sold memberships and collected donations: no donation too small. Observing what churches did, we organized Las Vegas Nights—one night of legal gambling in a local church hall made possible by our nonprofit status. We also used our nonprofit tax status to bring in carnivals. Our ability to access public space enabled carnival operators to bring their rides to densely populated areas—paying a substantial fee to us. We also raised money from foundations and wealthy donors.

The budget of the organization increased rapidly, growing from under $200,000 in that first year to more than $3 million in less than six years. We were proud that 90 percent of our funds were raised organizationally. I was always pushing for new ways to raise more. Money was the key to sustaining a large and ever-growing organization. And raising it ourselves meant we were only accountable to the members.

I am sure that outbound phone fundraising would have been invented sooner or later, but as far as I know, Fair Share was the first organization, at least in the Northeast, to use a dedicated phone bank of paid outbound callers to raise significant sums of money. Telethons from Jerry Lewis to public television had been doing phone campaigns for years where viewers urged on by TV called into a toll-free number to donate. Throughout the 1970s public radio was doing very successful on-air drives.

We had more than 100,000 households who, when a stranger knocked on their door and explained that they were collecting memberships and donations for Mass Fair Share, would give $15, $25, and $50. A year later they would give again. I kept mulling over ways to get them to give again sooner, to give more, and how to lower the cost of getting their donation.

One day, an old friend called looking for a job. Sandy Sokoloff was a talented artist, a painter who annoyed me enormously for decades by squandering his substantial talent. I had not heard from Sandy in several years when he called me and then came by. He was desperate for a job. He had been working multiple short-term jobs, including for the census and for WGBH, our local public television station, answering the phone for their pledge drives.

I asked him if he thought calling our canvass donors, especially ones who had given $15 or more, might work. Sandy was eager to try it. I told him, "Okay. You are hired to design a phone campaign calling the donors from the door-to-door canvass six months from the date of their last donation. We will do a very small test: you personally will call for a couple of days. If it goes well, you will call for several weeks. If that goes well, we will build a small team of callers, and you will train and direct them as well as make calls yourself."

The first call Sandy made was a success. The man on the other end of the phone said he would be delighted to give again to support Fair Share. "Given how much Fair Share has saved me, this is a bargain."

The calling went spectacularly well. Within several months, Sandy had a small team making calls and creating systems for sending out pledge packages and processing the checks that came back. Over a short time, the net funds raised by the phone canvass were over a half a million dollars a year.

Another unexpected source of financial support for Mass Fair Share came from the federal government. In 1977 President Jimmy Carter appointed Sam Brown as the head of ACTION, the agency that housed the Peace Corps and VISTA. I had a long history with Sam. He had been the appalled spokesperson for the National Student Association during the *Ramparts* exposé of CIA funding. Then he got his first taste of organizing as a volunteer with Vietnam Summer which led him to become the youth coordinator for Gene McCarthy's challenge to Lyndon B. Johnson. While at the Harvard Divinity School, he was one of the coordinators for the Moratorium. After a stint as state treasurer of Colorado, Carter chose Sam to head ACTION where he brought in two other people I had long known and admired, John Lewis of SNCC and Marge Tabankin. Marge had been an antiwar activist and then the first woman trained by the Saul Alinsky network, before becoming the head of a nonprofit, The Youth Project, that had been a source of funding for many organizing efforts. Together they reshaped VISTA so that community organizing was an approved role for the volunteers. Fair Share received a first batch of twenty and eventually as many as forty paid VISTA volunteer positions, allowing us to dramatically increase the number of organizers and organizer trainees.

While at Fair Share, I studied populist movements, in particular the Non-Partisan League of North Dakota. I was struck by how they had created an economic infrastructure to support their political movement. They had established cooperatives and even banks. We wanted to emulate the populists of those movements.[13] But if were to do so, we would need some help from people with a very different skill set than our organizers. We brought in Josh Posner to figure out how we might use the membership and name recognition of Fair Share to launch cooperatives that would provide tangible benefits for members, deepening their ties to the organization. Josh had been a student activist at Brown, a community organizer in Brockton, and then worked on low-income housing.

Josh set out to build an economic development arm. The first venture was a successful home heating oil cooperative. Bringing together hundreds of members to negotiate group contracts with oil companies, we were able to get significantly better prices than any individual could. From an oil co-op it was not a huge leap to energy conservation audits.

We created a new legal entity, the Fair Share Development Corporation, which outlasted Mass Fair Share. Over time, it became the Conservation Services Group led by Mark Dyen, Steve Cowell, and Adam Parker. They built it into a massive energy conservation services effort that, over thirty years, grew to operate in twenty-three states and employ 800 people. They would contract with utility companies and governments to run large-scale conservation efforts, doing home energy audits, weatherizing, and making improvements that would reduce energy use. The result was that energy companies would not have to build costly new plants and homeowners reduced their energy bills.

As Fair Share grew, we grappled with how to be part of something national. We knew that only a national effort could address the root causes of the economic dislocation all around us. Increasingly we looked for a path forward to build national power. We were not interested in another national effort that did not have a deep base of support in the states and communities. Our challenge was to build more state level organizations that could then band together.

Our first attempt was a national strategy around energy, led by Heather Booth. Heather convinced William Winpisinger, the head of the International Association of Machinists and Aerospace Workers (IAM), to create a coalition focused on a progressive energy policy. The coalition would be composed of labor unions and citizens, community, senior, and consumer organizations around the country. The IAM had 920,000 members back then. Heather convinced the unions— still wary of the movements of the 1960s—to work with our community groups, the National Council of Senior Citizens, and churches to form a Citizen Labor Energy Coalition (CLEC). Most of the financial support for CLEC came from the union. CLEC launched national campaigns around the energy crisis of the seventies that allowed groups such as Fair Share to participate on the national stage. Mark became the New England coordinator.

In Massachusetts, with CLEC joining us, Fair Share won the fight for unitary taxation of oil companies. The oil companies created many corporate entities in different states and countries. They made sure most of the profits were placed in the subsidiary in the lowest tax areas. Massachusetts was only taxing a fraction of the real economic activity and profits taking place in the state. Under the unitary method we passed, all the entities were combined, and the Massachusetts tax was based on a fair evaluation. Arcane stuff, but we found ways to simplify and make it clear that it was time for the oil companies to start paying their fair share.

Organizers in other states were starting new organizations like Fair Share. In Oregon, an organizer named Kim Clerc founded Oregon Fair Share. In Connecticut, Toby Moffet and Ralph Nader had created an organization in 1970 to work on consumer and environmental issues, the Connecticut Citizen Action Group (CCAG). In 1975 CCAG started a door-to-door canvass, as well as deployed organizers to cities and communities. In early 1979 CCAG, however, was in turmoil. Marc Caplan, the director, knew he needed help, and we at Fair Share were the nearest source. The only person I thought capable of leading a successful turnaround was the best organizer we had, Miles Rapoport. With some trepidation I suggested that Miles become their new director. We thought that it would only be for a short period; however, Miles forged a lifelong political partnership with Marc. Under his leadership, CCAG not only righted itself but rapidly grew and became a significant force in Connecticut politics.[14]

As we groped for a national strategy, the Midwest Academy became central to our efforts. Started by Heather Booth and employing another old SDS leader Steve Max, the Midwest Academy offered intensive training sessions for organizers. It provided an important development process for organizing talent and became the place where organizers could share their craft.

There was growth in new state organizations, many related to the Midwest Academy, that while working on the same issues as Mass Fair Share, approached the work differently. These organizations combined door-to-door canvasses with a coalition approach that brought together unions, senior citizen organizations, and some community-based organizations. These included the Illinois Public Action Coalition (IPAC), Indiana Citizen Action, and the Ohio Public Interest Campaign started by my old organizing pal, Ira Arlook.

In 1979 Heather, Miles, Bob Creamer of IPAC, and I convened a series of meetings to explore how to create a national organization. Too many of the decisions that would wipe out neighborhoods, close workplace after workplace, determine the cost of living, and shape the economy were made at a national level. To be serious about our organizing we needed a national strategy and organization. We agreed that the participating state organizations did not need to be uniform, that we would allow for state variation especially as we were all still testing and learning. With Ira as the executive director and Heather as the president, we launched Citizen Action.

Soon there were organizations in New York, Florida, Virginia, Wisconsin, New Jersey, and even Idaho. Within three years, Citizen Action grew to include twenty state organizations

Citizen Action tackled economic issues: rate hikes and the price of energy, plant closings, tax reform, and a variety of state issues. Its retreats brought together hundreds of organizers and leaders to share ideas and strategies.

As the decade drew to a close, we appeared to be on the cusp of creating a national effort that was rooted in state organizations. We thought we were ready to become a force in national politics. The growth of Citizen Action was running against the national political tide. Ronald Reagan's election in 1980 ushered in a new conservative dominance. His success among "Reagan Democrats" made the compelling case that if there was not a populism of the left, there would be ever-increasing success for a right-wing populism that appealed to those left behind. Globalization was beginning to empty out factories and communities as corporations raced to find the labor markets with the lowest cost. Unions and liberal organizations were reeling. Despite the rising tide of reactionary politics, it seemed as if Fair Share could alter what was possible in Massachusetts and perhaps Citizen Action could develop a successful national progressive populism.

At home we had welcomed a second daughter, Meg, who had arrived in a hurry that August of 1979. I missed the moment of her birth, frantically scurrying after a meeting in Worcester to find that she had been born within eight minutes of Amy arriving at the hospital. Two delightful daughters, leading a powerful statewide organization and helping form a new national organization. Life was full. I felt I was again at the center of a historic fight.

I was personally exhausted, however. Shortly, and way too soon, the bottom would drop out for me and for Fair Share.

THE END OF MY LONG SIXTIES

History is like water. It ebbs. It flows. History moves slowly. Until suddenly it doesn't. Social movements cannot be willed into existence, nor are they created by organizers and activists. They are the product of deep social and historical forces. Economic, social, political, and cultural forces converge. Wars, depressions, demographic changes, new technologies all disrupt old ways of doing things. These large-scale changes sometimes produce extraordinary moments, the moments of social movement when ordinary people feel pulled out of the quotidian trajectory of their lives to do remarkable things.

While leaders and organizers and activists do not bring a social movement into existence, leaders have a huge impact on its direction, its success or failure. Think: Nelson Mandela, Martin Luther King, Jr., Fannie Lou Hamer, or Vaclav Havel. Alongside the leaders there are always organizers working to turn feeling into program, emotion into action, action into lasting organization, working to educate and structure the great awakenings that come with social movements. Organizers prepare for the moments of social movement. Then they take advantage of the high tides of social movements to grab a bit of the ground the waves have made possible and hold some of it once the waves recede, as they always must.

I think of my "long sixties" as the twenty-three years when I went from a young boy to a man, to a father, from an activist to a skilled organizer. Two decades when I tried with every cell of my hyperactive brain to alter history. I started as a despairing adolescent; I traveled across amazing peaks of hope and desperation; I witnessed the dignity and audacity of so many "ordinary" people attempting the extraordinary. I felt a direct connection to history. For twenty-three years the "movement" gave my life purpose and meaning. And yet I emerged humbled and confused.

Starting in 1980, I went through a hideous three-year period. First my mother died an ugly death from cancer, the disease breaking most of the bones in her body. Dealing with her illness and protracted dying was unrelenting, depressing, and disruptive. After she died, my seventeen-year-old marriage reached a final crisis, unraveled, and ended in divorce, leaving me caring for two young daughters most of the time. For two years there had been endless sessions with marriage counselors and perpetual crises at home. Then in the year after Amy and I agreed to divorce, I received a call from my father's doctor. He had failed to show up at his appointment and was not answering his phone. After getting no answer, I went to his apartment with the police who broke the door, and we found my father dead on the floor by his desk. He had finally experienced the fatal heart attack we had been dreading for years.

As my personal life went from crisis to crisis, Fair Share encountered a severe financial challenge. The organization had grown faster than my ability to manage it. In 1981 we abruptly lost our forty Volunteers in Service to America (VISTA) slots as the new Reagan administration moved quickly to make sure no federal resources went into progressive organizing. The proper response should have been to make significant staff reductions and reduce spending. I refused. Feeling battered on all sides, I locked myself into a path of obstinately persevering. I was convinced that we could weather the storm, keep everyone on staff, and somehow will our way through it. Our inexperienced financial team agreed. Our phone fundraising was going remarkably well. The gross revenues from the canvass remained high.

The organization careened from one cash shortage to another. We delayed payments to our landlords and to other vendors. We episodically delayed payroll.

The financial crisis exacerbated tensions within the staff. In 1979 and 1980, as our reputation grew, older longtime organizers from across the country had asked to join Fair Share. While they brought a lot of prior experience and talent, they also brought their own ways of doing things and, in several cases, a distinctly competitive approach. The result was that as the organization experienced financial strain, there was, for the first time, the growth of factionalism inside the large staff and criticism of my leadership, which, to be accurate, was suffering acutely from my personal crises.

We seemed unable to get on top of what we thought were perpetual cash flow challenges. I replaced the finance director with someone who came with experience managing nonprofit finance departments. My choice was a serious mistake. He had neither the skill nor the character to deal with the complexities we faced.

Once we fired him, we discovered bookkeeping irregularities along with unsent checks to the IRS in his desk drawer.

Finally, our banker, John Marston, a good friend, requested that we bring in an outside accountant, Tom Feeley. Tom brought in a small team to pour through our books. He then sat me down to deliver the bad news. While we were indeed raising $3,000,000 a year, we had been spending $3,400,000 for the last three years. We had a deficit of $1,200,000 and there was no way we could pay off our debts. We owed money to the bank. We owed money to the IRS that was accumulating exorbitant interest and penalties. The canvass that raised such a large share of our budget had been so costly that there had been no net income for the last several years. We had no system of spending controls. Our books were a mess. The bank would be forced to call our loans. The IRS would demand payment immediately. "Michael," Tom said, "you are broke and out of options. You need to slash spending, tell everyone who cosigned loans that they must pay back the bank the guaranteed portion of the loans. I will work with you to get an agreement from the IRS to waive penalties and put you on a strict payment plan. The bank will have to eat the loans that are not guaranteed. But to start with, you need to make massive cuts in spending immediately."

I enacted devastating layoffs of two-thirds of the staff, beginning with myself. Everyone, including me, was in complete shock. At first, I slogged on, heartbroken, dazed. Without a paycheck I was not sure how I would survive, but I refused to abandon Fair Share, thinking I could figure out something.

For the first time in my life, I experienced profound failure on top of failure. I could not save my parents. I could not save my marriage. While I refused to admit it, I could not save Fair Share.

I had to tell friends and donors who had cosigned our loans that now they had to pay the bank. With Tom's help I was desperately negotiating payment plans with the IRS. I was dealing with irate vendors who had not been paid for months. I was miserable. I was a mess.

After several months of this, the senior women in the organization asked to take me out to lunch. At the meeting, one by one, gently, respectfully but firmly, they told me that it was time for me to leave Fair Share. "You have two small daughters that need your care," one emphasized. "You're a wreck and need to take care of yourself," another said. "While we appreciate your sense of responsibility, you need to resign and step away," they all said in one way or another. Listening to them I simultaneously felt waves of great sadness and relief. They were right. I was a wreck. I was not really doing anyone any good attempting to soldier on.

I told the Fair Share leaders, many of whom were still in shock and many of whom were furious with me, that I had to resign, and that they needed to find a replacement from within the remaining senior staff. I was delighted that they chose Mark Dyen, who, with some trepidation, was willing to do what he could in the face of enormous challenges. I felt great guilt about leaving Fair Share in such a state. But I was done. I was exhausted. I was a shell of myself, and I had two young daughters who needed me.

Fair Share would continue for several more years. It would even win important victories. But the financial crash had started it on a downward spiral that, despite the heroic efforts of the remaining staff, could not be reversed.

There certainly had been other weaknesses with the organization. We suffered from the inaccurate dichotomy between "organizers" and "leaders" that was common to community organizing in those days. We were too dependent on staff. We also experienced difficulty translating our power into the electoral arena. At the start we had positioned the organization as outside the corruption of Massachusetts politics. We always intended to enter that arena once we had built power and credibility. Having sharply criticized electoral politics, we encountered internal resistance when we proposed directly playing a role in elections. Yet to truly win what we were fighting for, we needed to be able to defeat politicians who opposed us and elect a new wave of leaders who emerged from the organization or supported our program. That new wave of leaders was emerging and beginning in small numbers to be elected to municipal positions, but they were running on their own, without the organization officially throwing its resources into their campaigns. After I left, many of the Boston leaders and many of the Boston staff organized the successful populist mayoral campaign of Ray Flynn and became his political organization. That demonstrated Fair Share's strength in Boston but also weakened it as they left the organization to join Flynn. With time, Fair Share could have made the needed transition, but our financial crisis short-circuited everything.

While Fair Share did not last, its impact persisted. A remarkable group of young Fair Share organizers went on to work for unions, electoral campaigns, environmental groups, and other organizations. They would lead other community organizations, revitalize several unions, elect mayors, run cities, enter state legislatures, run foundations, work on presidential campaigns, head think tanks, and organize undocumented immigrants. One became a lawyer who won major legal victories for Native Americans, and another filed successful suits against lead paint and tobacco companies. Others would become elected officials, judges, and beloved teachers. They all would say that their time at Fair Share was essential to who they became.

When I left Fair Share in 1983, I was worn out. Certainly, I was drained by three years of an unending succession of tragedies. I was also exhausted by the continuous effort to exert leadership for so many years, starting at such a young age. So much of what I had tried to do had been through acts of will. It is trite but true to say that I had focused so much on the work, I had done little to renew myself. I had believed that being part of the movement would in and of itself be nourishing. It was not enough.

Not only was I exhausted but so were the social movements I had been a part of for so many years. The New Left was no longer. The youth revolt had largely been turned into a marketing ploy. The heroic civil rights wave had accomplished so much but was now meeting an inevitable backlash. The antiwar movement had dissipated. The failure of the movements of the 1960s to create an effective political expression left a vacuum. Still, powerful currents had been unleashed that would travel on, gain steam, and change the country. The women's movement would forever alter what was possible for women. A growing environmental movement would force new ways of thinking about our world, nature, and our responsibilities. A new gay rights movement would over the next forty years change America, winning seemingly impossible transformations.

I left Fair Share, and my world changed dramatically. No longer was I a full-time organizer. My phone rarely rang. I had no meeting to organize or attend. I focused primarily on my two delightful daughters. And so, like many of my generation, I turned to the one area where, perhaps, I might feel some success: raising my children.

In the next years I would put my daughters first. I would work as a very part-time consultant to the Nuclear Freeze Campaign and the Central American Peace Campaign. Over time I would consult on voter registration strategies and work on political campaigns, including, ironically, Michael Dukakis's campaign for president. I would stumble into running several businesses. I would retain the fundamental values that had been formed in the movements of the 1960s. But I would no longer define myself as a full-time organizer. In many ways I was adrift without that identity.

In 1996 I would experience a profound midlife crisis and become unforgivably embroiled in a headline-producing scandal around the campaign of the reform president of the Teamsters Union. I would, unknowingly, participate in a conspiracy of money laundering, misuse of union dues, fraud, and extortion of union contractors. I was guilty of multiple felonies. Once I understood, way too late, what I had been part of, I took full responsibility, pleading guilty to one felony count. I would argue with supportive friends who claimed I was the victim of overzealous prosecution, "No," I would state, "I am guilty." My negligence was indefensible.

Over the years, I would slowly rebuild my life, become a poet and essayist, and volunteer for campaigns and with nonprofit organizations. However, I would never again have the heady sense that I was leading thousands, that I was making history. I remain acutely aware of my flaws. My hope is to be helpful to a new generation of leaders.

Looking back on my "long sixties," I was fortunate enough to have been one of roughly 10,000 women and men of my age group who participated full-time in the great efforts of those years: to split apart the relentless hold of racism, to end a war that should never have been waged, to create new organizations that were massive schools of democracy, to support the birth of a movement that irrevocably altered the role of women, to organize low-income and blue-collar communities to have a voice and to fight for their fair share.

Many people today ask me: don't you miss the sixties? I do miss that feeling of being part of something so much larger than myself. I do miss the sense of being connected to history in such a direct and raw way. I miss being a young, idealistic activist. I miss feeling the power of bending, or at least attempting to bend, the arc of history.

I do not miss the feeling of waking up every day thinking that so many people's lives depend upon what we—including me with all my shuddering imperfections and immaturities—will be able to do. The feeling, every single day, of not being good enough, not being smart enough, not being effective enough to live up to the imperatives we faced. I do not miss the fear, the experiences of detectives with large guns putting those barrels to my head, screaming, "One of these days I am going to blow your head off you motherfucking maggot!" No, I do not miss that.

I do not miss the feeling that I could not save those well-meaning boys who did not have my student draft deferment and were going to die because we could not awaken enough of the country. I do not miss the terrible sadness of Dr. King gunned down on a balcony in Memphis; of Fred Hampton shot to death in his bed in Chicago; of Michael Schwerner, Andrew Goodman, and James Chaney buried in the mud of Mississippi; of the protesting students at Kent State and Jackson State who were killed; of the countless children napalmed; of getting into my comfortable bed knowing that a half a world away, Vietnamese and Americans my own age would meet that night in cramped underground tunnels, and many of them would die.

I do not miss the weight of knowing that we, our band of desperate, hopeful young people, were all that stood in the way of an even wider war.

And I do not miss so much of what was the America of 1960. In twenty-six states, it was illegal for a man and woman of different races to marry. It was illegal for consenting adults of the same sex to make love. Girls were not allowed to play baseball. Law firms did not have women partners. It was a time when the overwhelming number of college students believed the president of the United States never lied. When men were supposed to be "real men." When people were just beginning to read *Silent Spring* and have a conception of something called the environment. The rivers in midwestern industrial cities regularly caught fire and no one thought it unusual. It was a time of unrestrained American imperial misadventures, not just in Asia but also in Central America and the Caribbean and the Middle East.

I do not miss the America we set out to change, and I do not miss the grind and fear and endless pressure of a war that had to be stopped.

I do miss the bountiful sense of hope and history, knowing for certain that I was a small part of something so much larger.

Of course, looking back now, I wish I had done better, been smarter. Oh, how I wish I had understood the necessity of always holding the moral high ground, the imperative to always and explicitly embrace nonviolence. I wish I could have grasped a strategy that included both disruptive protest and effective electoral action. I wish I had better understood how much symbolism and words matter; I wish that we had always marched only under the American flag. And of course, I wish that the weight of the war had not driven so many of us crazy. Despite all that I am proud of what we attempted. What we did was important.

And, of course, I would do it all again, in a heartbeat.

EPILOGUE
From the Vantage of Fifty Years

As I write these words, I am now further removed from the events of the 1960s than I was in 1964 from World War I, which then seemed unimaginably ancient history.

So much has changed in these fifty-plus years. Today there is an American Chamber of Commerce in the city that used to be named Saigon.[1] The old Soviet Union collapsed. Communist parties around the world imploded, transformed, or disappeared. The Chinese economy has grown into a juggernaut with a new form of state capitalism, with all the voraciousness and vitality of capitalism but with none of the liberal democratic forms associated with capitalism in the West.

Now young Vietnamese line up to enter McDonald's, Kentucky Fried Chicken, Starbucks, Pizza Hut, and Burger King; one can buy a cold Coca-Cola in Hanoi.[2] Nike makes Air Jordan sneakers in Vietnamese factories, employing the grand-daughters of those who fought us.[3] In a neighborhood where once tens of thousands of American GIs strolled the streets, workers at the Danu Vina factory turn out plush Mickey and Minnie Mouse dolls for Disney.[4]

US Navy ships make calls to Danang and Ho Chi Minh City. In the wake of anti-Chinese riots across Vietnam, and Chinese activity in the South China Sea, the US 7th Fleet suggested that it should make more stops in Vietnam.[5] In 2018 the US aircraft carrier *Carl Vinson* steamed into the port of Da Nang, welcomed by Vietnamese leaders. In the following days 6,000 American sailors engaged in "community service projects" in Da Nang and the 7th Fleet Band conducted free concerts.[6] In September 2023, Vietnam elevated its diplomatic relationship with the United States to its highest level, a "comprehensive strategic relationship."[7]

Coke. Plush Minnie Mouse dolls. The second fastest growing economy in Asia. Anti-Chinese riots. A close diplomatic relationship created in large part by concern about China. In 1964 anyone suggesting that a North Vietnamese victory would lead to this future would have been a candidate for a mental asylum.

During the war, we were told endlessly that failure to win in Vietnam inevitably meant that one domino after another would fall to communist aggression, threatening the security of America. That has been proved wrong. The dominoes that did fall fell instead to the powerful forces of global economics, culture, and technology.

From the vantage point of fifty years, some things are clear. The war that our leaders waged in our name, with our young men's lives, with the riches of our land, was the wrong war at the wrong time and in the wrong place.

History has shown that the basic world view that was the rationale for the Vietnam War was simply wrong. The world was and is a far more complex and nuanced place.

The Second World War ruptured the tectonic plates of history. While most American political leaders focused on the lessons of Munich ("appeasement"), the war cracked open space for strong independence movements in former colonies around the world. One of those was the French colony of Vietnam. We can never know what might have happened if the United States had continued to embrace the communist-led independence forces after World War II as it had when those forces fought the Japanese occupation. There is no way of knowing whether the Vietnamese Communist Party might have been even more of a maverick than Yugoslavia's party. The brief but very real Sino-Vietnamese war of 1979 certainly suggests that possibility.

The fact that the communist leaders of Vietnam, emerging from three extraordinarily bloody decades of revolution and war, were not, and are not, democratic does not change the fact that our country should never have prosecuted that war.

With all the benefits of hindsight, would I try again to create opposition to that war? Absolutely! But I hope we would be smarter and better. There is no question that our movement against the war mattered. It was a critical factor in driving Lyndon B. Johnson to reject his generals' request for more troops, not to run again, and to start peace negotiations. Richard Nixon was obsessed with the antiwar movement. We now know that the antiwar movement was a constant constraint stopping him from ever more outlandish escalations. Without the movement Nixon and Henry Kissinger might well have used nuclear weapons.[8] While we made mistakes, our efforts mattered.

The war destroyed so much. In that long list of losses, I count our original vision of a New Left, our political innovation, and our innocence. The politics of our country became distorted and fractured. In so many ways, in the admirable effort to end that war, we lost much of what was best in ourselves.

In a short time, we experienced the unimaginable: we went from a tiny band of the scorned to leaders of demonstrations of hundreds of thousands. We saw the war escalate and escalate, witnessed violence unceasing and unimaginable, and it felt as if we were the only ones there to stop it. We became the leaders of a massive youth insurrection at a time when all around the world, young people were shaking the foundations of society. And throughout, we were so incredibly young. That youth gave us our energy, our passion, and our ability to think in new ways. But it also meant we lacked a grasp of strategy and a mature understanding of how to succeed at the enormously difficult tasks we set for ourselves.

I know that many of my friends from those days will not like my account of our failures. I have read many books by former activists that let us off the hook of historical judgment. There is a great desire to either ignore the craziness that gripped so many of us in 1968, 1969, and 1970 or to see it as somehow a product of government repression, manipulation, agent provocateurs, and infiltration.

Indeed, there is now a well-documented history of how the government launched covert operations targeting both the civil rights and student movements. In the FBI's massive Counterintelligence Program, J. Edgar Hoover did order his agents to "expose, discredit, neutralize and otherwise eliminate" the activists of the Civil Rights Movement, the antiwar movement, and the New Left.[9] That did happen. It was serious. It was often illegal. There were undercover informants; there were agent provocateurs who promoted internal division and urged extremism.

However, to think that the craziness that overcame the student New Left was primarily the product of government infiltration is just not accurate. John Maher didn't accuse me of "objectively" working for the CIA because of government agents in the movement—although I am sure that those agents were happy to amplify such charges. The Weatherman in the New York townhouse didn't plan to bomb the dance at Fort Dix because some government provocateur seduced them into it.

Our youth and the wild ride of those years drove us. Guilt hung heavy. Guilt that we had not ended the war. Guilt that many of us could avoid the draft. Guilt over the many privileges provided us by the very systems we so passionately wanted to change.

Too many New Left leaders careened off the tracks of reality. I saw talented, brilliant friends of mine whose political journey started with a profound rejection of the old left's idolatry of foreign leaders and foreign countries, fall into a parody of all that they had rejected. Our intellectual journey had been launched by studying C. Wright Mills, Marcuse, Jefferson, and Emerson, by exploring American moral traditions, looking for new ways of extending and reinvigorating democracy. By 1969 too often that journey descended into deranged dogmas, secular cults, and a glorification of violence.

It is unlikely that even a sane New Left could have stopped the rise of the vicious conservative counterreformation that dominated the next fifty years of American politics. Once the voting rights bill had been signed, it would not have been possible to stop the consolidation of the white South into a Republican Party on its long march to becoming the party of white grievance, the party of Donald Trump. Equally there is probably little that in the end could have stopped the political and ideological mobilization of the insanely rich.

Still there could have been a more serious, intellectually rigorous, politically relevant resistance.

Counterfactual history is always a subjective, unprovable option. What would our history have been without assassinations? What would have happened had John Kennedy, Martin Luther King, Jr., Malcolm X, and Robert Kennedy lived? What might have developed had Tom Hayden and Rennie Davis crisscrossed the country in 1968 encouraging us to run insurgent antiwar candidates rather than demonstrate in Chicago? What would have happened if Hubert Humphrey had won in 1968 because, instead of his dogged support for the war, he had denounced it? Or if the antiwar movement had decisively mobilized young voters against Nixon? Or if Johnson had aggressively prosecuted Nixon and Kissinger for treasonously sabotaging the Paris peace negotiations?[10]

What could have happened had the New Left matured, not shattered but instead had made a long march through America's institutions, changing cities, media, businesses, and politics?

In the end, the answer is, of course, unknowable.

Many veterans of SDS and the New Left kept working and work to this day for social justice and economic reform. Many have stayed true to their values, lived moral lives, made countless contributions to decency. I could compile a long list of those people; they have my admiration and deep respect.

Yet many more of my generation set off on a long march through society's institutions as individuals. While we had an impact on those institutions, the institutions had a much greater impact on us, deflecting us from the path of serious seekers of change. We failed to challenge the extreme concentration of wealth, the poisonous increase in inequality. We failed to make the threat of climate change a political cause that could not be ignored years ago when there was still time to prevent the worst damage. And of course, tragically, we failed to vanquish the racism that, along with extreme inequality, deforms our politics and degrades our society.

Just as it is tantalizing to think how a successful New Left from the 1960s might have shaped the last fifty years of our nation's history, it is tempting for me to think about the populist road not taken. What if, instead of becoming a party focused on elites, the Democratic Party, or at least major forces within it, had taken up a progressive populism in the vein of Mass Fair Share? Where once it claimed to be the party of the common man, until very recently the Democratic Party was enthralled with elites. That those elites included university presidents, Hollywood actors and even a few writers, does not alter the fact that much of the Democratic agenda was shaped by the interests of the rich and powerful, the titans of tech, bank CEOs, and hedge fund managers.

That embrace occurred while the elites set the rules for a period of accelerated globalization of the economy. Democrats under Bill Clinton, and to an extent under Barack Obama, were as complicit as the Republicans in supporting ever more mobility for capital and allowing American corporations to dramatically lower costs by moving production abroad. Domestically, Democrats, as well as Republicans, worked to slash regulations, allow for ever more financial specula- tion, and did not vehemently fight the weakening of unions.[11] The elites failed to evince the slightest concern for the impact of these policies on vast swaths of America as factories closed, towns withered, and incomes decreased or stag- nated. The result has been extreme income inequality, the hollowing out of the heartland, the ruin of many families.

Intertwined with all this has been the infusion of ever larger sums of money into our politics. In an effort to roll back the tides of the sixties, corporate inter- ests and the wealthy poured money into Republican campaigns. By 1980 there was a clear imbalance. Republicans had won the campaign fundraising arms race. Democratic Congressman Tony Coelho proved that Democrats could compete. There was a new generation of elites who had come of age in the 1960s. They were more sympathetic to Democrats on social issues and, so long as one acquiesced to their economic agenda, they were willing to write large checks. Soon Democratic candidates were spending most of their days dialing for dollars—and talking with the wealthy. Steadily the Democratic economic agenda shifted. Democrats embraced "free trade" and failed to fight against the depredations of unfettered globalism. More and more Democrats supported deregulation and the economy of speculation.

Add to all this the lasting white backlash to the Civil Rights Movement, a wave of new immigrants, and the growth of radical connectivity and social media. The result has been the growth of an ugly populism of the right. It is reminiscent of other past populist moments and leaders: Father Charles Coughlin, Huey Long, George Wallace. America has a long history of populist xenophobia—the Know Nothings, the movements that led to the Chinese Exclusion Act and the Mexican

Deportation Act, the endless waves of racism directed at immigrants and, again and again at Black people first brought to this country in chains. Populism has now become identified with demagoguery, extremism, and white supremacy.

However, there is a significant, if troubled, history of a different sort of American populism. Its most vivid expression came in the People's Party of the 1890s, which campaigned against the banks, plutocrats, the railroads, and the elites. Rooted in agrarian communities in the Midwest and South, this populism rested on a foundation of organic organizations such as the Farmers Alliance. The populist third party in the presidential election of 1892 received 8.5 percent of the popular vote and carried five midwestern and western states. In the congressional elections of 1894, populists took 10 percent of the vote. These populists considered themselves part of the left, often allied with labor and in league with the Socialist Party. In the South they self-consciously organized alliances of Black and white farmers.[12]

The troubled aspect of that legacy is best represented by Tom Watson. In the 1890s he was famous as a leader of the populists, urging Black and white farmers in the South to fight together against "the money power." In 1890 he was elected to Congress and was able to pass the legislation that created Rural Free Delivery, which meant that families in rural areas no longer had to travel miles to get mail and parcels or pay private carriers. However, in Georgia the conservatives mobilized to suppress the votes of Black people. Watson was defeated for reelection. While early in his career, he had been famous for his support for Black farmers, for supporting Black people's right to vote, and for his vociferous opposition to lynching, in his later years Watson became equally vociferous attacking Black people, Catholics, and Jews and campaigning to protect a white Protestant America.[13]

Those of us who emerged from the New Left to become organizers of Mass Fair Share sought to create a new populism of the left. We recognized the beginnings of a profound process that has indeed played out over the last forty years. A large segment of the population, especially those who had no college education, faced new challenges; their incomes stagnated and then declined, their social world collapsing. It was clear that they would feel betrayed and could fall prey to demagogues. Or possibly they could be organized to see the sources of their problems as rooted in the growing inequality of wealth and power and could be organized to band together with people of different races and ethnicities who had long experienced the same inequality. We sensed it would be one or the other: the demagogues of the right or a progressive populism.

Mass Fair Share briefly showed that progressive populism was possible. It demonstrated that the appeal of such a populism went beyond the blue-collar and low-income neighborhoods and could create a remarkable suburban–urban political force. It showed that even in the wake of the racist backlash to court ordered school busing, it was possible to bring Black and white families together around a common economic justice agenda. Sadly, we were not capable of leading Fair Share through its massive growth, and we were not able to leave that political heritage for our children and grandchildren.

In recent years, the amazing response to police killings of unarmed African Americans has taken me back to my days in the Civil Rights Movement. For many in my generation, before the war in Vietnam shoved everything aside, the Civil Rights Movement was the defining moral issue. Yet we were not able to move from the success of ending legal segregation to realize full racial justice. The clearest evidence of this is the relentless racial disparity in household income and even more, the extreme racial wealth gap. The typical white household has ten times the net worth of the typical Black household.[14]

The cause of this is clear: one hundred years of policies and laws that prevented African Americans from gaining access to the same home ownership that was provided for white people. The Federal Housing Administration (FHA) and Veterans Administration (VA) aggressively promoted housing segregation. The postwar GI Bill that was so critical to the families of millions of white veterans, effectively excluded most of the 1.2 million Black veterans. The massive postwar boom in suburbs excluded Black families who were confined to inner-city ghettos. Explicit racially restrictive covenants, as well as the segregation policies of the VA loan guarantee program and other federal programs, denied home ownership to Black families.[15]

Without access to the new, affordable housing in the suburbs and restricted to racially segregated inner-city neighborhoods, Black families experienced a long-lasting wealth gap. While the Civil Rights Movement successfully ended legal segregation, it failed to redress the economic impact and betrayals of Black Americans that started with Reconstruction and continued through to the 1960s.

The heroic Civil Rights Movement that so inspired my first forays in activism spun apart in the late 1960s. The murder of key leaders played an important role: Evers, King, Malcolm X, Fred Hampton, and more, all murdered. The FBI's virulent campaign to undermine Black leaders. The turn to Black Nationalism. The enormous white backlash. The unrelenting racism and threats. The movement could not sustain an assault on the key systems of economic injustice: the segregated housing system, the decline of good-paying blue-collar jobs, the resegregation of school systems.

Now we have a Supreme Court determined to roll back so many of the hardwon gains, eager to strike down any race-specific solutions such as affirmative action. It is useful to remember that this is not the first time the court has acted in ways that should not be followed. In 1857 the court ruled that Americans of African descent, whether free or slave, were not citizens and could not sue in federal court. In 1883, despite the very clear language of the Thirteenth and Fourteenth Amendments, the court nullified the Civil Rights Act of 1875, which had outlawed discrimination in hotels, trains, and other public spaces. Those amendments are still part of the Constitution. There is no practical or legal way to remedy race-specific crimes without race-specific solutions.

Today the politics of the nation remain as polarized around race as at any point in my lifetime. White grievance is essential to the political forces working to undermine our democracy. While it is a hard time to continue the work of racial justice, it is an absolute imperative if we are to save American democracy.

America has been experiencing its fourth great wave of immigration. Over the last forty years thirty million legal immigrants have moved to the United States. Eighty percent of those immigrants came from Latin America and Asia.[16]This wave of immigration, like those that preceded it, has been essential to the country's economic growth and prosperity.

Before 1965, the United States had no numerical limits on immigration from any country in the Americas. Each year more than 500,000 Mexicans came across the border to work in the United States. Many returned South through the porous border. In 1965, legal immigration was capped. In 1986, as articulated by President Ronald Reagan, the Immigration Reform and Control Act was an attempt to curb the immigrant "invasion." The Southern border was militarized and enforcement dramatically beefed up. Still there was a constant inflow of people seeking work, many of whom have ended up staying in the United States, producing our estimated eleven million undocumented immigrants.[17]

Over this period the Republican Party, once the "party of Lincoln," became the party of white voters. For the last fifty years every Republican presidential candidate has won a majority of the white vote.[18] Race has remained the central fault line in American politics. As the country changes, Republicans have used all the undemocratic aspects of the system (the US Senate, the electoral college), along with gerrymandering, and stealing Supreme Court appointments, to work for minority rule.

Those of my generation who were so inspired by the Civil Rights Movement still believe in racial justice. But over these last fifty years we have failed to fight for it. Many like me have moved to almost all-white suburbs. We did not oppose mass incarceration. In our pursuit of comfortable lives, and our fixation on our own children, all too often we have forgotten children not our own. Once again, the country finds itself with the moral imperative to dismantle the deeply rooted systems of racism. Once again, we need more than words. Even more than protests. We need to put a stake through the heart of white supremacy and finally redress decades of segregation and racial injustice.

Over these fifty years I have often found myself pondering leadership, both my own experience of leading, and the culture and practice of leadership. In the student movement we were profoundly confused about the role of leaders. Surrounded by examples of command and control, top-down leadership, we rejected leadership all together. "We have no leaders" was a common refrain.

That was nonsense. Every social movement and every organization has leaders, formal or informal. The question is not whether we have leaders, but whether we have good leaders, leaders who empower others, who build successors, who are accountable. In SDS, the confusion over leadership inhibited our effectiveness, allowing young, arrogant men like me to lead without being accountable. All too often we lacked both the structures, and the culture needed for a democratic leadership that would build lasting organization. Leadership structures and a culture that promotes the intentional development of new leaders are important for any insurgent democratic movement. It is especially important for student organizations where every four years, older leaders cycle out and every year new people cycle in.

I loved being a leader. I loved inspiring people, helping them see what they could accomplish together. I loved the aspects of leadership that involved teaching and the development of others.

And of course, I came to love the power that comes from changing people's lives. It is intoxicating stuff.

For many years I exercised a furious will—we will do more; we will achieve the unexpected. My relentless drive, my furious will, my ever increasingly transactional approach, all combined to hollow me out and drain me.

I never thoughtfully engaged with the flaws in my own leadership practice. I look back over all these years, and I see a young man who believed deeply in empathy, in empowering others but who was consumed by stopping the war, by achieving great things, by fighting for justice.

It certainly did not help that the deep antiauthoritarian and individualistic culture of our movements threw up unending resistance to those who led. There was a constant stream of criticism and harsh personal attacks. Looking back, I am struck that we never engaged the question of how we might sustain and nourish our leaders.

A changed America, of course, demands a changed politics. The crises we face today include new challenges that our past movements did not anticipate. The COVID-19 pandemic highlighted the inequalities, the racial disparities, and the problem of disinformation. Climate change is now a profound threat to the future. The concentration of wealth and power has reached an extreme we could not have imagined. New technologies are profoundly altering how most Americans get information. We live in a period where more information is more easily available to more people from more sources than ever in human history. We also live in a period where disinformation and willful falsehoods are warping millions of Americans' perceptions of reality.

It is not easy to marry the just demands for racial and gender equity with a populism that embraces those left behind and left out. Not easy, but it is possible. Indeed, we are now seeing some signs of it.

The reaction to Trumpism has produced a new wave of activism. It has not yet cohered but its signs are everywhere: defending women's rights, pushing back against extreme economic inequality, demanding action on climate, mobilizing against attacks on immigrants and people of color. Union organizing has increased. Workers are more willing to strike. While our politics are often dominated by the effort of the old men of the Republican Party to create the conditions for minority rule, increasingly the young, people of color, and infuriated women are resisting.

Despite the profound changes of the last fifty years, I see some of the same dynamics as when I was young. A small group of old white men clinging desperately to power. The ongoing failure of the country to face up to the systems of racism that have settled bone deep in the land. And young people whose futures are at stake. Young people who want to live lives that have meaning and value, who want to be able to have a stake in shaping the decisions that will determine their lives.

Now looking around at America after those five decades, I am struck by how much I still believe in young people. When I am hopeful about our nation, it is because of our young people. They will fight for their futures. I believe that. And in fighting for their futures, they will make America a more decent, tolerant, democratic, creative country. They will force the country to deal with climate change. They will fight for racial equity. They will struggle against extreme economic inequality. They will win back reproductive freedom. They will challenge foreign misadventures. They will work to reinvigorate democracy. Even in the darkest times, they will continue the hard work of hope. That they will struggle to shape the future is a given. That they will succeed remains an open question. I hope they can learn something from my experiences, from my many mistakes. This book is, in the end, dedicated to them.

Acknowledgments

This book was more than nine years in the making, and all along the way I received invaluable assistance and support. Richard Hoffman, brilliant memoirist, poet, and friend, was the first to convince me to start the project and throughout has been a necessary source of guidance and encouragement. Alexis Rizzuto was a critical early editor; without her, I would have floundered. Grub Street's invaluable memoir workshop convinced me I was attempting to write two memoirs and to focus on what became this book.

The late Todd Gitlin was generous and supportive. I miss him. Miles Rapoport was a source of advice, encouragement, and constructive challenges, as he has been so often over the last fifty years. There has never been a better friend. Mark Dyen has been on this march with me for so many years and was willing, once again, to help me as I struggled to write this book. Amy Merrill was helpful and tolerant.

Some of the friends who supported and encouraged me along the way include: Heather Booth, Dick Flacks, Michael Kazin, Robert Kuttner, Nicco Mele, Richard Parker, Bob Ross, Richard Rothstein, Lee Webb, and so many more. Thank you all.

This is a work of remembering and so undoubtedly, I will have made mistakes, especially as I kept no papers, nor wrote diaries or journals. Obviously, any such mistakes are mine and mine alone.

I want to thank Kathleen Aguero for permitting me to use her wonderful poem, "Hard Work." Mass Poetry generously allowed me to steal the title, *The Hard Work of Hope*, from a series that they curated based on her poem.

I want to thank Jim Lance and the entire team at Cornell University Press. Without their faith in this book, you would not be reading it now.

The research librarians at the Joseph P. Healey Library of the University of Massachusetts Boston, the Northeastern University Archives and Special Collections, and the Harvard University Archives were exceedingly generous with their time and knowledge, assisting me to track down old photographs.

Essays based on earlier drafts of this memoir have appeared in *Solstice*, *Vox*, *Arrowsmith Journal*, *Cognoscenti*, and the *Lowell Review*.

I was constantly inspired to keep going by my six wonderful grandchildren, Cyrus, Ben, Tessa, Treat, Seamus, and Owen, as well as my three grown children,

Emma, Meg, and Zander, and my two sons-in-law, Steve and Joel. I hope this book in a small way helps make the world that they inherit a better one.

As has been the case over and over these last forty years, I would never have been able to write this memoir without the constant, patient support of Barbara Treat Arnold, who, although she is embarrassed every time I say it in public, is my companion, my accomplice, my love.

Notes

PREFACE

1. Larry Buchanan, Quoctrung Bui, and Jugal K. Patel, "Black Lives Matter May Be the Largest Movement in U.S. History," *New York Times*, July 3, 2020, https://www.nytimes.com/interactive/2020/07/03/us/george-floyd-protests-crowd-size.html.

1. GETTING ON THE BUS

1. Civil Defense Museum, "National Fallout Shelter Program—Public Fallout Shelter Signs," August 25, 2024, http://www.civildefensemuseum.com/signs/.

2. This is not hyperbole. Between 1882 to 1968, the NAACP has documented 4,743 lynchings. NAACP, "History of Lynching in America," accessed September 30, 2024, https://naacp.org/find-resources/history-explained/history-lynching-america. For more on the killings of African Americans see Equal Justice Institute, "Lynching in America, Confronting the Legacy of Racial Terror," 2017, https://eji.org/reports/lynching-in-america/.

3. Mel King, *Chain of Change: Struggles for Black Community Development* (Boston: South End Press, 1981), 97

4. King, *Chain of Change*, 98

5. "First National Bank of Boston Agrees to Hire 10 Negroes," *New York Times*, September 21, 1963.

6. *Statistics of the Congressional Election of November 6, 1962* (Washington, DC: United States Government Printing Office, 1963), https://clerk.house.gov/member_info/electionInfo/1962election.pdf.

7. Robert L. Levey, "10,000 on Common, Hub Rally Backs Alabama Negroes," *Boston Globe*, May 13, 1963, 1.

8. Richard Pearson, "Former Ala. Gov. George C. Wallace Dies," *Washington Post*, September 14, 1998, A1.

9. Jonathan Rieder, "The Day President Kennedy Embraced Civil Rights—and the Story Behind It.," *Atlantic*, June 11, 2013, https://www.theatlantic.com/national/archive/2013/06/the-day-president-kennedy-embraced-civil-rights-and-the-story-behind-it/276749/.

10. Rachel L. Swarns, Darcy Eveleigh, and Damien Cave, "The Day Medgar Evers Was Killed," *New York Times*, January 31, 2016, https://www.nytimes.com/interactive/projects/cp/national/unpublished-black-history/the-morning-after-medgar-evers-is-killed.

11. John A. Fenton, "Boston's Negroes Firm on Stay Out," *New York Times*, June 18, 1963, 20.

12. John Lewis, *Walking with the Wind: A Memoir of the Movement* (New York: Harcourt Brace, 1998), 219–28.

13. Lydia Saad, "On King Holiday, a Split Review of Civil Rights Progress, *Gallup*, January 21, 2008, https://news.gallup.com/poll/103828/civil-rights-progress-seen-more.aspx.

14. Saad, "On King Holiday."

15. "Noel Alger Day," Blacks@Dartmouth 1775 to 1960, 2024, https://badahistory.net/view.php?ID=176.

16. Pat Paterson, "The Truth about Tonkin," *Naval History* 22, no. 1 (February 2008), https://www.usni.org/magazines/naval-history-magazine/2008/february/truth-about-tonkin.

2. A NEW LEFT AND THE START OF THE STUDENT MOVEMENT

1. Richard Rothstein would go on to become a famed union organizer leading textile worker organizing in the South before becoming a writer, the national education columnist for the *New York Times* and then the author of the bestselling *The Color of Law*, which documented the intentional history of housing segregation, and, with his daughter Leah, *Just Action*, which explored citizen-led solutions to segregation.

2. Todd Gitlin, who would go on to be president of SDS, became a professor of sociology and journalism, the author of sixteen books, and the embodiment of an engaged public intellectual until his death in February 2022.

3. Lee became the national secretary of SDS in 1963. We would work together at *Ramparts*, and in Vietnam Summer. Lee would go on to found the Center for Policy Alternatives, the first national center focused on developing innovative ideas for state and local government. Lee then had a long career in public administration for New York State, Partners Health Care, and the New School.

4. Tom Hayden, "*The Port Huron Statement*, Written by Tom Hayden for the Students for a Democratic Society, June 15, 1962," https://images2.americanprogress.org/campus/email/PortHuronStatement.pdf.

5. Hayden, "*Port Huron Statement*."

6. David would stay active in politics his whole life, working for the senator Ted Kennedy for many years, and becoming the chief economist of the House Financial Services Committee, helping to shepherd the passage of the first Emergency Economic Stabilization Act of 2008 and then the Dodd-Frank Wall Street Reform Act in 2010.

7. C. Clark Kissinger, "SDS National Council," *Students for a Democratic Society Bulletin* 3, no. 4 (January 1965): 2.

8. Kirkpatrick Sale, *SDS: The Rise and Development of the Students for a Democratic Society* (New York: Random House, 1973), 15–17.

9. Milton Viorst, *Fire in the Streets: America in the 1960s* (New York: Simon & Shuster, 1979), 293–98.

10. Dwight D. Eisenhower, *Mandate for Change* (Garden City, NY: Doubleday & Company, 1963), 338.

11. Lyndon B. Johnson, "Statement by the President: 'Tragedy, Disappointment, and Progress' in Viet-Nam," American Presidency Project, April 17, 1965, https://www.presidency.ucsb.edu/documents/statement-the-president-tragedy-disappointment-and-progress-viet-nam.

12. "46,500 U.S. Troops in Vietnam," *New York Times*, May 13, 1965, 16.

13. Todd Gitlin, *The Sixties, Years of Hope, Days of Rage* (New York: Bantam Books, 1987), 242.

3. CREATING ROOM FOR DISSENT

1. FBI Memorandum of July 11, 1968, written by Special Agent Kenneth West, document ID: 32509982, released under the Freedom of Information Act, author's collection.

2. Kirkpatrick Sale, *SDS: The Rise and Development of the Students for a Democratic Society* (New York: Random House, 1973), 229–31.

3. Sale, *SDS*, 231.

4. Sale, *SDS*, 231.

5. Sale, *SDS*, 231–32.

6. Paul Booth, along with his wife Heather, would remain a friend until his death in 2018. He would have a long career as an organizer and strategist. He worked with Saul

Alinsky in Chicago before becoming a labor organizer, eventually rising to national leadership in the American Federation of State, County and Municipal Employees.

7. Tom Wells, *The War Within: America's Battle over Vietnam* (Berkeley: University of California Press, 1994), 58.

8. Florida Atlantic University Libraries, "Battle of Ia Drang 1965," accessed July 10, 2021, https://libguides.fau.edu/vietnam-war/us-military-la-drang.

9. Robert J. Samuelson, "Harvard's SDS Chapter May Begin Larger Anti-War Drive Next Term," *Harvard Crimson*, December 13, 1965, https://www.thecrimson.com/article/1965/12/13/harvards-sds-chapter-may-begin-larger/.

10. Digital History, "The Vietnam War: Interpreting Statistics," 2021, https://www.digital history.uh.edu/disp_textbook.cfm?smtID=11&psid=3844.

11. National Archives, "Vietnam War U.S. Military Fatal Casualty Statistics: Electronic Records Reference Report," August 23, 2022, https://www.archives.gov/research/military/vietnam-war/casualty-statistics.

12. Juleyka Lantigua-Williams, "40 Years Later, U.S. Invasion Still Haunts Dominican Republic," *Progressive Magazine*, April 21, 2005, https://progressive.org/40-years-later-u.s.-invasion-still-haunts-dominican-republic/.

13. Vincent Bevins, "What the United States Did in Indonesia," *Atlantic*, October 20, 2017, https://www.theatlantic.com/international/archive/2017/10/the-indonesia-documents-and-the-us-agenda/543534/.

14. Wells, *War Within*, 374; and Craig McNamara, *Because Our Fathers Lied: A Memoir of Truth and Family, from Vietnam to Today* (Boston: Little Brown, 2022).

15. Stanley Karnow, *Vietnam: A History* (New York: Viking, 1991), 491.

16. Selective Service System, "Induction Statistics," accessed July 15, 2023, https://www.sss.gov/history-and-records/induction-statistics/.

17. Bruce Dancis, *Resister: A Story of Protest and Prison during the Vietnam War* (Ithaca, NY: Cornell University Press, 2014), 44–45.

18. Sherry Gershon Gottlieb, *Hell No, We Won't Go! Resisting the Draft During the Vietnam War* (New York: Viking, 1991), 91.

19. Students for a Democratic Society, "National Vietnam Examination," accessed October 10, 2019, https://www.sds-1960s.org/exam.htm

20. Robert J. Samuelson, "SDS to Distribute Exam on Vietnam at Draft Test," *Harvard Crimson*, May 3, 1966, https://www.thecrimson.com/article/1966/5/3/sds-to-distribute-exam-on-vietnam/.

21. Eric Pace, "Thomas B. Adams Dies at 86; Descendant of Two Presidents," *New York Times*, June 9, 1997, https://www.nytimes.com/1997/06/09/us/thomas-b-adams-dies-at-86-descendant-of-two-presidents.html.

5. TAKING IT TO A NEW LEVEL: 1966–67

1. United Press International, "McNamara Heckled as War Critics Halt His Car at Harvard; HARVARD UPROAR BALKS M'NAMARA," *New York Times*, November 8, 1966, 1.

2. Robert S. McNamara, *In Retrospect: The Tragedy and Lessons of Vietnam* (New York: Crown, 1995).

3. Richard W. Lyman, *Stanford in Turmoil: Campus Unrest, 1966–1972* (Redwood City, CA: Stanford University Press, 2009), chapter 4.

4. "Battlefield: Vietnam," accessed July 20, 2023, https://www.pbs.org/battlefield vietnam/timeline/index1.html.

5. Bryan Marquard, "David Bird, 79, Civic Activist, Campaign Aide," *Boston Globe*, November 6, 2007, http://archive.boston.com/news/globe/obituaries/articles/2007/11/06/david_bird_79_civic_activist_campaign_aide/.

6. Karen Paget, *Patriotic Betrayal: The Inside Story of the CIA's Secret Campaign to Enroll American Students in the Crusade against Communism* (New Haven, CT: Yale University Press, 2015), chapter 15.

7. Peter Richardson, *A Bomb in Every Issue: How the Short, Unruly Life of Ramparts Magazine Changed America* (New York: New Press, 2010), 80.

8. Church Committee, *Final Report, Senate Select Committee to Study Governmental Operations with Respect to Intelligence Activities*, 93rd Cong., 1st sess., S. Rep. no. 94–755, April 29, 1976, https://www.intelligence.senate.gov/resources/intelligence-related-commissions. See in particular *Interim Report: Alleged Assassination Plots Involving Foreign Leaders* and *Book II: Intelligence Activities and the Rights of Americans*.

9. "The CIA Report the President Doesn't Want You to Read," *Village Voice* 21, no. 7 (February 16, 1976), https://www.cia.gov/readingroom/docs/CIA-RDP03-01541R0002 00420001-1.pdf.

10. James Risen and Thomas Risen, *The Last Honest Man: The CIA, the FBI, the Mafia, and the Kennedys—and One Senator's Fight to Save Democracy* (Boston: Little, Brown, 2023), 400–407.

11. "December 13–14—The village of Caudat near Hanoi is leveled by U.S. bombers resulting in harsh criticism from the international community." History Place, "The Vietnam War: The Jungle War, 1965–1968," 1999, https://www.historyplace.com/unitedstates/vietnam/index-1965.html.

12. "December 26, 1966—Facing increased scrutiny from journalists over mounting civilian causalities in North Vietnam, the U.S. Defense Department now admits civilians may have been bombed accidentally"; "December 27, 1966—The U.S. mounts a large-scale air assault against suspected Viet Cong positions in the Mekong Delta using Napalm and hundreds of tons of bombs." History Place, "Vietnam War."

13. Ron Milam, "1967: The Era of Big Battles in Vietnam," *New York Times*, January 10, 2017, https://www.nytimes.com/2017/01/10/opinion/1967-the-era-of-big-battles-in-vietnam.html.

14. J. Anthony Lukas, "Bad Day at Cairo, Ill," *New York Times*, February 21, 1971, SM22.

15. "Detroit under Fire, 12th Street Blind Pig," 2021, https://policing.umhistorylabs.lsa.umich.edu/s/detroitunderfire/page/blind-pig1.

16. Todd Gitlin, *The Sixties: Years of Hope, Days of Rage* (New York: Bantam Books, 1987), 245.

17. University Communications, "SF State experts say 'Summer of Love' Legacy Still Widely Felt," SF State News, May 15, 2017, https://news.sfsu.edu/archive/news-story/sf-state-experts-say-%E2%80%98summer-love%E2%80%99-legacy-still-widely-felt.html.

18. "Draft Memorandum from Secretary of Defense McNamara to President Johnson," May 19, 1967, in *Foreign Relations of the United States, 1964–1968*, vol. 5, *Vietnam, 1967* (Washington, DC: Government Printing Office, 2002), document 177.

19. Simon Hall, "On the Tail of the Panther: Black Power and the 1967 Convention of the National Conference for New Politics," *Journal of American Studies* 37 (2003): 59–78.

6. 1967 SITTING IN AND ARMIES OF THE NIGHT

1. Katie Mettler, "The Day Anti-Vietnam War Protesters Tried to Levitate the Pentagon," *Washington Post*, October 19, 2017, https://www.washingtonpost.com/news/retropolis/wp/2017/10/19/the-day-anti-vietnam-war-protesters-tried-to-levitate-the-pentagon/.

2. Tom Wells, *The War Within: America's Battle over Vietnam* (Berkeley: University of California Press, 1994), 195–203.

3. Robert Neer, *Napalm: An American Biography* (Cambridge, MA: Belknap Press, 2013), 34.

4. "Napalm," Wikipedia, July 10, 2024, https://en.wikipedia.org/wiki/Napalm.

5. Neer, *Napalm*, 111.

6. John A. Herfort, "Dow and the Faculty," *Harvard Crimson*, November 2, 1967, https://www.thecrimson.com/article/1967/11/2/dow-and-the-faculty-pthe-sit-in/.

7. Paul Lauter, *Our Sixties: An Activist's History* (Rochester, NY: University of Rochester Press, 2020), 132–40.

8. Ned Brandt, *Growth Company: Dow Chemical's First Century* (East Lansing: Michigan State University Press, 1997), 356.

7. 1968

1. Tom Wells, *The War Within: America's Battle over Vietnam* (Berkeley: University of California Press, 1994), 230–33.

2. History Place, "The Vietnam War: The Jungle War, 1965–1968," 1999, https://www.historyplace.com/unitedstates/vietnam/index-1965.html.

3. Peter Arnett, *Live from the Battlefield: From Vietnam to Baghdad, 35 Years in the World's War Zones* (New York: Simon & Shuster, 1993), 253–57.

4. Tom Wicker, "Johnson Says He Won't Run," *New York Times*, March 31, 1968, 1.

5. Virginia Hamill, "Rudi Dutschke, 39, Led German Student Revolt," *Washington Post*, December 26, 1979, https://www.washingtonpost.com/archive/local/1979/12/26/rudi-dutschke-39-led-german-student-revolt/fbab8efd-cbe4-4ef4-af0d-d2c2c2d93158/.

6. Mark Kurlansky, *1968: The Year That Rocked the World* (New York: Ballantine Books, 2003), 151–54.

7. Charles Kaiser, *1968 in America: Music, Politics, Chaos, Counterculture, and the Shaping of a Generation* (New York: Weidenfeld & Nicolson, 1988), 163.

8. "Metropolitan Briefs," *New York Times*, November 14, 1974, 51.

9. Alissa J. Rubin, "May 1968: A Month of Revolution Pushed France into the Modern World," *New York Times*, May 5, 2018, https://www.nytimes.com/2018/05/05/world/europe/france-may-1968-revolution.html.

10. Elisabeth Malkin, "50 Years After a Student Massacre, Mexico Reflects on Democracy," *New York Times*, October 1, 2018, https://www.nytimes.com/2018/10/01/world/americas/mexico-tlatelolco-massacre.html.

11. Nicholas Gagarin, "442 Harvard Students Pledge 'We Won't Go,'" *Harvard Crimson*, May 15, 1968, https://www.thecrimson.com/article/1968/5/15/442-harvard-students-pledge-we-wont/.

12. Joel R. Kramer, "The Fellows Beef Up Their Party by Doling Out the Honoraries," *Harvard Crimson*, June 12, 1969, https://www.thecrimson.com/article/1969/6/12/the-fellows-beef-up-their-party/.

13. Craig MacNamara, *Because our Fathers Lied: A Memoir of Truth and Family, from Vietnam to Today* (Boston: Little, Brown and Company, 2022).

14. Tad Szulc, "Czechoslovakia Invaded by Russians and Four Other Warsaw Pact Forces; They Open Fire on Crowds in Prague," *New York Times*, August 21, 1968, 1.

15. A. J. Liebling, "Do you Belong in Journalism," *New Yorker*, May 14, 1960, 105.

16. We were told the quote came from Karl Marx's *The Eighteenth Brumaire of Louis Bonaparte*. But it is not so simple. There Marx, in a reference to his beloved William Shakespeare play *Hamlet*, wrote, "Well grubbed, old mole." In an 1856 speech Marx said "we recognize our brave friend, Robin Goodfellow, the old mole that can work in the earth so fast, that worthy pioneer—the Revolutions." See Peter Stallybrass, "'Well Grubbed Old Mole': Marx, *Hamlet*, and the (Un)fixing of Representation," *Cultural Studies* 12, no. 1 (1998): 3–14, https://cpb-ap-se2.wpmucdn.com/global2.vic.edu.au/dist/5/3744/files/2016/12/Marx-and-Hamlet-1awo1ut.pdf.

17. John A Farrell, "Tricky Dick's Vietnam Treachery," *New York Times*, January 1, 2017, SR9.

18. Richard Nixon, "Acceptance Speech, August 8, 1968," Richard Nixon Foundation, accessed June 5, 2020, https://www.nixonfoundation.org/wp-content/uploads/2011/04/RNs-Annotated-Reading-Copy-Folder-28.pdf.

19. Dan Baum, "Legalize It All: How to Win the War on Drugs," *Harper's Magazine*, April 2016, https://harpers.org/archive/2016/04/legalize-it-all/.

8. SHUTTING DOWN HARVARD

1. Declan J. Knieriem, "Haunted by the War: Remembering the University Hall Takeover of 1969," *Harvard Crimson*, May 27, 2019, https://www.thecrimson.com/article/2019/5/27/university-hall-1969/.

2. "No Military Training at Harvard," *Harvard Crimson*, December 2, 1968, https://www.thecrimson.com/article/1968/12/2/no-military-training-at-harvard-pbtbhe/.

3. "Robert B. Watson, Harvard Dean, Dies at 86," *New York Times*, August 17, 2000, 38.

4. Tyler S. B. Olkowski, "The Great Harvard Sex Scandal of 1964," *Harvard Crimson*, May 29, 2014, https://www.thecrimson.com/article/2014/5/29/harvard-sex-scandal-1964/.

5. Peter Shapiro, "F. Skiddy von Stade: Dean of Freshmen, Harvard College," *Harvard Crimson*, September 1, 1972, https://www.thecrimson.com/article/1972/9/1/f-skiddy-von-stade-pbybou-might/.

6. "Von Stade Wrote Letter against Merger, Saw No Benefit in Educating More Women," *Harvard Crimson*, November 6, 1970, https://www.thecrimson.com/article/1970/11/6/von-stade-wrote-letter-against-merger/.

9. STRANGE DAYS: 1969–1970

1. Church Committee, *Intelligence Activities and the Rights of Americans*, book 2, *Senate Committee to Study Governmental Operations with Respect to Intelligence Activities*, 93rd Cong., 1st sess., S. Rep. no. 94–755, https://www.intelligence.senate.gov/sites/default/files/94755_II.pdf.

2. U.S. Government Memorandum to FBI Director 100–450214 from Boston FBI office, Subject Michael Stearns Ansara, August 23, 1968, author's collection: "An FD-122 has been submitted to the Bureau recommending the inclusion of the subject's name in the Security Index"; SAC Boston (100–36315) to Director FBI, October 8, 1968, author's collection: "Boston should promptly submit an amended succinct summary setting out specific reasons why subject should be considered for inclusion in the Agitator Index"; and US Government Memorandum 100–36315, from SAC Boston, to FBI Director Subject Michael Stearns Ansara, October 2, 1969, Rabble Rouser Index, author's collection.

3. Ward Churchill and Jim Vander Wall, *The COINTELPRO Papers: Documents from the FBI's Wars against Dissent in the United States* (Baltimore: Black Classic Press, 2022), 355n57.

4. Tom Wells, *The War Within: America's Battle over Vietnam* (Berkeley and Los Angeles: University of California Press, 1994), 382.

5. Mathew Fleischer, "Opinion: 50 Years Ago, LAPD Raided the Black Panthers. SWAT Teams Have Been Targeting Black Communities Ever Since," *Los Angeles Times*, December 8, 2019, https://www.latimes.com/opinion/story/2019-12-08/50-years-swat-black-panthers-militarized-policinglos-angeles.

6. Homer Bigart, "War Foes Here Attacked by Construction Workers," *New York Times*, May 9, 1970, 1.

7. Robert B. Semple, Jr., "Nixon Meets Heads of 2 City Unions; Hails War Support," *New York Times*, May 27, 1970, 1.

8. "An S.D.S. Founder Beaten in Chicago," *New York Times*, May 7, 1969, 26.

9. Mickey Flacks and Dick Flacks, *Making History/Making Blintzes: How Two Red Diaper Babies Found Each Other and Discovered America* (New Brunswick, NJ: Rutgers University Press, 2018), 299.

10. "Senate Committee Schedules Radical Group Investigation," *Pacifican*, April 19, 1970, 1.

11. Richard J. Connolly, "Businessman, Dummy Firm Fund Boston SDS," *Boston Globe*, July 12, 1969, 2.

12. James R Hagerty, "CVS Founder Had One Foot in Business, the Other in Counterculture," *Wall Street Journal*, January 23, 2020, https://www.wsj.com/articles/activism-disrupted-career-of-cvs-co-founder-ralph-hoagland-11579811162.

13. Todd Gitlin, *The Sixties: Years of Hope, Days of Rage* (New York: Bantam Books, 1987) n370.

14. Steve Estes, "Engendering Movement Memories: Remembering Race and Gender in the Mississippi Movement," in *The Civil Rights Movement in American Memory*, ed. Leigh Raiford and Renee Christine Romano (Athens: University of Georgia Press, 2006), 301.

15. Casey Hayden and Mary King, "A Kind of Memo," Civil Rights Movement Archive, November 18, 1965, https://www.crmvet.org/docs/kindof.htm.

16. Jo Freeman, "On the Origins of the Women's Liberation Movement from a Strictly Personal Perspective," jofreeman.com, accessed July 10, 2023, https://www.jofreeman.com/aboutjo/persorg.htm.

17. Wells, *War Within*, 290.

18. Wyatt Olson, "Hamburger Hill: For War-Weary Americans, 10-Day Battle Defined Futility of Vietnam War," *Stars and Stripes*, August 15, 2019, https://www.stripes.com/special-reports/vietnam-stories/1969/2019-08-15/hamburger-hill:-for-war-weary-americans,-10-day-battle-defined-futility-of-vietnam-war-1479397.html.

19. U.S. Army Center of Military History, "Vietnam War Campaigns," accessed September 5, 2023, https://history.army.mil/html/reference/army_flag/vn.html.

20. Vietnam Veterans Project, "Statistics about the Vietnam War," accessed September 5, 2023, https://vietnamveteranproject.org/statistics-2/.

21. Selective Service System, "Induction Statistics," accessed September 6, 2023, https://www.sss.gov/history-and-records/induction-statistics/.

22. Gitlin, *Sixties*, 412.

23. David Cortright, *Peace: A History of Movements and Ideas* (Cambridge, UK: Cambridge University Press, 2008), 164–65.

24. Giuseppe Valiante, "U.S. Vietnam War Draft Dodgers Left Their Mark on Canada," CTV News, April 16, 2015, https://www.ctvnews.ca/canada/vietnam-war-draft-dodgers-left-mark-in-canada-1.2329725.

25. Mark Shields, "Myths of Vietnam Still Alive and in Print," *Tampa Bay Times*, September 15, 2005, https://www.tampabay.com/archive/1996/04/29/myths-of-vietnam-still-alive-and-in-print/.

26. Jerry Lembcke, "The Myth of the Spitting Antiwar Protester," *New York Times*, October 13, 2017, https://www.nytimes.com/2017/10/13/opinion/myth-spitting-vietnam-protester.html; and Jerry Lembcke, *The Spitting Image: Myth, Memory, and the Legacy of Vietnam* (New York: NYU Press, 2000).

27. Lew Finfer, "RIP, Harry Gottschalk, Dot's 'Renaissance Man,' " *Dorchester Reporter*, May 15, 2014, https://www.dotnews.com/columns/2014/rip-harry-gottschalk-dot-s-renaissance-man.

28. Lydia Saad, "Gallup Vault: Hawks vs. Doves on Vietnam," Gallup, May 24, 2016, https://news.gallup.com/vault/191828/gallup-vault-hawks-doves-vietnam.aspx.

29. Hedrick Smith, "Nixon to Reduce Vietnam Force, Pulling out 25,000 G.I.'s by Aug. 31; a Midway Accord," *New York Times*, June 9, 1969, 1.

30. Bob Orkand, "'I Ain't Got No Quarrel with Them Vietcong,'" *New York Times*, June 27, 2017, https://www.nytimes.com/2017/06/27/opinion/muhammad-ali-vietnam-war.html.

31. Kirkpatric Sale, *SDS: The Rise and Development of the Students for a Democratic Society* (New York: Random House, 1973), 565.

32. Sale, *SDS*, 566.

33. Carol J. Williams, "Milosevic's Defiance Is Taking Its Toll on Him—and His Trial," *Los Angeles Times*, August 6, 2002, https://www.latimes.com/archives/la-xpm-2002-aug-06-fg-milo6-story.html.

34. Peter Knight, "Outrageous Conspiracy Theories: Popular and Official Responses to 9/11 in Germany and the United States," *New German Critique* 35, no. 1 (2008): 165–93.

35. Arthur M. Eckstein, *Bad Moon Rising, How the Weather Underground Beat the FBI and Lost the Revolution* (New Haven, CT: Yale University Press, 2016), 61.

36. Bertolt Brecht, "To Prosperity," trans. H. R. Hays, All Poetry, 2008, https://allpoetry.com/to-posterity.

37. Churchill and Vander Wall, *COINTELPRO Papers*, 138–41.

10. DAYS OF RAGE

1. Ron Carver, David Cortright, and Barbara Doherty, eds., *Waging Peace in Vietnam: US Soldiers Who Opposed the War* (New York: New Village Press, 2019).

2. Learning Network, "Nov. 15, 1969 | Anti-Vietnam War Demonstration Held," *New York Times*, November 15, 2011, https://archive.nytimes.com/learning.blogs.nytimes.com/2011/11/15/nov-15-1969-anti-vietnam-war-demonstration-held/.

3. David N. Hollander and Carol R. Sternhell, "Boston: 100,000 Rally," *Harvard Crimson*, October 16, 1969, https://www.thecrimson.com/article/1969/10/16/boston-100000-rally-pmore-than-100000/.

4. Carol R. Sternhell, "1000 Protestors at M.I.T. Ask End to War Research," *Harvard Crimson*, November 5, 1969, https://www.thecrimson.com/article/1969/11/5/1000-protestors-at-mit-ask-end/.

5. Parker Donham, "4 Officers Injured in BU Melee," *Boston Globe*, November 26, 1969, 1.

6. J. Anthony Lukas, "Chicago 7 Cleared of Plot; 5 Guilty on Second Count," *New York Times*, February 19, 1970, 1.

7. "Hub Police Head Issues Post-Trial Violence Alert," *Boston Globe*, February 18, 1970, 4.

8. Jerry T. Nepom, "The Shea Bill Testing the War," *Harvard Crimson*, April 11, 1970, https://www.thecrimson.com/article/1970/4/11/the-shea-bill-testing-the-war/.

9. Bryan Borroughs, *Days of Rage: America's Radical Underground, the FBI, and the Forgotten Age of Revolutionary Violence* (New York: Penguin Books, 2016), 100.

10. Todd Gitlin, *The Sixties: Years of Hope, Days of Rage* (New York: Bantam Books, 1987), 400; and Mark Rudd, *Underground: My Life with SDS and the Weathermen* (New York: HarperCollins, 2009), 189.

11. Arthur M. Eckstein, *Bad Moon Rising: How the Weather Underground Beat the FBI and Lost the Revolution* (New Haven, CT: Yale University Press, 2016), 70–71.

12. Eckstein, *Bad Moon Rising*, 98–99.

13. Eckstein, *Bad Moon Rising*, 42–44; Burroughs, *Days of Rage*, 5.

14. Eckstein, *Bad Moon Rising*.

15. Sam Roberts, "Danny Schechter, 'News Dissector' and Human Rights Activist, Dies at 72," *New York Times*, March 23, 2015, https://www.nytimes.com/2015/03/24/arts/television/danny-schechter-news-dissector-and-human-rights-activist-dies-at-72.html.

16. Agis Salpukas, "U.S. Foregoes Trial of Weatherman," *New York Times*, October 16, 1973, 89.

17. Charles R. Babcock, "Gray, 2 High-Ranking Aides Are Indicted in FBI Break-Ins," *Washington Post*, April 11, 1978, https://www.washingtonpost.com/archive/politics/1978/04/11/gray-2-high-ranking-aides-are-indicted-in-fbi-break-ins/ed0c09a0-f8bd-4192-b090-38fe9147efbc/.

11. A MARCH IN LOWELL

1. Peter Ward, "The Clash of Class over Vietnam Still Felt by Some," *Lowell Sun*, October 12, 2001, 11.

12. DORCHESTER AND THE PEOPLE FIRST

1. Robert Turner, "Judge Troy: Many Friends, Interests and Controversies," *Boston Globe*, April 11, 1973, 3.

2. John Fenton, "Massachusetts Speaker and 25 Indicted in Corruption Inquiry," *New York Times*, May 9, 1964, 1.

3. Bo Burlingham, "The Legend of Banquo's Ghost," *Boston Magazine*, May 15, 2006, https://www.bostonmagazine.com/2006/05/15/the-legend-of-banquos-ghost/.

4. "The Law: The Fight to Sack Troy," *Time*, June 5, 1972, https://time.com/archive/6839820/the-law-the-fight-to-sack-troy/.

13. HOW DOES A WAR END?

1. Lawrence O'Donnell, Jr., *Playing with Fire: The 1968 Election and the Transformation of American Politics* (New York: Penguin, 2017), 416.

14. TO BE AN ORGANIZER

1. Nussbaum has continued to be an organizer and leader, first with 9 to 5 for many years, then with the Service Employees Union, the Bill Clinton Department of Labor, and the AFL-CIO, where she created Working America. Cassedy also spent years leading 9 to 5 and then became a journalist, speech writer in the Clinton administration and award-winning novelist, translator, playwright, and filmmaker.

2. The Jane Collective that Heather helped lead has garnered a new round of appreciation in the wake of the *Dobbs* decision overturning *Roe v. Wade*. There is a book, *The Story of Jane: The Legendary Underground Feminist Abortion Service*, by Laura Kaplan, and an HBO movie, *The Janes*.

3. Jo Freeman, "The Tyranny of Structurelessness," JoFreeman.com, 2013, https://www.jofreeman.com/joreen/tyranny.htm.

4. Mel would go on to become a beloved longtime activist, a state representative, and the first serious Black candidate for mayor of Boston.

5. The Movement for Economic Justice had been founded by George Wiley, who had created and led the National Welfare Rights Organization. Tragically Dr. Wiley drowned in August of 1973, which deprived the new organization of the leadership it needed to fulfill his dream of a new national organization built to fight for economic justice.

6. Michael Corbett, "Oil Shock of 1973–74," Federal Reserve History, November 22, 2013, https://www.federalreservehistory.org/essays/oil-shock-of-1973-74.

7. "Referendums Fared Poorly," *Boston Globe*, November 4, 1976, 1.

8. Lew would remain an organizer in Boston and Massachusetts for the next fifty years, becoming an icon. In November 2022, he would spearhead the successful referendum campaign that enacted a 4 percent surtax on income above $1 million annually, known as the Fair Share Amendment. When he finally announced his official retirement, it was covered in the *Boston Globe*: Joan Vennochi, "Lew Finfer, a Quiet Leader for Social and Economic Justice in Boston," *Boston Globe*, October 19, 2022, https://www.boston globe.com/2022/10/19/opinion/lew-finfer-quiet-leader-social-economic-justice-boston/.

15. MASSACHUSETTS FAIR SHARE

1. Robert Carr, "Reinstein Pays Tax, Withholds Tardy List," *Boston Globe*, September 6, 1977, 3.

2. "Revere Woman Elected to Fair Share Board," *Revere Journal*, November 16, 1977, 7.

3. Edward Quill, "Taxpayers Smolder of Revaluation," *Boston Globe*, August 28, 1978, 25.

4. William Doherty, "Kelly Is Found Guilty of Extortion," *Boston Globe*, December 24, 1982, 1.

5. Laurence Collins, "Legislators Fill 'Goody Box,'" *Boston Globe*, May 12, 1978, 10.

6. Kirk O'Donnell would go on to be a key aide to O'Neill when he was the speaker of the House. Fred Salvucci would become known as he architect of Boston's "Big Dig" completely changing Boston's road ways. Micho Spring would go on to be a fixture in Boston politics and business for four decades.

7. David Rogers, "It Was 'All Aboard' for Question 1 Forces," *Boston Globe*, November 5, 1978, 15.

8. "It's Official—the Election Winners and Figures," *Boston Globe*, November 30, 1978, 30.

9. Norman Lockman, "Auto Rate Fight Brewing for 78," *Boston Globe*, September 25, 1977, 4.

10. Norman Lockman, "Insurance Rates Cut for 60% of Drivers," *Boston Globe*, December 29, 1977, 1.

11. U.S. Department of Commerce, "1970 Census of Population: Distribution of the Negro Population by County," June 1971, https://www2.census.gov/prod2/decennial/documents/31679801n1-40ch01.pdf.

12. Charles A. Radin, "Citizen Group Charges Racial Bias in T Service." *Boston Globe*, March 1, 1980, 13.

13. Harry C. Boyte and Frank Riessman, *The New Populism: The Politics of Empowerment* (Philadelphia: Temple University Press, 1986).

14. Miles would go on to be elected to the state legislature and then secretary of state in Connecticut. Every time Marc was his campaign manager.

EPILOGUE: FROM THE VANTAGE OF FIFTY YEARS

1. "American Chamber of Congress in Vietnam," accessed October 15, 2016, https://www.amchamvietnam.com/.

2. Mike Ives, "McDonald's Opens in Vietnam, Bringing Big Mac to Fans of Banh Mi," *New York Times*, February 7, 2014, B1.

3. Mark Landler, "Making Nike Shoes in Vietnam," *New York Times*, April 28, 2000, https://archive.nytimes.com/www.nytimes.com/library/world/asia/042800vietnam-nike.html.

4. Sheridan Prasso, "Made in Vietnam," November 20, 2006, https://money.cnn.com/magazines/fortune/fortune_archive/2006/11/13/8393175/index.htm.

5. Chris Buckley and Chau Doan, "Anti-Chinese Violence Convulses Vietnam, Pitting Laborers against Laborers," *New York Times*, May 16, 2014, A15.

6. Jon Simkins, "Carl Vinson First Carrier to Visit Vietnam since War," Navy Times, March 5, 2018, https://www.navytimes.com/news/your-navy/2018/03/05/carl-vinson-first-carrier-to-visit-vietnam-since-war/.

7. Peter Baker and Katie Rogers, "Biden Forges Deeper Ties with Vietnam as China's Ambition Mounts," *New York Times*, September 10, 2023, A1.

8. Tom Wells, *The War Within: America's Battle over Vietnam* (Berkeley and Los Angeles: University of California Press, 1994), 356, 357.

9. Ward Churchill and Jim Vander Wall, *The COINTELPRO Papers: Documents from the FBI's Secret Wars against Dissent in the United States* (Baltimore: Black Classic Press, 2022), 92.

10. John A. Farrell, "When a Candidate Conspired with a Foreign Power to Win an Election," Politico, August 6, 2017, https://www.politico.com/magazine/story/2017/08/06/nixon-vietnam-candidate-conspired-with-foreign-power-win-election-215461/.

11. Matt Welch and Alexis Garcia, "When Democrats Loved Deregulation," *Reason*, December 12, 2018, https://reason.com/2018/12/12/when-democrats-loved-deregulation/; and Mychael Schnell, "Democrats Defend Deregulation Vote amid Banking Blame Game," *Hill*, March 18, 2023, https://thehill.com/business/banking-financial-institutions/3905108-democrats-defend-deregulation-vote-amid-banking-blame-game/.

12. Lawrence Goodwyn, *The Populist Moment: A Short History of the Agrarian Revolt in America* (New York: Oxford University Press, 1978).

13. C. Vann Woodward, *Tom Watson: Agrarian Rebel* (Oxford: Oxford University Press, 1963).

14. Rakesh Kochhar and Anthony Cilluffo, "How Wealth Inequality Has Changed in the U.S. since the Great Recession, by Race, Ethnicity and Income," Pew Research Center, November 1, 2017, https://www.pewresearch.org/short-reads/2017/11/01/how-wealth-inequality-has-changed-in-the-u-s-since-the-great-recession-by-race-ethnicity-and-income/.

15. Richard Rothstein, *The Color of Law, A Forgotten History of How Our Government Segregated America* (New York: W. W. Norton, 2018)

16. Pew Research Center, "Facts on U.S. Immigrants, 2018," August 20, 2020, https://www.pewresearch.org/hispanic/2020/08/20/facts-on-u-s-immigrants/.

17. Jorge Durand, Douglas S. Massey, and Emilio A. Parrado, "The New Era of Mexican Migration to the United States," Organization of American Historians, accessed May 15, 2020, http://archive.oah.org/special-issues/mexico/jdurand.html.

18. Steve Phillips, "What about White Voters?," Center for American Progress, February 5, 2016, https://www.americanprogress.org/article/what-about-white-voters/.

Selected Bibliography

Arnett, Peter. *Live from the Battlefield: From Vietnam to Baghdad, 35 Years in the World's War Zones.* Simon & Shuster, 1993.

Borroughs, Bryan. *Days of Rage: America's Radical Underground, the FBI, and the Forgotten Age of Revolutionary Violence.* Penguin Books, 2016.

Boyte, Harry C., and Frank Riessman. *The New Populism: The Politics of Empowerment.* Temple University Press, 1986.

Brandt, Ned. *Growth Company: Dow Chemical's First Century.* Michigan State University Press, 1997.

Carver, Ron, David Cortright, and Barbara Doherty. *Waging Peace in Vietnam: US Soldiers Who Opposed the War.* New Village Press, 2019.

Churchill, Ward, and Jim Vander Wall, *The COINTELPRO Papers: Documents from the FBI's Secret War against Dissent in the United States.* Black Classic Press, 2022.

Cortright, David. *Peace: A History of Movements and Ideas.* Cambridge University Press, 2008.

Dancis, Bruce. *Resister: A Story of Protest and Prison during the Vietnam War.* Cornell University Press, 2014.

Eckstein, Arthur M. *Bad Moon Rising: How the Weather Underground Beat the FBI and Lost the Revolution.* Yale University Press, 2016.

Eisenhower, Dwight D. *Mandate for Change.* Doubleday, 1963.

Flacks, Mickey, and Dick Flacks. *Making History/Making Blintzes: How Two Red Diaper Babies Found Each Other and Discovered America.* Rutgers University Press, 2018.

Gitlin, Todd. *The Sixties: Years of Hope, Days of Rage.* Bantam Books, 1987.

Goodwyn, Lawrence. *The Populist Moment: A Short History of the Agrarian Revolt in America,* Oxford University Press, 1978.

Kaiser, Charles. *1968 in America: Music, Politics, Chaos, Counterculture, and the Shaping of a Generation.* Weidenfeld & Nicolson, 1988.

Karnow, Stanley. *Vietnam: A History.* Viking, 1991.

King, Mel. *Chain of Change: Struggles for Black Community Development.* South End Press, 1981.

Kurlansky, Mark. *1968: The Year That Rocked the World.* Ballantine Books, 2003.

Lauter, Paul. *Our Sixties: An Activist's History.* University of Rochester Press, 2020.

Lembcke, Jerry. *The Spitting Image: Myth, Memory, and the Legacy of Vietnam.* New York University Press, 2000.

Lyman, Richard W. *Stanford in Turmoil: Campus Unrest, 1966–1972.* Stanford University Press, 2009.

McNamara, Craig. *Because Our Fathers Lied: A Memoir of Truth and Family, from Vietnam to Today.* Little Brown & Company, 2022.

McNamara, Robert S. *In Retrospect: The Tragedy and Lessons of Vietnam.* Crown, 1995.

Neer, Robert. *Napalm: An American Biography.* Belknap Press, 2013.

O'Donnell, Jr., Lawrence. *Playing with Fire: The 1968 Election and the Transformation of American Politics.* Penguin Press, 2017.

Paget, Karen. *Patriotic Betrayal: The Inside Story of the CIA's Secret Campaign to Enroll American Students in the Crusade against Communism.* Yale University Press, 2015.

Richardson, Peter. *A Bomb in Every Issue: How the Short, Unruly Life of Ramparts Magazine Changed America.* New Press, 2010.

Risen, James, and Thomas Risen. *The Last Honest Man: The CIA, the FBI, the Mafia, and the Kennedys—and One Senator's Fight to Save Democracy.* Little, Brown & Company, 2023.

Rothstein, Richard. *The Color of Law: A Forgotten History of How Our Government Segregated America.* W. W. Norton, 2018.

Sale, Kirkpatrick. *SDS: Student for a Democratic Society.* Random House, 1973

Viorst, Milton. *Fire in the Streets: America in the 1960's.* Simon & Shuster, 1979.

Wells, Tom. *The War Within: America's Battle over Vietnam.* University of California Press, 1994.

Woodward, C. Vann. *Tom Watson: Agrarian Rebel.* Oxford University Press, 1963.

Further Reading

Ayres, Bill. *Fugitive Days: A Memoir.* Beacon Press, 2001.

Branch, Taylor. *At Canaan's Edge: America in the King Years, 1965–68.* Simon & Shuster, 2006.

Embree, Alice. *Voice Lessons.* Briscoe Center for American History, 2023.

Gottlieb, Sherry Gershon. *Hell No, We Won't Go! Resisting the Draft During the Vietnam War.* Viking, 1991.

Harris, David. *Dreams Die Hard: Three Men's Journey through the Sixties.* St. Martin's, 1982.

Hayden, Tom. *Reunion: A Memoir.* Random House, 1988.

Kazin, Michael. *What It Took to Win: A History of the Democratic Party.* Farrar, Straus & Giroux, 2022.

Knight, Peter. *Dark Powers: Conspiracies and Conspiracy Theory in History and Literature.* Duke University Press, 2008.

Lewis, John. *Walking with the Wind: A Memoir of the Movement.* Harcourt Brace, 1998.

Miller, James. *Democracy Is in the Streets: From Port Huron to the Siege of Chicago.* Simon & Shuster, 1987.

Raiford, Leigh, and Renee Christine Romano. *The Civil Rights Movement in American Memory.* University of Georgia Press, 2006.

Ricks, Thomas E. *Waging a Good War: A Military History of the Civil Rights Movement.* Farrar, Straus and Giroux, 2022.

Rudd, Mark. *Underground: My Life with SDS and the Weathermen.* William Morrow, 2009.

von Hoffman, Nicholas. *We Are the People Our Parents Warned Us Against: The Classic Account of the 1960s Counter-Culture in San Francisco.* Quadrangle, 1968.

Wilkerson, Cathy. *Flying Close to the Sun: My Life and Times as a Weatherman.* Seven Stories Press, 2007.

Wright, James. *Enduring Vietnam: An American Generation and Its War.* St. Martin's Press, 2017.

Zaroulis, Nancy, and Gerald Sullivan, *Who Spoke Up? American Protest against the War in Vietnam 1963–1975.* Holt, Rinehart & Winston, 1984.

Index

Illustrations are indicated by italicized page numbers. All locations are in Massachusetts unless otherwise indicated.

abortion, 206, 271n2
Abrams, Eliot, 127
ACTION (government agency), 239–40
Adams, Thomas Boylston, campaign of, 56–57, 61, 87
Agent Orange, 130
Agnew, Spiro, 53, 133
Aguero, Kathleen: "Hard Work" (poem), xi
Albert, Michael, 154
Ali, Muhammad, 145
Alinsky, Saul, 205, 207, 213, 240, 264–65n6
Allen, Jesse, 29
Allende, Salvador, 72
Alper, Rika, 3
Alperovitz, Gar, 78, 79
American Friends Service Committee, 79
American Legion, 145
Anderson, Marc, 237
Angleton, James, 97
Ansara, Amy (wife): at Brandeis, 61, 79, 106; Cuba travel (1968), 104; at Lowell action (1970), 167, 169, 172, 175; March on Pentagon (1967), 87–88; marital problems and divorce, 106, 244; nursing career, 203; at post-protest social gathering (1968), 113; pregnancy and motherhood, 204; San Francisco summer (1967), 79–81; Vietnam Moratorium march and, 154, 159; in women-only "consciousness raising" groups, 139. *See also* Merrill, Amy (maiden name)
Ansara, Emma (daughter), 204, 207
Ansara, Jim (brother), 61
Ansara, Meg (daughter), 242
Ansara, Michael: anti-drug use, 58, 147–48; arrests and beating in Boston (1971), 195, 198; *Boston Globe* columnist, 207; change of appearance in 1972, 202, *202*; community activism in Boston black neighborhoods, 9–11; as consultant, 247; conventional personal life, 58–62; as "democratic communist," 232; despair and

sense of failure, 132, 152, 166, 245, 252; as door-to-door canvasser, 237–38; draft exam rejection, 140–44; Europe trip (1968), 96–99; exhaustion of, 140, 242, 246–47, 258; family background, 4, 23, 33–34, 39; as father, 204, 207, 242, 245, 247; on FBI lists as dangerous individual, 133; high school years and education, 1–4, 6–7; hindsight of, 243–49, 251; joint disease, 3, 5, 140; listening skills, 175–76, 201–2; marriage to Amy and divorce, 61, 106, 134, 244; mentors from Civil Rights Movement, 7–8, 11–12, 25; midlife crisis, 244, 247; parents' deaths, 244; photos of, *126, 202, 220*; as poet and essayist, 247; police threatening, 133, 134, 248; on poster of "100 Most Dangerous Radicals in America," 137; student painting crew of, 18–19, 39; as volunteer for campaigns and nonprofits, 247. *See also* antiwar movement; Dorchester; Harvard; Harvard Strike; Mass Fair Share; The People First
antiwar movement: 1968 and, 95–114; 1969 and, 129; 1972–1975 and, 198–99; active-duty military and, 153, *153*, 164; Ansara throwing brick at police car, 158–59; Boston and Cambridge protest (October 1965), 42–43, *42*; Boston regional gathering (December 1965), 46–48; Boston University picketing and police ambush (1969), 155–56; brochures (1972), 199; "Call to Resist Illegitimate Authority" (1967), 92–93; changing minds and gaining supporters, 41–57, 67, 74–77, 114, 145, 150, 154–55; Columbia University action (1968), 100–101, 117; counter demonstrators, 43, 53, 85; The Day After (Chicago Eights Verdict) march (1970), 157, *158*; Dow Chemical Company protests (1967), 89–93; effect on US as a nation, 252; electoral politics and, 84, 110–12, *111*; FBI and, 110,

antiwar movement (*continued*)
133; fractious nature of, 41, 79; guilt of students in, 56, 131, 140, 152, 252; Harvard Square demonstration, 159–62, *160–62*; in hindsight, 251; indictment rumors (1969), 156–57; International Days of Protest (1965), 42–43; lessons learned from, 207; Lexington/Concord march to Bunker Hill (1971), 192; London march (1968), 97; Lowell action (1970), 167–77; March on the Pentagon (1967), 85–88, *88*; March on Washington (April 1965), 31, 32, 34–37, *35*, 39; March on Washington (November 1965), 45–46; mindset of, 46, 53–54, 78–84, 88, 94, 104, 150; MIT action (1969), *151*, 154–55; New Left Caucus and, 116; New Politics coalition and, 82; Nixon and, 133, 154, 163, 251; Northeastern demonstration (1970), 157–59, *159–60*; NYC construction workers' attack on student activists (1970), 133, *134*; Richardson and, 235; SDS at head of, 38, 39–57; self-immolation, 45; Senate Subcommittee on Internal Security investigation, 135–37; social gatherings after protests, 113; Spring Mobilization (NYC 1967), 74–75, 80; unclear in how to end the war, 105–6; Vietnam Moratorium and, 112; war on drugs and, 109–10; Washington demonstrations (April & May 1971), 194. *See also* Harvard Strike; SDS; Vietnam Veterans Against the War
apartheid, 31, 32, 93
Appleby, Mike, 25
Árbenz, Jacobo, 51, 72
Arlook, Ira, 168–71, 176, 177, 182, 198–99, 242
Arnett, Peter, 95

Bailey, F. Lee, 225
Benenson, Hal, 64–65, 78, 113
Berkeley, 32, 35. *See also* Free Speech Movement
Berrigan, Daniel and Philip, 54
Bevel, James, 75, 85
Billy C. (Boston cop), 197–98
Bird, David, 69, 71
Birmingham: Baptist Church bombing, 16; civil rights protests, 12
Black equality. *See* Civil Rights Movement
Black liberation struggle, 129, 136; San Francisco State University student strike and (1970), 157
Black Nationalism, 256
Black Panthers, 75–76, 81–82, 133, 146, 148–49, 163, 235

Black Power, 75, 82–83
Black radicals, split with white progressives, 82–84
Black studies programs, 125, 128, 129
Bond, Julian, 82
Booth, Heather, 139, 205–6, 241, 242, 271n2
Booth, Paul, 31, 44–45, 82, 205–6, 264–65n6
Bosch, Juan, 51
Boston: canvassing in Black neighborhoods, 9–11; The Day After (Chicago Eight Verdict) march (1970), 157, *158*; highway construction and, 207; nonviolent sit-in at federal building (May 1971), 194–95, *196*; racial discrimination and school segregation, 9, 12; school desegregation and busing, 56, 207–8, 213, 234, 256; Vietnam Moratorium march (1969), 154, 159. *See also* Dorchester
Boston Action Group (BAG), 7, 9–11, 28, 201, 208
Boston Draft Resistance Group (BDRG), 54–55, 136, 142
Boston Edison, 222
Boston Fair Share, 224, 225
Boston Five, 95, 105
Boston Legal Assistance Project (BLAP), 188–90
Boston Organizing Project, 209, 210
Boston Tactical Police Force (Tac Squad), 181, 195, 198
Boston University picketing and police ambush (1969), 155–56
Brandon, Peter, 29
Bread and Roses (feminist organization), 139
Brecht, Bertolt: "To Posterity" (poem), 147
Breeden, Jim, 7, 8, 9–12, *13*, 19, 154
Brooke, Edward, 187
Brookline, 1–6, 11
Brookline Lunch (Central Square), 107
Brower, Reuben, 59
Brown, H. Rap, 75
Brown, Sam, 239–40
Build Not Burn, 44
Bulger, Whitey, 215
Burlage, Robb and Dorothy, 25
Burlingham, Bo, 152, 163–65

Cairo riot (Illinois 1967), 76
California: farm worker organizing, 213; Proposition 13 and tax relief, 218–19
"Call to Resist Illegitimate Authority" (1967), 92–93
Cambodia bombing/invasion (1969–70), 109, 130, 140, 162, 194

Campaign for Human Development (CHD), 209, 210

Canny, Jim, 182

Cantor, Jay, 127

CAP-Energy, 205, *206*, 207–8, 210

Caplan, Marc, 241

Carmichael, Stokely, 75

Carter, Jimmy, 239

Carter, Vernon, *13*

Carver, Ron, 6, 11, 14, 17–18, 101, 153, 164

Casady, Simon, 82

Cassedy, Ellen, 205, 271n1

Castro, Fidel, 72, 104

Catholics and Catholicism, 179–80; Catholic Worker Movement, 54; right-wing forces and, 84; social justice and, 206–7; Vatican II, 209

Celtic Club (Lowell), 170

Central American Peace Campaign, 247

Central Square (Cambridge, Mass.), 106–7

Chaney, James, 21, 28, 131, 248

Chase Manhattan Bank, 31

Chavez, Cesar, 213

Chelsea Fair Share, 209–10

Chelsea Street Bridge, 233

Cheney, Dick, 73

Chicago: community activism in, 205–6, 237; police, 93–94, 131, 134, 148–49, 152

Chicago Eight, 133, 149, 156–57, *158*

China, 250–51

Chomsky, Noam, 40, 43

Church, Frank, and Church Committee, 72–73

CIA: Bird and, 69; Harvard and, 91, 120, 128; in Indonesia, 51; Maher and PL labeling Ansara as agent of, 134–35, 252; National Student Association and, 71; secret operations and covert funding of, 70–73, 96, 99, 106; September 11 attacks (2001) and, 146

Citizen Action, 242

Citizen Labor Energy Coalition (CLEC), 241

Citizens for a Better Environment, 237

Citizens for Human Rights, 12

civil defense drills, 1–3, *2*, 28

civil disobedience, 87, 88, 92

Civil Rights Act of 1875, 257

Civil Rights Movement: anti-Vietnam war stance and, 75; in Birmingham, 12, 16; Black challenges to Jim Crow, 5–6; in Boston area, 6, 12–13; FBI targeting of, 252; Hoagland and, 136; inspiration of, 257; JFK and, 12, 16; liberal consensus and, 22; March on Washington (1963), 13–15, *15*;

nonviolence and, 12, 16, 75; organizers of, xiii, 6; Richardson and, 235; SDS origins and, 30; shift from interracial to all-Black movement, 75, 77, 82–83; sit-ins, 5, 6; uncompleted work of, 256; white backlash against, 247, 254, 256

Clark, Mark, 149

Clark, Owen, 226

Clerc, Kim, 241

climate change, 253, 259

Clinton, Bill, 254

Clive, John L., 78

Coelho, Tony, 254

COINTELPRO, 72, 133, 252

Colburn, Judith, 71

Colby, William, 73

Cold War, 12, 24, 26–27, 33, 41, 45–46, 71; US interventions overseas, 51, 68, 72–73. *See also* Vietnam war

Columbia University action (1968), 100–101, 117

Commonwealth School (Boston), 6–7, 16

communism: in Vietnam, 34, 36; Vietnam war as part of struggle against, 33, 49, 170. *See also* Cold War

Communist Party (CP), 24, 44–45; post-Soviet era of, 250; Progressive Labor Party and, 116; Vietnamese, 251

community organizing. *See* Mass Fair Share

Congress of Racial Equality (CORE), 7, 11

Connecticut Citizen Action Group (CCAG), 241

Connolly, Richard, 136

conscientious objectors, 44, 141, 193

Conservation Services Group, 240

conservatism, 114, 253

Continental Baking Company, boycott of, 11

CORE (Congress of Racial Equality), 7, 11

corporate bureaucracy and corporate liberals, 22, 24, 26, 39, 50

Corrigan, Tom, 209

Coughlin, Charles, 254

Council of Federated Organizations (COFO), 17

counterculture (1967), 79–81, 86

COVID-19 pandemic, 258–59

Cowell, Steve, 240

Coyote, Peter, 87

Cram, Bestor, 193, *194*

Crane, Bobby, 229–30

Creamer, Bob, 242

Cuban Missile crisis, 12, 16

Curley, James Michael, 180, 186

Czechoslovakia, 96, 101, 105

Daley, Richard J., 105
Dammond, Peggy Trotter, 12, *13*
Davidson, Tom, 204
Davis, Rennie, 93–94, 133, 157
Day, Noel, and Day campaign, 7, 8, 9–12, *13*, 18–20, 24, 28, 29, 76
Days of International Protest (1966), 53–54
Debray, Régis, 87
De Fronzo, Anna, 212
Dellinger, Dave, 87, 157
Democratic Party: congressional majority opposed to war funding, 199; Dorchester and, 180, 186; elite capture of, 254; Massachusetts governor primary (1978), 217, 227; populism and, 254; Southern Democrats, 26, 108; Vietnam war and primaries, 96. *See also* Humphrey, Hubert; Johnson, Lyndon; National Democratic Convention (1964) *and* (1968); *specific politicians*
despair: in antiwar movement, 54, 132, 176; failure and, 152, 245; in family life, 4–8; in school, 3
Detroit riot (1967), 76, *76–77*
DiCarlo, Joe, 226
Dickinson, Tim, 6
Diggers (theater collective), 80, 87
Dohrn, Bernadine, 163
Dolan, Jim, 190
Dominican Republic, 51, 68
domino theory, 41, 251
Donaldson, Ivanhoe, 75
Donham, Flora, 12
Donham, Parker, 124
Dorchester, 177–90; Ansara and Amy's residence in, 179, 181, 203–4; Anti-Troy Day, 188; economic campaigns for local community, 184; failure to develop stable community-based organization, 190; food cooperative, 181; locals against the war, 150, 182; organizing headquarters, 181; political unrest in, 180; racial change in, 179, 203; Reilly's Tavern meeting, 183; removing Judge Troy from the bench, 184–90, *189–90*, 194, 197, 238; tragic lives in, 184; Vietnam veterans in, 182, 183–84, 193. *See also* The People First
Dorchester Fair Share, 215, 225
Dorchester Community Action Council (DCAC), 215
Dow Chemical Company protests (1967), 89–93
draft exam rejection of Ansara, 140–44

draft resistance, 42, 54–56, 82, 85, 93, 95, 150, 168; alternative service for conscientious objectors, 44; draft card burnings, 54–55, 74, 85, *86*; draft evasion, 55, 141; end of draft, 198–99. *See also* Boston Draft Resistance Group
Drinan, Robert, 193
Dubček, Alexander, 96
Dudley Street Action Center (Boston), 19–20, 27, 76
Dukakis, Michael, 217–19, 227–28, 231, 247
Dutchke, Rudi, 97–100, *98*, *100*, 106
Dyen, Mark, 115, 152–53, 203, 205, 210–11, 221, 240, 241, 246
Dylan, Bob, 33, 152–53

East Boston Maverick Street Mothers, 212
economic justice: Citizen Action and, 242. *See also* Mass Fair Share
Economic Research and Action Project (ERAP) organizers, 30–33, 47, 203
Eggleson, Nick, 54
Ehrlichman, John, 53, 109–10
Eisenhower, Dwight D., 143; *Mandate for Change*, 34, 50
election day protests (1968), 110, *111*
elites: Democratic Party in thrall of, 254; saving sons from Vietnam draft, 141; split between parents and children in view of Vietnam war, 51–53, 104
Ellsberg, Daniel, 197
Emergency Detention Program, 133
Emerson, Ralph Waldo, 23, 253
energy crisis (1970s), 210, 241
environmentalism, 114, 247, 253
Epps, Archie, 13, 118
Erlichman, John, 53
Europe trip (1968), 96–99
Evans, Rowland, 41
Evers, Medgar, 12, 131, 256

Fair Fighter (Fair Share newspaper), 220–21
Fair Share: in states other than Massachusetts, 241. *See also* Mass Fair Share
Fair Share Amendment, 272n8
Fair Share Development Corporation, 240
Farmers Alliance, 255
FBI: Ansara on registries of, 133; Burlingham and, 164–65; COINTELPRO operation, 72, 133, 252; Communist Party members as informants for, 45; on domestic bombings (1971–72), 163; Hoagland and, 137; illegal wiretaps and tactics, 163, 165;

informants inside Black Panthers, 149; investigating Harvard students, 39; murder of Fred Hampton and, 148–49; Nixon and, 110; student movements and, 147, 252; undermining Black leaders, 256
Federal Communications Commission (FCC), 165
Federal Housing Administration (FHA), 256
Feeley, Tom, 245
Feinberg, Gerald, 225–26
Feldman, Michael, 188
feminism, 114, 137–40, 146, 175–76, 205. *See also* women's liberation movement
Ferber, Michael, 85, 95
Finfer, Lew, 215, 272n8
Finn, Donna, 181, 182, 185
Finnegan, John J., 227–28
First National Bank, Boston, 224, 229
Flacks, Dick, 30, 133–34
Flaschner, Franklin N., 188
Flynn, Ray, 246
Fonda, Jane, 199
Ford, Franklin, 120–21, 126, 128
Fort Dix, New Jersey, 163, 252
Fourteenth Amendment, 257
France: demonstrations and strikes by students and workers, 101, *102*; in Indochina, 34, 49, 95; WWII resistance, 93
Frank, Barney, 67–68, 228–29
freedom of speech, 54, 63, 66
Freedom Riders, 5
Freedom Summer and Freedom Schools: Boston alternative Freedom Schools, 12–13; Mississippi, 17–18, *18*, 20, 21, 29, 31, 32, 40, 78, 206
Freeman, Jo: "The Tyranny of Structurelessness," 207
Free Speech Movement (Berkeley), 28–29, 32, 86
FTA ("fuck the army" musical tour), 183

Gabriel, Vernice, 236
Gauthier, Gouch, 170, 172, 176
gay rights, 114, 247
General Electric strike (1969), 155–56
Geneva Accords (1954), 34, 50, 65, 143
gentrification, 204
German Socialist Student Union (German SDS), 97–100
Germany: 1968 student unrest, 97–100, *100*, 129; in World War II, 50
Gerstacker, Carl, 93
Gibbs, Phillip Lafayette, 131

GI Bill's exclusion of Black veterans, 256
Ginsberg, Allen, 60, 80, 86
Gitlin, Todd, 25, 31, 264n2
Glimp, Fred, 90–91
globalization, 242, 251, 254
global scope of student militancy, 101–2, 129. *See also specific countries*
Glynn, Seamus, 178, 180–81, 185
Gold, Paula, 188, 189–90
Gold, Ted, 162–63
Goldberg, Arthur, 67
Gold Star families, 145
Gold Star Mothers for Peace, 145
Goldwater, Barry, 21
Goodman, Andrew, 21, 28, 131, 248
Goodman, Mitch, 95
Gottschalk, Ruth and Harry, 145, 188
Green, James Earl, 131
Gregory, Chris, 193
Grizzard, Vernon, 54
Grossman, Jerry, 12, 193
Guatemala, 51, 68
Guevara, Che, 87
guilt of students in antiwar movement, 56, 131, 140, 152, 252

Haber, Al, 30, 138
Haber, Barbara, 138
Haldeman, H. R., 53
Hamer, Fannie Lou, 8, 21, 28, 82, 243
Hampton, Fred, 131, 148–49, 248, 256
Hanley, Martin J. (Marty), 180, 186–88
Harmon, John, *13*
Harrington, Kevin B., 227–28
Harrington, Michael: *The Other America*, 29
Harris, Cheryl, 236
Hartman, Chester, 11, 78
Harvard (1964–67, Ansara's undergraduate years): Adams House, 50–51, 59–60; as Ansara's first choice, 17; Booth as speaker to SDS at, 44; cultural events, 60–61; discipline of leaders of Dow Chemical protest, 92; Dow Chemical Company protests (1967), 89–93; entry as advanced placement sophomore, 23–24; faculty opposed to Vietnam war, 53, 92; McNamara protest, 63–67, *64*, 74, 92; organizing on campus, 48–51; Quincy House visit by McNamara, 63–64; SDS and, 27, 29; senior-year thesis and graduation, 78–79, 96, 103–4; shah of Iran as graduation speaker (1968), 103–4; Student–Faculty Advisory Council, 92; teach-in, 39–41; teach-out, 78

Harvard Afro, 125
Harvard Corporation, 121, 126, 128
Harvard Square demonstration (1970),
  159–62, *160–62*
Harvard Strike (1969), 115–29; African
  American studies department, demand
  for, 125, 128; Ansara as chair of strike
  committee, 124, 127; broader import of,
  129; called "Harvard Riots" by faculty and
  administration, 129; exposing Harvard's
  work with CIA and military support, 120,
  128; faculty and administration's reaction
  to, 126–27; initiation of strike, 124–25;
  moderates' role, 124; nonviolence and, 121;
  occupation of University Hall, 117–24, *120*;
  opposition to building occupation and tactics,
  121; police violence and arrests of protestors,
  121–24, *123*; posters and t-shirts, 127–28,
  128; ratification in Harvard Stadium, 125–26,
  125–26; ROTC program and, 115–16, 124,
  127–28; SDS and, 124–26; student anger in
  reaction to police treatment, 123; women
  on strike committee, 139; Worker Student
  Alliance and, 116. *See also* ROTC program
Havel, Vaclav, 243
Hayakawa, S. I., 157
Hayden, Casey, 139; "A Kind of Memo" (with
  King), 139
Hayden, Tom, 25–26, 30–32, 93–94, 133, 157,
  199
Hersh, Seymour (Sy), 72
Hershey, Lewis Blaine, 55
Hicks, Louise Day, 208
Hinkle, Warren, 69, 71–72, 80
Hispanic Young Lords, 146
Ho Chi Minh, 34, 143, 174
Hoagland, Ralph, 136–37
Hoffman, Abbie, 56–57, 86–87, 157
Hoffman, Julius, 156–57
Hoover, J. Edgar, 110, 133, 147, 252
hope for future, 259
Hornstein, Harriet, 3
housing: affordable, 207; restrictive covenants,
  256
Houston, Julian, 7
Hubbard, Al, *194*
Huggins, George, 236
Hughes, H. Stuart, 11–12, 25, 193
Humphrey, Hubert, 21, 105, 109, 110, 112
Hunt, Robert, 76

illegal wiretaps and strategies of government
  agencies, 163, 165
Illinois Public Action Coalition (IPAC), 242
immigration and xenophobia, 254–55, 257–58

Immigration Reform and Control Act (1986),
  257
Independence Foundation, 69–71
Indiana Citizen Action, 242
Indochina Peace Campaign (IPC), 199
Indonesia, 51, 68
Institute for Defense Analysis, 100
International Association of Machinists and
  Aerospace Workers (IAM), 241
International Days of Protest (1965), 42–43, *42*
International Women's Day march (1970), 157
interracial movement, 30, 32, 47, 75, 94,
  234–36
Iran, 51, 68, 97, 103–4
IRS, 69–70, 72, 245
Israel, 82–83
Israel, Jared, 117, 146

Jackson State killings of protesting students,
  110, 131, 162, 248
Jacobs, Arlo, 164. *See also* Burlingham, Bo
Jane Collective, 206, 271n2
Jefferies, Sharon, 30
Jefferson, Thomas, 252
Jews: Ansara's mother's family as, 4; anti-
  Semitism, 83, 255; in Civil Rights
  Movement, 82–83; white flight of, 179
Jim Crow, 1, 5, 24
Johene, Fran, 208
Johnson, Art, 193, *194*
Johnson, Lyndon B. (LBJ): antiwar movement
  and, 37, 46, 251; arrogance of, 67; CIA and,
  72, 73; criticism of, 40; Gulf of Tonkin and,
  20–21, 34, 41; as likely Democratic Party
  nominee in 1968, 81, 93–94; not running
  for reelection (1968), 96; Vietnam war
  escalation, 20–21, 34, 50, 53, 68, 85, 95, 130
Joyce, Joe, 215
Judge, Darwin Lee, 199–200

Katz, Jim, 210, 221
Katzenbach, Nicholas, 42
Kazin, Michael, 117, *120*, 124, 152
Kelly, Jim (Senate ways and means chair),
  227–28
Kelly, Jimmy, 183–84, 215
Kennedy, John F., 1, 4, 12, 16, 109
Kennedy, Robert F., 96, 104–5, 131
Kennedy, Sargent, 104
Kennedy, Ted, 11–12, 208
Kent State protests and killing of students, 110,
  131, 162, 164, 248
Kerry, John, 193, *194*
King, Coretta Scott, 103
King, Ed, 217, 219, 227, 231

King, Martin Luther, Jr.: assassination of, 99, 131, 248, 256; "the beloved community" concept and, 30; Birmingham arrest and "Letter from Birmingham Jail," 12; as impactful leader, 243; March on Washington and (1963), 14–15; National Conference for a New Politics and, 82; National Democratic Convention (1964) and, 21; as possible presidential contender, 79, 82; Spring Mobilization (1967) and, 75; Vietnam Summer (1967) and, 79
King, Mary, 139; "A Kind of Memo" (with Hayden), 139
King, Mel, 7, 208, 212, 234, 271n4
Kinkead, Maeve, 60, 61
Kissinger, Henry, 66, 73, 108–9, 154, 199, 251, 253
Klotz, Gretchen, 97, 99
Krause, Allison, 131

labor unions, 47–48, 84, 93, 215, 241, 247, 254–55, 259, 265n6
Landau, David, 135
landlords as tax cheats, 225–26
Laquidara, Charles, 164
Leavitt, Fred, 90–91
Legal In-Service Project (LISP), 193
Legion of Justice (right-wing group), 134
Leichman, Ivy, 156
Leninism, 116, 146–47
lessons learned: from antiwar movement and Civil Rights Movement, 207; author offering to young people, 259; from California farm worker organizing, 213; referendum passage and, 212, 228
Levertov, Denise, 60
Levin, Larry, 199
Levine, Eric, 29
Levy, Allyn, 225–26
Lewis, John, 14–15, 240
Lexington/Concord march to Bunker Hill (1971), 192
liberals and liberal consensus: antiwar march organized by (November 1965), 45–46; criticism of, 24, 109; in mid-1960s, 22; New Politics coalition and, 82
liberation theology, 209
Liebling, A. J., 106
Lodge, George Cabot, 40
Logan Airport expansion protests, 93, 212, 224, 227, 229
Long, Huey, 254
Loud, David, 29, 67, 78, 147–48
Loving v. Virginia (1967), 14
Lowell action (1970), 167–77

low-income neighborhoods, 31, 177, 205, 208–9, 213, 218, 220, 236, 238, 240, 248
Lucas, Carolyn, 218–19, 229
Luria, Sal, 40
Lynd, Staughton, 29, 40
Lynn, 177, 205, 216, 226

MacEachern, Richard G., 157
Maguire, Dusty, 181
Maher, John, 11, 54, 134–35, 252
Mailer, Norman, 40, 86
Malcolm X, 16, 75, 131, 256
Mandela, Nelson, 243
Manning, Frank, 212
Maoism, 116, 146
March on the Pentagon (1967), 75, 85–88, *88*
March on Washington (April 1965 anti-Vietnam war), 31, 32, 34–37, *35*, 39
March on Washington for Jobs and Freedom (1963), 13–15, *15*, 118
March on Washington (November 1965 anti-Vietnam war), 45–46
Marcuse, Herbert, 28, 87, 253
Margolin, Barry, 221
Marston, John, 245
Martilla, John, 230
Marxism and Karl Marx, 78, 108, 116, 146, 267n16
Massachusetts: budget surplus, allocation of (1978), 227; residential conservation program, 223
Massachusetts Bar Association, 188–89
Massachusetts Bay Transportation Authority (MBTA), 236
Massachusetts Community Center, 205–7
Massachusetts Crime Commission, 187
Massachusetts Department of Public Utilities (DPU), 211, 223
Massachusetts Freedom Movement, 7, 20
Massachusetts State Police Red Squad (Red Squad), 167, 170, 173, 195, 198
Massachusetts Supreme Judicial Court (SJC), 188
Massachusetts tax reform: initiatives of Mass Fair Share, 223–31; tax cap referendum, 230
Mass Fair Share, xiii, 217–42; access to and release of information by, 222, 226; actions and confrontations with decision makers, 222; Ansara in director role, 216, 219, *220*; Ansara's resignation, 245–46; Black organizers, 234–36; Black women and, 234, 236; budget of, 238; "circuit breaker" bill limiting property tax payments and, 217–19, 226–28; "Covenant of Racial Justice and Harmony," 236; door-to-door

Mass Fair Share (*continued*)
canvassers, 237–38; electoral politics and, 246; electric rates and, 211–12, *232*; end of, 246; factionalism in, 244; financial crisis (1981), 244–45; fundraising for, 238–39; home heating oil cooperative and, 240; house meetings and, 214; launch of, 209–16; layoffs, 245; leadership structure and training, 214, 216, 219, 221, 233, 241, 246; name recognition of, 219; national initiative and, 240–42; new chapters, formation of, 214–16; nonprofit status of, 238; organizing committees, formation of, 213–14; phone campaign to get donations, 238–39; as populist force, 219–20, *232*, 255; racism and, 234–36; range of issues, 215, 233; referendum campaigns for flat rate electric rates and graduated income tax (1976), 211–12, *212*, 222, 228; self-interest as best way to appeal to community, 232–33; staff of, 236–37, 244, 246; steps in community organizing, 213–14; successful initiatives of, 220–21, 233; tax abatements and, 224; tax reform initiatives, 223–31, 241; tax revaluation/overassessment of residential property, 224, 226, 230; unitary taxing of oil companies and, 241; utility companies, rate protests against, 222–23, *223*, *232*; women's role in, 221, 245
Maverick Street Mothers, 93, 212, 229
Max, Steve, 241
Mayer, Tim, 60–61
McCarthy, Eugene, 79, 83, 96, 239
McCarthy, Joseph, 189
McCormack, John, 18
McDonough, Sonny, 187, 189–90
McDowell, Banks, 40
McGee, Thomas, 227–28
McGovern, George, 154
McKissick, Floyd, 82
McMahon, Charles, 199–200
McNamara, Craig, 104
McNamara, Robert: children of, 53; at Harvard and encounter with Ansara, 63–67, *64*, 74, 92, 229; *In Retrospect: The Tragedy and Lessons of Vietnam*, 64
media: counterculture newspapers, 108; social media, 254; support for antiwar demonstrators, 106; underground newspaper *Old Mole* (1968–70), 107–8, 119, 128; Vietnam war and, 46, *68*
Meisel, Lisa, 163–65
Merrill, Amy (later Amy Ansara): at Commonwealth School, 16–17; marriage to Ansara, 61; at Pembroke (Brown University), 27–28, 59; at SDS National Council meeting (1964), 29–30, 31; transfer to Brandeis, 61, 79
Merrill, Catherine, 80
Merrill family, 16–17, 61
METCO (voluntary school busing program), 208
Mexico student protests (1968), 101, 113, 129
Mickiewicz, Al, 224
Midwest Academy, 206, 241–42
Milford, New Hampshire, 147–48
military draft. *See* draft resistance; Selective Service
Miller, Jeffrey, 131
Mills, C. Wright, 28, 253
Milošević, Slobodan, 146
Mississippi delegation to National Democratic Convention (1964), 21
Mississippi Freedom Democratic Party (MFDP), 21, 28, 31–32
MIT action (1969), *151*, 154–55
Mitchell, John N., 133
Moffet, Toby, 241
Monro, John, 66, 67
Montgomery, Richard, 235
Moore, Frederick R., 19
Moran, Peg, 182
Moratorium. *See* Vietnam Moratorium
Morrison, Norman, 45
Morse, Wayne, 20, 53
Mosaddegh, Mohammad, 51, 72
Moses, Bob, 36
Mothers for Adequate Welfare (MAW), 20, 56, 76, 93, 116
Movement for Economic Justice, 209, 271n5
Muse, Robert, 187

NAACP, 12
Nader, Ralph, 241
National Committee for a Sane Nuclear Policy (SANE), 79, 82
National Conference for a New Politics (NCNP), 82–83
National Coordinating Committee to End the War in Vietnam, 53
National Council of Senior Citizens, 241
National Democratic Convention (1964), 21, 28, 32
National Democratic Convention (1968): Ansara's choice not to participate in protests at, 94, 105; antiwar protests at, 93–94, 105–6
National Emergency Committee of Clergy and Laymen Concerned about Vietnam, 74, 79
National Liberation Front (NLF, aka Vietcong), 74, 95, *131*, *151*, 152, 171, 174–75, 200

National Mobilization Committee to End the War in Vietnam (the "Mobe"), 85, 87, 159
National Student Association (NSA), 70, 71–72, 239
Neustadt, Richard, 66
Newark riot (1967), 76
New England Life, 225
New Left: Bread and Roses and, 139; building student-based movement, 23–24, 37; in coalition to form New Politics, 82; congressional investigations of (1969–70), 137; electoral politics and, 84; FBI targeting, 252; in Germany, 97; McCarthy presidential campaign and, 83; nonexistent by 1960s, 247; PL faction vs., 116–17; *Ramparts* (magazine) and, 69; scorning old left, 24, 33, 44, 252; SDS and, 12, 116, 146; Senate Subcommittee on Internal Security investigation of, 135–37; significance of, 45; veterans still working for social justice, 253; Vietnam war and, 251. *See also* SDS
New Left Caucus, 116
"New Politics," 74, 81–83
New York: construction workers' attack on antiwar student activists (1970), 133, *134*; march to end Vietnam war (March 1966), 53; march to support US in Vietnam (fall 1966), 50; Spring Mobilization (1967), 74–75. *See also* Columbia University action (1968)
New York Police Department (NYPD), 101
9 to 5, 205, 207, 271n1
Nixon, Richard: 1960 election, 1; 1968 election, 110–12; 1972 election, 199; antiwar movement and, 133, 154, 163, 251; Cambodia and, 140, 162; electoral failure of left to organize against, 84, 110, 112; FBI and, 110, 133; lying by, 140, 197; prolonging Vietnam war, 108–9, 140, 145, 192, 194, 197–99; racism of, 109–10; as Republican presidential nominee (1968), 105, 108–9; Southern Strategy reshaping Republican Party, 108; Vietnam Moratorium and, 154; Watergate and, 72, 189, 199, 200
Non-Partisan League of North Dakota, 240
nonviolence: antiwar protesting and, 192; arguing against violence, 152; Civil Rights Movement and, 12, 16, 75; Harvard (1969) protests, 121; regrets over failure to always follow, 249
Northeastern demonstration (1970), 157–59, *159–60*
Northern Student Movement, 6, 7
North Vietnam. *See* National Liberation Front (NLF, aka Vietcong); Vietnam war

Novak, Robert, 41
November Action Coalition (NAC), 153, 154–56
nuclear weapons and disarmament, 1–4, 11, 16, 28, 66, 247
Nussbaum, Karen, 205, 271n1

Obama, Barack, 254
O'Connor, Buddy and Mikey, 178, 180–81, 185
O'Connor, Mike, 156
October Days of Rage, 152
O'Donnell, Kirk, 229, 272n6
O'Donnell, Lawrence F., 188–89
Oglesby, Carl, 44, 46
Old Mole (underground newspaper 1968–70 and later office space), 107–8, 119, 128, 136, 139, 153, 178–79, 199
O'Neill, Tip, 233, 272n6
Operation Rolling Thunder (1965), 34
optimism, 2, 6, 8, 38, 258–59
Oregon Fair Share, 241
organizing: with Adams campaign, 56–57, 61, 87; as author's passion, 9, 15, 61; beliefs behind, 9; Black organizers, 234–36; with Day campaign, 7, 8, 9–12, *13*, 18–20, 24, 28, 29, 76; democratic structuring and, 207; electoral politics and, 84, 110, *111*; first encounter with, 5; leaders vs. organizers, 246; professionalization of, 213; raising money for, 238; recognizing areas in which to improve, 190, 201–3; social movements and, 243; training of organizers, 214, 216, 219, 221, 233, 241; Vietnam Summer (local organizing of antiwar movement), 78–79. *See also* antiwar movement; Mass Fair Share; SDS; SNCC; The People First
Osborn, Frances, 39
Oughton, Diana, 162–63
"Our Bodies, Ourselves," 139

Pahlavi, Mohammed Reza, 103–4
Paine, Thomas, 191
Palladino, Elvira "Pixie," 208
Paris student demonstrations (1968), 101, *102*, 129
Parker, Adam, 240
patriotism, 41, 47, 142, 170, 192, 197
Payne, Dan, 230
Peace Corps, 44
Pentagon Papers, 66, 197, 199
People's Party (1890s), 255
Peretz, Marty, 78, 79, 83
Phillips, A. Robert (Bob), 7–8
Pillsbury, George, 222

police violence and brutality, 76, 101, 105, 121–23, *123*, 124, 150; recent killings of unarmed African Americans, 256. *See also* antiwar movement *for specific actions and demonstrations*
populism: Mass Fair Share and, 219–20, *232*, 255; right-wing, 254; road not taken by Democratic Party, 254; study of populist movements, 240; white supremacy and, 255. *See also* right-wing forces
Port Huron Statement, 25–26, 28
Posner, Josh, 240
Potter, Paul, 29, 36–37
Prague Spring (1968), 96, 101, 105, 113, 129
presidential election: (1960), 1; (1968), 109–12; (1972), 199
Progressive Labor Party (PL), 115–29; effect of, 152; Harvard Strike of 1969 and, 118–19, 121, 124–26; Maher and, 134; Maoism and, 146; SDS and, 115–16, 136, 145–46; sentenced and sent to prison for violent action in Harvard Strike, 129
Prosten, Jesse, 47
protests. *See specific marches and locations of protests*
Pusey, Nathan, 92, 117, 121, 123–24, 126–28
Putnam, Hilary, 92

Quincy Community College, 177
Quinsigamond Community College, 177

race riots: (1967), 76–77, *76–77*, 79; (1968), 99
racism and racial discrimination, 9; failure to vanquish, 253; MBTA and, 236; National Conference for a New Politics and Black caucus, 82–83; Nixon and, 109–10; police and, 76; racial justice, need to fight for, 257; restrictive covenants and, 256; school desegregation and antibusing movement, 207–8, 213, 234, 256; US Supreme Court and, 256–57; violence and, 5, 10, 16, 76, 255. *See also* Civil Rights Movement; Jim Crow
Ramparts (magazine), 63; Ansara's CIA book for, 106; Ansara's part-time position with, 71, 73, 77, 81; Burlingham as editor, 165; CIA money laundering exposé, 68–69, 71–72, 239; European research for, 96–97; summer job (San Francisco 1967), 79–81
Randolph, A. Phillip, 14
Rapoport, Miles, 156, 177, 205, 207, 210, 213–14, 241–42, 272n14
Raskin, Marcus, 95
Reagan, Ronald, 242, 244, 257

Red Squad. *See* Massachusetts State Police Red Squad
Regan, John, 212, 215
Regan, Mike, 218, 233
Reinstein, William, 226
Reisen, Beth, 203
Republican Party: campaign funding of, 254; minority rule of old white men, 259; Nixon's transformation of, 108–9; as party of white grievance, 108, 253; as party of white voters, 257; resistance to, 259. *See also specific politicians*
Reserve Officer Training Corps (ROTC): Harvard's abolition of, 128; Harvard Strike of 1969 and, 117–18, 128; SDS campaign to shut down, 115–16
resistance: meaning of, 93; move from protest to, 57, 73, 92–93. *See also* antiwar movement; draft resistance
Reston, James, 43
Restore Our Alienated Rights (ROAR), 208
Reuther, Walter, 21
Revere, 216–19, 226, 228
Revolutionary Youth Movement (RYM), 146
Richardson, Peter: *A Bomb in Every Issue*, 72
Riepen, Ray, 165
right-wing forces, 84, 113, 242, 254
Robbins, Terry, 162–63, 164
Ronan Park, Boston, 178, *179*, 180–81
Ross, Bob, 30, 32
Ross, Fred, 213
Rothstein, Richard, 25, 264n1
Rothstein, Vivien, 139
Rottman, Lenni, 193
Rubin, Jerry, 86–87, 157
Rumsfeld, Donald, 73
Rushing, Byron, 7
Russell, Bill, 13
Ryan, Robert, 224

Sagan, Carl, 92
Salvucci, Fred, 229, 272n6
Salzman, Marilyn, 139
San Francisco (1967): counterculture, 79–81; *Ramparts* summer job, 79–80; Spring Mobilization, 74
Sasso, John, 230, 231
Savio, Mario, 32
Scalese, Dominick, 132–33, 134
Schechter, Danny, 96–97, 99, 120, 165
Scheer, Bob, 63, 68–69, 71–72, 79, 80, 82–83
Scheuer, Sandra Lee, 131

schools: desegregation and busing (Boston), 56, 207–8, 213, 234, 256; resegregation after Civil Rights Movement, 256
Schroeder, William, 131
Schwartz, Jon, 108
Schwerner, Michael, 21, 28, 131, 248
SDS (Students for a Democratic Society): 1968 and, 111–12; as Ansara's political home, 25–39; attacks by US government officials on, 41–42, 43–44; changing minds of students to support, 50–51, 111; Columbia University action (1968), 100–101; craziness as offshoot of, 135, 150–53, 162–63, 166, 252; Days of International Protest (1966), 53–54; decision making by consensus vs. leadership, 30, 44, 258; Economic Research and Action Project (ERAP) organizers, 30–33; electoral politics and, 110–12, *111*; factions breaking apart and end of, 112, 135, 140, 145–49, 152; FBI informants and, 147; final convention (Chicago 1969), 145–46; funding from Hoagland, 136; government targeting of, 133–41; growth of and dominance among student organizations, 37; Harvard ROTC program and, 115–16, 124, 127–28; Harvard Strike of 1969 and, 124–26; Humphrey as presidential candidate and, 109; lessons learned from, 207, 258; life after disintegration of, 150–54; male domination of, 138–39; March on Washington (April 1965), 31, 32, 34–37, *35*, 39; McCarthy presidential campaign and, 83; the "Mobe" and, 85; as multi-issue organization, 30; National Council meeting (1964), 29–32; NCNP conference and, 81–82; New England organization of, 27–29; origins of, 30; parasitic organizations and, 116; Revolutionary Youth Movement and, 146; role models to Ansara, 11–12; Rosa Luxemburg chapter at MIT, 154; San Francisco State University student strike and (1970), 157; *SDS Bulletin*, 44; Spring Mobilization (NYC 1967), 74; veterans of still working for social justice, 253; Vietnam Summer (1967) and, 78–79. *See also* antiwar movement
Seale, Bobby, 133, 156–57, 160, 171
Seaver, Tom, 154
segregation. *See* Civil Rights Movement; racism and racial discrimination
Selective Service, 54–56; Massachusetts Shea Act (1970) exempting state citizens from serving in illegal war, 159; testing of college students along with class ranking and GPA to determine deferments, 55; during Vietnam war years, 140. *See also* draft resistance
Sellman, Dottie, 236
Senate Subcommittee on Internal Security, 135–37
September 11 terrorist attacks (2001), 146
Sharpeville massacre (South Africa), 31
Shaw, Sarah-Ann, 7, 8
Shea Act (Massachusetts 1970), 159
Sheet Metal Workers Union, 215
Shephard, Art, 236
Shirley, Lillian, 204
Shuttlesworth, Fred, 12
Sidney & Esther Rabb Foundation, 69–71
silent majority, 133
sit-ins, 5, 6, 30, 117
Skiddy von Stade, Francis, 118
Sloan Coffin, William, 85, 95
Smith, Bernice, 236
Smith, David, 27, 264n6
SNCC (Student Nonviolent Coordinating Committee), 12; becoming all-Black organization, 75, 82; "the beloved community" concept and, 30; college students as organizers, 6; decision making by consensus, 30; Freedom Summer and, 17; Friends of SNCC, 25, 57, 206; as inspiration, 8–9; lessons learned from, 207; male superiority and, 139; March on Washington (1963) and, 14–15; March on Washington (April 1965) and, 36; renunciation of nonviolence, 75; Vietnam Summer (1967) and, 78–79; white women as members, 139
Social Democratic Party (Germany), 97
socialism: avoidance of term, 26–27; in Czechoslovakia, 101
Socialist Party, 24, 30, 255
social justice, 206–7, 209
social media, 254
Sokoloff, Sandy, 239
Sommaripa, George, 69–70
Sourwine, Jules, 135–36
South Africa. *See* apartheid
South Boston, Fair Share organizing efforts in, 215
South Boston Marshals, 215
Southern Christian Leadership Conference (SCLC), 12
South Vietnam. *See* Vietnam war
Soviet Union, 45, 96, 101, 105, 250. *See also* Cold War
Spiegel, Mike, 152
Splain, Barbara Bowen, 209, 213

Splain, Mark, 209–11, 216
Spock, Benjamin, 75, 79, 82, 85, 95, 105
Spring, Micho, 229
St. Clair, James, 189
St. Mark's Church and Social Center (Boston), 7–9, 19
Staples, Lee, 209, 210, 213
Stay Out for Freedom Day, 12–13, *13*, 19
Stern, Sol, 68–69, 71
Stone, I. F. (Izzy), 34, 36, 40
Stone, Jim, 231–32
Studds, Gerry, 230
Student Afro Society (Columbia University), 100–101
Student League for Industrial Democracy (SLID), 30
Student Nonviolent Coordinating Committee. *See* SNCC
Students for a Democratic Society. *See* SDS
Supreme Court, US, 256–57
SWAT team, 133

Tabankin, Marge, 240
tax reform initiatives, 217–19, 223–31; property tax abatements, 224, 226, 230; referendum campaign for graduated income tax (1976), 211–12, 222; tax delinquents, pursuit of, 225–26; unitary taxing of oil companies, 241
teach-ins, 35, 39–41
Teamsters Union scandal (1996), 247
The Day After (TDA) protests (1970), 156–57, *158*
The People First (TPF), 181–82, 184, 188, 190, *190*, 192, 201, 203, 238
Thirteenth Amendment, 257
Thompson, Bill, 235–36
Thompson, John, 186–87
Thurmond, Strom, 135–36
Tonkin Resolution. *See* Gulf of Tonkin incident/resolution
Travers, Herbert, 187
Troy, Jerome, 184–90, *189–90*, 194, 197, 238
Trump, Donald, xiii, 108, 253, 259
Turner, Chuck, 234
Tuttle, Betsy, 226

U Mass Boston, 177, 182
United Auto Workers (UAW), 25, 30
United Packing House Workers of America, 47–48
University at Nanterre, 101
University of Alabama, 12
University of Michigan teach-in (1965), 35
utility rates protests, 211–12, 222–23, *223*, 231

Vellucci, Al, 124
Veterans Administration (VA), 256
Veterans of Foreign Wars, 145
Vietcong. *See* National Liberation Front
Vietnam Moratorium (1969), 112, 154, *155*, 159, 193, 239
Vietnam Summer (1967), 79–81, 83, 239
Vietnam today, 250
Vietnam veterans, 102–3, 112, 144–45, 150, 154; in Dorchester, 177, 182, 183–84, 193; in Lowell, 169, 171, 174, 175; returning medals, 192
Vietnam Veterans Against the War (VVAW), 181, 184, 192–94, *193–94*; "Winter Soldier Investigation" documenting war crimes, 193
Vietnam war: active duty military refusing to go, 153, *153*; bombings and civilian casualties, 74, 130, 194, 197; congressional power to cut off funding for, 199; Democratic primaries and, 96; end of (1975), 199–200; family divisions over, 51–53; government lies about, 140, 197; Gulf of Tonkin incident/resolution, 20–21, 34, 41, 53, 130; "Hamburger Hill" battle (1969), 140, *141*; Harvard deaths in, 141; Harvard students' apology to McNamara for protestors, 66; Ia Drang Valley battle (1965), 46, *47*, 130; LBJ escalation of, 20–21, 34, 50, 53, 68, 81, 85, 95, 130; lies and deceit of government, 41, 68, 130; Massachusetts Shea Act (1970) challenging legality of, 159; media depictions as turning point of public opinion, 46, *68*, *131–32*; My Lai massacre (1968), 130; napalm, 88–89, *89*, 91, 93, *132*, 248; national support for, 39, 43, 105; Nixon's policies, 108–9, 140, 145, 192, 194, 197; Operation Junction City (1967), 74; peak of US troops in, 140; rationale for, assessed with today's knowledge, 251; reaction to end of, 191–92, 200; South Vietnamese government and, 68; Tet Offensive (1968), 95–96; US abandonment of South Vietnamese at end, 200; US commitment to, 67, 102; in US pattern of foreign interventions, 51, 68, 72–73; weight of responsibility to end, 130–32; withdrawal of US from Vietnam (1973), 191, *192*, 198. *See also* antiwar movement; Vietnam Moratorium
VISTA (Volunteers in Service to America), 44, 237, 239–40, 244

Wald, George, 92
Wallace, Chris, 124
Wallace, George, 12, 96, 254
Walls, Chaka, 146

Walzer, Michael, 67, 78, 92
war on drugs, 109–10
Washington marches. *See headings starting* "March on"
Watergate, 72, 189, 199, 200
Watson, Robert, 118
Watson, Tom, 255
WBCN (Boston FM station), 106, 164, 165
wealth gap, racial disparity, 256
Weatherman, 113, 147, 152–53; Black Panthers and, 163; Burlingham and Meisel leaving, 163–64; crazy and morally bankrupt, 163; Dyen and, 152; Greenwich Village explosion (1970), 162–63, 252; meeting with Vietnamese, 163; October Days of Rage and, 152
Webb, Lee, 11, 25, 71, 79, 264n3
Weiner, Jon, 96
Weld, Bill, 60
Wenner, Jan, 80
Westmoreland, William, 81
White, Kevin, 228–30
white backlash against civil rights, 247, 254, 256
white grievance, 108, 253, 257
white privilege, 146, 152

white supremacy, 255, 258
Wiley, George, 271n5
Wilkins, Inez, 236
Winpisinger, William, 241
Winship, Tom, 207
Womack, Jack, 92
women's liberation movement, 137–40, 157, 175, 247. *See also* feminism
Worcester, 57, 87, 177, 216, 219, 226, 232–33
Worker Student Alliance, 116, 146
working-class outreach: Dorchester, 177, 179–80; Lowell, 173–76; Mass Fair Share and, 213; Ronan Park, Boston, 178, *179*, 180–81
World War II, 251; Hitler–Stalin Pact, 45; Munich appeasement (1938), 41

Yippies (Youth International Party), 87
Young, Andrew, 79
Young, James, 224
Young Americans for Freedom, 35, 43
Youth Project, 240

Zellner, Bob and Dottie, 25
Zevin, Robert, 153
Zinn, Howard, 40, 182

www.ingramcontent.com/pod-product-compliance
Lightning Source LLC
Chambersburg PA
CBHW020357220126
38614CB00021B/216